Between Resistance and Revolution

Cultural Politics and Social Protest

Edited by Richard G. Fox and Orin Starn

Rutgers University Press

New Brunswick, New Jersey, and London

Library of Congress Cataloging-in-Publication Data

Between resistance and revolution : cultural politics and social
    protest / edited by Richard G. Fox and Orin Starn.
        p.   cm.
    Includes bibliographical references.
    ISBN 0-8135-2415-6 (cloth : alk. paper). — ISBN 0-8135-2416-4
(pbk. : alk. paper)
    1. Protest movements.   2. Direct action.   3. Dissenters.
4. Culture.   I. Fox, Richard Gabriel, 1939–   . II. Starn, Orin.
HN17.5.B433   1997
303.48'4—DC21   97-9638
                                                                              CIP

British Cataloging-in-Publication information available

Manufactured in the United States of America

Contents

Acknowledgments

This book was made possible by a grant from the Harry Frank Guggenheim Foundation. We are grateful to the foundation for its generosity, and to Karen Colvard and Joel Walman for their enthusiasm for the project. Clare Talwalker and Jennifer Hirsch provided invaluable research assistance. For astute and helpful readings of earlier drafts of the manuscript, we thank John Borneman, Charles Hale, Robin Kirk, Donald Moore, Frances Starn, and Randolph Starn. Martha Heller at Rutgers University Press was a wonderfully energetic and supportive editor, and we thank her for her help in bringing the book to press.

Richard G. Fox and Orin Starn

Introduction

It happened so quickly that some of us had to be reminded afterward that rocks had broken the taillights of the bus. We had just got off the plane in Quito, Ecuador, from different corners of the world, eleven academics and two foundation officers. The bus was to take us to a country hotel for a conference on social protest. Real protest refused to wait for our discussion, however. On the highway north, we came upon a bonfire blocking traffic. Men and children in ponchos, windbreakers, and baseball caps came out of the shadows and asked for money. A few coins having passed hands, we drove on, weaving around burning tires and branches—and then the taillights shattered as protesters rained rocks down from the hills above. We took temporary shelter at a police checkpoint and fortified ourselves with beer and coffee at the adjacent café.

A policeman explained that we had stumbled into a massive protest by Ecuadorian Indians.[1] Rock throwing and highway blockades had paralyzed the country. The next morning at the hotel (which we reached safely), the newspapers reported on the nonviolent marches that had also taken place and on the new agrarian law that had provoked the protests by limiting the water rights of Quichua villagers. The evening news broadcast footage of what the anchorman promised was the "normalization" of trade and transport: tanks lumbering down a highway and gangs of troops lifting tree trunks, pushing boulders, and filling ditches.[2]

We learned more in the next few days. The protesters did not advocate Marxist revolution, like the Maoist guerrillas who were fighting just to the

1

south in Peru. The immediate aim of the highway blockade was only the repeal of a new law that the protesters believed favored the big, the powerful, and the multinational. Yet the mobilization was far more than the atomized or surreptitious politics of scattered confrontation, evasion, or footdragging. This was a public protest where those involved risked jail or worse. Leaders interviewed in the newspapers spoke of "native dignity" and "Quichua unity," challenging the old view of the passivity and inferiority of the poor and brown-skinned people in Ecuadorian society and advancing a shared cultural vision that recoded the category of Indianness from a mark of subordination to an emblem of pride. "We do not want to be strangers in our own land," declared a manifesto of the Indian coalition that organized the mobilization.

Social Protest "In Between"

The theme of our conference was precisely the terrain in between mass revolution and small-scale resistance. An intermediate zone of what can be labeled "dissent" and "direct action" is prominent in the topography of protest in the late twentieth century.[3] Whereas the old dream of total transformation through armed revolution may have faded in recent years, mobilization around a stunning diversity of causes signals continued willingness to enter into open confrontation with the powers-that-be, warning against the facile view of the present as a "postideological" or "postpolitical" epoch. Under the auspices of the Harry Frank Guggenheim Foundation, our small group was to focus on the development of dissent and the organization of direct action, examining patterns of similarity and difference in this kind of opposition to the status quo that mobilizes such commitment and passion in so many corners of the world.

The intermediate forms of mobilization of concern to our group tend to be marginalized in the analysis of protest and insurgency. Many scholars of political change in the 1960s and 1970s focused on the drama of revolutionary war, as the upheaval in Vietnam threw into relief the wrenching force of national liberation struggles in Africa and Asia.[4] Although this large body of literature brought needed attention to the role of Indians, peasants, workers, and other subaltern groups in shaping national histories, we realize with hindsight that large-scale revolution was never common, no matter what the 1960s and 1970s seemed to promise. It takes an unlikely alignment of desperation, opportunity, leadership, and commitment to lead people to be willing to kill and to die to overthrow a system. As the travails of postrevolutionary societies from Cuba to Ethiopa have underscored, many of these full-scale revolutions did not even accomplish fundamental social changes that they had promised and expected.

During the 1980s, much academic inquiry swung to the opposite pole of the small, and often surreptitious, acts of footdragging, false deference, gossip, evasion, and pilfering that James Scott dubbed the "weapons of the weak."[5] Critics have charged that studies of everyday resistance romanticize the clarity of the political vision of the downtrodden and overvalue the transformative potential of small-scale and stealthy acts of opposition. On the positive side, the work of Scott and others demonstrated that subordinate groups may maintain feelings of opposition behind masks of compliance with the state and ruling classes, even developing what Scott called "hidden transcripts" that represent a "critique of power spoken behind the back of the dominant."[6] By challenging the view of the political as understandable only from speeches, marches, and elections, studies of everyday resistance encouraged and expanded understanding of the dialectic of compliance and opposition that takes into account the concealed as well as the visible, the scattered as well as the organized, the small as well as the massive.

For all the robust and insightful work of three decades, however, we still know relatively little about the ample and charged territory between the cataclysmic upheaval of revolutionary war and the small incidents of everyday resistance, namely the thousands of social struggles where people enter into open protest yet do not seek the total overthrow of the social order. This collection seeks to contribute to careful yet creative thinking about the midways of mobilization. One way it tries to achieve this is by focusing on the cultural politics of social protest. Our premise is that protest necessarily involves struggle over ideas, identities, symbols, and strategies within and across regional and national borders, and we assert the inextricability of the culture of politics and the politics of culture in mobilization. We also cut across disciplinary boundaries. This collection draws together work by the scholars from anthropology, political science, history, sociology, and ethnomusicology who gathered in Ecuador. Their essays examine dissent and direct action in Australia, Brazil, Colombia, India, Korea, Peru, and the United States. Taken together, they offer a comparative view that moves beyond national and regional confines. Further, the contributors use the case study method to look at a broad range of (overlapping) debates in political economy, literary studies, feminism, and theories of nationalism and state making. In contrast with much unanchored inquiry in recent cultural studies and postcolonial theory, each essay uses the detailed investigation of a particular case as an entry point into inquiry into broader themes of cultural theory and social analysis.[7] We hope the collection will deepen the dialogue about social protest across the geographical and professional borders that can make for parochial, in-bred views and advance the case for joining close research with theoretical agility in social inquiry.

Readers will be struck first by the sheer range of "in between" protest. What Ramachandra Guha calls the "environmentalism of the poor" in rural India proves to be nonviolent yet confrontational in "tree hugging" to stop logging. In the Andes of Peru, Orin Starn shows how self-defense committees fight Maoist revolutionaries without ceding control over local life to military authorities. The "webs" of public protest that Sonia Alvarez studies in Brazil operate above ground and publicly yet outside established political parties. Ingrid Monson explores how African American jazz musicians go beyond quietly coding resistance into their music to become activist musicians vocally engaged in the civil rights movement. Each of these initiatives refuses the stark choice between foot-dragging resistance or all-out revolt to forge instead an independent vision of opposition and mobilization.

The national and global characters of many of these social protests reinforce their in betweenness: it is hard enough to mobilize for revolution nationally and even harder transnationally; it is impossible to broadcast a muffled resistance at any great distance, and certainly not around the world. Several papers in this collection pursue the possibilities for global or transnational mobilization that in between social protest enables. Faye Ginsburg, for instance, shows how the burgeoning worldwide indigenous rights movement becomes outspoken but reformative as it turns to national media, as in Australia, and as it travels trasnationally. Along Colombia's Atlantic coast, Arturo Escobar finds a different relationship: here, global environmentalism leagues with local-level ethnic separatism in protest against Western-style progress and development.[8] The social activism that Yoshinobu Ota finds in Okinawa takes place in between Japanese hegemony and U.S. imperialism, a space where language, rather than the bomb, serves as the chief means of a dissent, which is, however, necessarily vocal. Along the same lines, Richard Fox argues that Gandhian nonviolent resistance coming from India had to be de-Orientalized and de-Christianized before it could provide African American activists with an effective form of protest that was neither Marxian revolutionary nor Christian pacific.

Social protest that stops short of advocating revolution often gets written off as a poor substitute for the "real thing." Conversely, some scholars have presented small-scale resistance as the only option under repressive regimes. The real possibilities and concrete results of social protest can disappear in these views, as several papers in this collection remind us. For instance, Nancy Abelmann notes that in Korea an in between social protest replaced a revolutionary leftist movement. Although or perhaps because it is nonrevolutionary, the new Korean social protest has proved less doctrinaire and more flexible than previous activism. Meanwhile, Nathan Stoltzfus confronts the argument that everyday resistance is all that is possible under certain repressive regimes and finds it wanting, at least in East Germany just before the Berlin Wall fell. Under an Orwellian state, individuals nevertheless dissented and communicated their misgivings to others; obviously, they were guarded and very careful, but they took risks well beyond passive resistance. Alvarez suggests that flexibility can be an asset of an in between social protest. Although Brazilians began to forge coalitions of activist groups under military dictatorship, these networks have survived and even expanded with the return of electoral democracy. For more than what one observer calls the "glory of slaves," the powerful and sometimes unexpected force of initiatives in the midways of mobilization can make a real difference against the grain of poverty and injustice, and they can develop even under conditions of almost impossible danger. We agree with the claim of Gilles Deleuze and Félix Guattari that "the middle is by no means an average; on the contrary, it is where things pick up speed."[9]

Many of these cases might appear to be instances of the so-called new social movements that cut across class lines to organize around issues of autonomy and identity—for example, environmentalism in Latin America, feminism in Brazil, indigenous activism in Australia and Okinawa, and antiracism in the United States.[10] However, new social movements can be a misleading rubric if it is taken to mean that current social movements are unprecedented and altogether novel. Such a view overlooks the persistence of dissent and direct action along old lines of social status and economic interest, as in the examples in this collection of peasant activism in Peru and India. Moreover, the claim of newness ignores the fact that social movements were never a simple matter of the mobilization of peasants or proletarians under a common banner of class struggle. As in the book burning of sixteenth-century Dominicans in Italy or the uprising of Andeans to restore the Inca empire in the eighteenth century, protest has taken historically diverse and eccentric paths. Perhaps more than anything else, the rise of a literature on new social movements reflects a new sensitivity on the part of scholars to the multiple vectors of political activity that always exist in any society.

Our choice of in between (in place of new social movements) signals a desire to dodge the trap of seeing only discontinuity between the past and the present. To do so, we define this category not by qualities it may possess so much as by how it differs from resistance or revolution. Elusiveness for us represents less a weakness than a strength, as it opens a broad area of social protest for investigation and debate yet without smothering inquiry under static categories or singular definitions.

From Dissent to Mass Action

This collection examines an additional in betweenness that we feel needs greater attention in studies of social protest. This additional area is the terrain between individual dissent and mass action and the issue of why and when the opposition of few may grow into the cause of many. As we understand it, individual dissent is both more and less than simple resistance. It is more in that it is forthright and (usually) public; it is less in that it may be the work of only one person or a handful of people. At the other end of the range, mass action, as it appears in this collection, is always less than revolutionary: it aims for confrontation and revision, not sabotage and upheaval. By exploring how individual dissent does (or does not) turn into mass action, we underscore that social protest should be understood as a process of becoming rather than an already achieved state, the typical premise in too much of the literature on social movements.

Thus: how do individuals make their dissenting consciousness known to others, that is, how do they "go public"? These essays point to the many different means of communication by which the process can occur. At one end of the spectrum, there is the guarded and small-scale communication in Stoltzfus's study of East Germany, where opposition is expressed in whispers and by "pass-the-secret" means. A wider, more open, but still primarily face-to-face transmission of dissent occurs in the Colombian coastal communities studied by Escobar and in the upland peasant villages of northern India that Guha presents (although outside forces are also influential). In still another form of communication, Abelmann's Korean politicians and Fox's erstwhile Gandhians in the United States present their dissenting narratives at pep-talks and speeches. Although still face-to-face in terms of the presentation, the distance increases between dissenter and what has now become an audience. Broadcasting dissent through mass media depends on communicating protest to an audience that cannot be seen—whether in the jazzy lyrics sung in support of civil rights, the case that Monson explores; in films made by indigenous Australian activists, as studied by Ginsburg; or in TV comedy routines that Ota claims "joke-start" Okinawan ethnic identity. Once fully developed into social movements, such as Starn finds in Peru and Alvarez finds in Brazil, dissent has become institutionalized, and the resulting social movement has internal organization, methods of self-policing, public demonstrations of unity, and routinized means of communication.

Culture and Protest

A common theme in all the essays is that cultural representations play a pivotal role in the formation and maintenance of social protest. In many, for example, "dissenting narratives" come in over the air waves and on screen—and thus through media representations. Ginsburg shows that media productions made by indigenous producers are—when they circulate into television and film festivals—an act of protest against the denial of Aboriginal rights in broader society. The public presence of indigenous media counters negative stereotyping and erasure of Aboriginal perspectives and histories in national institutions such as television. Indigenous media makers, therefore, construct a cultural conception of the indigenous not only by expressing an Aboriginal perspective. By the act of circulating these oppositional versions of history and culture, they can also have an important influence on struggles for rights to land, language, and culture. Monson extends the point to show how jazz conveyed political messages. The musicians who spoke out in their music then went on to confront the racial inequality built into white control over clubs, record companies, and even the cultural understanding of what jazz was or should be. Ota introduces us to theater and television on Okinawa, where island activists compose a distinctive identity from elements of Japanese, U.S., and Okinawan traditions.

Of course, media representations can also short-circuit social protest. This was the case in the mid-twentieth century, according to Fox, when newspapers and radio showed Gandhian nonviolent protest either in Christian or Orientalist stereotype. As Fox shows, these cultural misrepresentations were only overcome by the personal re-representations of transnational subjects. Fox and the other contributors view media culture as a fundamental ground for protest politics as the world wires up and plugs in to an electronic age.[11]

Other papers focus on how protest builds and sometimes transforms the cultural meanings shared by communities or groups. The environmental movements studied by Escobar and Guha, for example, prosper because they develop among populations that are clearly labeled—and are therefore sharply self-represented—within their societies: the low-caste peasantry in India and the black coastal workers of Colombia. Stern sees rural activism in Peru emerging in part from collective village efforts to protect life and property. Alvarez and Abelmann also show the way in which culturally labeled groups like farmers in Korea and women in Brazil could build protest organizations on the basis provided by cultural stereotypes, in the process reworking and even redefining the meaning of these categories in national society.

The collection, then, advances the proposition that protest must be understood as culturally laden and historically specific. At first glance, this combination may seem contradictory: how can we claim, it might be asked, that the structure of culture comes together with the contingency of historical events to create social protest? For our assertion to make sense, we must dismiss the notion of culture as a deeply anchored and long-standing tradition. Culture gets made into (usually temporary and short-lived) structure as people become conscious and learn to cope with historical events.[12] Individual dissent and mass action grow from dangerous thinking and painstaking labor. Contemplating the sins of the system, painting banners, making speeches, marching—these bold actions are wound around an armature of cultural meanings before they power up social protest. As dissent grows and protest erupts, there may be improvisation, there must be inclusion (and exclusion), there can be persistence and success, and, very often, there will be failure. Every step in the process involves the creation and diffusion of cultural meanings. At every step, too, historical events create new social conditions within which these meanings deploy.

Each essay underscores that if activist social protest depends on the culturing of meanings and action, this process, in turn, depends on the purposeful decisions of individuals. But the importance of individual initiative does not mean a retreat into atomistic or Great Man theories of history. The novelist Eduardo Galeano warns us against this kind of thinking when he laments the orthodox understanding of Latin America's past as a "military parade of bigwigs in uniforms fresh from the drycleaners."[13] The individual histories found in this collection exhume unremembered actors and buried stories, covered up by official accounts from the public theater of war, government, and diplomacy. An Indian exile, memorialized neither in India nor in the United States, translates Gandhian protest methods for U.S. civil rights activists. An Okinawan performer adds a string to a traditional instrument and plays a new music of local identity and protest upon it. African American jazz artists sing new, liberating lyrics; indigenous Australian film makers satirize colonialism on screen; peasant leaders in India and Peru hug trees and whip people into line; and a few East Germans begin to go to church to sing new hymns to freedom. This dissent and these oppositional actions occur within specific conditions of time, place, gender, race, sexuality, and sectarian identity; but portraying these conditions as determining events can efface individual effort and innovation. The conviction confirmed by these essays is that the themes of personal desire, local initiative, and human inventiveness must be starting points for analysis of social protest.

Culture and Protest Late in the Twentieth Century

Institutions of transportation and communication in the late twentieth century are changing the role of cultural representations and individual initiatives in the genesis and spread of protest, as many of these essays show. The rhetoric of rupture in theories of "postmodern hyperspace" and "time-space compression" forgets that the world has long been interconnected by the flow of ideas, people, and goods.[14] Still, the intensification of globalization makes it ever clearer that movements or mobilizations cannot be thought of as self-contained or separate units, any more than cultures or societies. To the contrary, protest develops in the interplay of transculturation and creolization across regional and international borders. As Stoltzfus shows for East Germany, "local knowledge" (as Clifford Geertz [1983] labels it) enables protesters to maneuver in the treacherous waters of family divisions or neighborhood politics. Yet, dissent and direct action almost always turn out to implicate a widening circle of interests and institutions, as when East German dissidents discovered that programs broadcast from West Berlin spread news about protests kept from official airwaves by Stasi censors.

Our contributors borrow or invent labels such as "movement webs" and "flexed networks" to evoke the fluid ways in which activists interconnect in a shrinking world. In Brazil, for example, Alvarez documents the flexible ties of personal contact and political affiliation linking feminist and shantytown activists, research centers, church groups, and international aid agencies around the cause of women's rights and social justice. Guha shows the same elasticity in the web of alliances that connects Indian villagers and urban activists into a local ecology movement that is sometimes in league with and other times at odds with the international one. Fluidity gives local activists a panoply of difficult and sometimes contradictory choices about whether and how to link to global initiatives.

As the presence at New York film festivals of Aboriginal filmmakers whom Ginsburg initially met in "remote communites" suggests, protest moves with people across borders. The current fascination with borderlands and diasporas can gloss over the profound differences in the predicament of the millions of people in motion in a restless world where the reasons for migration and mobility can range from the luxury of tourism to the terror of genocide. Nevertheless, these essays suggest that the role of mobility in one form or another would be difficult to overestimate in spreading as well as transforming or containing ideologies and strategies of dissent and direct action. The farmers studied by Escobar find themselves displaced by plantation agriculture, yet in the cities find an identity politics of Afro-Colombian pride that then challenges the terms of development on Colombia's Pacific coast. Guha shows how the arrival of international groups for ecological preservation offers poor villagers in India a source of financing and advice for defending land and livelihood, even as it threatens to result in a more depoliticized view of environmental activism. Dislocation and movement in a nomadic world make interlinkages across the leaky borders of regions and nations more the norm than the exception in protest today.

Of course, ideas can also migrate on video or by satellite—hence the concern, once again, of so many of our contributors with the media. Although the use of camcorders and satellites by Aboriginal Australians displays the possibilities of communications technology, corporate monopoly over the airwaves can also cut off protest possibilities: the cultural activists whom Ota studied in Okinawa find themselves blocked from TV channels by *General Hospital* and *Dallas*. More intricately, a communications glut may even generate coexisting, contradictory messages that may weaken or divide local dissent and protest, as the papers by Monson, Fox, and Guha indicate. The dispute over whether jazz was art or ethnic music—especially as whites who controlled the music industry entered into it—impeded African American jazz activists in their search for autonomy. Whether Gandhi was a Christian martyr or an Oriental saint—these alternative media representations, both false, made it hard for American protest groups to understand the range of meanings of *satyagraha*. Never just an encouraging parable of unlimited communication or a sinister story of corporate mastery, the advent of global media presents an array of opportunities and obstacles to change.

As a product of the alchemy of the local and the global, the parochial and the cosmopolitan, the regional and the international, social protest today therefore travels along and takes place in spaces once unused or nonexistent, whether on jumbo jets or the electronic pulses and silicon chips of the information age. This volume pushes us to recognize the ever more heterogeneous and unexpected fronts of organized protest and dissenting consciousness in today's world. We are used to thinking about mobilization and protest by way of a familiar, yet limited, constellation of images: marches, speeches, rallies, strikes. In contrast, these essays advocate an expanded sensitivity to the diverse arenas of current strategies for social transformation—new ways of speaking in Okinawa; religion in East Germany when dissidents took advantage of the safe haven of Protestant churches; an "abstract" form of cultural expression like jazz. When Abbey Lincoln and Max Roach connected music and the civil rights movement, they redrew the boundaries between aesthetics and activism, performance and organizing, art and politics. Jazz music made into protest politics—this progress from dissent to direct action anticipates later, equivalent developments in Okinawa and Australia. As we learn from these essays, collective protest at the dawn of the new century can just as readily emerge from battles over a TV program, a religious service, or a song lyric as over land tenure or factory wages.

Protest and Progress?

Social movements, especially today under the impact of globalization and post–cold war international relations, cannot be cast as marching lock-step toward human emancipation. Some contemporary theorists, like Ernesto Laclau and Chantal Mouffe, have sought to restore a sense of the multiple tracks and uncertain destinations of social protest in today's diverse world. We are confronted with the emergence of a "plurality of subjects," they assert.[15] At the same time, some scholars have persisted in an unreconstructed faith in salvation history. For example, the South Asian historian Ponna Wignaraja tells us that "people's movements . . . release creative energies . . . and move society to a developmental and democratic alternative."[16] This shaky claim to the liberating potential of social movements also sometimes emerges in the new materialism of New Class or Regulation theory, both of which presume the inevitability of crisis of capitalism and the transformation to a better society.[17]

The authors here assert a less predetermined, more nuanced view of political struggles late in the twentieth century (and one that is probably applicable to earlier ones, as well). They highlight the diverse, and often contradictory, origins of mass mobilization. Talk of grassroots mobilization and popular uprising suggests a spontaneous, even natural, initiative of the poor and dispossessed. Our cases suggest otherwise. Whether in Indian environmentalism or Andean self-defense organizations, the outbreak of social protest is seldom, if ever, just an upswell from the bottom. Political parties, development groups, military officials, state bureaucracies, and international aid organizations turn out to be just some of the major forces in social struggles. Basic desires for political justice and economic survival often drive protest. Just as often, however, dissent and direct action depend on the explosive interaction of an array of constituencies, institutions, and ideologies. Social forces not just from below but also from above and across come into play in social movements.

Moreover, there is never a straight vertical line from misery to protest nor a straight historical line from dissent to mobilization. Ginsburg, Guha, Ota, Fox, Alvarez, and Abelmann show how elites—sometimes local; other times, national; and still other times, transnational—get mixed up in protests by the impoverished and excluded. These cases also indicate that the specific character of the mobilization includes some and excludes others: an Abbey Lincoln but not an Ornette Coleman; James Farmer but not W.E.B. DuBois; certain Australian indigenous filmmakers and Okinawan performance artists and Brazilian NGOs to the exclusion of others. Peruvian peasant committees against the Shining Path have the patronage of authoritarian and even fascist generals in the Peruvian military.

Nor does this volume presume that dissent and opposition are invariably benign. Although most of our studies deal with movements with a progressive agenda, we allow that if they are progressive today, they need not continue to be in the future—and that even at present, they use cultural representations that might be turned to reactionary and sometimes frightening ends. A Shining Path that once offered hope soon turns from benefaction to oppression. The celebration of jazz as black music against white cultural superiority could later come to support claims to racial purity. Gandhian nonviolent protest looked benign when Martin Luther King, Jr., practiced it back in the 1950s; it does not look so clear-cut when used by the Animal Liberation Army to block research on cancer and AIDS. Radical environmentalism in the United States has led to violence and virulent antigovernment stances akin to the practices of white-supremacist groups. Is this possibility out of the question in India and Colombia? How, in any case, to distinguish the progressive from the reactionary? Why demonize at all? But then: how and what and whether to celebrate? A recognition of the unruliness and unpredictability of protest's course opens the charged question of position and judgment in the relation of scholarship to dissent and direct action.

Academic Culture and Protest

The paradoxes are no less poignant for being obvious when social protest is studied from the privileged halls of U.S. and European universities, scholarly seminars, and international conferences. What of a conference in Ecuador on protest at a resort hotel in what was once a hacienda, the supreme symbol of feudal oppression for Andean villagers? The stack of dollars for the airfares and expenses of the participants, fifty times the annual income of an average family in a poor nation like Ecuador? These and other ironies of the conference point to an array of issues too little discussed in the academy: what is the role of upper-middle-class academics vis-à-vis political struggles? How to bridge, or at least negotiate, the distance between the protected hallways of Duke or Washington University and the mean streets of the Third World? How do we meet the obligations incurred as we convert the initiatives of the downtrodden into the means by which to advance professional careers? The essays by Ginsburg and Monson, in particular, take up these questions. Overall, they emphasize that there can be no escape for scholars to a prelapsarian paradise of political innocence and virtue. They examine ways in which scholars studying social protest can make positive (albeit limited) contributions to social change through writing, teaching, and research.[18]

Monson gives us her experiences dealing with the politics of essentialism in her classes on jazz. When whites chastize black students for an Afrocentric essentialism about jazz, Monson reminds them that they need to understand how Afrocentricity has helped generate progressive black protest. Ginsburg stresses the moral imperative of melding activism and research to encourage as well as study the precarious enterprise of indigenous media. Like Stuart Hall, all the contributors advocate an "academic practice which always thinks about its intervention in a world in which it would make some difference."[19] As pain and injustice proliferate across the world, the project of scholarly activism remains one of desperate urgency.

Between Hope and Despair

Late in the twentieth century, Nietzsche's credo about the "defiant unruliness" of human history seems prophetic. It encapsulates a cumulative message of this book. Some critics purvey a socialist nostalgia for an earlier (perhaps largely imagined) period of popular protest that reduces the present to a time "after the revolution" or even "after the masses."[20] However, the eclipse of hopes for radical transformation can also force a renewed appreciation of the politics of the possible. Many of the studies in this volume portray brave and persistent efforts to break with systems of exclusion and prejudice. Even the most heartening initiatives will always be crosscut by ironies and compromises, and mass mobilization from our present vantage should not be understood within the comforting vision of a utopian destiny. Whether it be Korean students or Afro-Colombian farmers, however, many social protests have made a serious difference in local lives and even intervened for the good in global society. These movements offer encouraging flashes of struggle and vision to remind us that, *pace* Frances Fukuyama, there is much more to come in history.

In the days after our departure from Ecuador, the fight over water and land rights raged. There were setbacks, including a dispute between the National Federation of Indigenous Ecuadorians and the National Agrarian Federation over leadership of indigenous protest. As the protest stretched into a second week, however, the highway blockades led to rising discontent at market shortages among the middle classes. Pressure mounted on the government to settle, and the Ecuadorian president called a meeting at the presidential palace with the leaders of the protest. The leaders arrived in the dark hats, ponchos, and knee-high pants that announced a cultural vision where being Indian would no longer mean exclusion from the halls of power. They left with a temporary agreement to suspend the law, able to claim success when they returned to villages across the Andes. The interests of the majorities had carried the day for the moment, even if this was only a modest and partial victory. One can only hope for more of these cultures of protest that proffer visions of possibility and renewal to a hard world that needs them more than ever.

Notes

1. See a special issue of *Latin American Perspectives* for more on indigenous protest in Ecuador (forthcoming, 1997).
2. We are indebted for much of this description and analysis of the mobilization to a chapter in a forthcoming dissertation by Suzanna Sawyer, Anthropology Department, Stanford University.
3. As we understand it, dissent means a conscious and public opposition to the status quo, whether by an individual or group. Direct action refers to public and active protest against the existing state of society. If dissent represents the social-learning processes by which people come to disagree with their circumstances, then direct action stands for the agency of individuals and small groups to activate opposition into larger movements for change.
4. Among the books that shaped the debates on revolution and decolonization were Wolf (1969), Scott (1976), Paige (1975), and Popkin (1979). For useful overviews of this scholarship, see Theda Skocpol's (1979) classic article and Steve J. Stern's (1987) general introduction to an anthology on rebellion in the Andes.
5. This is the title of Scott's (1985) influential and intelligent book, which has shaped the debate on everyday resistance. For criticism of the book, see Mitchell (1992) and Kondo (1990, especially 218–228).
6. Scott (1990, xii).
7. For strong, and sometimes overstated, criticism of the problem of politics and groundedness in cultural studies and postcolonial theory, see Dirlik (1994a), Ebert (1992–93), and Shohat (1992).
8. Ferguson (1990) and Escobar (1994) offer provocative criticism of the ideology and implementation of development in the Third World.
9. Deleuze and Guattari (1987, 25).
10. The work of Touraine (1988) and Melucci (1989) have been especially influential in the literature on new social movements. See McCrea (1989) for an overview of the literature. More recent attempts to rethink the concept of new social movements in the Third World include Escobar and Alvarez (1992) and Wignaraja (1993).
11. We draw the term "media culture" from Kellner (1995), who offers a broad view of recent developments in media studies.
12. Here we differ from Sahlins's (1985) notion of the "structure of the conjuncture" because we assume people put culture into practice only self-consciously and usually in confrontation with the status quo (see Fox [1989]).
13. Galeano (1985, xv).
14. Neo-Marxist efforts to theorize global interconnection have included the famous debate between Wallerstein (1974) and Brenner (1977). For other useful contributions to the mushrooming literature on globalization and transnationalism, see Wolf (1980), Harvey (1989), Featherstone (1990), Clifford (1993), and the journals *Public Culture* and *Diaspora*.
15. Laclau and Mouffe (1985, 181).
16. Wignaraja (1993, 5–6).
17. For a critique of the literature on New Class and Regulation Theory, see Steinmetz (1994).
18. See Starn (1994), Scheper-Hughes (1995), and Burdick (1995) for recent efforts to grapple with the issue of engagement and activism in relation to social movements.

Introduction 15

19. Hall (1992, 286).
20. The phrases come from titles of recent work by Dirlik (1994b) and Hebdigge (1989).

References

Brenner, Robert (1977). The Origins of Capitalist Development: A Critique of Neo-Smithian Marxism. *New Left Review* 104:25–93.

Burdick, John (1995). Everyday Resistance Is Not Enough: Anthropology and Social Movements. *Dialectical Anthropology*, in press.

Clifford, James (1993). Diaspora. *Cultural Anthropology* 9(3):302–338.

Deleuze, Gilles and Félix Guattari (1987). *A Thousand Plateaus: Capitalism and Schizophrenia*. Translated by Brian Massumi. Minneapolis: University of Minnesota Press.

Dirlik, Arif (1994a). The Postcolonial Aura: Third World Criticism in the Age of Global Capitalism. *Critical Inquiry* 20(2):328–356.

Dirlik, Arif (1994b). *After the Revolution: Waking to Global Capitalism*. Hanover, N.H.: Wesleyan University Press.

Ebert, Teresa (1992). Luddic Feminism: The Body, Performance and Labor: Bringing Materialism Back into Feminist Cultural Studies. *Cultural Critique* (Winter:5–50).

Escobar, Arturo (1994). *Encountering Development*. Princeton: Princeton University Press.

Escobar, Arturo and Sonia Alvarez, Eds. (1992). *The Making of Social Movements in Latin America: Identity, Strategy, and Democracy*. Boulder: Westview Press.

Featherstone, Mike, Ed. (1990). *Global Culture: Nationalism, Globalization, and Modernity*. London: Sage Publications.

Ferguson, James (1990). *The Anti-Politics Machine: "Development," Depoliticization, and Bureaucratic Power in Lesotho*. Oxford: Oxford University Press.

Fox, Richard (1989). *Gandhian Utopia: Experiments with Culture*. Boston: Beacon.

Galeano, Eduardo (1985). *Memory of Fire: Genesis*. New York: Pantheon.

Geertz, Clifford (1983). *Local Knowledge: Further Essays in Interpretive Anthropology*. New York: Basic Books.

Hall, Stuart (1992). Cultural Studies and Its Theoretical Legacies. In *Cultural Studies*, ed. L. Grossberg et al., pp. 277–294. New York: Routledge.

Harvey, David (1989). *The Condition of Postmodernity*. London: Basil Blackwell.

Hebdigge, Dick (1989). After the Masses. In *New Times: The Changing Face of Politics in the 1980s*, ed. Stuart Hall and Martin Jacquess, pp. 76–93. London: Lawrence and Wisshart.

Kellner, Douglas (1995). *Media Culture: Cultural Studies, Identity, and Politics in Between the Modern and the Postmodern*. New York: Routledge.

Kondo, Dorrine (1990). *Crafting Selves: Power, Gender, and Discourses of Identity in a Japanese Workplace*. Chicago: University of Chicago Press.

Laclau, Ernesto and Chantal Mouffe (1985). *Hegemony and Socialist Strategy: Towards a Radical Democratic Politics*. London: Verso.

McCrea, Frances (1989). *Minutes to Midnight: Nuclear Weapons Protest in the United States*. Newbury Park, Calif.: Sage Publications.

Melucci, Alberto (1989). *Nomads of the Present: Social Movements and Individual Needs in Contemporary Society*. Philadelphia: Temple University Press.

Mitchell, Timothy (1990). Everyday Metaphors of Power. *Theory and Society* 91:545–577.

Paige, Jeffrey (1975). *Agrarian Revolution: Social Movements and Export Agriculture in the Underdeveloped World.* New York: Free Press.

Popkin, Samuel (1979). *The Rational Peasant: The Political Economy of Rural Society in Vietnam.* Berkeley: University of California Press.

Sahlins, Marshall (1985). *Islands of History.* Chicago: University of Chicago Press.

Scheper-Hughes, Nancy (1995). The Primacy of the Ethical: Notes for a Militant Anthropology. *Current Anthropology* 36(3):409–421.

Scott, James (1976). *The Moral Economy of the Peasant: Rebellion and Subsistence in Southeast Asia.* New Haven: Yale University Press.

Scott, James (1985). *Weapons of the Weak: Everyday Forms of Peasant Resistance.* New Haven: Yale University Press.

Scott, James (1990). *Domination and the Arts of Resistance: Hidden Transcripts.* New Haven: Yale University Press.

Shohat, Ella (1992). Notes on the "Post-Colonial." *Social Text* 31–32:99–223.

Skocpol, Theda (1979). What Makes Peasants Revolutionary? *Comparative Politics* 14(3):35–75.

Starn, Orin (1994). Rethinking the Politics of Anthropology: The Case of the Andes. *Current Anthropology* 35(1):13–38.

Steinmetz, George (1994). Regulation Theory, Post-Marxism, and the New Social Movements. *Comparative Studies in Society and History* 36(2):176–212.

Stern, Steve J., Ed. (1987). *Resistance, Rebellion, and Consciousness in the Andean Peasant World, 18th–20th Centuries.* Madison: University of Wisconsin Press.

Touraine, Alan (1988). *The Return of the Actor: Social Theory in Postindustrial Society.* Minneapolis: University of Minnesota Press.

Wallerstein, Immanuel (1974). *The Modern World System, Vol. 1.* New York: Academic Press.

Wignaraja, Ponna, Ed. (1993). *New Social Movements in the South: Empowering the People.* New Delhi: Vistaar.

Wolf, Eric (1969). *Peasant Wars of the Twentieth Century.* New York: Harper and Row.

Wolf, Eric (1982). *Europe and the People without History.* Berkeley: University of California Press.

Ramachandra Guha

The Environmentalism
of the Poor

The Origins of Conflict

When India played South Africa in a recent international cricket game in Calcutta, Sunil Gavaskar, the great Indian cricketer, was asked by another television commentator to predict the likely winner. "I tried to look into my crystal ball," answered Gavaskar, "but it is clouded up by the Calcutta smog." He might well have added: "To clear it I then dipped my crystal ball in the river Hooghly [which flows alongside the city's cricket stadium], but it came up even dirtier than before."

The quality of air and water in Calcutta is representative of conditions in all Indian cities; little wonder that foreign visitors to India come sturdily equipped with masks and bottles of Bisleri. Less visible to the tourist, and to urban Indians themselves, is the continuing environmental degradation in the countryside. Over 100 million hectares, or one-third of India's land area, has been classed as unproductive wasteland. Much of this was once forest and grazing ground; the rest, farmland destroyed by erosion and salinization. The uncontrolled exploitation of groundwater has led to an alarming drop in the water table, in some areas by more than 5 meters. There is also an acute shortage of safe water for domestic use and for drinking. As ecologist Jayanta Bandyopadhyay has remarked, water rather than oil will be the liquid whose availability (or lack of it) shall have a determining influence on India's economic future (Bandyopadhyay, 1987).

The physical facts of the deterioration of India's environment are by now well established.[1] But even more serious are its human consequences, as all social groups face chronic shortages of natural resources in their daily lives. Peasant women have to trudge further and further for fuelwood for their hearth. Their menfolk, meanwhile, must dig deeper and deeper for a trickle of water with which to irrigate their fields. Forms of livelihood crucially dependent on the bounty of nature—such as fishing, sheep rearing, or basket weaving—are being abandoned all over India. Those who once subsisted on these occupations are joining the band of "ecological refugees," flocking to the cities in search of employment. Urban people themselves complain of shortages of water, power, construction material, and (for industrial units) raw material.

Such shortages flow directly from environmental abuse in contemporary India, the too-rapid exhaustion of the resource base without consideration of its replenishment. Shortages lead, in turn, to sharp conflicts between competing groups of resource users. Indian society is a veritable cauldron of conflicts, many of which pertain, directly or indirectly, to the control and use of natural resources. These conflicts often pit poor against poor, as when neighboring villages fight over a single patch of forest and its produce, or when slum dwellers come to blows over the trickle of water that reaches them, one hour every day from a solitary municipal tap. Occasionally, the conflicts pit rich against rich, as when the wealthy farmers of the adjoining states of Karnataka and Tamil Nadu quarrel over the water of the Kaveri River. But the most dramatic environmental conflicts oppose rich to poor. Such, for instance, is the case with the Sardar Sarovar Dam on the Narmada River in central India. The benefits from this project will flow primarily to already pampered and prosperous areas of the state of Gujarat, while the costs will be disproportionately borne by poorer peasants and tribals in the upstream states of Madhya Pradesh and Maharashtra. These latter groups, who will be displaced by the dam, are being organized by the Narmada Bachao Andolan (Save the Narmada Movement), which is indisputably the most significant environmental initiative in India today.

This cycle of environmental degradation, resource shortages, and social conflict has given rise to a vigorous environmental movement that mocks the conventional wisdom of Northern social science. Thus, in 1980 U.S. economist Lester Thurow had claimed that "if you look at the individuals who support environmentalism within each country, one is struck by the extent to which environmentalism is an interest of the upper middle classes. Poor countries and poor individuals simply aren't interested" (pp. 104–105). Thurow's views were echoed by other writers, for whom environmentalism was quintessentially a "postmaterialist" or "full stomach" phenomenon, a luxury, leisure-time concern that emerged only after basic material needs of food, clothing, and shelter had been met (cf. Inglehart, 1977; Nash, 1982).

Events over the last two decades, in societies as varied as India, Brazil, and Kenya suggest, however, that poor countries, and quite often poor individuals and groups within them, can be deeply concerned with environmentalism. Of course, the environmental impulse here has quite different origins and ways of expression. In the words of the Spanish economist and historian, Juan Martínez Alier, there is an "ecology of affluence" characteristic of the advanced industrial (or postindustrial) societies of the North, and there is an "environmentalism of the poor," more typical of the less urbanized, less industrialized, societies of the South (1990a, 1990b, Introduction).[2] However, the study of Northern environmental movements has been for some time an object of close professional interest on the part of sociologists and historians (among these are Lowe and Goyder, 1983; Fox, 1985; Bramwell, 1989; Dominick, 1992; Jamison et al., 1992). By contrast, scholarly work on Southern environmentalism is as yet in its infancy. This essay, on conflicts over nature in contemporary India, might be taken as one attempt toward redressing this imbalance. It is prompted by the question—what are the origins and characteristic expressions of the environmentalism of the poor?

Resources and Rights

The Indian environmental movement is an overarching, umbrella term covering a multitude of local conflicts, initiatives, and struggles. Its origins can be dated to the Chipko Andolan (Movement that Hugged the Trees) that broke out in the Garhwal Himalaya in April 1973. Between 1973 and 1980, over a dozen instances were recorded wherein, through an innovative technique of protest, unlettered peasants—men, women, and children—threatened to hug forest trees rather than allow them to be logged for export outside the hills. The peasants were not interested in saving the trees per se, but in using their produce for agricultural and household requirements. In later years, however, the movement turned its attention to broader ecological concerns, such as the collective protection and management of forests and the diffusion of renewable energy technologies (Guha, 1990).

Chipko was the forerunner of, and in some cases the direct inspiration for, a series of popular movements in defense of community rights to natural resources. Sometimes these struggles revolved around forests; in other instances, they involved the control and use of pasture, mineral, or fish resources. The most characteristic of these conflicts has pitted rich against poor: logging companies against hill villagers, dam builders against forest tribals, multinational corporations deploying trawlers against artisanal fisherfolk rowing country-boats. In these cases, one party (e.g., loggers or trawlers) seeks to accelerate the pace of resource exploitation to service an expanding commercial-industrial economy. This is a process that often involves the partial or total dispossession of those communities that earlier had control over the resource in question, and whose own patterns of utilization were both less energy and capital intensive and less destructive of the environment.

More often than not, resource-intensification agents are given preferential treatment by the state (which usually claims formal proprietary rights over the resource in contention), through the grant of generous long-term leases over mineral or fish stocks, for example, or the provision of raw materials at enormously subsidized prices. The injustice so compounded, local communities at the receiving end of this process have no recourse except direct action, resisting both the state and outside exploiters with a variety of protest techniques. These struggles might perhaps be seen as the manifestation of a new kind of class conflict. Whereas traditional class conflicts were fought in the cultivated field or in the factory, these struggles are waged over the gifts of nature (such as forests and water), gifts that are coveted by all but increasingly monopolized by some.

There is, then, an unmistakable material context to the upsurge of environmental conflict in India: the shortages of, threats to, and struggles over natural resources. No one could suggest, with regard to India, what two scholars claimed some years ago about U.S. environmentalism, namely that it had exaggerated or imagined the risk posed by ecological degradation (Douglas and Wildavsky, 1982).[3] All the same, the environmentalism of the poor is neither universal nor pregiven—there are many parts of India (and the Third World generally) where the destruction of the environment has generated little or no popular response. To understand where, how, and in what manner environmental conflict articulates itself requires the kind of location-specific work, bounded in time and space, that social scientists in India have thus far reserved for studies of worker and peasant struggles. This essay focuses, then, on a particular environmental conflict that was played out between 1984 and 1991 in the southern Indian state of Karnataka. The conflict I write of is perhaps not as well known outside India as the Chipko or Narmada movements. But, as I hope to show, its unfolding powerfully illustrates the same countrywide processes of resource deprivation and local resistance.

Claiming the Commons in Karnataka

On 14 November 1984, the government of Karnataka entered into an agreement with Harihar Polyfibres, a rayon-producing unit in the north of the state, that forms part of the great Indian industrial house of the Birlas. By this agreement, a new company was formed. It was to be called the Karnataka Pulpwoods Limited (hereafter KPL), in which the government had a holding of 51 percent, with 49 percent vesting in Harihar Polyfibres. KPL was charged with growing eucalyptus and other fast-growing species for the use of Harihar Polyfibres. For this purpose, the state had identified 30,000 hectares of common land, spread over four districts in the northern part of Karnataka. This land was nominally owned by the state (following precedents set under British colonial rule, when the state had arbitrarily asserted its rights of ownership over noncultivated land all over India)—however, the grass, trees, and shrubs standing on it were extensively used by surrounding villages for fuel, fodder, and other materials.[4]

This land was granted by the state to KPL with a lease of forty years and a ridiculously low annual rent of one rupee per acre. As much as 87.5 percent of the produce was to go directly to Harihar Polyfibres; the private-sector company even had the option of buying the remaining 12.5 percent. All in all, this was an extraordinarily advantageous arrangement for the Birla–owned firm. The government of Karnataka was even willing to guarantee the loans that were to finance KPL's operations: loans to be obtained from several nationalized banks, one of which was, in a telling irony, the National Bank of Agriculture and Rural Development.

For years before the formation of KPL, the wood–based industry had been clamoring for captive plantations. For at least two decades, industrial units had been faced with chronic shortages of raw material. Forests were being depleted all over India; this deforestation had itself been caused primarily by overexploitation of green trees to meet industrial demands. Although the state had always granted them handsome subsidies in the provision of timber from government forests, paper, rayon, and plywood factories were eager to acquire firmer control over their sources of supply. Indian law prohibited large-scale ownership of land by private companies: in the circumstances, joint sector companies (i.e., units jointly owned by state and capital) provided the most feasible option. Indeed, no sooner had KPL been formed than industrialists in other parts of India began pressing state governments to start similar units with their participation and for their benefit.

Of course, paper and rayon factories were not alone in complaining about shortages of woody biomass. A decade previously, the Chipko Andolan had highlighted the difficulties faced by peasants in gaining access to the produce of the forests. In the wake of Chipko a wide-ranging debate on forest policy had arisen, with scholars and activists arguing that the state's forest policies had consistently discriminated against the rights of peasants, tribals, and pastoralists, while unduly favoring the urban-industrial sector (Anon., 1982; Fernandes and Kulkarni, 1983; Guha, 1983).

There was little question that, as a result of these policies, shortages of fuel and fodder had become pervasive throughout rural India. In Karnataka itself, one study, conducted around the time of the formation of KPL but independent of this happening, estimated that although the annual demand for fuelwood in the state was 12.4 million tonnes (mt), annual production was 10.4 mt—a shortfall of 16 percent. In the case of fodder, the corresponding figures were 35.7 and 23 mt respectively—a deficit of as much as 33 percent (Gadgil and Sinha, 1985).

The fodder crisis, in turn, illustrated the crucial importance of species choice in programs of reforestation. From the early sixties on, the government's Forest Department had enthusiastically promoted the plantation of eucalyptus on state-owned land. In many parts of India, rich, diverse natural forests were felled to make way for single species plantations of this tree of Australian origin. This choice was clearly dictated by industry, for eucalyptus is a quick-growing species coveted by both paper and rayon mills. But it is totally unsuitable as fodder—indeed, one reason eucalyptus was planted by the Forest Department was that it was never browsed by cattle and goats, thus making regeneration that much easier to achieve. Environmentalists deplored this preference for eucalyptus, which was known to have negative effects on soil fertility, water retention, and biological diversity generally. Eucalyptus was, moreover, a "plant which socially speaking has all the characteristics of a weed," (Bandyopadhyay and Shiva 1984) in that it benefited industry at the expense of the rural poor, themselves hard hit by biomass shortages. These critics advocated the plantation and protection instead of multipurpose, indigenous tree species more suited for meeting village requirements of fuel, fodder, fruit, and fiber (Bandyopadhyay and Shiva, 1984; Agarwal and Narain, 1985).

In the context of this wider, all-India debate, the formation of KPL seemed a clear move in favor of industry as the noncultivated lands allotted to it had long constituted a vital (and often irreplaceable) source of biomass for small peasants, pastoralists, and wood-working artisans. Thus, within months of its coming into existence, the new company became the object of sharp criticism. In December 1984, the state's preeminent writer and man of letters, Dr. Kota Shivram Karanth, wrote an essay in the most widely circulated Kannada daily, calling upon the people of Karnataka to totally oppose "this friendship between Birlas and the government and the resulting joint sector company."

The opposition to KPL picked up after 15 July 1986, the date on which the state actually transferred the first installment of land (3,590 hectares) to KPL. Even as the company was preparing the ground for planting eucalyptus, petitions and representations were flying thick and fast between the villages of north Karnataka (where the land was physically located) and the state capital of Bangalore, 400 kilometers to the south. The chief minister of Karnataka, Ramkrishna Hegde, was deluged with letters protesting the formation of KPL. The letters came from individuals and organizations all over the state; one letter, given wide prominence, was signed by a former chief minister, a former chief justice, and a former minister. Meanwhile, protest meetings were organized at several villages in the region and the matter was raised in the state legislature.[5]

In the forefront of the movement against KPL was the Samaj Parivartan Samudaya (Association for Social Change—hereafter SPS), a voluntary organization working in the Dharwad district of Karnataka. The SPS had, in fact, cut its teeth in a previous campaign against Harihar Polyfibres. This was a movement it had organized against the pollution of the Tungabhadra River by the rayon factory, whose untreated effluents were killing fish and severely impairing the health and livelihood of villages downstream. On 2 October 1984, (Mahatma Gandhi's birth anniversary), SPS held a large demonstration outside the production unit of Harihar Polyfibres. Then, in December 1985, it filed a public interest litigation in the High Court of Karnataka against the State Pollution Control Board, for its failure to check the pollution of the Tungabhadra by the Birla factory.[6]

Before this petition was heard, SPS filed a public interest writ against KPL, this time in the Supreme Court of India in New Delhi. This action was motivated by a similar writ in the state High Court, filed by a youth organization working among the farmers in the Sagartaluka (county) of the adjoining Shimoga district. Here, in a significant judgment, Justice Bopanna issued a stay order, instructing the deputy commissioner of Shimoga to ensure that common lands were not arbitrarily transferred to KPL and that villagers be allowed access to fodder, fuel, and other usufruct from the disputed land (Kanvalli, 1990).

Submitted in early 1987, the Supreme Court petition was primarily the handiwork of SPS. The petitioners spoke on behalf of the 500,000 villagers living in the region of KPL's operations, the people most directly affected by the action of the state in handing over common land to one company. The transferred land, said the petition, "is the only available land vested in the village community since time immemorial and is entirely meant for meeting their basic needs like fodder, fuel, small timber, etc. Neither agriculture could be carried out, nor the minimum needs of life, such as leaves, firewood, and cattle fodder could be sustained without the use of the said lands."

In this context, went on the petition, the arbitrary and unilateral action of the state amounted to the passing of "control of material resources from the hands of common people to capitalists." This was a "stark abuse of power," violative not just of the general canons of social justice but also of two provisions of the Indian Constitution itself: the right to fair procedure guaranteed by Article 14, and the right to life and liberty (in this case, of the village community) vested under Article 21 of that document. Finally, the petitioners contended that the planting of monocultures of eucalyptus, as envisaged by KPL, would have a "disastrous effect on the ecological balance of the region."[7]

The arguments of equity and ecological stability aside, this petition is notable for its stubborn insistence that the lands in contention were common rather than state property, "vested in the village community since time immemorial." Here, the claims of time and tradition were counterposed to the legal status quo, wherein the state both claimed and enforced rights of ownership. In this respect, the petition was perfectly in line with popular protests in defense of forest rights, which since colonial times have held the Forest Department to be an agent of usurpation, taking over by superior physical force land that by right belonged to the community (see Guha and Gadgil, 1989).

On 24 March 1987, the Supreme Court responded to the petition by issuing a stay order, thus preventing the government of Karnataka from transferring any more land to KPL. Encouraged by this preliminary victory, SPS now turned to popular mobilization in the villages. In May, it held a training camp in nonviolence at Kusnur, a village in Dharwad district where 400 hectares of land had already been transferred to KPL. A parallel organization of villagers, the Guddanadu Abhivruddi Samiti (Hill Areas Development Committee) was initiated to work alongside SPS. The two groups held a series of preparatory meetings in Kusnur and other villages nearby, for a protest scheduled for 14 November 1987, to coincide with the third anniversary of the formation of KPL.

On 14 November, about two thousand people converged at Kusnur. Men, women, and children took an oath of nonviolence in a school yard, and then proceeded for a novel protest, termed the *Kithiko-Hachiko* (Pluck-and-Plant) *satyagraha*. Led by drummers, waving banners and shouting slogans, the protesters moved on to the disputed area. Here, they first uprooted 100 saplings of eucalyptus before planting in their place tree species useful locally for fruit and for fodder. Before dispersing, the villagers took a pledge to water and tend the saplings they had planted (Bhattacharjea, 1987).[8]

The next major development in the KPL case was the partial vacation, on 26 April 1988, by the Supreme Court of the stay it had granted a year previously. Now it allowed the transfer of a further 3,000 hectares to KPL (such interim and ad hoc grants of land were also allowed in 1989 and 1990) (Hiremath, 1992).

The court appearing to have let them down, SPS prepared once again for direct action. They commenced training camps in the villages, planning to culminate in a fresh Pluck–and–Plant satyagraha. Meanwhile, journalists sympathetic to their movement intensified the press campaign against KPL (Bhattacharjea, 1988a, 1988b).

The mounting adverse publicity and the prospect of renewed popular protest forced the government of Karnataka to seek a compromise. On 3 June 1988, the chief secretary of the state government (its highest-ranking official) convened a meeting attended by representatives of SPS, KPL, and the Forest Department. He suggested setting up a one-person commission, comprising the distinguished ecologist, Madhav Gadgil, to enquire into the conflicting claims (and demands) of the villagers and KPL. Until the commission submitted its report, KPL was asked to suspend its operations in Dharwad district and SPS to withdraw its proposed monsoon satyagraha.

The setting up of committees and commisions is, of course, a classic delaying tactic. In India it is used by colonial and democratic governments alike to defuse and contain popular protest. In this case, the government had no intention of formally appointing the Madhav Gadgil Commission, for the ecologist was known as a critic of the industrial bias of state forest policy (Gadgil, Prasad, and Ali, 1983), and thus likely to report adversely on KPL. So the commission never materialized; in response, SPS set about organizing another Pluck–and–Plant satyagraha for 8 August 1988. This time, however, the protesters were arrested and hustled off before they could actually reach KPL's eucalyptus plot.

In later years, nonviolent direct action continued to be a vital plank of SPS's strategy. Thus, in an attempt to more closely link the issues of industrial pollution and the alienation of common land, it organized, in August 1989, in the towns of Hangal and Ranibennur, public bonfires of rayon cloth made by Harihar Polyfibres. The burning of mill-made cloth was reminiscent of the bonfires of Manchester textiles during India's freedom movement. Where that campaign stood for national self–reliance (*swadeshi*), this one affirmed *village* self–reliance by rejecting cloth made of artificial fiber. However, the following year, 1990, SPS reverted to its own, patented method of protest. Therefore, on Indian Independence Day (15 August), it invited the respected Chipko leader, Chandi Prasad Bhatt, to lead a Pluck–and–Plant satyagraha in the Nagvand village of the Hirekerrur *taluka* of Dharwad (*The Hindu*, 20 August 1990).

Where these protests kept the issue alive at the grassroots, SPS continued to work the wider political and legal system to its advantage. Through friendly contacts in the state administration, it obtained copies of four orders issued in 1987 by the chief conservator of forests (general), an official known to be particularly close to the Birlas. By these orders, he had transferred a further 14,000 hectares of forest land to KPL, an area far in excess of what the Supreme Court had allowed. On the basis of these "leaked" documents, SPS filed a further Contempt and Perjury petition in October 1988.

The SPS had, meanwhile, also persuaded public-sector banks to delay the release of funds to KPL, pending the final hearing and settlement of the case in the Supreme Court. More crucially, it had lobbied effectively with the government of India in New Delhi to clarify its own position on KPL-style schemes. In February 1988, an official of the Union Ministry of Environment and Forests, deposing in the Supreme Court, stated unambiguously that the raising of industrial plantations by joint sector companies required the prior permission of the government of India. Later the same year, a new national forest policy was announced, which explicitly prohibited monocultural plantations on grounds of ecological stability. Then, in June 1989, the secretary of the Ministry of Environment and Forests wrote to the government of Karnataka expressing his concern about the KPL project.

Within Karnataka itself, resolutions asking the government to cancel the KPL agreement were passed by local representative bodies, including several Mandal Panchayats, each representing a group of villages, as well as the Zilla Parishad (district council) of Dharwad. This was followed by a letter to the chief minister, signed by fifty-four members of the state legislature and sent on 11 July 1990, asking him to close KPL so as "to reserve village common land for the common use of villagers." With public opinion and the central government arrayed against it, and possibly anticipating an adverse final judgment in the Supreme Court, the government of Karnataka decided to wind up KPL. The company's closure was formally announced in a board meeting of 27 September 1990, but by then it was already nonfunctional. Thus, its report for the previous financial year (April 1989 to March 1990) complained that "during the year the plantation activity has practically come to a standstill, excepting raising 449 hectares of plantations"—a tiny fraction of the 30, 000 hectares of common land it had once hoped to capture for its exclusive use.

A Vocabulary of Protest

The struggle against KPL had as its mass base, so to speak, the peasants, pastoralists, and fisherfolk directly affected by environmental abuse. Yet key leadership roles were assumed by activists who, although they came from the region, were not themselves directly engaged in production. Of the SPS activists who were involved more or less full time in the movement, one had been a labor organizer, a second a social worker and progressive farmer, and a third an engineer who had returned to India after working for years in the United States. Crucial support was also provided by intellectuals more distant from the action. These included the greatest living Kannada writer, Dr. Shivram Karanth, a figure of high moral authority and the first petitioner in the Supreme Court case against KPL. A copetitioner was the Centre for Science and Environment, a greatly respected Delhi-based research and advocacy group whose influence in the media and in the government was shrewdly drawn upon by the activists from Karnataka.

This unity, of communities at the receiving end of ecological degradation and of social activists with the experience and education to negotiate the politics of protest, has been characteristic of environmental struggles in India. In other respects, too, the SPS-led struggle was quite typical. For underlying the KPL controversy was a series of oppositions that frame most such conflicts in India: rich versus poor, urban versus rural, nature for profit versus nature for subsistence, the state versus the people.[9]

In more explicitly ecological terms, these conflicts oppose "ecosystem people"—that is, those communities that depend almost exclusively on the natural resources of their own locality—to "omnivores," individuals and groups with the social power to capture, transform, and use natural resources from a much wider catchment area (sometimes, indeed, the whole world). The ecosystem people category includes the bulk of India's rural population; small peasants, landless laborers, tribals, pastoralists, and artisans. The category of omnivores comprises industrialists, professionals, politicians, and government officials—all of whom are based in the towns and cities—as well as a small but significant fraction of the rural elite, the prosperous farmers in tract of heavily irrigated, chemicalized, Green Revolution agriculture. The history of development in independent India can thus be interpreted as being, in essence, a process of resource capture by the omnivores at the expense of ecosystem people. This process has, in turn, created a third major ecological class: that of "ecological refugees," peasants-turned-slum dwellers, who eke out a living in the cities on the droppings of omnivore prosperity (Gadgil and Guha, 1995).

It is not accidental that conflicts over nature and natural resources were muted in the first two decades of Indian independence, only to suddenly erupt and spread all over the country beginning in the mid-seventies. One reason for this is, of course, the accumulating impacts of ecological degradation. But another, equally important factor is the changing popular perception of the Indian state. Through the fifties and sixties, the Indian National Congress (which has held power in New Delhi for all but five years since 1947) was widely acknowledged to be the authentic legatee of a genuinely mass-based national movement. After independence, the state was no longer regarded as the instrument of a colonial power bent on subjugation and the extraction of surplus; rather, it was held to be the vehicle for bringing about all-round social and economic development. With time, however, the Indian state has lost much of its legitimacy and is seen increasingly as being captive to the interests of the omnivores; the corrupt politician and official, the industrialist, and the rich farmer. At the same time, the democratic system has afforded both ecosystem people and ecological refugees a modicum of clout, creating a space for the prosecution of social protest.

In this framework, the environmentalism of the poor might be understood as the resistance offered by ecosystem people to the process of resource capture by omnivores. This is embodied in movements against large dams by tribals to be displaced by them, or struggles by peasants against the diversion of forest and grazing land to industry. In recent years, the most important such struggle has been the Narmada Bachao Andolan (hereafter NBA), the movement representing the ecosystem people who face imminent displacement by a huge dam on the Narmada River in central India. The movement has been led by the forty-year-old Medha Patkar, a woman of courage and character once described (by a journalist) as an "ecological Joan of Arc." As I write this (December 1994), the national newspapers are covering the latest initiative of the NBA, an indefinite hunger strike by Patkar, demanding that the government immediately halt work on the dam.

I cannot provide a detailed analysis of the origins and development of the Narmada conflict (Morse and Berger, 1993; Gadgil and Guha, 1995, Chapter III; Baviskar, forthcoming). But I can briefly describe one aspect of the movement that is of particular relevance to this conference: namely, its flexible and wide-ranging "vocabulary of protest."

I offer the term vocabulary of protest as an alternative to Charles Tilly's concept of the "repertoire of contention." Tilly and his associates have done pioneering work on the study of dissent and direct action. This work has focused on the techniques most characteristic of different societies, social groups, or historical periods. While acknowledging this contribution, I feel, however, that Tilly's own understanding of direct action tends to be a narrowly instrumental one, with actors drawing on those techniques from a broader repertoire of contention that most effectively defend or advance their economic and political interests (Tilly, 1978, 1993). But in my own work on social protest, I have considered techniques of direct action as having simultaneously a utilitarian and an expressive dimension. In adopting a particular strategy, protesters are both trying to defend their interests *and* passing judgment on the prevailing social arrangements. This latter, so to speak, ideological dimension of social protest needs to be inferred even when it is not formally articulated— that protesting peasants do not pass around a printed manifesto does not mean that they do not have developed notions of right and wrong. In field or factory, ghetto or grazing ground, struggles over resources, even when they have tangible material origins, have always also been struggles over meaning. Thus, I prefer the term vocabulary of protest—for "vocabulary" more than "repertoire" and "protest" more than "contention" helps clarify the notion that most forms of direct action, even if unaccompanied by a written manifesto, are simultaneously statements of purpose and of belief. In the act of doing, protesters are saying something, too. The Kithiko-Hachiko satyagraha was not simply an affirmation of peasant claims over disputed property: as a strategy of protest, its aim was not merely to insist, "This land is ours," but also (and equally significantly) to ask, "What are trees for?"

With this caveat in place, let us return to the Narmada Bachao Andolan. Like the anti-KPL struggle, the Narmada movement has operated simultaneously on several flanks: a strong media campaign, court petitions, and lobbying of key actors (such as the World Bank, which was to fund a part of the dam project). Most effectively, though, it has deployed a dazzlingly varied vocabulary of protest, in defense of the rights of the peasants and tribals to be displaced by the dam.

These strategies of direct action might be classified under four broad heads. First, there is the collective *show of strength*, as embodied in demonstrations (Hindi: *pradarshan*) organized in towns and cities. Mobilizing as many people as they can, protesters march through the town, shouting slogans, singing songs, and wending their way to a public meeting that marks the procession's culmination. The aim here is to assert a presence in the city, which is the locus of local, provincial, or national power. The demonstrators carry a message that is at once threatening and imploring: in effect, they tell the rulers (and city people in general), "do not forget us, the dispossessed in the countryside. We can make trouble, but not if you hand out justice."

There is also *disruption of economic life* through more militant acts of protest. One such tactic is the *hartal* or *bandh* (shut-down strike), wherein shops are forced to lower shutters or buses are pulled off the roads, thus bringing normal life to a standstill. A variant to this is the *rasta roko* (road blockade), through which traffic on an important highway is blocked by squatting protesters, sometimes for days. These techniques are rather more coercive than persuasive, foreshadowing the economic costs to the state (or to other sections of the public) if they do not yield to the dissenters.

Where the hartal or rasta roko aim at disrupting economic activity across a wide space, a third type of action is more sharply focused on an individual target. Thus, the *dharna* (sit-down strike) might be used to stop work at a specific dam site or mine. Sometimes the target is a figure of authority rather than a site of production; for example, protesting peasants might *gherao* (surround) a high public official, allowing the official to move only after the official has heard their grievances and promised to act upon them.

The fourth, generic strategy of direct action aims at putting moral pressure on the state *as a whole*, not merely on one of its functionaries. Preeminent here is the *bhook hartal*, the indefinite hunger strike undertaken by a charismatic leader of a popular movement. This technique was once used successfully by Sunderlal Bahuguna of the Chipko Andolan; in recent years, it has been resorted to on several occasions by Medha Patkar, the remarkable leader of the Narmada Bachao Andolan. In the bhook hartal, the courage and self–sacrifice of the individual leader is directly counterposed to the claims to legitimacy of the state. The fast is usually carried out in a public place and is closely reported in the media. As the days drag on, and the leader's health perilously declines, the state is forced into a gesture of submission—if only by constituting a fresh committee to review the case in contention.

The bhook hartal is most often the preserve of a single, heroic, exemplary figure. A sister technique, also aimed at *shaming the state*, is more of a collective undertaking. This is the *jail bharo andolan* (lit: movement to fill the jails), through which protesters peacefully and deliberately court arrest by violating the law, hoping the government will lose face by putting masses of its own citizens behind bars. The law most often breached is Section 144 of the Criminal Procedure Code, invoked, in anticipation of social tension, to prohibit gatherings of more than five people.

The pradarshan, hartal, rasta roko, dharna, gherao, bhook hartal, and jail bharo andolan are some of the techniques that make up the environmental movement's vocabulary of protest. This is a vocabulary shared across the spectrum of protesting groups, but new situations constantly call for new innovations. Thus, peasants in Garhwal developed the idiosyncratic but truly effective Chipko technique; the SPS in Dharwad, opposing eucalyptus plantations, thought up the Kithiko-Hachiko satyagraha; and, most dramatic of all, the NBA has threatened a *jal samadhi* (water burial), saying its cadres would refuse to move from the villages slated for submergence even after the dam's sluice gates are closed and the waters start rising to where they are.

A Rhetoric of Betrayal

The techniques of direct action itemized above have, of course, deep and honorable origins. They were first forged, in India's long struggle for freedom from British rule, by Mohandas Karamchand "Mahatma" Gandhi. In developing and refining this vocabulary of protest, Gandhi drew both upon Western theories of civil disobedience and traditions of peasant resistance within India itself.[10]

Mahatma Gandhi is indeed the usually acknowledged and sometimes un-acknowledged patron saint of Indian environmentalism. From the Chipko Andolan to the Narmada Bachao Andolan, environmental activists have heavily relied on Gandhian techniques of direct action, and drawn abundantly on Gandhi's polemic against heavy industrialization. Moreover, the movement's best-known figures—Chandi Prasad Bhatt and Sunderlal Bahuguna of the Chipko Andolan, for example, or Medha Patkar and Baba Amte of the Narmada Bachao Andolan—have repeatedly underlined their own debt to the figure of Gandhi.

One must not deny other influences, however, for under the broad umbrella of the environmental movement are many groups with little connection to Gandhi. For example, there is the Kerala Sastra Sahitya Parishad, the organization of radical scientists in southern India that arises from a background of Marxism, but whose contribution to the environmental movement is second to none. Other voluntary groups in the environmental field are variously influenced by socialism, liberation theology, and traditions of self-help. Nonetheless, it is probably fair to say that the life and practice of Gandhi are the single most important influence on the Indian environmental movement (Guha, 1988).

This invocation of Gandhi is conducted through what might be called a rhetoric of betrayal. For the sharpening of environmental conflict has vividly brought to light the failed hopes of India's freedom struggle. That movement commanded a mass base among the peasantry; its leaders promised a new deal for rural India. And yet, after 1947 the political elite has worked to ensure that the benefits of planned economic development have flown primarily to the urban-industrial complex.

The KPL controversy illustrates this paradox as well as any other case does. On one side were the peasants and pastoralists of north Karnataka; on the other, an insensitive state government in league with the second-largest business house in the country. As one protester expressed it in Kusnur: "Our fore-fathers who fought to get rid of the foreign yoke thought that our country would become a land of milk and honey once the British were driven out. But now we see our rulers joining hands with the monopolists to take away basic resources like land, water and forests from the [village] people who have traditionally used them for their livelihood." In much the same vein, a Chipko activist once told me: "After independence, we thought our forests would be used to build local industries and generate local employment, and our water resources to light our lamps and run our flour mills." But to his dismay, the Himalayan forests continued to service the paper and turpentine factories of the plains, even as the hill rivers were dammed to supply drinking water to Delhi and electricity to the national grid which feeds into industries and urban agglomerations all over India. While private industry has thus gained privileged access to natural resources, the burden of environmental degradation has fallen heavily on the rural poor. In a bitter commentary on this, the common people of Dharwad district have come to refer to the noxious air outside Harihar Polyfibres as "Birla Perfume," to the water of the Tungabhadra river as "Birla Teertha" (holy water of the Birlas), and to the eucalyptus as "Birla Kalpataru" (the Birla wonder tree) (Kanvalli, 1990, 1).

In his own way, Gandhi had anticipated that a bias toward urban-industrial development would result in a one-sided exploitation of the hinterland. As he put it in June 1946, "the blood of the villages is the cement with which the edifice of the cities is built."[11] Or, to quote a statement made in 1928, where the ecological implications are more explicit still: "God forbid that India should ever take to industrialization after the manner of the West. The economic imperialism of a single tiny island kingdom [England] is today keeping the world in chains. If an entire nation of 300 million [India's population at the time of writing] took to similar economic exploitation, it would strip the world bare like locusts."[12] For Gandhi, "to make India like England and America is to find some other races and places of the earth for exploitation." As it appeared that the Western nations had already "divided among themselves all the known races outside Europe and there are no new worlds to conquer, he asked, pointedly, "what can be the fate of India trying to ape the West?"[13]

Taking these (and other) clues of an environmental nature that are strewn across the vast corpus of Gandhi's writings, the environmentalists of today insist that, since 1947, the attempt has been precisely to "make India like England and America." But without access to the resources and markets enjoyed by those countries when they began to industrialize, India, inevitably, has had to rely on the exploitation of its own people and environment. The natural resources of the countryside have been increasingly channelized to meet the demands of the cities and the factories. This diversion of forests, water and so on, to what might be termed the omnivore sector, has accelerated processes of environmental degradation and dispossesed rural communities of their traditional rights of access and use. To invoke a slogan made famous by the Narmada Bachao Andolan, this is a process of "destructive development"—destructive both of rural society and of the natural fabric within which it rests. The task, then, is to move beyond this to a new, "nondestructive" model of development, wherein (to quote Gandhi) "the blood that is today inflating the arteries of the cities run[s] once again in the blood vessels of the village."

In this manner, Mahatma Gandhi provides the environmental movement both with a vocabulary of protest and an ideological critique of development in independent India. The return to Gandhi is thus also a return to his vision for free India: a vision so completely disregarded in practice. Perhaps it is more accurate to see this as a rhetoric of betrayal *and* of affirmation, as symbolized in the dates most often chosen to launch (or end) programs of direct action. These are 2 October, Gandhi's birth anniversary; 15 August, Indian Independence Day; and most poignantly, 8 August, the day in 1942 when Gandhi's last great anticolonial campaign, the Quit India movement, was launched. In invoking this last date, environmentalists are asking the state and the capitalists, the rulers of today to "quit" their control over forests and water.

Two Kinds of Environmentalism

In the preceding sections of this essay, I have used the controversy surrounding the KPL to outline the origins, trajectory, and rhetoric of the environmental movement in India. In conclusion, let me broaden the discussion by briefly contrasting the environmentalism of the poor with the more closely studied phenomenon of First World environmentalism. This contrast can be sharply etched by juxtaposing two episodes of direct action, one carried out in California, the other attempted in central India.

In May 1979, a young American environmentalist, Mark Dubois, chained himself to a boulder in the Stanislaus River in California. The canyon where he lay formed part of the reservoir of the New Melones Dam, whose construction Dubois and his organization, Friends of the River, had long but unsuccessfully opposed. In October of the previous year (1978), the Army Corps of Engineers had completed the dam, and the following April it closed the floodgates. The level of the reservoir started rising, and it appeared as if the campaign to "Save the Stanislaus" had failed. Then, in an act of rare heroism, Mark Dubois went into the waters and chained himself to a rock. He chose a lonely hidden spot; only one friend knew of his location (Palmer, 1982, Chapter VIII).

Fourteen years later, an uncannily similar strategy of protest was threatened against another dam, on another river in another continent. In August 1993, with the onset of the Indian monsoon, the vast reservoir of the Sardar Sarovar Dam on the Narmada River began filling up to capacity. It seemed that the decade-long Narmada Bachao Andolan had irrevocably lost its fight. But then the leader of the movement, Medha Patkar, decided to drown herself in the swollen waters. Patkar announced her decision to walk into the river on 6 August, along with a group of colleagues, but at a place and time not to be disclosed. Fearing detention by the police, Patkar disappeared into the countryside weeks before the appointed date.

I dare say Medha Patkar had not heard of Mark Dubois, but the parallels in their modes of protest are striking indeed. Both individuals formed part of ongoing, popular movements against large dams. Only when the movements seemed to have failed did Patkar and Dubois decide to throw the last card in their pack, so to speak, offering their lives to stop the dam. In both cases, the political system was alert (or open) enough not to allow the environmentalists to make this supreme sacrifice. In Stanislaus, the Corps of Engineers stopped filling the reservoir and sent search parties by air and on land to find and rescue Dubois. In the Narmada Valley, Patkar and her band were found and prevailed upon to withdraw their *samarpan dal* (martyrs' squad), in return for the Indian government's promise for a fresh, independent review of the Sardar Sarovar project.

Although the strategies of direct action might have been superficially similar, their underlying motivations were not. Mark Dubois and his colleagues were striving, above all, to save the Stanislaus Canyon as one of the last remaining examples of the unspoiled, California wilderness. As Dubois wrote to the colonel of the Corps of Engineers prior to entering the river:

> All the life of this canyon, its wealth of archaeological and historical roots to our past, and its unique geological grandeur are enough reasons to protect this canyon *just for itself*. But, in addition, all the spiritual values with which this canyon has filled tens of thousands of folks should prohibit us from committing the unconscionable act of wiping this place off the face of the earth (Mark Dubois to Colonel Donald O'Shea, reproduced in Palmer, 1982, 163–164, emphasis added).

By contrast, Patkar and her colleagues hoped not only to save the Narmada River itself, but also (and more crucially) the tens of thousands of peasants to be displaced by the dam being built on it. When completed, the Sardar Sarovar project will submerge 245 villages, with an estimated total population of 66,675 people, most of whom are tribals and poor peasants (Anon., 1988). True, the dam will also inundate old growth forests and historic sites, but it will most dramatically destroy the living culture of the human communities that live by the Narmada River. The project has thus become a symbol of a destructive and grossly inequitous pattern of development, and the struggle of Patkar and her associates becomes, as they put it (in a message written on the forty-second anniversary of Gandhi's martydom), a move "towards our ultimate goal of [a] socially just and ecologically sustainable model of development."[14]

The Stanislaus/Narmada or Dubois/Patkar comparison illustrates a fundamental difference between the ecology of affluence and the environmentalism of the poor. Mark Dubois's action, heroic though it was, was quite in line with the dominant thrust of the environmental movement in the North, toward the protection of pristine, unspoiled nature—a reservoir of biological diversity and enormous aesthetic appeal that serves as an ideal (if temporary) haven from the workaday world. In protecting the wild, it asserts, we are both acknowledging an ethical responsibility toward other species and enriching the spiritual side of our own existence (cf. Nash, 1989). By contrast, Medha Patkar's action was consistent with the dominant thrust of the environmental movement in India, which powerfully features questions of production and distribution within human society. The concern here is with "the use of the environment and who should benefit from it; not with environmental protection for its own sake" (Agarwal, 1987, 167). It is impossible to say, for instance, of the Indian environmental movement what Jurgen Habermas has claimed of the European green movement: namely, that it is sparked not "by problems of distribution, but by concern for the grammar of forms of life" (Anon., 1981).[15]

These distinctions are important but they are not necessarily culture bound or culture specific. Thus, the Western wilderness crusade has its vanguard representatives in the Third World; they spearhead the setting aside of vast areas as national parks and sanctuaries, strictly protected from human interference. Southern lovers of the wilderness come typically from patrician backgrounds and show little regard for the fate of the human groups who, after a parkland is designated as protected, are abruptly displaced without compensation for territory that they have lived on for generations and have come to regard as their own (Guha, 1989; West and Brechin, 1991). Such is the ecology of affluence within the countries of the South that, like their counterparts in the North, they have tended to underplay and more often to ignore questions of equity within the human species. But there is also a growing environmentalism of the poor in the most prosperous countries of the North. This is exemplified by the movement for environmental justice in the United States, the struggles of low-class, often black communities against the toxic waste sites that, by accident and frequently by design, come to be sited near them (and away from affluent neighborhoods). One U.S. commentator, Ruth Rosen, has nicely captured the contrast between the environmental justice movement and the wilderness lovers. "At best," she writes, "the large, mainstream environmental groups focus on the health of the planet—the wilderness, forests, and oceans that cannot protect themselves. In contrast, the movement for environmental justice, led by the poor, is not concerned with overabundance, but with the environmental hazards and social and economic inequalities that ravage their communities" (Rosen, 1994, 229; see also Szasz, 1994).

These words could also have been used to contrast the concerns of the Indian branch of the World Wide Fund for Nature, for instance, with the activities and struggles of the Narmada Bachao Andolan.[16] The ecology of affluence in the North and in the South affirms that there can be "No Humanity without Nature!" To this the environmentalism of the poor, in the North as much as in the South, responds with the equally compelling slogan, "No Nature without Social Justice!" (see Kothari and Parajuli, 1993).

Notes

1. This was shown most authoritatively, perhaps, in the first two Citizens' Reports on the Indian environment, published by New Delhi's Centre for Science and Environment in 1982 and 1985.
2. Martínez Alier's arguments have been extended in Brechin and Kempton (1994). His writings apart, the arguments also derive from conversations over the years with Martínez Alier and with Indian ecologist Madhav Gadgil—two colleagues whose insights on the origins of environmental conflict have greatly influenced my own work.
3. I am aware that the provocative argument made by Douglas and Wildavsky has been disputed with regard to the ecology of affluence itself—see the critical review of the book by James Boon in *Raritan* (Spring 1983, 4[2]).
4. Aside from specific sources, which are cited, this discussion of the KPL case also draws on numerous unpublished and locally printed documents, as well as on my own fieldwork and interviews in the region.
5. *Jagruta Vani* (quarterly newsletter of the Samaj Parivartan Samudaya, Dharwad) (December 1986, 2[4]).
6. Writ Petition Number 19483 in the High Court of Karnataka, Bangalore (SPS and others versus Karnataka State Pollution Control Board and others). On the antipollution movement, see also Hiremath (1987).
7. Writ Petition (Civil) Number 35 of 1987 in the Supreme Court of India, New Delhi (Dr. K. Shivram Karanth, SPS et al. versus the State of Karnataka, KPL et al.).
8. Coined by Gandhi, the term "*satyagraha*" (literally, "truth-force") is used generically in India to denote any form of nonviolent direct action.
9. But the KPL case was atypical in one telling respect—environmental movements of the poor rarely end in emphatic victory.
10. In contemporary India these "Gandhian" techniques are by no means the sole preserve of the environmental movement. They are used in all sorts of ways by all sorts of social struggles: farmers wanting higher fertilizer subsidies, hospital workers wanting greater security of tenure, or ethnic minorities fighting for a separate province.
11. *Harijan*, 23 June 1946, in *Collected Works of Mahatma Gandhi*, Volume 84, page 226 f.
12. *Young India*, 20 December 1928, in *CWMG*, Volume 38, pp. 243–244.
13. *Young India*, 7 October 1926, in *CWMG*, Volume 31, pp. 478–479. A more detailed assessment of Gandhi's foresight in environmental matters can be found in Guha (1993), an abbreviated version of which was published in *Seminar* (New Delhi), annual number, January 1994.
14. Circular letter from Medha Patkar and others, dated 30 January 1990.
15. I am grateful to Amita Baviskar for this reference
16. But with the caveat that with regard to popular support and geographical spread, the movements of ecosystem people, rather than the work of groups such as the WWF, would qualify as the mainstream of the environmental movement in India.

References

Agarwal, Anil (1987). Human-Nature Interactions in a Third World Country. *The Environmentalist* 6(3):167.

Agarwal, Anil and Sunita Narain, Eds. (1985). *The State of India's Environment: A Citizens Report, 1984–1985*. New Delhi: Centre for Science and Environment.

Anon. (1981). New Social Movements. *Telos* (49):33–37.

Anon. (1982). *Undeclared Civil War: A Critique of the Forest Policy*. New Delhi: Peoples' Union for Democratic Rights.

Anon. (1988). *The Narmada Valley Project: A Critique*. New Delhi: Kalpavriksh.

Bandyopadhyay, J. (1987). Political Economy of Drought and Water Scarcity. *Economic and Political Weekly* (12 December).

Bandyopadhyay, J. and Vandana Shiva (1984). *Ecological Audit of Eucalyptus Cultivation*. Dehradun: Natraj Publishers.

Baviskar, Amita (forthcoming). *In the Belly of the River: Adivasi Battles over Nature in the Narmada Valley*. New Delhi: Oxford University Press. Also available in an earlier version as a doctoral dissertation undertaken at the Department of Rural Sociology, Cornell University.

Bhattacharjea, Ajit (1987). Satyagraha in Kusnur (in two parts). *Deccan Herald* (Bangalore) (19 and 20 November).

Bhattacharjea, Ajit (1988a). KPL Strikes Back. *Deccan Herald* (Bangalore) (5 May).

Bhattacharjea, Ajit (1988b). Kusnur: Significant Success. *Deccan Herald* (Bangalore) (15 June).

Bramwell, Anna (1989). *Ecology in the Twentieth Century: A History*. New Haven: Yale University Press.

Brechin, Stephen R. and Willet Kempton (1994). Global Environmentalism: A Challenge to the Postmaterialism Thesis? *Social Science Quarterly* 75(2):245–269.

CWMG (1958–1984). Collected Works of Mahatma Gandhi. Delhi: Publications Division, Ministry of Information and Broadcasting, Government of India.

Dominick, III, Raymond H. (1992). *The Environmental Movement in Germany: Prophets and Pioneers, 1871–1971*. Bloomington: Indiana University Press.

Douglas, Mary and Aaron Wildavsky (1982). *Risk and Culture: An Essay on the Selection of Technical and Environmental Dangers*. Berkeley: University of California Press.

Fernandes, Walter and Sharad Kulkarni (1983). *Towards a New Forest Policy*. New Delhi: Indian Social Institute.

Fox, Stephen (1985). *The American Conservation Movement: John Muir and His Legacy*. Madison: University of Wisconsin Press.

Gadgil, Madhav and Ramachandra Guha (1995). *Ecology and Equity: The Use and Abuse of Nature in Contemporary India*. London: Routledge.

Gadgil, Madhav, Narendra S. Prasad, and Rauf Ali (1983). Forest Policy and Forest Management in India: A Critical Review. *Social Action* 27(1).

Gadgil, Madhav and Madhulika Sinha (1985). The Biomass Budget of Karnataka. In *The State of Karnataka's Environment*, ed. Cecil J. Saldanha. Bangalore: Centre for Taxonomic Studies.

Guha, Ramachandra (1983). Forestry in British and Post-British India: A Historical Analysis. *Economic and Political Weekly*, in two parts (29 October and 5–12 November).

Guha, Ramachandra (1988). Ideological Trends in Indian Environmentalism. *Economic and Political Weekly* (3 December).

Guha, Ramachandra (1989). Radical American Environmentalism and Wilderness Preservation: A Third World Critique. *Environmental Ethics* 11(1):71–84.

Guha, Ramachandra (1990). *The Unquiet Woods: Ecological Change and Peasant Resistance in the Himalaya*. Berkeley: University of California Press.

Guha, Ramachandra (1993). *Mahatma Gandhi and the Environmental Movement*. Pune: Parisar Annual Lecture.

Guha, Ramachandra and Madhav Gadgil (1989). State Forestry and Social Conflict in British India. *Past and Present* (123):141–177.

Hiremath, S. R. (1987). How to Fight a Corporate Giant. In *The Fight for Survival*, ed. Anil Agarwal, Darryl D'Monte, and Ujjwala Samarth. New Delhi: Centre for Science and Environment.

Hiremath, S. R. (1992). The Karnataka Pulpwoods Limited Case. Paper presented at the training workshop on Environment, People and the Law, at the Centre for Science and Environment, in New Delhi, 12–15 October.

Inglehart, Ronald (1977). *The Silent Revolution*. Princeton: Princeton University Press.

Jamison, Andrew, Ron Eyerman, Jacqueline Cramer, and Jeppe Lessoe (1992). *The Making of the New Environmental Consciousness: A Comparative Study of the Environmental Movements in Sweden, Denmark and the Netherlands*. Edinburgh: Edinburgh University Press.

Kanvalli, Sadanand (1990). *Quest for Justice*. Dharwad: SPS and others.

Kothari, Smitu and Pramod Parajuli (1993). No Nature without Social Justice: A Plea for Ecological and Cultural Pluralism in India. In *Global Ecology: A New Arena of Political Conflict*, ed. Wolfgang Sachs. London: Zed Books.

Lowe, Philip and Jane Goyder (1983). *Environmental Groups and Politics*. London: George Allen and Unwin.

Martínez Alier, Juan (1990a). Ecology and the Poor: A Neglected Dimension of Latin American History. *Journal of Latin American Studies* 28(3):621–639.

Martínez Alier, Juan (1990b). *Ecological Economics: Energy, Environment, Society*. Paperback edition. Oxford: Basil Blackwell.

Morse, Bradford and Thomas R. Berger (1993). *The Sardar Sarovar Project: The Report of the Independent Review*. Washington: The World Bank.

Nash, Roderick (1982). *Wilderness and the American Mind*. Third edition. New Haven: Yale University Press.

Nash, Roderick (1989). *The Rights of Nature: A History of Environmental Ethics*. Madison: University of Wisconsin Press.

Palmer, Tim (1982). *Stanislaus: The Struggle for a River*. Berkeley: University of California Press.

Rosen, Ruth (1994). Who Gets Polluted: The Movement for Environmental Justice. *Dissent* (Spring):229.

Szasz, Andrew (1994). *Ecopopulism: Toxic Waste and the Movement for Environmental Justice*. Minneapolis: University of Minnesota Press.

Thurow, Lester (1980). *The Zero-Sum Society: Distribution and the Possibilities for Change*. New York: Basic Books.

Tilly, Charles (1978). *From Mobilization to Revolution*. Reading, Mass.: Addison-Wesley Publishers.

Tilly, Charles (1986). *The Contentious French*. Cambridge, Mass.: Harvard University Press.

Tilly, Charles (1993). *European Revolutions 1492–1992*. Oxford: Blackwells.

West, Patrick C. and Steven R. Brechin (1991). *Resident Peoples and National Parks: Social Dilemmas and Strategies in International Conservation*. Tucson: The University of Arizona Press.

Arturo Escobar

Cultural Politics and Biological Diversity

State, Capital, and Social Movements in the Pacific Coast of Colombia

Introduction: The Cultural Politics of Nature

The centrality of nature for politics of diverse kinds—from the reactionary to the progressive—has become increasingly clear in recent times. The invention and reinvention of nature is, in the words of theorist Donna Haraway, "perhaps the most crucial arena of hope, oppression and contestation for inhabitants of the planet earth of our times" (1991, 1). Inherent in this claim is the belief that what counts as nature can no longer be taken for granted. While most of us continue to adhere to an anachronistic ideology of naturalism—the belief in an external and even untouched nature, preexisting any construction and independent of human history—recent technoscientific advances promise to free us from the shackles of this tradition. From recombinant DNA on, the inroads of technoscience into the molecular fabric of nature have advanced steadily. Today, life forms can be patented, the human genome perfected, reproduction conducted under conditions that seemed impossible only yesterday, and crops strengthened with genes borrowed from microorganisms—all instances of a profound transformation in the relation between humans and nature. As Paul Rabinow put it in explaining the regime of biosociality that he sees as emerging, "Nature will be made and remade through technique and will finally become artificial, just as culture becomes natural" (1992, 141).

If there is a place on earth where the ideology of naturalism is alive and well, it would be the tropical rainforests. They are instances of "violent nature, resilient life . . . one of the last repositories on earth of that timeless dream [of primeval nature]," as Edward Wilson tells us in his much-cited treatise on biological diversity (1992, 5). The humid forests of the tropics are, with good reason, perceived as the most natural form of nature left on earth, inhabited by the most natural people (indigenous peoples) possessing the most natural knowledge of saving nature (indigenous knowledge). As we shall see, however, tropical rainforests worldwide are being ineluctably thrust into the technoscientific and managerial project of designing nature. In places as diverse as Costa Rica, Thailand, the Ivory Coast, Colombia, Malaysia, Cameroon, Brazil, and Ecuador, projects of "biodiversity conservation"—most often funded by Northern environmental NGOs and the World Bank's Global Environment Facility (GEF)—are incorporating national planners and local communities alike into complex politics of technoscience that sees in the genes of rainforest species the key to the preservation of these fragile ecosystems. As the basic argument goes, the genes of rainforest species constitute a veritable library of genetic information, a source of wonder drugs and perhaps a cornucopia of foods, all of which could be converted into valuable products by biotechnology. The rainforest would thus be preserved at the same time that sizable profits are made, benefiting local people along the way.

The reason why so much attention is given to rainforests today lies in what may be termed "the irruption of the biological" as a central social fact in the global politics of the late twentieth century. After two centuries of systematic destruction of nature and life, and through a dialectical process set in motion by capitalism and modernity, the survival of biological life has emerged as a crucial question in the global landscape of capital and science. Conservation and sustainable development seem to have become inescapable problems for capital, thus forcing it to modify its older reckless logic according to which nature was chiefly seen as an external domain of raw materials to be appropriated at any cost; but the irruption of the biological into the global theater of development, environment, and security concerns is fostering a new look at life itself. As Wilson puts it, "the key to the survival of life as we know it today is the maintenance of biological diversity" (1992, 12). The rising discourse about biodiversity is the result of this problematization of the biological. It places tropical rainforest areas in key positions in global biopolitics.

This chapter examines the reconversions of nature and culture that are taking place around this discourse. Its geographical focus is the Pacific Coast region of Colombia, a rainforest area of almost legendary biodiversity. In this region, the cultural politics of nature is circumscribed by three main processes that have developed simultaneously after 1990: the radical policies of economic *apertura* (opening to world markets) pursued by the government in recent years, particularly the push toward integrating the country into the Pacific Basin economies; the novel strategies of sustainable development and biodiversity conservation; and growing and increasingly visible forms of black and indigenous mobilization.

I consider cultural politics the process enacted when social actors shaped by or embodying different cultural meanings and practices come into conflict with each other. The notion of cultural politics assumes that cultural meanings and practices—particularly those theorized as marginal, oppositional, minority, residual, emergent, alternative, dissident, and the like, all conceived in relation to a given dominant cultural order—can be the source of processes that must be accepted as political. That this is rarely seen as such is more a reflection of entrenched definitions of political culture than an indication of the social force, political efficacy, or epistemological relevance of cultural politics. A given cultural politics has the potential to redefine existing social relations, political cultures, and knowledge circuits. Culture becomes political when meanings become the source of processes that, implicitly or explicitly, seek to redefine social power. In tropical rainforest areas, this redefinition is mediated by forms of knowledge production and political mobilization intimately related to the construction of ethnic identities. This cultural politics unsettles familiar understandings and practices of nature as it attempts to wrest away local ecologies of mind and nature from entrenched networks of class, gender, cultural, and ethnic domination.

Part One of this essay describes the Pacific Coast region of Colombia as it has become the object of recent interventions by capital and the state in the context of apertura and in the name of sustainable development. Part Two surveys briefly the discourse of biodiversity as it emerged in the 1990s out of Northern NGOs and international organizations and its particular application in Colombia. Part Three analyzes in detail the black movement that has arisen as a response to the developmentalist onslaught and the ways in which this movement engages in biodiversity discussions. Lastly, Part Four elaborates the notion of a cultural politics of nature by imagining a strategy of hybrid natures that would rely on new articulations between the organic and the artificial. It will argue that social movement activists and progressive intellectuals concerned with the nature of nature are thrown into a situation of defending local modes of consciousness and practices of nature the success of which might depend on alliances with the advocates of biotechnological applications of biodiversity—that is, with the advocates of the artificial. Like the concept of hybrid cultures, the strategy of hybrid natures is seen as a medium for new representations of Third World situations and a possibility for postdevelopment.

1. The Arrival of Development to the Pacific Coast Region

Tropical rainforest areas constitute a social space in which the rein-vention of nature, the search for alternative social and economic approaches, and the changing modes of capital can be observed. In fact, the interweaving of these three processes can serve as an interpretive framework for investi-gating the political practices of the various social actors. This interweaving of forces suggest the following questions. First, in what particular ways is the re-lation between people and nature being transformed? What lessons can this transformation teach us about postmodern theorizations of nature and culture that have been derived mostly in First World contexts? Second, what can be gleaned from struggles and debates in tropical rainforests about alternative socioeconomic designs and the possibility of transcending the imaginary of development (Escobar, 1995)? Third, do events in these areas substantiate the claim that capital is entering an "ecological phase," where modern destructive forms would coexist with postmodern conservationist forms (O'Connor, 1993)? Finally, what do the socioeconomic and cultural struggles to define tropical rainforests tell us about oppositional politics, dissenting imaginations, and col-lective action by social groups? In what follows, I will explore the meaning of these questions by drawing on fieldwork in a particular rainforest region of Colombia.

The Pacific Coast region is a vast rainforest area, about 900 kilometers long and 80–160 kilometers wide, stretching from Panama to Ecuador, and between the westernmost chain of the Andes and the Pacific Ocean. About 60 percent of the region's 900,000 inhabitants live in a few cities and large towns, the rest sparsely settling the areas along the large number of rivers flowing from the Andes toward the ocean. Afro-Colombians, descendents of slaves brought from Africa beginning in the sixteenth century to mine gold, make up most of the population, but there are also about 50,000 indigenous people, particularly Emberas and Waunanas living mostly in the northern Chocó province. Black groups, with which this paper is primarily concerned, have maintained and de-veloped a significantly different set of cultural practices of both Spanish and African origin. These include multiple and shifting economic activities, ex-tended families, matrilineality, unique dance, musical, and oral traditions, funerary cults, sorcery, and the like—even if such practices are increasingly hybridized with urban, modern forms due to in- and out-migration and the im-pact of commodities, media, and development programs from the interior of the country. Although the region has never been isolated from the world mar-kets—"boom and bust" cycles of gold, platinum, precious woods, rubber, tim-ber, and (as we shall see shortly) genes have successively tied black communities to the world economy—it was only in the 1980s that the region became subjected to coordinated policies of development (Whitten, 1986; Friedemann, 1989).

What is happening in the Pacific Coast region is in many ways unprecedented: large-scale development plans; new fronts for capital accumulation, such as African palm plantations and artificial shrimp cultivation; and growing black and indigenous mobilization. Three main actors—state, capital, and social movements—struggle over the definition of the present and future of the region. Behind these three sets of actors lie different cultural and political economies whose genealogies and links to cultural and socioeconomic rationalities have to be elucidated. The investigation of the cultural politics of these actors is important to the extent that the future of the region will largely depend on how the region is defined and represented. Let us then analyze how state, capital, and social movements seek to deploy their discourses and practices in the Littoral.

Discourses of the State: Apertura and Sustainable Development. Until recently, almost every document on the Pacific Coast started with the same image of the Littoral as a region forgotten by God and government, its inhabitants living under primitive subsistence conditions, the environment unhealthy, hot and humid as almost no other part of the world—a sort of no man's land where only rugged capitalists, colonists, missionaries, and the occasional anthropologist ventured to work among "blacks and Indians." The region is, indeed, very poor by conventional indicators such as income per capita, literacy rates, and levels of nutritional status; malaria is rampant, linked to the fact that the region, especially its northern part, has one of the highest indices of rain and humidity in the world.

Since the early 1980s, these features have been emphasized in such a way as to make development interventions ineluctable and undisputable. The geographical and ecological determinism with which the region is endowed in these representations—backward and diseased, needing the white hand of government, capital, and technology to free it from its lethargy of centuries—sets it up as an empirical reality to be dealt with through appropriate economic and technical interventions. Almost four decades after the rest of the country, the region entered the development era with the launching of the "Plan for the Integral Development of the Pacific Coast" (Plan de Desarrollo Integral para la Costa Pacífica, PLADEICOP) in 1983 (DNP, 1983). The plan changed significantly the policy of neglect the government had maintained for centuries with regard to this region. It was designed and implemented by a regional development corporation based in Cali, the Autonomous Corporation of the Cauca, CVC, set up in the mid-1950s with World Bank funding and the advice of David

Lilienthal of the Tennessee Valley Authority. Since its inception, the CVC has been the chief social force shaping the dynamic capitalist development of the fertile Cauca River Valley area in southwestern Colombia (Escobar, 1995, 87–89).

In keeping with the regional development approach followed by the corporation in the Andean Cauca Valley, the new plan for the Pacific Coast had three basic components: the building of infrastructure (roads, electrification, water supply, etc.); social services (health, education, nutrition, women's income-generating programs); and rural development projects for small farmers in the riverine settlements. The main achievement of the plan, however, was that, for the first time in the country's history, it created an image of the Pacific Coast region as an integrated ecocultural and geographic whole in need of systematic and well-concerted development. This "developmentalization" was the most important resignification to which the region has been subjected in the modern period. It placed the region into a new regime of representation in which capital, science, and the institutions of the state provide the signifying categories. In this way, PLADEICOP began and then intensified the project of modernity in the Littoral by creating the necessary infrastructure for capital to arrive in an ordered way and by initiating the process of expert-based social intervention, so central to modernity, throughout the towns and riverine communities of the Littoral. In fact, reversing the conventional development philosophy of seeing economic growth as the driving force for social development and following UNICEF's lead and the basic human needs approach that became trendy in the early 1980s, PLADEICOP attempted to place social programs at the center of their strategy for "integral development."

Nevertheless, the design and implementation of the basic social services programs were marred by many problems, including the fact that the programs followed technocratic blueprints crafted for the extremely different conditions existing in the Andean interior of the country. Despite some attempts at enlisting local participation, the programs did not take into account local cultures and conditions. For instance, in the late 1980s and early 1990s, agriculturalists in river communities were offered a package of credit and technical assistance for the cultivation and commercialization of cocoa and coconut that mimicked the integrated rural development packages designed more than a decade earlier for Andean peasants. The program overlooked the very different social, ecological, and farming conditions and practices of the local Afro-Colombian families. By introducing practices such as the "farm planning methodology"—which called for profit-oriented models of cultivation and accounting, unheard of previously in the region—the program fostered the cultural reconversion necessary for the successful commodification of land, labor, and subsistence agriculture. Indeed, some of the farmers participating in the program seem to be undergoing this transformation, although still retaining many of their traditional beliefs and practices concerning the land, nature, the economy, and life in general. They thus start the process of cultural hybridization of nonmodern and modern forms fostered by development interventions in so many parts of the Third World.

Since the late 1980s, the government has been pursuing an overarching policy of integration with the Pacific Basin economies. The Pacific Ocean—rebaptized "the sea of the 21st century"—is seen as the socioeconomic and, to a lesser extent, cultural space of the future. Within this nascent imaginary, the Pacific Coast Littoral occupies an important place as the launching platform for the macroeconomics of the future. As we will see, the discovery of the region's biodiversity is an important component of this imaginary. It coexists in contradiction, however, with the radical policy of economic apertura (opening) inaugurated by the government after 1990. In the midst of this contradiction, development approaches have taken two directions. On the one hand, there is the dominant intervention, an ambitious plan for sustainable development, the so-called Plan Pacífico (DNP, 1992). This plan is even more conventional in its design than PLADEICOP and its results will be more devastating. It self-consciously promotes capitalist development. As such, it is opposed by black and indigenous communities, who see in the discourse of apertura an ominous trend for wresting away from them control of the rich resources of the region. On the other hand, the government has also started a more modest project for the conservation of the region's biological diversity ($9 million as compared with the $250 million allocated to Plan Pacífico for a four-year period), under the sponsorship of the World Bank's Global Environment Facility, GEF (GEF/PNUD, 1993). We shall return to this project in the next section.

New Forms of Capital in the Pacific Coast Region. Timber and mining have been extractive activities in the Pacific Coast rainforest for decades, although the scale of operations has increased with the use of technologies such as industrial gold mining, fueled partly by drug money. Timber is harvested by large multinational and Colombian companies and by poor colonists. Deforestation from all sources reaches 600,000 hectares a year by some estimates. In recent years, besides an increase in capital accumulation in these sectors, and in the wake of Pacific Basin integration and apertura strategies, investment in the new sectors has increased, such as African palm plantations for the production of oil, artificial shrimp cultivation, hearts of palm canning, coastal and off-shore fishing, shrimp and fish processing and packaging for export, and tourism.

Each of these new forms of investment is producing noticeable cultural, ecological, and social transformations, most visible perhaps in the Tumaco region
in the southern part of the Littoral, near the border with Ecuador, where African palm oil production and shrimp cultivation have reached sizable levels.
Land for African palm plantations has been seized from black farmers by force
or purchase, causing massive displacement from the land and intensive prole-
tarianization. Displaced people now work for meager wages in the plantations
or, in the case of women, in shrimp- and fish-packaging plants in the port city
of Tumaco. Colombia is now the fifth-largest producer of African palm oil; production has increased sharply especially in the Tumaco area since 1985, mostly
in large plantations of several thousand hectares, set up by well-known capitalist groups from Cali. In dollar terms, African palm now comprises 3.9 percent of the GDP in agriculture; it is a significant operation that has transformed
the biocultural landscape of the area, from small patches of land cultivated by
local people in the midst of the forest to the interminable rows of palm trees
so characteristic of modern agriculture. The army of workers start their jour-
ney from the rivers of adjacent towns to the plantations before daybreak, returning to their homes at the end of the day, day after day, unable to engage
in their own farming activities any longer.

The construction of large pools for shrimp cultivation has similarly modified the local cultural and physical landscapes. It has disrupted the fragile balance of river/sea borderline ecosystems, destroying large areas of mangroves
and estuaries essential to the reproduction of marine and river life. The destruction is more advanced in neighboring Ecuador, where the farm production of shrimp reaches many times that of Colombia. The shrimp is processed
and packaged locally by women under conditions reminiscent of those faced
by the women studied by Aihwa Ong (1987) in multinational electronic factories in Malaysia. Many of these women previously practiced subsistence agriculture, fishing, or charcoal making and have now joined the ranks of the new
proletariat under extremely precarious conditions. In both African palm and
shrimp cultivation sectors, nineteenth-century forms of work coexist alongside
late twentieth-century technology; African palm production has benefited
greatly from genetic improvement carried out in the larger producer countries,
such as Malaysia and Indonesia (Escobar, 1996a). Shrimp cultivation is also a
highly technologized operation requiring the laboratory preparation of the seed,
artificial feeding, and careful monitoring of the conditions of cultivation. Science and capital thus operate as apparatuses of capture (Deleuze and Guattari,
1987) that have remade and disciplined the landscape, money, and labor alike
in one single, complex operation.

In the past, as anthropological studies suggest, integration of Afro-

Colombians into the capitalist world economy was based on limited boom-and-bust cycles that did not produce enduring transformations in the local cultural fabric and social structures. Local communities were able to resist, utilize, and adapt to the boom and bust dynamics without very significant permanent alterations (Whitten, 1986; Arocha, 1991). The scale and form of new capital forces, however, are making long-standing adaptive strategies untenable. Socially, new forms of poverty and inequality are appearing as displaced people move to crowded slums in booming cities like Tumaco, which has doubled its population (now about 100,000) in less than a decade. Politically, a new black elite has appeared that wants to take control of their part of the "development pie," "modernize" black culture and institutions, and finally bring blacks into the twentieth century. Capitalists foster these changes with some degree of consciousness, forming convenient alliances with the nascent local elites. Although they are beginning to fear widespread violence as in other parts of the country, they are not willing to slow the pace of accumulation.

2. Biodiversity: New Imaginary of Nature and Culture

Nothing is more inimical to the much-touted conservation of rainforest biodiversity than gold mining, plantation agriculture, uncontrolled timber extraction, and the like. Yet the argument has been made that capital might be entering an "ecological phase" in which capital's modern, reckless logic would coexist with a postmodern, conservationist tendency (O'Connor, 1993). The label "green capitalism" is an expression of this change, even if the concrete modes of operation and the mutual articulation and conflict of the two forms of capital—modern and postmodern, let us say—are not well understood yet and certainly escape the superficial connotations suggested by green capitalism. The fact is that a powerful discourse emphasizing the preservation of the earth's species, ecosystem, and genetic diversity as one of the most important issues of the times has arisen in recent years, and its credo is spreading transnationally. It is by no means an arbitrary event; after two centuries of systematic destruction of nature, the biodiversity discourse responds to what might be called the irruption of the biological, that is, the survival of biological life as a central problem for the modern order.

The discourse of biodiversity promises to deliver nature from the grip of destructive practices and establish in its stead a conservationist culture. It constitutes a new way to talk about nature deeply mediated by technoscience, and a new interface between nature, capital, and science. The origins of this discourse is very recent indeed; they can be traced to two founding texts, the *Global Biodiversity Strategy* (WRI/IUCN/UNEP, 1991), and the Biodiversity Convention signed at the Earth Summit in Rio de Janeiro in 1992. The chief architects of the discourse are easily identifiable: Northern environmental NGOs, particularly the Washington, D.C.–based World Resources Institute (WRI) and the Swiss-based World Conservation Union (previously IUCN); the World Bank's Global Environment Facility (GEF), a multibillion-dollar fund with 40 percent of its budget earmarked for biodiversity conservation; and the United Nations Environment Program (UNEP). Dozens of documents, reports, and expert meetings on the scientific, institutional, and programmatic aspects of biodiversity conservation have succeeded in consolidating the discourse and deploying around it an institutional apparatus of growing reach and sophistication.

The key to biodiversity conservation, in the view propagated by dominant institutions, is to find ways of using rainforest resources that ensure their long-term conservation. These uses must be based on the scientific knowledge of biodiversity, acknowledged to be extremely inadequate at present since only a relatively small percentage of the world's species is known to science; appropriate systems of management; and adequate mechanisms of intellectual property rights to protect those discoveries that might lead to commercial applications. According to the subtitle of the *Global Biodiversity Strategy*, modified by one of the world's foremost biodiversity experts, Daniel Janzen, "You've got to know it to use it, and you've got to use it to save it." Biodiversity prospecting—the surveying and screening of nature by taxonomists, botanists, and others with the goal of finding species that might lead to valuable pharmaceutical, agro-chemical, food, or other commercial applications—is emerging as a leading practice among those adhering to the "know it–save it–use it" equation (WRI, 1993). Also known as "gene hunting" since the promise of conservation-cum-profits is believed to lie in the genes of the species, biodiversity prospecting is presented as a respectable protocol of saving nature (WRI, 1993). In various "hot spots" of diversity in the Third World, prospecting activities of this sort are under way, involving prospectors such as U.S. and European botanical gardens, pharmaceutical companies, independent biologists, and Third World NGOs. Often, prospecting and biodiversity inventories rely, as in Costa Rica, on the labor of parataxonomists and paraecologists, who act as paramedics of nature under the guidance of highly trained biologists belonging to what Janzen calls the "international taxasphere" (Janzen and Hallwachs, 1993; Janzen, Hallwachs, Jiménez, and Gómez, 1993).

The apparatus for biodiversity production encompasses a host of disparate actors—from Northern NGOs, international organizations, botanical gardens, universities, and corporations to newly created national biodiversity institutes in the Third World, Third World planners and biologists, and local communities and activists—each with their respective interpretive framework of what biodiversity is, should be, or could become. These frameworks are mediated by machines of all kinds, from the magnifying lens of the botanist to the computer-processed satellite data fed to Geographical Information Systems (GIS) programming and forecasting. Species, humans, and machines participate in making biodiversity as a historical discourse in what can be seen as another example of the mutual production of technoscience and society (Hess, 1995). This discursive formation can be theorized as a network with multiple agents and sites where knowledge is produced, contested, utilized, and transformed. We will see how black activists of the Pacific Coast have attempted to insert themselves in this network.

One interesting feature characterizing the biodiversity network is that, despite the dominance of Northern discourses and perhaps for the first time in the history of development, a number of Third World NGOs have been successful in articulating an oppositional view that is circulating in some of the network sites, thanks in part to new practices and media such as electronic networks and U.N. preparatory meetings. Although this issue cannot be elaborated upon in this essay, it is important to point out that these NGOs—most of them from South and Southeast Asia, a few in Latin America—see the dominant strategy as a form of bioimperialism. GEF projects, for instance, usually are paired with other conventional initiatives of rainforest utilization and privatization. More importantly, critics argue that biotechnology-based biodiversity conservation will erode biodiversity, given that all biotechnology depends on the creation of uniform market commodities. The diversity of commodities cannot result in the diversity of cultures and species. The history of the genetic manipulation of seeds, for example, is also the history of its progressive commodification and the loss of seed diversity (Kloppenburg, 1988). Habitat destruction by development projects and monocultures of minds and agriculture are the main sources of biodiversity destruction, not the activities of poor forest peoples. With GEF and biodiversity prospecting, the disease is offered as the cure; dominant strategies amount to placing the wolf in charge of the sheep (Shiva 1993, 1994; von Weizsacker, 1993).

From a biological standpoint, biodiverse ecosystems are characterized by a multiplicity of interactions and the coevolution of species in such a way that biological disturbances are reduced, biological threats minimized, and multiple outcomes favored. Culturally, Third World critics strategically argue, diverse societies in forest areas have favored self-organization, production based on the logic of diversity, and cropping practices that favor diversity, such as multiple cropping, crop rotation, extractive reserves, and multiple outcomes. Critics like Vandana Shiva maintain that a notion of biodemocracy predicated on the termination of large-scale development projects, the recognition of community rights, a redefinition of productivity and efficiency to reflect multiple outcome ecosystems, a recognition of the cultural character of biodiversity, and local control of the resources by communities should be opposed to the regime of bioimperialism.

Without attempting to analyze the rationality of these claims—and avoiding the trap of assuming a priori any sort of "primitive environmental wisdom" or the existence of a benevolent relation between local culture and sustainabilty, as many environmentalists are prone to do (Dahl, 1993; Milton, 1993)—it is possible to underscore, from an anthropological point of view, the necessary connection that exists between a system of meanings of nature and concrete practices of nature. This relation is not static. New ecological, cultural, and political orders are continuously being crafted at the local level as communities are brought into the politics of development, capital, and expert knowledge. There is a connection between history, identity, and meanings that regulate local environmental practices. In the rainforests of the world, most often than not, the use-meanings in place account for practices of nature that are ostensibly different from those characteristic of Western modernity.

The biodiversity discourse embodies the postmodern form of capital (Escobar, 1996b); it effects a resignification of the rainforest (as a reservoir of value at the genetic level), its peoples (as "custodians of nature"), and their knowledge (as traditional knowledge of saving nature). Whether this set of resignifications will necessarily result in new forms of colonization of the biophysical and human landscapes, or contribute to creating new economic and political possibilities for local communities, is still an open question. The answer to this question will depend largely on the extent to which local communities succeed in appropriating and utilizing the new significations for their own ends, linking them to other identities, circuits of knowledge, and political projects. This, in turn, brings into consideration the strength of local social movements. Will rainforest social movements be able to become significant social actors in the conversations that are shaping rainforest futures? Will they be able to participate in the coproduction of technoscience and society, nature and culture, set into motion by the biodiversity network?

3. Collective Action, Ethnic Identity, and the Politics of Nature

The events of recent years in tropical rainforest areas suggest that the stakes go beyond the politics of resources, the environment, and even representation. At issue is the existence of multiple constructions of nature in all of its complexity: contrasting practices of meanings-use; entire groups with different outlooks on life; the dreams of collectivities. They also make visible power configurations in the making, woven by the development apparatus out of the fabric of capital and technoscience. In short, rainforest events present us with a cultural politics of nature the lessons of which go beyond the rainforests themselves. One of the most salient aspects of this cultural politics is the organized response from social movements.

In Colombia, attempts at black organizing in recent decades have taken place since the early 1970s, mostly in urban areas, inspired by the U.S. black movement. These efforts emphasized the exploitation and resistance of black people since their arrival as slaves in the New World. Studies of the history of black people in the country became important in this regard; politically, the strategies of early and most present-day urban black movement organizations have emphasized the pursuit of equality and integration within society at large. Only in recent years, particularly as a result of the emergence of a black movement in the Pacific Coast, has cultural difference become the key banner of black organizing. Two factors have been most important in this regard: the developmentalist and capitalist onslaught on the region, fostered by the process of apertura and the country's integration to the Pacific Rim; and the process of constitutional reform that culminated with the election in 1991 of a National Constituent Assembly and the reform of the 1886 constitution.

Intended to build a multicultural, pluriethnic society—and thus reversing the nineteenth-century project of constructing a homogeneous national identity through race blending and assimilation into mestizo (coded white) culture—the new constitution granted unprecedented rights to indigenous, ethnic, and religious minorities. The reform of the constitution served as a historical conjuncture for a variety of social processes, black and indigenous organizing being the most visible of them. For the black communities of the Pacific Coast, it was a question of unprecedented identity construction under the guise of cultural, political, and socioeconomic demands and proposals. While blacks were unsuccessful in securing their own representatives in the Constituent Assembly, the plight of Pacific Coast blacks was presented in the assembly by the indigenous representatives. Initially approved by the assembly as a provisional measure (Transitory Article 55, A.T. 55), the cultural and territorial rights of the black communities were finally enshrined in the constitution as a law (Ley 70) two years later, in July 1993.

Black organizing in the Pacific Coast and other parts of Colombia grew in intensity and complexity from the initial drive to obtain representation in the Constituent Assembly, to the ensuing mobilization to draft and vote the transitory article into law during 1991–1993, to today's complex and conflictual negotiations entailed by the demarcation of the collective territories under Ley 70. By the time Ley 70 came into effect, the conjunctural character of the organizing process fostered by the constitutional reform had been largely superseded and a widespread and heterogenous movement had come into place. The fact that the new constitution allocated several seats in the national congress to ethnic and religious minorities motivated the opportunistic appearance of black leaders associated with the traditional political parties and the nascent black elite. Despite these difficulties and increasing divisions within the black movement itself, particularly between the Northern Chocó organizations and those from the southern part of the Littoral, an increasingly articulate movement continued to grow throughout the first half of the decade.[1]

The organizing drive for A.T. 55 and Ley 70 made manifest to the rest of the nation the presence of unsuspectedly vibrant black communities along the rivers of the coast. The fact that these communities had maintained significantly different cultural practices and social relations also became visible, thus contributing to reverse the long-standing Andean-based representations of the region as a jungle inhabited by indolent people unable to exploit its resources. The rich cultural traditions of the people; the exploding discourse around the region's biodiversity; the government's commitment to its sustainable development; and the possibility of collective land titling for the local communities became the most important elements for activists in their attempt at launching a well-coordinated, massive campaign for black rights. This determination crystallized in important events such as the Third National Convention of Black Communities, which took place in a predominantly black town in the southern tip of the Cauca River valley in September 1993. At this event, attended by more than three hundred activists from various parts of the country, it was agreed that the goal of the strategy should be "the consolidation of a social movement of black communities of national scope capable of undertaking the reconstruction and affirmation of black cultural identity," a process to be based in turn "on the construction of an autonomous organizing process aimed at struggling for our [black people's] cultural, social, economic, and territorial rights, and for the defense of natural resources and the environment."[2]

The same declaration identified and explained the movement's main principles for political organizing as follows. First, the right to an identity, that is, the right to being black according to the cultural logic and worldview rooted in black experience, opposed to dominating national culture; this principle also called for the reconstitution of black consciousness itself and the rejection of the dominant discourse of equality, with its concomitant obliteration of difference. Second, the right to a territory as a space for being and an essential element for the development of culture. Third, the right to political autonomy as a prerequisite for the practice of being, with the possibility of fostering social and economic autonomy. Fourth, the right to construct their own vision of the future, development, and social practice based on the customary forms of production and social organization. Fifth, a principle of solidarity with the struggles of black peoples for alternative visions throughout the world.

The approval of these principles as the basis for the articulation of a black movement of national scope was not achieved at the convention because the black organizations of the Chocó refused to endorse them; once Ley 70 was approved, they argued, the direction of the movement could not be dictated only by those who had been prominent in the organizing effort around A.T. 55, but should be expanded to all communities and social actors, presumably the traditional political parties as well. As the only black province in the nation, the Chocó region had a long history of traditional party activity; this became sharply visible when the time came for electing black representatives to the national congress, in which their candidates predominated. The debate on electoral participation thus acted as a divisive force among the black communities of the southern Littoral, the Chocó, and the Atlantic Coast. Confronted with these divisions, the organizations from the south, particularly those gathered around the Organization of Black Communities of Buenaventura—the major city of the entire region, with about 250,000 inhabitants, mostly black—decided to constitute themselves into a Network of Black Communities (Proceso Nacional de Comunidades Negras, PCN), while continuing to push for the creation of a national movement of black communities (Grueso and Rosero, 1995; Grueso, Rosero, and Escobar, In press).

The most distinctive feature of the PCN is the articulation of a political proposal with a primarily ethnocultural character and basis. Their vision is not that of a movement based on a catalogue of needs and demands for development, but a struggle couched in terms of the defense of cultural difference. In this lies the most radical character of the movement. The shift to emphasizing difference was a pivotal decision, as some of the leading activists explain:

> We don't know exactly when we started to talk about cultural difference. But at some point we refused to go on building a strategy around a catalogue of "problems" and "needs." The government continues to bet on democracy and development; we respond by emphasizing cultural autonomy and the right to be who we are and defend our own life project. To recognize the need to be different, to build an identity, are difficult tasks that demand persistent work among our communities, taking their very heterogeneity as a point of departure. However, the fact that we do not have worked out social and economic proposals make us vulnerable to the current onslaught by capital. This is one of our foremost political tasks at present: to advance in the formulation and implementation of alternative social and economic proposals.[3]

The persistent work has been impressive indeed. As mentioned before, the

conceptualization and actual drafting of Ley 70 was the linchpin for the organizing process, particularly in river communities and much less in urban areas, where organizing the communities has proven to be much more difficult
and ineffective. From 1991 to 1993, activists organized information and discussion workshops in a large number of river communities on topics such as the
concept of territory, traditional production practices, natural resources, the
meaning of development, and the question of black identity. Results of these
workshops in the local communities were subsequently taken up to subregional
and finally national forums, where all of the multiple conceptions were discussed. This construction was advanced as a dual process: first, according to
"the logic of the river," that is, taking as a point of departure the everyday life
and aspirations of the local communities; second, by engaging in a more thorough conceptual elaboration on identity, territory, development, and political
strategy at the regional and national levels. Out of this double process emerged
the five principles proposed at the Third National Convention.[4]

The choice of cultural difference as an articulating concept for political strategy was informed by various historical factors, although it was, of course, related to the broader debates propitiated by the constitutional reform. In this
reinterpretation of the history of the region, Pacific Coast activists not only
moved away from the integrationist perspective, strongly denouncing the myth
of racial democracy (see also Wade, 1993); they also highlighted the fact that
black communities of the coast have historically favored isolation from the national society and economy, while recognizing that this ethics of isolation and
independence is increasingly untenable under today's forceful policies of integration and the inevitable presence of modern media, commodities, and the
like. The relationship between territory and culture is of paramount importance
in this regard. Activists conceptualize the territory as "a space for the creation
of futures, for hope and the continuation of existence." The loss of territory is
likened to "a return to the times of slavery."[5] The territory is also an economic
concept to the extent that it is linked to natural resources and biodiversity.

The interest in biodiversity stems from this recognition. It provides an opening toward the future. It is not a coincidence that several articulate black professionals associated with the movement have decided to participate in the
national biodiversity project. Although they recognize the risks entailed by this
participation, they believe that the discourse of biodiversity affords possibilities they cannot afford to ignore. Biodiversity might also be an important element in the formulation of alternative development strategies. As activists are
quick to mention, they know they do not want any form of conventional development, but they are less clear about what they want.[6] They also recognize
that experts (planners, ecologists, anthropologists, biologists, etc.) might be

important allies in this regard. This suggests the possibility for a new practice of collaboration between experts and social movement activists. The role of mediation that experts fulfill between the state and social movements needs to be theorized further (Fraser, 1989). Dissident, oppositional, and solidarity practices on the part of those holding the expert discourses of modernity need to be imagined.

The notion of territory is a new concept in rainforest social struggles. All over Latin America, peasants have engaged in struggles over land. The right to a territory—as an ecological, productive, and cultural space—is a new political demand. This demand is fostering important reterritorialization (Deleuze and Guattari, 1987)—that is, the formation of new territories fueled by novel political perceptions and practices. Social movement activists fulfill this role as well: to make evident both the processes of deterritorialization and reterritorialization effected by the apparatuses of capture of modernity, such as capital, media, and the development apparatus (for example, the centrifugal forces of media on local cultures and the reorganization of the landscape by African palm plantations and shrimp cultivation), and the potential reterritorializations by the mobilized communities. During the organizing for Ley 70, this process took a literal form, that of physically traveling up and down the rivers with local people in order to identify long-standing patterns of land use, signs of new occupations (e.g., by colonists of the interior), and signaling possibilities for reterritorialization of forest "empty" lands. This was an important movement practice. The collective traveling of the territory was shaped and favored by the fractal character and contours of littoral, rivers, estuaries, forest edges, and patterns of cultivation.

Like territory, the question of identity is at the heart of the movement. Most Pacific Coast activists see identity as based on a set of cultural practices believed to characterize black culture—practices such as shifting and diverse economic activities, the importance of oral traditions, the ethics of nonaccumulation, the importance of kindred and extended families, matrilineality, local knowledge of the forest, and the like. However, activists are increasingly drawn to understanding identity as a construction, thus converging in some ways with current scholarly trends. Social movement theorists have underscored that the construction of collective identities is an essential feature of contemporary struggles.[7] Recent work in cultural studies has contributed additional insights regarding ethnic identities. Stuart Hall (1990), for instance, has suggested that the construction of ethnic identities is marked by a certain doubleness. On the one hand, identity is thought of as rooted in a shared culture embodied in concrete practices, a collective self of sorts. This conception of identity has played an important role in anticolonial struggles and it involves an imaginative rediscovery, the importance of which cannot be overestimated, to the extent that it contributes to lending coherence to the experience of fragmentation, dispersal, and oppression. On the other hand, while recognizing continuity and similarity, another view of identity highlights the difference created by history. It emphasizes becoming rather than being; it involves positioning rather than essence, discontinuity as well as continuity.

The coexistence of difference and sameness constitutes the doubleness of cultural identity today. Identity is thus seen as something that is negotiated in economic, political, and cultural terms. For communities of the African diaspora, cultural identity involves a retelling of the past "by another route" (Hall, 1990, 399): Africa not as ancestral land but as it has become in the New World, mediated by colonialism. This retelling takes place in two other contexts: that of the European and Euro-American presence—a dialogue of power and resistance, recognition of the inevitable and irreversible influence of modernity; and the context of the New World, where the African and the European are always creolized, where cultural identity is characterized by difference, heterogeneity, and hybridity.

The doubleness of identity operates in the Pacific Coast black movement. For the activists, the defense of certain cultural practices of the river communities is a strategic question to the extent that they are seen as embodying resistance to capitalism and modernity. Although often couched in a culturalist language, they are aware that the intransigent defense of black culture is less desirable than a cautious opening toward the future, including a critical engagement with modernity. The challenges they see the movement as facing stem from this recognition. They include: acknowledging the heterogeneity of the movement(s); addressing the specificities of the movement, particularly the inclusion of gender as an organizing principle for the movement as a whole, without decontextualizing it from the overall cultural and ethnic struggle; consolidating the organizations of river communities, particularly through the creation of local councils for the implementation of territorial law; and reaching black people in urban areas, which has proven difficult until now. One of the most pressing needs, of course, is to articulate alternative socioeconomic proposals, lest they be swept away by green redevelopment in the fashion of Plan Pacífico. The increasing presence of drug money after 1995, particularly in industrial gold mining, is one of the toughest forces impinging upon the movement, given the tremendously deleterious effects it is having on the physical and cultural ecologies. It is, indeed, a problem they feel unable to face without national and international support.

The discourse of biodiversity and the potential for biotechnology-based economic projects appeal to the movement, to the extent that they might present opportunities for improving living standards while avoiding the destruction of nature and local cultures. Unlike the state and the ecodevelopment apparatus, the movement sees the scope for using natural resources sustainably from the perspectives of territory and identity. It is, in short, a question of cultural politics. Unfortunately, the bargaining position of local communities is weak. In addition, black movement organizations have to compete with stronger institutions and organizations for the political space generated around environment and development. Timber extraction, gold mining, shrimp cultivation, hearts of palm canning, and other extractive activities continue apace in some areas even in contravention of Ley 70, often with the complicity of local authorities and without the movement being able to stop them. However, social movement organizations have been able to negotiate successfully with the state in several cases involving environmental conflict (Grueso, 1995).

In sum, the discourses of biodiversity and the dynamics of capital in its ecological phase open up spaces that activists try to seize as points of struggle. This dialectic posits a number of paradoxes for the movement, including the contradictory aspects of defending local nature and culture by relying on languages that do not reflect the local experience of nature and culture. The alliance between social movements and the state effected by the biodiversity project is tenuous at best; it is foreseeable that the tension will grow as the project's national staff continue their attempts at tempering the political nature of the project by emphasizing its scientific aspects instead, and as prospecting activities and agreements with private agents start to take place. Community needs and aspirations will not be easily accommodated into these schemes, as the experience with GEF projects in other countries indicate. As we shall see below, however, there are theoretical grounds for envisaging alliances between local communities and technoscience, the political expediency of which should not be discarded beforehand.

4. Conclusion: The Cultural Politics of Hybrid Natures

The ways of understanding and relating to nature that have existed in the Pacific Coast region are being transformed by the increased presence of capital, development, and modernity, including the discourses of sustainable development and biodiversity. Programs for small farmers in river communities, for instance, affect conceptions of land and the forest, even if they do not displace completely older systems of meanings-use. Nature starts to be conceived of in terms of "natural resources," an idiom that local people are increasingly adept at using. Even the concept of biodiversity is beginning to circulate locally as a currency of sorts, with ambiguous and imprecise meanings.

What lends tropical rainforest areas worldwide specificity in today's politics of nature and culture is the coexistence—even in stark contrast—of different modes of historical consciousness and practices of nature. Black and indigenous communities, African palm and artificial shrimp production capitalists, and advocates of biodiversity prospecting, respectively, seem to enact different modes of nature. We may speak of three different regimes for the production of nature—organic, capitalist, and technonature—that can be characterized only briefly in this essay. Broadly speaking, organic nature represents those modes that are not strictly modern; from the perspective of the anthropology of local knowledge, they may be characterized in terms of the relative indisociability of the biophysical, human and spiritual worlds, vernacular social relations, nonmodern circuits of knowledge, and forms of meanings-use of nature that do not spell the systematic destruction of nature. Capitalized nature, on the contrary, is based on the separation of the human and natural worlds, capitalist and patriarchal social relations; from the perspective of historical materialism, it appears as produced through the mediation of labor. Technonature, finally, is nature produced by new forms of technoscience, particularly those based on molecular technologies. As studied by poststructuralist and feminist studies of science and technology, it appears as produced more by technoscientific intervention than by labor-based production of value. But meanings, labor, and technoscience are important to all three regimes.

These three regimes for the production of nature, it must be pointed out, do not represent stages in the history of social nature; it is not a linear sequence, since the three regimes co-exist and overlap. Although the three of them represent instances of constructed nature—to the extent that nature never exists for humans outside of history—the respective practices of construction are relatively distinct. The terms organic, capitalized, and technonature are used to convey particular intensities and practices of meanings-use. More importantly, the three regimes produce each other symbolically and materially; they represent relational elements in the forms of nature's production. Moreover, the dominant capitalist nature necessarily invents its own forms of the organic (for instance, ecotourism and a large part of environmentalism, which are forms of capitalist organicity) and technonatures—most biodiversity prospecting applications today could be thought of as capitalist technonature. It is important to emphasize that within organic nature the rainforest is not an external resource but an integral part of social and cultural life. In this resides its difference, to the extent that capitalist forms of the organic cannot reconstitute this integral relationship.

One could then posit that today's landscapes of nature and culture are characterized by what can be called "hybrid natures." Hybrid natures would take a special form in tropical rainforest areas, where popular groups and social movements would use novel practices to defend organic nature against the ravages of capitalist nature, with technonature—biotechnology-based conservation and use of resources—as a possible ally. Many intellectual and political questions arise in relation to the feasibility of this strategy. For instance, what sort of collective practices—by cultural activists, scientists, ecologists, feminists, planners, prospectors—could foster hybrid natures that contribute to the affirmation of local cultures and postdevelopment? How can local activists position themselves effectively in the network of biodiversity production? How might anthropologists and others contribute to invent new ways of talking about nature appropriate to the new tools for conceiving of and producing nature that are now in place?[8]

The obstacles to this strategy of hybrid natures are immense and remain to be explored. Activists in the Pacific Coast seem aware of the need to take traditions in new directions, some of which will perhaps be unrecognizable from today's vantage point, in their attempt to reconfigure traditions and infuse them with an operational measure of diversity. This might be the only way in which, with their limited power and the odds stacked against them, Afro-Colombians might retain a degree of autonomy in a world where not only traditions but also many of the markers of modernity seem to be increasingly weakened. At the margins of the "Black Atlantic" (Gilroy, 1993), they seem to make us aware of the recombinant aspects of nature and culture from a place in which organicity and artificiality might not be mortal enemies, and where the unbounding of culture and ethnicity might not spell the end of local communities rich in diverse traditions.

In places like the Pacific Coast of Colombia, struggles for cultural difference are also struggles for biological diversity. What kinds of nature will be possible to design and protect under these conditions? Is it possible to construct a cultural politics of biodiversity that does not deepen the colonization of natural and cultural landscapes characteristic of modernity? Perhaps in the tropical rainforests of the world we might have the chance to weave together sociosphere, biosphere, and machinosphere in novel "ecosophical" practices (Guattari, 1993). By envisaging other forms of being modern, we might be able to renew our solidarity with what until now we have called nature.

Struggles in the world's rainforests turn out to be exemplary histories of what nature has been, is, and might be in the future (see Guha, this volume). Here may lie one of the deepest meanings of dissent: in the creation of life possibilities and modes of existence through new concepts and practices, particularly those that most people might find unthinkable or impracticable. If it is true that the task of philosophy is the creation of concepts—a construction of life possibilities through novel practices of thought, imagination, and understanding (Deleuze and Guattari, 1993)—and that this task today entails a recasting of the resistance to capitalism, activists in the world's rainforests may keep alive the dream of other peoples and lands of the future. Utopian? Perhaps. But let us keep in mind that "utopia designates the conjunction of philosophy with the present. . . . It is with utopia that philosophy becomes political, carrying to its extreme the critique of its era" (Deleuze and Guattari, 1993, 101). Some of these utopias of nature and culture continue to circulate in the dissenting practices of black activists of the Pacific Coast of Colombia, even if against all odds.

Notes

This chapter is based on fieldwork carried out from January to December 1993 and July to November 1994. The research was conducted by a small research team coordinated by Alvaro Pedrosa and myself, including two researchers from the Pacific coast. The project was funded by grants from the Division of Arts and Humanities of the Rockefeller Foundation, the Social Science Research Council, and the Heinz Endowment. I am greatful for their support. I also thank Alvaro Pedrosa (Universidad del Calle, Cali, Colombia); Libia Grueso and Carlos Rosero (Organización de Comunidades Negras de Buenaventura); Tracey Tsugawa, Jesús Alberto Grueso, and Betty Ruth Lozano (members of the research team); and the participants at the Harry Guggenheim Conference in Ecuador—particularly Sonia E. Alvarez, Orin Starn, and Faye Ginsburg—for their concern and support when I was hospitalized in Quito. And I thank my Quito friends Beatriz Andrade and Susana Wappenstein in this regard.

1. This brief account of the black movement is based on my own research with Alvaro Pedrosa (Escobar and Pedrosa, 1996) and on the work of two of the main activists of the movement in the southern part of the Littoral, Libia Grueso and Carlos Rosero (Grueso and Rosero, 1995; Grueso, Rosero, and Escobar, In press). I should point out that this account refers mostly to the experience of the black movement in the southern Pacific Coast, especially that led by the Organization of Black Communities of Buenaventura, to whom Grueso and Rosero belong.

2. Declaration of the Tercera Asamblea de Comunidades Negras, Puerto Tejada, September 1993.

3. Interview with Libia Grueso, Carlos Rosero, Leyla Arroyo, and other members of the Organización de Comunidades Negras de Buenaventura (OCN), 3 January 1994 (Escobar and Pedrosa, 1996).

4. A word about the activists of the movement is in order. In the southern part of the coast, the most important leaders are social science professionals who grew up in the rivers and traveled to cities like Cali, Bogotá, or Popayán for university training. These leaders are very articulate, and despite disagreements, their political vision is impressively clear. The presence of women in the higher echelons of groups like the Organization of Black Communities of Buenventura, and in the movement as a whole, is extremely important. But the strength of the movement lies in a relatively large cadre of activists in the Littoral itself, only a few of whom have received university training. Often, the pace of activities is dictated by young activists involved

with the various aspects of the growing cultural politics, such as local radio stations, dance and theater groups, local newsletters, and the preparation of workshops for the discussion of Ley 70. This impressive, though still fragile, process of organizing is yet to be chronicled adequately. An initial analysis is found in Grueso, Rosero, and Escobar (In press). For an account of the black movement in Colombia, see Wade (1995).

5. Encuentro de Comunidades de Buenaventura held in Puerto Merizalde, November 1991. This meeting was attended by 1,600 people.

6. The difficulty of formulating alternative proposals is a worldwide phenomenon. Once the failure of development became evident, and after its radical deconstruction as a discourse of domination, there are few clues for re/constructing regimes of representation and practice. The increasingly widespread call for "alternatives to development" is a recognition of this fact (Escobar, 1995).

7. See Escobar and Alvarez (1992) for a review of the literature.

8. I will not discuss here the various criticisms that the notion of hybridity or hybridization has motivated in its various conceptions. Suffice it to say that there are significant differences between the Anglo-Saxon and the Latin American versions of it. In Latin American anthropology and cultural studies, emphasis is placed on hybridization as a cultural process, rather than on hybridity as a state or mode of being. Hybridization is a collective, not an individual process; it characterizes entire social groups; it is not a means to erase differences but rather to affirm them. In analyzing cultural hybridization, emphasis is placed in identifying those experiences that are politically powerful. Hybridization might be a transitional notion toward a more satisfactory account of the dynamics of the production of culture and cultural difference in today's globalized world. When applied to nature, I seek to highlight similarly that the production of social nature is an uneven and complex process ranging from the organic to the artificial and the many combinations that culture, economy, and technology seem to allow today.

References

Arocha, Jaime (1991). La ensenada de Tumaco: Invisibilidad, incertidumbre e innovación. *América Negra* 1:87–112.

Dahl, Gudrun, Ed. (1993). *Green Arguments for Local Subsistance*. Stockholm: Stockholm University Press.

Deleuze, Gilles and Félix Guattari (1987). *A Thousand Plateaus*. Minneapolis: University of Minnesota Press.

Deleuze, Gilles and Félix Guattari (1993). *Qué es la filosofía?* Barcelona: Anagrama.

DNP (Departamento Nacional de Planeación de Colombia) (1983). *Plan de desarrollo integral para la Costa Pacífica, PLADEICOP*. Cali: DNP/CVC.

DNP (Departmento Nacional de Planeación de Colombia) (1992). *Plan Pacífico. Una estrategia de desarrollo sostenible para la Costa Pacífica Colombiana*. Bogotá: DNP.

Escobar, Arturo (1995). *Encountering Development: The Making and Unmaking of the Third World*. Princeton: Princeton University Press.

Escobar, Arturo (1996a). Viejas y nuevas formas de capital y los dilemas de la biodiversidad. In *Pacífico: Desarrollo o Diversidad?*, ed. A. Escobar and A. Pedrosa, pp. 106–131. Bogotá: CEREC/Ecofondo.

Escobar, Arturo (1996b). Constructing Nature: Elements for a Poststructuralist Political Ecology. In *Liberation Ecologies*, ed. R. Peet and M. Watts, pp. 46–68. London: Routledge.

Escobar, Arturo and Sonia Alvarez, Eds. (1992). *The Making of Social Movements in Latin America: Identity, Strategy and Democracy*. Boulder: Westview Press.

Escobar, Arturo and Alvaro Pedrosa, Eds. (1996). *Pacífico: Desarrollo o diversidad? Estado, capital y movimientos sociales en el Pacífico Colombiano*. Bogotá: CEREC/Ecofondo.

Fraser, Nancy (1989). *Unruly Practices*. Minneapolis: University of Minnesota Press.

Friedemann, Nina S. de (1989). *Críele críele son*. Bogotá: Planeta.

GEF/PNUD (Global Environment Facility/United Nations Development Program) (1993). *Conservación de la biodiversidad del Chocó biogeográfico. Proyecto Biopacífico*. Bogotá: DNP/Biopacífico.

Gilroy, Paul (1993). *The Black Atlantic*. Cambridge: Harvard University Press.

Grueso, Libia (1995). Diagnósticos, propuestas y perspectivas de la Región del Chocó Biogeográfico en relación con la conservación y uso sostenido de la biodiversidad. Report presented to Proyecto Biopacífico, Bogotá.

Grueso, Libia and Carlos Rosero (1995). El proceso organizativo de comunidades negras en el Pacífico sur colombiano. Unpublished manuscript.

Grueso, Libia, Carlos Rosero, and Arturo Escobar (In press). The Process of Black Community Organizing in the Pacific Coast of Colombia. In *Cultures of Politics/Politics of Cultures: Revisioning Latin American Social Movements*, ed. Sonia E. Alvarez, Evelina Dagnino, and Arturo Escobar. Boulder: Westview Press.

Guattari, Félix (1993). *El constructivismo guattariano*. Cali: Universidad del Valle Press.

Hall, Stuart (1990). Cultural Identity and Diaspora. In *Identity, Community, Culture, Difference*, ed. J. Rutherford, pp. 392–403. London: Lawrence & Wishart.

Haraway, Donna (1991). *Simians, Cyborgs, and Women: The Reinvention of Nature*. New York: Routledge.

Hess, David (1995). *Science and Technology in a Multicultural World*. New York: Columbia University Press.

Janzen, Daniel and H. Hallwachs (1993). *All Taxa Biodiversity Inventory*. Philadephia: University of Pennsylvania.

Janzen, Daniel, H. Hallwachs, J. Jiménez, and R. Gómes (1993). The Role of the Parataxonomists, Inventory Managers and Taxonomists in Costa Rica's National Biodiversity Inventory. In: World Resources Institute, *Biodiversity Prospecting*, pp. 223–254. Washington, D.C.: WRI.

Kloppenburg, Jack (1988). *First the Seed. The Political Economy of Plant Biotechnology, 1492–2000*. Cambridge: Cambridge University Press.

Milton, Kay, Ed. (1993). *Environmentalism: The View from Anthropology*. London: Routledge.

O'Connor, Martin (1993). On the Misadventures of Capitalist Nature. *Capitalism, Nature, Socialism* 4(4):7–34.

Ong, Aihwa (1987). *Spirits of Resistance and Capitalist Discipline*. Albany: SUNY Press.

Rabinow, Paul (1992). Artificiality and Enlightenment: From Sociobiology to Biosociality. In *Incorporations*, ed. J. Crary and S. Kwinter, pp. 234–252. New York: Zone Books.

Shiva, Vandana (1993). *Monocultures of the Mind. Perspectives on Biodiversity and Biotechnology*. London: Zed Books.

Shiva, Vandana, Ed. (1994). *Close to Home: Women Reconnect Ecology, Health and Development Worldwide*. London: Zed Books.

von Weizsacker, Christine (1993). Competing Notions of Biodiversity. In *Global Ecology*, ed. W. Sachs, pp. 117–131. London: Zed Books.

Wade, Peter (1993). *Blackness and Race Mixture: The Dynamics of Racial Identity in Colombia*. Baltimore: Johns Hopkins University Press.

Wade, Peter (1995). The Cultural Politics of Blackness in Colombia. *American Ethnologist* 22(2):341–357.

Whitten, Norman (1986). *Black Frontiersmen: Afro-Hispanic Culture of Ecuador and Colombia*. Prospect Heights, Ill.: Waveland Press.

Wilson, Edward O. (1992). *The Diversity of Life*. New York: W. W. Norton & Co.

World Resources Institute (WRI), IUCN (World Conservation Union), UNEP (United Nations Environment Program) (1991). *Global Biodiversity Strategy*. Washington, D.C.: WRI/IUCN/UNEP.

World Resources Institute (WRI) (1993). *Biodiversity Prospecting*. Oxford: Oxford University Press.

Richard G. Fox

Passage from India

Today in North Carolina, Operation Rescuers, mostly women, blockade an abortion clinic, just as in 1930 Gandhi's women volunteers sealed off liquor shops in Delhi.[1] César Chávez began a fast in 1968 to atone for the increasing belligerence of the farm workers he represented, thereby imitating and celebrating the many fasts Gandhi undertook in penance for the misdeeds of his fellow Indians. Animal liberators currently free mice, rabbits, cats, monkeys, and other slaves of science, just as Gandhi wrenched Indians free of British colonial domination. Nowadays, Captain Paul Mitchell sails the high seas to discover whaling ships and then to scuttle them; Gandhi, too, traveled across India, leaving in his wake bonfires of British imported cloth.

The question is: how do we explain this local U.S. replication of an originally Indian protest method? This is also to ask: what do we learn about the nature and possibility of social protest as specific forms of it radiate globally?

Anthropology especially will find it hard to shift from a problematic of difference to an analysis of "likeness." We should take Bruno Latour seriously (1993, 116) when he worries: "is anthropology forever condemned to be reduced to territories, unable to follow networks?" Can anthropology today, he inquires, follow the topologies, twists, and switchbacks of time and place that connect the local with the global and then spin back down to the local somewhere else?

Transnational studies, globalization approaches, and cultural-flow models, as proposed by Arjun Appadurai (1991) and Ulf Hannerz (1992) among others, establish the importance of global diffusion and even analyze the maintenance of parochial social life within an all-pervasive transculturalism. These initiatives begin to convert anthropology to the study of likeness and likenesses late in the twentieth century. They carry us along the new ways of cultural connection, they may even navigate "the bumpy path that leads from the local to the global" (Latour, 1993, 118). Often, however, these approaches attribute the bumpy paths, the detours and twists, in global diffusion to structural inconsistencies and contradictions brought about by crosscurrent culture flows—when, for example, the diffusion of consumer expectations through the media runs far ahead of the transit of the actual consumer goods (cf. Appadurai 1990). But the nature of cultural flow itself remains unproblematic, because the assumption is that a steady and powerful diffusion stream—a coursing river of information, migration, and commodity flows—floods the globe with new cultural patterns.

Late in the twentieth century, to be sure, cultural diffusion has become pandemic, and global exposure is a permanent condition. Still to come, however, are theoretical forays—anthropology's new and promising safaris—into the complex twists produced by a modern world that is saturated with transcultural knowledge and connection.

Familiarity, as Mark Twain said, breeds contempt and children, but what does today's transcultural *exposure* beget? Cultural flows are no longer, if they ever were, simple riverine currents, moving unidirectionally upstream or down. As they flow globally, they encounter oceanic depths, countercurrents, rip tides, and adverse beachings. They course and eddy with the intentions of human agents and the contingencies of history, and, as they do, they twist around to form the strange topologies Latour notes. We then find many odd cases of what Taussig (1993) refers to as the "mimesis of mimesis." For example, Cuna women weave the RCA Victor-dog motif into clothing sold in the United States, or a British anthropologist films the way in which Trobriand Islanders rubbished British cricket and then it gets screened worldwide (see Taussig, 1993). Similar twists, from familiarity not exposure, happen within a single society, when, for example, subalterns speak diglossically or black jazz musicians rubbish mainstream pop music by knowledgeable parody (see Monson, 1994).

There is a difference, however, between the twists produced by familiarity within a single society and those emerging from global exposure. Familiarity depends on continuous and direct exchanges through ongoing social relations, whereas global exposure depends on indirect, mediated transfers through print, film, electronics, or even word of mouth carried by itinerant culture bearers.

The essays by Faye Ginsburg, Arturo Escobar, and Yoshinobu Ota in this collection indicate the actual human agencies, rather than some presumed structural contradictions, that may carry forward, but also detour, disrupt, or pervert a cultural flow. Set in the present, their work analyzes the way local groups can alter cultural flows by commandeering the global media through which they are transported. My article deals with a time anterior to such complete global saturation, when an equivalent protesting consciousness—Gandhian nonviolent resistance—had much less access to transnational currents of communication and migration.

Under these circumstances, the topologies produced when mindsets of dissent and methods of direct action travel transculturally are especially likely to eddy because they mostly flow outside the main circuits of global capitalism and international institutional relations. Their crossings are made in steerage or even as stowaways; either way, they pass from local to global and then to another locale, at the bottom of or hidden from existing power relations. Such freedom-train transport necessarily privileges individual agents and historical vagaries as significant parties to their spread. Only afterward, when actions and actors are forgotten, can they come to appear as an inevitable and obvious culture flow.

In the mid-1950s, Martin Luther King, Jr. made Gandhian nonviolence seem a "natural" for U.S. protests against racism. What happens, however, if we look at a time before King, and we set aside the certainty manufactured after the fact that Gandhian nonviolence in the United States was inevitable? To this end, we could adopt the methodology that Clifford Geertz (1971, 60) calls "doing history backward." We must work back from what we know happened historically to why it happened that way and not another. By placing chronology on its head, we avoid the linearity and determinism of Whiggish history as well as the unidirectionalism of much transnational research. Much like running backward, we are more likely to stumble over general processes as we carefully try to retrace past steps.

From the 1920s to the 1940s, the period that is my focus, today's globalization was in an early stage but growing apace. In a world system with large-scale knowledge transfer, likely much of it is selective, misleading, or even false by purpose, and the result is that cultural flows may twist and circle rather than simply diffuse. One sort of global twist depends on a magnification of difference, a supposition that a cultural practice located elsewhere cannot travel anywhere else. I am going to call this twist a topology of "hyper-difference." Alternatively, the modern condition of information-saturation about culture elsewhere, like an overexposed photograph, may minimize real contrasts and may so wash out difference that we see similarity when it is not there. This transnational linkage produces a topology of "over-likeness." Moving between hyper-difference and over-likeness, culture in transit can shape up into an extremely exaggerated Otherness or, at the opposite extreme, it can turn into a complete assimilation to Self.

Over-likeness and hyper-difference both made the passage of a truly Gandhian nonviolent resistance from India to the United States dubious and difficult, not certain and easy. As I shall soon show, hyper-difference created an Orientalist image of Gandhian nonviolence, which made it appear to work only in a deeply spiritual culture like India (was said to be) or only under the saintly direction of an Indian ascetic like Gandhi (was considered). The only way this Orientalist hyper-difference was broken with in the United States before 1940 was through assertions of over-likeness. In this case, Gandhian nonviolent resistance would be assimilated to existing protest methods known in the West. Gandhi's program would then be understood as the same as passive resistance, (Christian) nonresistance, or civil disobedience.

Hyper-difference and over-likeness made the actual passage around 1940 contingent on the intervention of only a few individuals—not migrants or simply exiles, but some of the earliest transnationals in spirit—each of whom created enabling images that represented Gandhian nonviolent resistance for what it was: an invention of a new form of mass protest, neither singularly Indian nor generically Christian. In the event, Gandhian nonviolent resistance understood in this way proved remarkably generative. New and powerful forms of mass protest appeared in America, replacing increasingly jejune practices like passive resistance and pacifism. Freed from over-likeness and hyper-difference, Gandhian nonviolence activated King, CORE, and the civil rights protest in the 1960s; the Berrigans, Dellinger, and many other anti-Vietnam activists in the 1970s; César Chávez and Mitch Snyder in the 1980s; and the rights advocates for ecology, animals, reproduction, and gays today. Such is the twisting transcultural typology I hope to chart by doing history backward.

Hyper-difference and over-likeness—these two characteristics of transcultural transfers in an age of globalization—were already quite strong by the middle of the twentieth century, as the Gandhian case will show. They have only grown more powerful—and impedimentary—as the century closes. If I am right, then we must scale the topologies so produced into our theoretical analyses of, and practical hopes for, the birthing and husbanding of social protest today—we must give special attention to the way in which individual consciousness and creative understanding today can straighten out global twists, as they did when Gandhian nonviolent protest finally took passage from India.

Gandhi's Truth

Is Gandhi not exemplary of a spiritual India or at least of an Indian ascetic tradition? Then make him out as a proper Christian martyr or pacifist. Or if that won't fly transculturally, figure him as a Western passive resistor.

Or, in the final analysis, find him to be a Western anarchist. Each Gandhian persona legitimates a different explanation of his protest method. Gandhi as Indian ascetic generates social protest out of a Hindu commitment to *tapasya* (spiritual austerity). Gandhi the Christian martyr practices nonresistance to evil in the noble pursuit of heavenly reward. Pacifist Gandhi refuses to engage in violence at any cost and therefore refuses to cooperate with those who make war on others. Gandhi through passive resistance acknowledges his inability to force his will on others and protests in the only, weak way he can. Anarchist Gandhi dissents by offering civil disobedience, that is, by undertaking individual acts of conscience against unjust laws.

Neither the real Gandhi nor Gandhi's truth appears in this list, which summarizes the representations produced by Orientalist hyper-difference or by Western over-likeness. How these representations twist up the passage of Gandhian nonviolence to the United States is the subject of the following section. Before that, the real Gandhi and actual Gandhian nonviolence had better make a brief appearance.[2]

Gandhi departed from Hindu spiritual orthodoxy in two prominent ways, therefore he could hardly be the exemplary Hindu or Otherworldly Indian that Orientalist hyper-difference required. Over the course of several encounters with poisonous snakes in South Africa and rabid dogs in India, Gandhi redefined the orthodox concept of *ahimsa* (nonviolence or nonkilling). Orthodoxy required that all killing should be avoided, in order to accrue spiritual merit. Gandhi's version mandated violence and even killing for humanitarian purposes, as in the euthanasia of rabid dogs (Fox, 1995; also see Fox, 1989). Many Hindus chastised the Mahatma for failing, on this issue, to be an orthodox votary of ahimsa. Many more, however, fell out with Gandhi over his opposition to Untouchability. In the India of the 1920s, orthodox Hindus usually accepted Untouchability as an essential element in Hinduism: it was for them a scripturally enjoined inequality, a product of individual *karma* (action) and performance of *dharma* (dedication, in the sense of a calling), and a proof of the cycle of *sansar* (reincarnation). Gandhi never succeeded in justifying his stance against Untouchability with orthodox opinion, and in the end, he simply asserted that Hinduism needed to change (Parekh, 1989).

Gandhi's practice fares no better if it is misconceived as a by-product of Indian asceticism. Although Gandhi followed various ascetic regimens, such as *brahmacharya* (celibacy), his purpose was to gain the strength for successful worldly action, rather than to accumulate spiritual merit.

Just as mistakenly, Gandhi and Gandhian protest, as they appear in Western over-likenesses, lose their Orientalized uniqueness and take on the guise of things we already know well. Gandhian nonviolence assimilated to Christian nonresistance dismisses the activist, confrontational element in Gandhism, in favor of a quietist resistance. Gandhi, however, wanted worldly success, the independence of India, not divine martyrdom. He made salt, he burned cloth, he led boycotts, he was thrown in prison, but he never waited around to be thrown to the lions.

Gandhian nonviolence and pacifism are not at all close, because Gandhi did not believe in turning the other cheek in every situation. Pacifists abhor all violence and refuse to engage in it at any cost. Gandhi believed that cowardice was worse than violence. Evil had to be resisted, best done nonviolently, but better by violence than not at all.

Passive resistance was the term that Gandhi originally used for his South African protest, but he soon disowned the term in favor of his neolocution, "*satyagraha*" (soul-force or truth-force). For Gandhi, passive resistance was a weapon of the weak, used expediently (not morally) when violence was impossible or too costly. When Gandhi observed British suffragettes and Irish Republican hunger-strikers offer passive resistance in jail, he located an essential coercive element in these protests, which made them akin to violent resistance. Such passive resistors perpetrated nonviolence to extract concessions from their enemies. Gandhian nonviolent resistors, so at least Gandhi said, suffered nonviolently to engender trust and respect in their opponents (Fox, 1996).

Civil disobedience against the state, and the anarchist spirit of protest it represented, is another presumed likeness that Gandhian protest is really unlike. The civil disobedience that Thoreau proposed and later anarchists practiced depended on individual acts of conscientious protest. Mass action was suspect because participants might not share the same conviction or some might feel coerced into action (the anarchist U.S. Catholic Worker movement was therefore never reconciled to Gandhism). In Gandhian protest, civil disobedience could begin with individual acts, but always with the purpose of mobilizing mass protest. Otherwise, civil disobedience was an ego-trip, not a moral action.

Gandhi's truth was therefore not a product of his Indian tradition; neither was it his parroting of protest methods already known in the West. It was an innovative syncretism of Western and Indian ideas and practices, as well as Gandhi's lived experience in England, South Africa, and India (Fox, 1989). By about 1918, at which time Gandhi had put its three most important elements together—namely, morally informed nonviolence, mass civil disobedience, and courageous suffering—Gandhian nonviolent protest is almost as strange to Indians as it is foreign to Americans. The next section explores the way in which Orientalist hyper-difference and Western over-likeness delayed the passage of Gandhian nonviolence from India to the United States. Although Gandhi's protest methods get recognized and appreciated in the United States from the

1920s, it is only from 1940 that they get truly understood and practiced. Even afterward, there are relapses, when Gandhian nonviolence gets made into the likeness of passive resistance or nonresistance, or when it is rejected because supposedly it only works in a spiritual culture. These results show just how difficult transcultural flows can be despite or, rather, because of globalization. In the final section, I discuss the agents and agencies by which Gandhian non-violence was "dislocated" from an Orientalized India and "relocated" in America as a protest method unlike any existing one.

Orientalist Hyper-Difference and Western Over-Likeness

American activists in the 1920s and 1930s began to take interest in Indian nationalism and Gandhian nonviolent protest, as the 1919 All-India strike, the 1920 Non-Cooperation Movement, and the 1930 Salt March and civil-disobedience campaign earned increased attention for India in world media. The problem was that expanded media coverage often fixed Orientalist under-standings of Gandhi even more securely and widely. A common conclusion in mainstream media, therefore, was that Gandhi and Gandhian protest would only work in India. For example, coverage in the *New York Times* from the early 1920s to the mid-1940s explains that the Indian masses follow Gandhi because he is a holy man and therefore appeals to their traditional religiosity. Gandhi's program is not presented as an attempt to raise the Indian people to altogether new levels of political consciousness, nonviolent action, and self-discipline. Rather, the newspaper accounts claim that the masses listen because Gandhi articulates ancient themes in Indian (Hindu) culture. The message itself ap-pears almost entirely as a moral philosophy, which emerges from Gandhi's re-ligious principles, self-sacrifice, and love. It is not a political culture that could endure, never mind prevail, independently of Gandhi and outside of India. In 1921, for example, Gandhi appears as an "ascetic . . . whose popularity among the Hindus appeared to have attained almost Messianic proportions" (*New York Times*, 17 May 1921, 2, 7). Gandhi "preaches" his "new revelation" and inspires the Indian masses to believe in his superhuman powers (*New York Times*, 11 March 1922, 2, 2). For the West, Gandhi's most important power was to hold back the mob violence that threatened to erupt from the Indian masses, evi-dently because such violence always threatened to erupt in an India riven by caste and sect. Gandhi's power is not reported as superhuman in the West, but it is taken as spiritual, otherwise it would have no influence over the In-dian masses (see, for example, *New York Times*, 12 March 1922, 2, 2). Gandhi "suffers himself to be adored," as one commentator put it (*New York Times*, 23 April 1922, section VII: 2, 2), and another takes Gandhi's penitential fasting for political ends as illustrating the "difference between East and West" (*New

York Times, 20 September 1924, 14, 6). Still another labels Gandhi as "the holy man of present-day India," but a practical (political) one, and speaks of him as "revered" (*New York Times*, 5 October 1924, 9, 5). These examples from early newspaper accounts establish a story line on Gandhi that continues throughout the interwar years.

A Gandhi sanctified by Orientalist hyper-difference in this manner spoke to American social activists only as a saint—which meant that he was heard best by Christian militants, rather than secular ones, and that his word was taken as prophecy, not politics. Even this depended on assimilating Gandhi to Christ and conforming his nonviolent resistance to Christian nonresistance and pacifism. This over-likeness, as I have called it, grows stronger from the 1920s on, partly as Gandhi's influence over Indian nationalism develops and partly as more and more American ministers go to India to meet the Mahatma and bring his ideas home (see Kapur, 1992, 72–100 for a summary of these excursions[3]). Taking passage with the ministers, Gandhi's ideas are sanctified—and crucified.

For example, in 1921, an editorial in the *A.M.E. Church Review* called Gandhi an Indian messiah and saint, and, in the same year, a columnist in the black newspaper the *Chicago Defender* applauded Gandhi for adopting Christ's message of mercy and suffering (Kapur, 1992, 28–29). A Howard University professor in 1930 over-likened Gandhian protest methods to Christian ones and praised the Mahatma for recognizing the weakness of the Indian people and their lack of power to end British rule except by Christ's method of passive resistance (Kapur, 1992, 42). John Haynes Holmes, a Protestant minister, pacifist, and activist with A. J. Muste's Fellowship for Reconciliation (FOR) was a major agent of Western over-likeness. He began to preach a Christianized version of Gandhi and Gandhism as early as 1918 and met the Mahatma in 1931. In a 1922 sermon, Holmes said that "'Gandhi is thus undertaking to do exactly what Jesus did when He proclaimed the kingdom of God on earth'" (*New York Times*, 13 March 1922, 2, 1). Another typical example of his over-likeness is the following: "This Indian is a saint in his personal life; he teaches the law of love, and non-resistance as its practice; and he seeks the establishment of a new social order which shall be the kingdom of the spirit" (Holmes, 1970 [1922], 60). Sudarshan Kapur aptly summarizes this collective misunderstanding, which continued to grow apace throughout the 1920s and 1930s, as "the notion that in Gandhi the world had a Christ-like figure" (1992, 40).[4]

For many U.S. activists in the 1930s, even Christian ones, a Christ-like Gandhi gave no political direction. A. J. Muste, who later came to personify Christian protest and who, as we shall see, underwrote Gandhian methods for U. S. activists, remembered this period with regret: "In the Thirties . . . we faced a terrible situation. . . . I did not know how to apply nonviolent methods effectively to the situation. The effort to apply Gandhian methods to American conditions had scarcely begun. Pacifism was mostly a middle-class and an individualistic phenomenon" (Muste in Hentoff, 1967, 136–137). Rejecting Christ and a Christ-like Gandhi, Muste turned to Trotsky and Communism, at least for a short period.

As late as 1943, Orientalist hyper-difference, on the one hand, and Western over-likeness, on the other, defined the twists in the terms of debate about Gandhian protest method in the United States. In this year, W.E.B. Du Bois, disputed with Ralph Templin, associated with the Harlem Ashram and the Kristagraha movement (for which, see the next section) over the worth of launching a Gandhian mass action, but their exchange never broke free of the twists. Du Bois argued that austerities—fasting, prayer, self-sacrifice, and personal abnegation—had been bred into "the very bone" of India for more than three thousand years, whereas a U.S. movement that embraced such tactics would be judged a joke or an insanity. The reason was that "our culture patterns in East and West differ so vastly, that what is sense in one world may be nonsense in the other" (Du Bois, 1943, 10).[5]

Templin replied that Gandhian protest took its methods from Thoreau and the American abolitionists, so it was eminently suitable to the United States (Templin, 1943, 10, 5–6). In effect, Gandhian method was either immobilized in India or came across as U.S. protest in a Christian tradition.

The terms of the debate were already being changed even before this dispute erupted, however. The twists were initially straightened out in practice primarily in Chicago and Washington by a small number of people, James Farmer, George Houser, A. Philip Randolph, Bayard Rustin, and A. J. Muste, chief among them; by an even smaller number of activist organizations, in the main, FOR, CORE, and MOWM; and just as World War II began.

Gandhian Nonviolent Protest Arrives and Prevails

In the fall of 1941, James Farmer recollects that he began to plan a Gandhian campaign for racial equality in the United States (Farmer, 1985, 74). At that time, he worked for the Fellowship of Reconciliation, the Christian pacifist organization run by A. J. Muste. Early in 1942, Farmer sent Muste a memo asking FOR to support a major effort at reforming U.S. race relations. Farmer wrote, "we must withhold our support and participation from the institution of segregation in every area of American life—not an individual witness to purity of conscience, as Thoreau used it, but a coordinated movement of mass noncooperation as with Gandhi. . . . Like Gandhi's army, it must be nonviolent. . . . Gandhi has the key for me to unlock the door to the American dream"

(Farmer, 1985 [1942], 356). This quotation indicates that as World War II came to the United States, Farmer had come to appreciate the three essentials of Gandhian method—activism, nonviolence, and mass protest—and also appreciated how they differed from existing American forms of protest.

August Meier and Elliott Rudwick (1973, 3) tell the story with much less emphasis on Farmer's individual contribution. They speak of an interracial cell of FOR that formed around Farmer, George Houser, and several others at the University of Chicago in 1941, who were, as one of them attested "'afire with Gandhian nonviolence'" (Bernice Fischer, quoted in Meier and Rudwick, 1973, 6). CORE (Congress of Racial Equality) was the spin-off of this group, which Muste agreed to underwrite as an independent association dedicated to activism against racism. CORE began to put Gandhian nonviolence into practice in 1942, first against racially restrictive covenants on housing around the University of Chicago and then in the successful use of satyagraha to integrate an ice skating rink.

In his 1942 memo, Farmer (1985, 356) gives credit to Krishnalal Shridharani and Jay Holmes Smith for his Gandhian fervor, and presumably this would be true of the others in CORE. I discuss these two individuals in the following section.

By the fall of 1942, Gandhian rhetoric has spread to MOWM (March on Washington Movement) and its leader, A. Philip Randolph. Now, with its successful passage, Gandhian nonviolence began to remake existing U.S. protest forms in *its* own likeness, and Randolph's metamorphosis is a good example.

Randolph's methods previously arose from labor militancy, and they emphasized mass action over spirituality and passive resistance. In July 1941, Randolph had called for a mass march on Washington to convince Roosevelt of the need for antidiscrimination laws in war industry. He exhorted his followers to concerted mass action, such as marches and petitions. There is no mention of Gandhi, India, or any other Gandhian technique; instead, Randolph invokes earlier black leaders like Nat Turner, Denmark Vesey, and Harriet Tubman (Randolph, in Meier et al., 1965, 221–224).

Soon after, Randolph comes to a more radical consciousness and rhetoric, strongly influenced by Gandhian methods. In his September 1942 address to MOWM, Randolph speaks of a "Negro Liberation Movement," (Randolph, in Meier et al., 1965, 232), and he has Indian nationalism much in mind. "'Witness the strategy and maneuver of the people of India,'" he exhorted, "'. . . mass civil disobedience and non-cooperation and the marches to the sea to make salt'" (Randolph, in Meier et al., 1965, 230). He calls for marches, picketing, and civil disobedience, and then, for the courage to accept courtroom battles and even imprisonment.

By 1943, Randolph writes in celebration of his proposed method of "non-violent, good-will direct action," which is a modification of "the principle of non-violent civil disobedience and non-cooperation set forth by Gandhi in India" (Randolph, 1943a, 13, 3–6). Randolph recognized that U.S. deployment of Gandhian methods would stop short of bringing down the civil administration, as Gandhi aimed to do in India (or so Randolph thought), but the civil rights leader dismissed any criticism based on the fact that the "strategy . . . was born in a foreign and oriental situation" (Randolph, 1943b, 13, 4–6).

Bayard Rustin seems to have linked Farmer's CORE, Muste's FOR, and Randolph's MOWM. Like Muste, Rustin had renounced secular radicalism to revert to a Christian activism. Rustin was a member of FOR and also was one of the early members of the Chicago CORE. He joined MOWM in 1941. Rustin described his use of Gandhian methods in a July 1942 article published by the FOR. On a bus trip through Tennessee, he refused to sit at the back and ended up in jail (1971 [1942], 5). In his "The Negro and Nonviolence," written in October 1942, Rustin rejects the "pink tea" protests of the black middle class and white intellectuals. He argues for nonviolent protest or what he also calls "nonviolent direct action," even though it demands a great capacity for suffering. Rustin associates this form of protest with Gandhi and Jay Holmes Smith and calls it "Christian and workable" (Rustin, 1971, 11).

Rustin, the intermediary among several U.S. protest groups, is also intermediary in his understanding of Gandhian nonviolence: he has de-Orientalized it and can put it into practice but he places something of a Christian likeness on it, which neither CORE nor MOWM did. The next section does the "forward history" by which Gandhian protest first was de-Orientalized and then under-likened to Christian pacifism and nonresistance.

Cultural Dislocation and Relocation

In successfully relocating Gandhian nonviolence to the United States, the first move was to "dislocate" it from the Orientalist hyper-difference that condemned it as an India-only phenomenon. The initial effort came from Richard Gregg, a lawyer whose extensive experience in dispute settlement came from service on the Labor Relations Board during World War I (Robert Brainerd, interview, 23 May 1994). Gregg traveled to India and lived in Gandhi's Sabarmati ashram for several months in the mid-1920s; he returned to India as an observer during the 1930 Salt March (Gregg, 1934, 13). Published in 1934, Gregg's *Power of Nonviolence* was read or cited by most of the activists mentioned earlier, or at least they mentioned the powerful image of Gandhian protest that Gregg introduces; he calls it "moral jiu-jitsu" (Gregg, 1934, 47) because it uses active protest and love against an opponent, to throw him off-balance rather than to beat him down by violence. The martial-arts image "dislocates" Gandhism from Indian spirituality and ascetic practice (even though it replaces it with another Orientalism). Jiu-jitsu highlights the this-worldly strength and skill Gandhian nonviolence requires: it is a matter of political training, not spiritual election. By moral, Gregg wishes to emphasize that Gandhian nonviolence is not coercive; it compels through superior social leverage, personal dedication, and moral balance. The first instance of dislocation, then, comes from the replacement of spirituality with athleticism.

Gregg also began to "relocate" Gandhian protest in the United States by emphasizing how unlike existing ones it was. He condemned American pacifists as ineffectual, or worse, selling out to the government whenever their beliefs are tested (Gregg, 1934, 158–160).

Although Gregg minimized their otherworldly and ascetic elements, he still thought Gandhian methods depended on religion and faith (Gregg, 1942, 3, 1).

Jay Holmes Smith, a missionary to India, also helped relocate Gandhian methods through the Harlem Ashram he established in 1940. Early in 1941, he formed the Non-Violent Direct Action Committee "to study the application of Gandhi's way to American life" (Anon., 1941 3:1, 1). Their protests against draft registration and participation in mass marches began at the same time. By later instigating nonviolent resistance against discriminatory hiring by Harlem businesses and using the ashram as a staging ground for such protests (see Smith, 1942b, 2, 1; Anon., 1943 5:2, 3), Smith highlighted Gandhism as confrontational and, in practice, as subordinating spiritual merit to secular action. His ashram anticipated many later developments that saw Christian protest redefined in the image of Gandhism—often to the point that a deep pedigree for nonviolent resistance within Christianity is advanced. Smith and his ashram represent a transitional point, however, when the attempt to redefine Christianity by Gandhian principles was conscious and obvious—and also embattled. In India, Smith and several other missionaries associated with what became known as the Kristagraha (Christ-force) movement had espoused Indian nationalism and had called on their church to work actively against racial inequality, imperialism, and all other instances of domination. Britain's declaration of war against the Axis in 1939 "on behalf" of an India it dominated (and despite protests from the Indian National Congress) prodded these missionaries into a more pronationalist stance. The mission authorities then called them home, where they began, as I have indicated, to reform Christianity by an activist Gandhian creed (see the brief retrospective in Templin, 1965, 323–330; see also Shridharani, 1941, 303–309, 342–345).

Moral jiu-jitsu and Kristagraha still conserved many notions of "oriental" self-discipline or, alternatively, Christ-like understandings. When James Farmer left Chicago in 1943 and came to New York, he initially put up in the Harlem Ashram but was soon put off by the voluntary poverty and renunciation in place there. Farmer says (1985, 150) he was "not one for asceticism," and the final step in dislocating Gandhian nonviolence was to remove the fasting and personal austerities to which Du Bois had taken exception as fundamentals of such protest. The faith in it had to be made a secular and political, not religious, one.

To do so required relocating Gandhism even more outside Orientalism and even further apart from existing Christian protest methods. The moving force turned out to be Krishnalal Shridharani, who acted with profound, albeit brief and now almost completely forgotten, influence on would-be Gandhian activists in the United States. He was the joker or wild card that makes determinist Whiggish histories look foolish. Self-exiled from India in 1934, Gandhian nationalist from childhood, poet and playwright in his native Gujarati language, Shridharani completed a Ph.D. in sociology from Columbia University with a dissertation on Gandhian nonviolence and its application to the United States. It was published in 1939 (Shridharani, 1939).

Shridharani widely broadcast the message that Gandhian nonviolence was "war without violence" (Shridharani, 1939). It was "the emergence of a new institution, a novel mode of solving group and national conflicts" (Shridharani, 1939, xxvii). The war image was obviously appropriate to a time when Europeans were busy with death. By it, he emphasized Gandhian confrontation even more strongly than had Gregg. For Shridharani, conflict over goals and interests is endemic to society, no matter what pacifists and Christian nonresisters might preach, and "nonviolent direct action" (another term he uses, which becomes standard in the vocabulary of American activists thereafter) is superior to other means of resolution because it acknowledges conflict and solves it without false claims of loving reconciliation, on the one hand, or mass killings, on the other (Shridharani, 1939, xxiv).

Shridharani strongly relocates Gandhian nonviolence as distinct from passive resistance, nonresistance, pacifism, and conscientious objection (Shridharani, 1939, 6). Harshly condemning American pacifists for their lack of any activist program, he accuses them of "religious appeasement," that is, instead of building a nonviolent program to thwart war, "they merely talked of 'love and good will.'" Whereas, in Shridharani's view, nonviolent resistance was basically a secular technique and the religious trappings were mainly there to satisfy Gandhi, "American pacifism is essentially religious and mystical." Pacifists follow the Christian idea of nonresistance, and that is why they fail (Shridharani, 1941, 14; see also p. 278 for his condemnation of the Quakers;

and Shridharani, 1939, 273). The irony of Shridharani's de-Orientalizing was obvious to one reviewer: "there has long been a tendency in casual western thinking to identify India with Mysticism and the exotic . . . we are confronted with the curious anomaly of having to learn from a follower of Gandhi . . . that American pacifism is too "'unworldly'" and "'essentially religious and mystical'" (Klieger, 1942, 5, 1–4).

Shridharani's book was probably the most widely read primer on Gandhian nonviolent resistance until after World War II. The Fellowship for Reconciliation published a pamphlet containing selections from it that sold for 15 cents. The Harlem Ashram used it as a study "text" (Anon., 1941, 1, 1), and J. Holmes Smith took its message on tour, calling it a must for every pacifist (Smith, 1942a, 4:1, 2). Its imprimatur no doubt rested on Shridharani's "authentic" Indian-ness and his authority as a Gandhian activist, but its vogue also depended on the force of Shridharani's prose and his impatience with existing American protest methods.

Shridharani spoke as well as wrote. He made the rounds of American protest organizations. In 1943, he spoke in Chicago to James Farmer and thirty others involved with CORE (Farmer, 1985, 110). A. J. Muste also convened a meeting with him and American activists, and he advised a nonviolent direct action in Pennsylvania (Shridharani, 1941, 273 lists the American activists he met very early on).

As for Shridharani himself, self-exile promoted his reflection and recollection of the Gandhian program, his highly public and vocal advocacy of Indian independence, and his intervention in U.S. activism. Shridharani was acutely conscious of being an Indian "on parade" in the United States and he strenuously resisted stereotypes of India and of Gandhi in his books and articles, and, we may presume, in his personal dealings and formal addresses. One time, for example, a Brooklyn waitress put her hand in his, not from love at first sight, but because she hoped he would tell her fortune. Shridharani comments laconically: "Not all Indians are fortune-tellers, not even a good many of them" (Shridharani, 1941, 89). He also recounts how he failed American hosts by admitting he was not a maharaja or, on another occasion, by refusing to do the Rope Trick of the Indian fakir. Salman Rushdie (1991, 13ff.) suggests that the experience of exile or transnationality often promotes a historical consciousness that resists official versions. Shridharani (1941, 607) said it more simply: in the United States, he had truly become "twice-born."

Moreover, Shridharani affected behaviors that produced a new transnational consciousness in the Americans who read and met him. When a very young and very committed James Farmer met Shridharani in 1943, he was, as we came to say in the 1960s, "blown away." Perhaps it was the wrap-up for any residual Orientalist, ascetic notion of Gandhism. Shridharani surprised Farmer by being exceedingly dapper and sharply dressed, Western-style. He also greatly enjoyed big cigars.[6] Sometimes a cigar need not (only) be a phallic symbol. With his cigar, Shridharani smoked out and dismissed stereotypes about Indian abnegation at the same time he asserted his comfort with Western forms of pleasure.

Richard Gregg and Jay Holmes Smith, although they did not have quite the same precocious transnational consciousness that twice-born Shridharani achieved, nevertheless also had uncommon lived experiences. Both were self-exiles. Gregg went to India to find new ways of managing disputes and returned with an empowering Gandhism. Smith's original Christian mission to India radicalized him, and when he was exiled from that mission and forced to go home to the United States, he returned filled with a Gandhian Christ-force that had no place in his church but was to have a future place in U.S. social protest, thanks in part to his efforts. The dislocation and relocation of Gandhian nonviolent resistance by Gregg, Smith, and, most of all, Shridharani depended on their personal dislocation and relocation. Gandhi, too, wore top hats in England, then the turban of an indentured laborer in South Africa, until finally, he bared his head in India.

Conclusions

Late in the twentieth century, understanding social protest means acknowledging transnational cultural movements. To this end, anthropology needs to "recycle" its early interest in diffusion; it must, in effect, move this concept transculturally, so that it no longer is something that only happens in the primitive world.[7] Modern communications and transport supposedly marked the "end of diffusion," because, it was presumed, there was no longer any need to map and historicize distribution in a world of mostly unimpeded cultural flows. But globalization also creates new conditions for cultural topologies that get twisted in transit. Anthropology must now recognize that cultural practices "flutter between worlds," just like the souls of innocents blown up in international air space by the new transnational terrorism.[8]

For a start, we need to reconceptualize diffusion late in the twentieth century away from flow models and toward analyses that take bumps as characteristic. I have suggested that globalization generates hyper-difference and over-likeness. They, in turn, can create very bumpy transcultural movements in a world saturated with information that is not necessarily knowledge, in a world where there is much exposure but little familiarity. Cultural dislocation and relocation were other concepts detailed in this paper; they emphasize what must happen before culture can make it over the bumps. Whereas hyper-difference and over-likeness are macroconditions of the current global system, dislocation and relocation depend on the interested activities of individuals, like Krishnalal Shridharani, suitably or, perhaps more likely, fortuitously placed in history. His precocious transnational consciousness, his public advocacy, his networking, his interventions against stereotypes, yet his uncompromising Indian identity—all helped work out the twists in the transfer of Gandhian protest methods to the United States.

Shridharani (1941, 125) gently chided his fellow "countryman," a Bengal tiger in the Bronx Zoo, for "selling out" to the West. The tiger ate peanuts it begged from zoo goers. It's lucky that Shridharani's transnational consciousness proved stronger than the tiger's biological instinct.

Notes

1. I thank the other participants in the conference for their probing comments, especially Sunita Parikh. I also thank John Bowen for pointing out weak points in the argument and Robert Brainerd for saving me from some errors about Richard Gregg and A. J. Muste.

2. The assertion here, to be absolutely clear, is that there is *a* Gandhian protest method, no matter how many so-called Gandhian methods his followers may have fastened upon. The Gandhian method is the one he was so careful to proclaim as different from passive resistance, pacifism, and anarchist individual civil disobedience. No better proof that such a method existed and that it differed substantially from the foregoing is the extent to which it generated new forms of protest in the United States when it was finally understood for what it was.

3. The title of this book, *Raising Up a Prophet: The African-American Encounter with Gandhi*, is an instance of over-likeness.

4. Kapur's book is also an indication that over-likeness continues to confuse understanding of Gandhian protest even today, especially as current laundering of Martin Luther King, Jr.'s, image and that of the civil rights movement continues to wash away its activist and confrontational aspects.

5. Du Bois was responding to A. Philip Randolph's avowal of "nonviolent direct action" in the March on Washington Movement, which I discuss later in this essay.

6. In a 1993 interview, Shridharani's widow (he returned to India after World War II and died quite young in 1960) explained that he was addicted to Cuban cigars. "He had highly aristocratic tastes." He believed in Gandhian philosophy, she said, but he did not live the Gandhian way. I thank Ajantha Subramanian for conducting this interview in New Delhi.

7. Michael Taussig (1992) recommends that an anthropology of the present, an engaged anthropology, must turn the concepts that anthropology used to "primitize" the rest back onto the West, for example, totemism or sympathetic magic. I believe the concept of diffusion also qualifies, to the extent that it was defined as a characteristic of primitive societies or only to be studied there.

8. "Like my husband's spirit, I flutter between worlds" (Mukherjee, 1988, 185).

References

Anon. (1941). New York Committee Studying Means of Non-Violence. *Conscientious Objector* 3 February–March:1, 1.

Anon. (1943). Ashram Offers Course on U.S. Race Problems. *Conscientious Objector* 5 July 7:2, 3.

Appadurai, Arjun (1990). Disjuncture and Difference in the Global Cultural Economy. *Public Culture* 2:1–24.

Appadurai, Arjun (1991). Global Ethnoscapes: Notes and Queries for a Transnational Anthropology. In *Recapturing Anthropology: Working in the Present*, ed. Richard G. Fox, pp. 191–210. Santa Fe: School of American Research.

Brainerd, Robert (1994). Personal communication. 23 May.

Du Bois, W.E.B. (1943). As the Crow Flies. *New York Amsterdam News* 13 March, 10, 2.

Farmer, James (1985). *Lay Bare the Heart*. New York: New American Books.

Fox, Richard G. (1989). *Gandhian Utopia: Experiments with Culture*. Boston: Beacon Press.

Fox, Richard G. (1995). Cultural Dis-Integration and the Invention of New Peace-Fares. In *Articulating Hidden Histories*, ed. Rayna Rapp and Jane Schneider, pp. 275–290. Berkeley: University of California Press

Fox, Richard G. (1996). Gandhian Fasting as Cultural Invention. *Gandhi Marg* 410–422

Geertz, Clifford (1971). *Islam Observed*. Chicago: University of Chicago Press, Phoenix edition.

Gregg, Richard B. (1934). *The Power of Nonviolence*. Philadelphia: Lippincott.

Gregg, Richard B. (1942). West Can Solve Problems with Non-Violent Action. *Conscientious Objector* 4, 8 August:1, 1+.

Hannerz, Ulf (1992). *Cultural Complexity*. New York: Columbia University Press.

Hentoff, Nat (1967). *The Collected Essays of A. J. Muste*. N.p.: Clarion Books.

Holmes, John Haynes (1970). *A Summons Unto Men*. New York: Simon & Schuster.

Kapur, Sudarshan (1992). *Raising Up a Prophet: The African-American Encounter with Gandhi*. Boston: Beacon Press.

Klieger, Harry (1942). Gandhi's Methods Applied to America. *Conscientious Objector* 4 January 1:5.

Latour, Bruno (1993). *We Have Never Been Modern*. Cambridge, Mass.: Harvard University Press.

Meier, August and Elliott Rudwick (1973). *CORE, A Study of the Civil Rights Movement*. Urbana: University of Illinois Press.

Meier, August, Elliot Rudwick, and Francis L. Broderick, Eds. (1965). *Black Protest Thought in the Twentieth Century*. Second edition. Indianapolis: Bobbs-Merrill.

Monson, Ingrid (1994). Doubleness and Jazz Improvisation: Irony, Parody, and Ethnomusicology. *Critical Inquiry* 20:283–313.

Mukherjee, Bharati (1988). *The Middleman and Other Stories*. New York: Fawcett Crest.

Parekh, Bhikhu (1989). *Gandhi's Political Philosophy*. South Bend, Ind.: University of Notre Dame.

Randolph, A. Philip (1943a). A Reply to My Critics. *Chicago Defender* 12 June, 13, 3–6.

Randolph, A. Philip (1943b). A Reply to My Critics. *Chicago Defender* 26 June 13, 3–6.

Rushdie, Salman (1991). *Imaginary Homelands*. London: Granta Books.

Rustin, Bayard (1971). We Challenged Jim Crow. In *Down the Line* Chicago: Quadrangle Books.

Shridharani, Krishnalal (1939). *War Without Violence.* New York: Harcourt, Brace.

Shridharani, Krishnalal (1941). *My India, My America.* New York: Duell, Sloan and Pearce.

Smith, J. Holmes (1942a). War Without Violence. *Conscientious Objector* 4, 3 March:1–2.

Smith, J. Holmes (1942b). Satyagraha in Race Struggle. *Conscientious Objector* 4, 8 August:2, 1+.

Taussig, Michael (1993). *Mimesis and Alterity.* New York: Routledge.

Templin, Ralph (1943). Letter to Editor. *New York Amsterdam News* 29 May, 10, 5–6.

Templin, Ralph (1965). *Democracy and Nonviolence.* Boston: Porter Sargent.

Sonia E. Alvarez

Reweaving the Fabric of Collective Action

Social Movements and Challenges to "Actually Existing Democracy" in Brazil

... theory should expose the limits of the specific form of democracy we enjoy in contemporary capitalist societies. Perhaps it can thereby help inspire us to try to push back those limits, while also cautioning people in other parts of the world against heeding the call to install them (Fraser, 1993, 27).

Introduction: Rethinking Social Movements' Contributions to Democratizing Brazil

During Brazil's singularly protracted, elite-controlled transition from authoritarian to civilian rule,[1] a vast array of social movements—ranging from human rights organizations, to urban struggles for adequate social services, to church-linked Christian base communities, to second-wave feminist and black rights organizations—helped push the military's planned "slow, gradual, and secure" political liberalization process well beyond the narrow limits envisioned by the military regime and its bourgeois allies.[2] Movements became variously entangled with the political opposition to the dictatorship, creatively occupying and often subverting what little political space remained after the military closed down or severely restricted preexisting channels of participation and representation. And, as I shall suggest here, social movements also created new public spaces in which the socially, culturally, and politically marginalized could re/construct identities, needs, and interests and challenge authoritarianism—in politics *and* in society.

During the transition period, social movements were widely hailed as heroic forms of resistance to dictatorship; for some progressive analysts, their defiant actions portended radical social transformations (Brant, 1980; Gohn, 1982, 1985; Moises, 1982).[3] Even mainstream analyses of transition politics viewed "the resurrection of civil society" (O'Donnell and Schmitter, 1986, especially Ch. 5) in general, and social movements in particular, as important forces in resisting and thereby undermining authoritarian rule and "reconstructing public space."[4]

Since the return of civilian rule in 1985, however, the actual or potential role of social movements in expanding or deepening "actually existing democracy" in Brazil and other Latin American nations has been largely ignored or downplayed by mainstream analysts. Indeed, a relative demobilization of "resurrected" civil society in the posttransition period is often presented as inevitable:

> The wave [of mobilization] crests sooner or later, depending on the case. A certain normality is subsequently reasserted as some individuals and groups depoliticize themselves again, having run out of resources or become disillusioned, and as others deradicalize themselves, having recognized that their maximal hopes will not be achieved. Still others simply become tired of constant mobilization and its intrusion into their private lives . . . and later on, return to some form of relatively depoliticized citizenship (O'Donnell and Schmitter, 1986, 26).

A certain degree of demobilization and a moderation of political conflict, moreover, is considered not only inevitable but also desirable by some: "Nothing is more destructive to democracy than frequent confrontations in the streets, the legislature, the state administration, and elsewhere. . . . The lifting of authoritarian repression and the return to democratic liberties to organize, petition, and demonstrate should not lead to widespread disorder and violence" (Valenzuela, 1992, 82).

Though too much "antisystemic" mobilization is considered destabilizing for democracy, other analysts insist that a loyal civil society is essential to democratic consolidation: "Just as democracy requires an effective but limited state, so it needs a pluralistic, autonomously organized civil society to check the power of the state and give expression democratically to popular interests" (Diamond and Linz, 1989, 35). Still, most mainstream analyses conclude that social movements and civic associations play, at best, a secondary role in democratization and therefore have focused scholarly attention on political institutionalization, which is viewed as "the single most important and urgent factor in the consolidation of democracy" (Diamond, 1994, 15).

Consequently, discussions of Latin American democratization today center almost exclusively on the stability of formal representative political institutions and processes, e.g., "the perils of presidentialism" (Linz, 1990; Mainwaring, 1990); the formation and consolidation of viable parties and party systems (Mainwaring, 1988); the "requisites of governability" (Martins, 1989; Huntington, 1991; Mainwaring, O'Donnell, and Valenzuela, 1992); and the like. These neoinstitutionalist analyses, in short, center on what political scientists have dubbed the "institutional engineering" required to consolidate representative democracy in the south of the Americas. Though the fragile, elitist, particularistic, and often corrupt institutions of Latin America's new democracies certainly warrant scholarly attention, such analyses too often disregard the possibility that nongovernmental or extrainstitutional public arenas—constructed principally by (often less-than-loyal) social movements—might be equally essential to the consolidation of meaningful democratic citizenship for subaltern social groups and classes.

A recent trend in the study of Brazilian social movements would appear to endorse this exclusive focus on the formally institutional.[5] Many recent analyses maintain that, although the early literature on movements of the 1970s and early 1980s praised their putative eschewal of institutional politics, their defense of absolute autonomy, and their emphasis on direct democracy, these postures gave rise to an "ethos of indiscriminate rejection of the institutional" (Doimo, 1993; Pereira da Silva, 1994) that made it difficult for movements to effectively articulate their claims in formal political arenas once civilian rule was restored in 1985. Other recent theorists of Brazilian social movements have highlighted the movements' parochial, fragmentary, and ephemeral qualities and emphasized their inability to transcend the local and engage in the realpolitik necessitated by the return of representative democracy (Cardoso, 1988; Coelho, 1992).

An excessively narrow or reductionist conception of democracy underlies both mainstream approaches to democratization and some recent treatments of social movements. The former assume that, if properly engineered and consolidated, the institutions traditionally associated with liberal democracy in the West would adequately represent the interests of subaltern citizens in highly stratified societies such as those of late twentieth-century Latin America. The latter presume that the principal challenge facing Brazilian social movements today is to learn to better interact with precisely those formal institutional arenas that have historically excluded the interests of the vast majority of citizens and to work to have their demands incorporated and processed within those arenas.

Following Nancy Fraser's critique of Habermas's account of the liberal public sphere, I maintain that such conceptions are "informed by an underlying evaluative assumption, namely, that the institutional confinement of public life to a single, overarching public sphere is a positive and desirable state of affairs, whereas the proliferation of a multiplicity of publics represents a departure from, rather than an advance toward, democracy" (Fraser, 1993, 13). This critique is particularly relevant in the case of Brazil and other Latin American nations where—even in formally democratic political contexts—information about, access to, and influence in the governmental arenas in which collectively binding policy decisions are made has been restricted to a very small, privileged fraction of the population and effectively denied to subaltern groups and classes.

Moreover, the rigid social hierarchies of class, race, and gender that typify Brazilian social relations prevent the vast majority of de jure citizens from even imagining, let alone publicly claiming, the "right to have rights." For Brazilian political theorist, Evelina Dagnino, popular movements, along with feminist, Afro-Brazilian and other liberation movements, have been instrumental in constructing a new concept of democratic citizenship. This concept claims rights in society, not just from the state, and challenges the rigid social hierarchies that dictate fixed social "places" for its (non)citizens on the basis of class, race, and gender:

> . . . social authoritarianism engenders forms of sociability and an authoritarian culture of exclusion which underlies the totality of social practices and reproduces inequality in social relations on all levels. In this sense, its elimination constitutes a fundamental challenge for the effective democratization of society. A consideration of this dimension necessarily implies a redefinition of that which is normally viewed as the terrain of politics and of the power relations to be transformed. And, fundamentally, this requires an expansion and deepening of the conception of democracy, so as to include the totality of social and cultural practices, a conception of democracy which transcends the formal institutional level and spills over into the totality of social relations permeated by social authoritarianism and not just by political exclusion in the strict sense (Dagnino, 1994, 14–15).

Because the subaltern in Brazil have been relegated historically to the status of de facto noncitizens, the multiplication of public arenas in which social/cultural, gendered, racial, and economic, and not just political, exclusion might be contested and resignified, then, must also be seen as integral to the expansion and deepening of democratization.

The proliferation of alternative social movement publics—configured, I will argue, out of intra- and intermovement political/communicative networks—is thus positive for democracy not only because they serve to "check the power of the state," or because they "give expression" to structurally preordained "popular interests," as Diamond and Linz would have it (1989, 35), but also because it is in these alternative public spaces that those very interests can be continually re/constructed. Fraser conceptualizes these spaces as *"subaltern counterpublics* in order to signal that they are parallel discursive arenas where members of subordinated social groups invent and circulate counterdiscourses, so as to formulate oppositional interpretations of their identities, interests and needs" (1993, 14). Social movements' principal contribution to Brazilian democracy, then, is to be found precisely in the proliferation of multiple public spheres.

Whereas some movement analysts claim that the "heroic" collective actors of yesteryear have today demobilized or even disappeared—echoing the predictions of the mainstream transitions literature—I suggest that, since the return to civilian rule, the fabric of collective action in Brazil has, instead, been rewoven or reconfigured. I will draw attention to the less visible, less heroic, but perhaps equally valiant, efforts of what I shall call an emergent social movement sector—composed of numerous multifaceted formal and informal political/communicative networks of movement organizations and their advisers and sympathizers in NGOs, parties, unions, government, the church, the media, the liberal professions and the universities—to deepen and expand the democratization of *both* state and society in postauthoritarian Brazil.

In this interpretive essay, I explore only a few of the myriad ways in which Brazilian social movements—articulated through inter- and intramovement networks or what I will call *social movement webs*—have enabled dissenting voices to challenge the consolidation of a class-based, masculinist, racist, and exclusionary "democracy," and to critically and proactively engage formal political institutions in order to adapt, without capitulating, to the requisites of the actually existing Brazilian democracy. The social movement sector has also devised alternative forms of political mediation in response to the manifest crisis of representation that afflicts Brazil along with most post- *and* prewelfare state political democracies in the late twentieth century. These alternatives, though still emergent, mostly partial, and sometimes contradictory, pose significant challenges for "actually existing democracy," its theorists, and its apologists. Finally, I briefly examine some of the democratic contradictions evident in practices *within* the social movement sector. I point to some power "knots" and democratic "snags" often found in social movement webs—in an effort to contribute to their political and theoretical disentanglement.

Reconceptualizing the Social Movement "Field" in Brazil

The present effort to reconceptualize the social movement field was prompted by a recurrent epistemological puzzle encountered over my many years of field research on Brazilian social movements. At the outset of each of my several field research trips to Brazil since at least 1985, some of my Brazilian social science colleagues as well as many friends involved in social movements would (gently) suggest that I was perhaps wrongheaded in insisting on continuing to study movements because these were "weakened" or "demobilized," "in crisis," "irrelevant" to democracy (or not as relevant as they used to be), or just plain old "dead."[6]

Yet, somehow, I always readily found these putatively disappeared, dead, or dying movements; attended their (still) numerous meetings, events, and rallies; and had animated conversations/interviews with long-time activists who told me of new developments in the movements, new strategies, new challenges confronted, new groups that had emerged, and new issues that had surfaced since my last visit. Many of these conversations were on-going ones with, for example, feminist activists whose location in the social and political fabric of Brazil had shifted significantly over time. The one-time *guerrilheiras* or student activists turned autonomous feminist militants in the 1970s had, by the 1990s, become leaders of women's sections of progressive parties, become elected officials, joined university faculties, or founded nongovernmental organizations—and each still considered herself a "feminist militant" and a member or part of the feminist movement. Each still regularly interacted with other feminists in a wide variety of public and private spaces—engaging in "kitchen table debates" about feminist theory and practice, participating in an occasional rally, mobilizing around a particular policy issue, working together on the campaign of a profeminist candidate, attending the yearly international women's day celebrations, and so on. Other ongoing conversations were with women who were still active members of autonomous feminist movement organizations and whose seemingly indefatigable energies and unwavering political commitment helped keep afloat the more visible, public face of feminism in Brazil, by, for example, organizing or articulating the varied events, rallies, and campaigns attended and sustained by the women mentioned above.

In light of these observations, I (slowly) arrived at the conclusion that either I or my so-called key informants were deluding ourselves about the vitality of these purportedly dead social movements, or there was a problem with the conceptual lenses through which some social scientists were viewing movement dynamics in postauthoritarian Brazil. The manifold ties that linked together feminists now dispersed in a variety of social, cultural, and political arenas—across time and space and between the mobilizational "peaks" of the movement—suggested an alternative conceptualization. Movement mobilizations—feared for their destabilizing potential by mainstream analysts—were indeed less frequent in postauthoritarian Brazil, and, when they occurred, were perhaps less militant and generally less massive than in the turbulent early years of the struggle against military rule. But social movements remained very much alive and articulated through precisely the (mostly informal) political/communicative networks or webs that now configure ever more heterogeneous, spatially and organizationally fragmented and polycentric social movement fields—such as the reconfigured feminist movement field of the 1990s, briefly described above.

To better understand how such webs were woven during the transition period and then rewoven to adapt to the contours of postauthoritarian political realities, we must first realize that Brazilian social movement organizations—even the smallest, most localized, neighborhood-based community struggles for adequate social services and infrastructure—cannot be conceptualized as self-contained, discrete, or isolated actors, somehow pure and disconnected from one another or from the larger constellation of social and political actors that surrounds them.

Much of the early literature on Brazilian grassroots movements, in particular, tended to emphasize the radical potential of community struggles through which the "autonomous popular classes" were taking command of their own political destinies, untainted by the tutelage of political parties and unfettered by the state. Subsequent analyses criticized this pristine characterization of popular movements. They highlighted the critical role played by what were variously called "external actors" (Cardoso, 1983), "catalyzers" (*catalizadores*) (Ferreira dos Santos, 1981), or "extracommunity agents" (Alvarez, 1990a)—such as feminists, party activists, leftist militants, and progressive clergy—in promoting "critical consciousness" among local residents, mobilizing them into action against government authorities, and advising them on how best to press their demands on the state. Still other analyses rejected the "exteriority" implicit in such nomenclature. They referred to these putatively external actors as "political articulators" (Coelho, 1991; Alvarez, 1993) who play a crucial role in shaping the *internal* dynamics of movement groups (even when they do not belong to the community or identity group in question) and in linking or articulating localized groups with other movements, civic organizations, parties, and government.

Taking this last line of argument a step further, I suggest that the discourses and dynamics of most contemporary Brazilian social movement organizations—including not just popular movements but also feminist groups, racial/ethnic movements, ecology movements, and the like—were shaped from the outset by their embeddedness in larger oppositional discursive organizational networks or webs. Movement networks or webs of interpersonal and interorganizational communication and interaction—though fluid and most frequently informal—are sustained over time by (formal or informal) movement leaders, advisers, and articulators. These webs intersect to constitute political/discursive fields and together configure an emergent social movement sector that has come to play an increasingly important role in Brazilian politics. Movement webs have today acquired a considerable degree of permanence and remain very much alive and articulated even in times of supposed decline or demobilization of social movements.

I prefer the term webs over the more common networks, precisely to try to convey the intricacy and precariousness of the manifold imbrications of and ties established among movement organizations, individual participants, and other actors in civil and political society and the state over the course of the last two decades. The metaphor of webs also enables us to more vividly imagine the *multilayered entanglements* of movement actors with the political-institutional and cultural-discursive terrains in which they are embedded. Indeed, when evaluating the impact of social movements on larger processes of political change, such as transitions to formal democracy, we must understand the reach of social movements as extending beyond their conspicuous constitutive parts and visible manifestations of protest. That is, we must move beyond measuring the policy effectiveness of specific movement organizations, their number of active members, or the size of the demonstrations or militant actions they organize. As Ana Maria Doimo argues in her incisive study of the popular movement in Brazil:

> In general, when we study phenomena relative to explicitly political participation, such as parties, elections, parliament, etc., we know where to look for data and instruments to 'measure' them. This is not the case with the movement field in question . . . such a field rests upon interpersonal relationships which link individuals to other individuals, involving connections that go beyond specific groups and transversely cut across particular social institutions, such as the Catholic church, protestantism—national and international—the scientific academy, nongovernmental organizations (NGOs), leftist organizations, trade unions and political parties (Doimo, 1993, 44).

The political demands, discourses, and practices and the mobilizational and policy strategies of movements are spread widely, and sometimes invisibly, through the social fabric, as their political/communicative webs stretch to envelop the institutional and the cultural and thus reach into parliaments, the academy, the church, the media, and the like. That is, movement webs encompass more than movement organizations and their active members. When we examine the impact of movements, then, we must gauge the extent to which their demands, discourses and practices circulate (e.g., are deployed, adopted, appropriated, coopted, reconstructed, as the case may be) in larger institutional and cultural arenas. We must also consider how movement dynamics and discourses are shaped by the important social, cultural, and political institutions that traverse them and how movements, in turn, shape the dynamics and discourses of those institutions.

These webs serve as a counterweight to the movements' parochial and fragmentary propensities. Organizationally fragile movement webs were and are held together not only by the multiple, overlapping memberships and horizontal ties established among movement participants and leaders but also by political articulators. And they are sustained by sympathizers or sporadic participants in movement organizations and events who may or may not also belong to political parties, NGOs, civic associations, universities, the media, the legislature, or the state apparatus itself.

In the last decade in particular, the social movement sector has also come to play a compensatory as well as complementary role in relation to conventional forms of political mediation and articulation embodied in crisis-ridden parties, parliaments, and corporatist systems of political representation. Moreover, because the threads of movement webs span vertically and horizontally, they construct crucial linkages between movements and the institutional political arena, linkages that have enabled movement demands and discourses to be translated into programmatic items on party platforms and, occasionally, into public policies.

In the remainder of this essay, I will illustrate—drawing examples principally from the popular movement field—how social movement webs were constituted and sustained over time and how those webs were and are deeply entangled with other actors and organizations of civil and political society and the state. I will first describe and analyze the embeddedness of the popular movement field in the larger field of oppositional and movement discourses and practices. Next, I will trace the reach and democratizing impact of popular movement practices into the official public sphere during the postauthoritarian period. Finally, I will examine some of the internal contradictions evident in movement webs, which themselves pose complex challenges for democratic theory and practice in the late twentieth century.

The Political Invention of the "Popular Movement": Urban Movement Webs and Alternative Democratic Discourses and Practices

Somewhat belatedly adopting an oppositional stance against military authoritarian rule and fostering community organization and mobilization among the poor and working classes in the 1970s, the progressive Catholic church became the foremost articulator of the popular movement field.[7] The political/communicative and discursive webs woven among the tens of thousands of groups (the majority of which owe their origins to the church) composed what came to be known as "The Popular Movement" (*O Movimento Popular*, or MP). They made possible the re/construction of the identities, needs, and claims of the subaltern and enabled these to reach *across* local community movements, *over into* networks of political advisers from NGOs, militant left organizations, the church and the academy, and ultimately, *up into* the sphere of institutional politics.

The popular movement field deployed a common set of practices developed within intermovement webs that loosely linked a wide array of sectoral and territorially based movements. Doimo vividly illustrates how these, in part, were fashioned out of the multiple, overlapping memberships of movement activists:

> Predisposed to continual participation, members of these networks appeared on the public scenario throughout the '70s and '80s interacting with an immense array of *carências* or needs and increasing the number of demand-based direct action movements. From the struggle for day care one moved to confront the problem of the cost of living which, in turn, suggested the struggle for health care and which, moreover, was connected to the problem of sewage. And in the place of residence, one discovered readily the absence of regularized or legalized land parcels or lots which, to be sure, unveiled the unequal distribution of lands and the scarcity of housing. But, what of the bus to take one to work? And how many can even find work? (Doimo, 1993, 110).

Thus, multilayered ties were forged among a vast array of localized, community struggles. These included, among others, the progressive Catholic church's Christian base communities; organizations of the urban landless, shantytown dwellers or *favelados*; grassroots women's organizations; and cost-of-living, day care, and health care movements. These ties helped develop a common set of oppositional discourses and practices that departed significantly from both preexisting populist-corporatist forms of association, participation, and representation and from the "para-liberal" forms prevailing in "redemocratized" Brazil.

Much of the extensive literature on urban popular movements characterizes these as struggles guided by new political methodologies (or, in movement parlance, "new ways of doing politics").[8] Indeed, despite the heterogeneity of demands articulated by Brazilian popular movements, there is considerable homogeneity in their discourses and practices. Though the actual political practices of these movements vary considerably and do not always conform fully to their stated egalitarian ideals, popular movement groups that proliferated in São Paulo and most other Brazilian urban centers during the 1970s and 1980s eschewed clientelistic ties and adopted a confrontational, often quite disloyal stance vis-à-vis both the authoritarian and postauthoritarian state. Moreover, their discourses and practices demarcated what Doimo, Sergio Baierle (1992), and others have called a distinctive "ethical-political field": "a common field of references and differences for collective action and political contestation" (Baierle, 1992, 320), that radically distinguished popular movement or MP webs from the clientelistic relations that tied older neighborhood associations to both the populist-corporatist and authoritarian political establishments.

The common repertoire of discourses and practices of these newer popular movements—which appeared in fullest force during the two decades of struggle against military rule—differs markedly from those of older neighborhood civic organizations that are crucial links in the urban chain of traditional clientelistic politics. In São Paulo, these older neighborhood civic associations, the most common of which are called *Sociedades de Amigos do Bairro* (SABs, or Societies of Friends of the Neighborhood), expanded steadily from the 1940s through the 1960s. Though originally organized by residents of the urban periphery who sought the expansion of social services to their neighborhoods, the SABs began to flourish when local politicians found them fertile ground for the extension of urban clientele networks. As Paul Singer notes, many of the SABs grew directly out of neighborhood electoral committees for populist politicians. He argues that "[t]he SABs functioned as links between the population lacking basic services and public authorities who had the possibility of responding, at least in part, to the demands presented. This involved, at bottom, exchanging public works and services, financed by the public treasury, for the vote of those benefited" (1980, 87). The politics of *troca de favores* (exchange of favors) thus provided the primary impetus for the expansion of the SABs throughout the populist period.[9] After 1964, Brazil's military authoritarian rulers also availed themselves of these representative neighborhood associations to control and coopt poor residents of the urban periphery.

In comparison to the formalistic structures of associations such as the SABs, the MP typically adopted informal, collective decision-making forms and established fluid intergroup linkages, gathering in innumerable, sporadic "popular assemblies" and movement "encounters," sometimes forming citywide or regional unions, forums or councils of neighborhood-based or issue-specific movement groups in which shared carencias were discussed and common strategies for demanding urban services or infrastructure were determined consensually.

The MP's emphasis on direct community participation led to a mistrust of classical liberal and populist-corporatist forms of representation; assemblies and forums were open to all to enable each individual member of the community to speak for her- or himself. Typically, in dealings with public authorities, caravans or busloads of movement participants would arrive at the mayor's office or the municipal legislature and demand that public officials speak with the entire group rather than with select movement representatives. Where representational schemes were required—as in the case of citywide, regional, or national movement encounters—rotational systems were often established or nonelected community leaders, whose authority was forged out of "the popular struggle," would be selected to participate.

In enacting alternative political practices and generating new arenas for the construction and reconstruction of popular needs and interests, these new movement articulations disputed the representativeness of older civic associations, formulated demands about issues ignored or excluded from debate within the elite-controlled official public sphere, and created alternative public spaces in which new collective identities could be forged. In these spaces, the purported marginality of poor and working-class urban residents was resignified and their demands as citizens legitimized, "removing the discriminatory weight built into words already consecrated by use: the *urban squatter*, for example, is now called the *urban landless* or *homeless*; the *land invasion*, the *occupation*; the *colored* now is recognized as *black* (Pereira da Silva, 1992, 12). Rigid social hierarchies were challenged as the MP sought to create "communities of equals" and to imbue participants with a new sense of citizenship that entailed not just the right to demand rights from the state or to belong to the political system but, as Dagnino points out, to also "effectively participate in the very definition of that system" (1994, 109). Thus, in the waning years of authoritarian rule, and especially when the political opposition won control of several state administrations in the early 1980s, the MP began to demand popular participation in the formulation of urban and social policies.

This posture gave rise to new popular movement practices that now sought to encroach on the terrain of the official public sphere. Since the late 1970s, for example, Popular Health Movement, one of São Paulo's most militant, had organized into popular health councils. In these, movement participants monitored the services provided by the neighborhood clinics that the movement had won from the state and municipal governments after years of struggle. Movement councils secured official recognition from the state and local health departments, but established their own internal rules and selected their own representatives in elections designed and supervised by the movement (Jacobi, 1989; Cardoso and Simões, 1990; Martes, 1990).

Significantly, the Popular Health Movement was, from the outset, advised by progressive doctors and other health professionals from the *movimento de medicos sanitaristas* (public health doctors' movement), leftist party activists, health-focused NGOs, and the progressive wing of the Catholic church. As Doimo's exhaustive study of the discourses of five popular movements—the Cost-of-Living Movement, the Popular Housing Movement, the Struggle against Unemployment Movement, the Health Movement, and the Movement for Collective Transportation—demonstrates, the MP's common discursive repertoire and shared ethical-political imaginary thus were also fashioned out of the multifold entanglements of these movements with progressive sectors of the Catholic church, certain sectors of the left, NGO professionals, intellectuals, and other middle-class dissidents (Doimo, 1993).

The militant left's strategic decision to organize at the community level in the wake of the severe government repression of the late 1960s and early 1970s, for example, led many to begin working in urban peripheral neighborhoods, attending and often organizing the activities of local mothers' clubs, youth organizations, health care groups, and so on. Shielded from military repression by the progressive church, members of (sometimes still clandestine) leftist organizations often served as advisers to community groups and worked with movement participants to unveil "the structural and political roots" that shaped the felt carencias of the poor and working classes. Feminists, drawn to popular movements because the overwhelming majority of participants in the new movements were and are women, worked to instill a critical gender consciousness among neighborhood activists.[10] Progressive intellectuals also riveted their attention on these new, grassroots forms of collective action that seemed to hold the promise of social transformation and their participant-observation often led to deep immersion in local movement activities. Opposition party activists—in seeking to enlist the electoral support of popular movement participants—also formed part of the dense tangle of social forces that traversed, helped shape, and were, in turn, shaped by the MP field. Feminists, leftists, opposition party militants, and engaged intellectuals also helped forge connections among local movement leaders and sometimes articulated protests and other joint movement strategies—helping compose fluid webs of horizontal linkages among popular movement organizations.

From the origins of second-wave Brazilian feminism onward, for example, feminists have been deeply entangled with both that vast subset of popular movements that Brazilians and other Latin Americans typically refer to as the *movimento feminino* or *movimento de mulheres* (popular women's movement) and with the left-intellectual-oppositional field that traversed MP webs since their origins (Moraes Nehring, 1981; Saffioti, 1987; Sarti, 1989; Alvarez, 1990a, 1994; Teles, 1993; Soares, 1994). Most of the early feminist groups that emerged

in Brazil in the 1970s were themselves products of the multilayered ties established among women involved in student movements, militant left organizations (in Brazil or in exile), and Marxist currents then prevailing in the Brazilian
academy.

When the left turned toward organizing a "mass base for the revolution" in
Brazil's urban periphery in the mid-1970s, many former guerrilheiras and student activists directed their efforts at women of the popular classes. Early feminists saw themselves as the vanguard of what was to be a united, cross-class,
mass-based Brazilian women's movement. The legacy of the left led early feminists to conceptualize women's oppression principally in class terms (e.g., focused on the binomial "production" and "reproduction") and to promote the
expansion of the grassroots women's movement. As the number of mothers'
clubs and other women's community organizations expanded and the day care,
cost-of-living, and feminine amnesty movements grew, so did feminist determination to capture the political significance of these struggles and to articulate them with the larger opposition.

The manifold imbrications of feminists with popular women's organizations
significantly re/shaped the discourses and practices of both movement fields.
Feminists at first shied away from raising issues such as abortion, domestic
violence, or power relations within the family with the poor and working-class
women with whom they worked—partly due to fears of losing crucial allies
on the left and in the progressive church. But they soon discovered that participants in popular women's groups were anxious to discuss such issues. Indeed, women's organizations in the urban periphery provided a new context
within which poor and working-class women could share their experiences not
only as residents of the *periferia* but also as wives, mothers, lovers—as women.
The involvement of feminist advisers or political articulators helped create a
discursive space in which participants in grassroots movement groups could
openly discuss problems they shared in their marriages, their sexual lives, their
desire to control fertility, their yearning for more information about the world
outside the domestic sphere, and their relationships to family and community.
And these organizing experiences, in turn, emboldened feminists to develop a
more strident critique of the left's relegation of the "woman question" to a secondary plane in the struggle for social transformation, to deploy more radical
discourses about the specificity of women's oppression, and to ultimately forge
a feminist political identity distinct from that of both the militant left and the
larger popular women's movement.

Whereas in the late 1970s and early 1980s, feminist practices often reflected
the "democratic centralism" and (often implicit) organizational hierarchies in-
herited from the left—for example, organizing women's congresses and cen-

tralized coordinations in which different sectors of the larger women's movement would be represented—by the late 1980s and 1990s, feminists had adopted many of the more fluid, nonhierarchical organizational practices that also typified the MP field in which many continued to operate. As growing numbers of poor and working-class women, African-Brazilian women, lesbians, women trade unionists, and other sectors of the larger women's movement came to embrace (and, often, radically redefine) feminism as their own, the distinctive feminist political identity of the late 1970s was transformed into a common ethical-political field of discourse and practice that now also spanned into a variety of public spaces in civil and political society and the state.

In the 1990s, the existence of many feminisms was widely acknowledged and the diversity of feminist visions, approaches, organizational forms, and strategic priorities appeared to be increasingly respected within the movement. Also, importantly, with the growth of popular feminism, the dichotomy between feminine and feminist struggles was also increasingly being abandoned or blurred. The various pieces of this "feminist mosaic of diversity" combined and recombined in a variety of forms and forums.[11] Periodic national and regional meetings or encounters brought together all strands of feminism and other sectors of the larger women's movement; groups working on women's health and reproductive rights created the Rede Nacional Feminista de Saude (the National Feminist Health Network) to coordinate their activities; feminist ecologists coordinated their input into the 1992 U.N. Conference on the Environment, held in Rio in June 1992, sponsoring a series of activities in a separate women's space, the Planeta Femea (Women's Planet), during that important global summit, and formalized their growing network in December 1992, forming the Coalizão de ONGs de Mulheres Brasileiras para o Meio Ambiente, a População e o Desenvolvimento (Coalition of Women's NGOs for the Environment, Population, and Development). Similar feminist coalitions—always imbricated at various levels with the popular women's movement—were established in relation to U.N. conferences on Population and Development (Cairo, 1994) and on Women (Beijing, 1995).

The internally heterogeneous and multicentric feminist movement field in Brazil today also includes a strand of more formal, institutionalized NGOs who advocate on behalf of poor and working-class women's rights and provide a wide variety of services—from legal assistance, to reproductive health information and services, to occupational training courses and the like. Leilah Landim's (1993) pioneering study of the "Invention of NGOs: From an Invisible Service to a Nameless Profession" shows how some feminists, along with many of the middle-class dissidents who advised the MP, gradually configured their own political/communicative networks and came to constitute their own distinctive ethical-political field, creating NGOs focused on providing "assistance to popular movements," thus stretching the reach of MP webs far beyond the community. Landim demonstrates that more than two thousand NGOs estimated to be active in Brazil today themselves are "composed of the crossing of people from universities, churches, parties and organizations of the left . . . diverse crossings or 'intersections' which occurred and continue to occur in time, in different moments, in diverse conjunctures" (1993, 154). She highlights the centrality of particular political organizations through which people "transit" (p. 167) and the importance of "*o pessoal que costura*" (p. 164) (literally, people who sew or stitch together) in weaving these personal/organizational intersections into increasingly coherent political NGO/MP webs.

Indeed, the Brazilian NGO field today stretches globally, as electronic conferences, newsletters, and publications and the innumerable periodic international and regional meetings/workshops of issue-specific movement groups and NGOs—often financed and sometimes organized by philanthropic foundations or bilateral or multilateral aid and development agencies—foster regularized communicative/political exchanges among people working on similar problematics in a variety of country or regional settings. Rubem Cesar Fernandes describes the multiplicity of strands that tie together Latin American NGOs:

> The key word in this new process of articulation was imported from the field of computer communications—they come together through "networks" which combine the autonomy of each point of the system with an intense flow of information. Multiple and transversal, NGO networks combine in a variety of forms, membership in one of them not excluding the possibility of affiliation with others (Fernandes, 1994, 130).

What Landim calls "Popular Movement Assistance NGOs" (hereafter, MPA-NGOs) became, over time, the quintessential nodal points through which the popular movement field increasingly was articulated and mobilized. As the NGO field was consolidated and the institutional church retracted considerably from its "preferential option for the poor" in the late 1980s and 1990s, the NGOs' more institutionalized, formal organizations—which command resources crucial to mobilization such as permanent support staff, telephones, duplication, and fax machines and connections with the media, the academic community and public policy community—played an increasingly important role in sustaining, rearticulating, and sometimes repairing the constitutive webs of the MP field. When a movement rally needed to be staged; a manifesto produced; a conference, course, or encounter organized; or citizen pressure mobilized to secure the passage of specific legislation, these articulatory nodes reactivated sometimes dormant movement networks. And because NGO webs are themselves the product of multiple intersections of the academy, political parties, the media, the church, and so on, their mobilizational and discursive reach can be quite extensive.

Like the popular movements they served, MPA-NGO networks developed a common set of discourses and practices grounded in concepts such as "'participation,' 'self-help,' 'self-promotion,' 'leadership training,' 'change of habits and behaviors,' . . . stressing that the 'communities' must organize from their 'felt needs' and take the reins of their own 'development,' in a process of 'self-determination'" (Landim, 1993, 193). Doimo shows that these MPA-NGOs, along with the Catholic church and other political articulators, helped diffuse common discourses and practices throughout the MP field through the promotion of innumerable training courses for movement leaders, guided by popular education based on the methods of Paulo Freire, and the production of a wide array of popular communication materials such as "manuals, bulletins, flyers, calls-to-action, audio-video, public loudspeakers, dramatizations, etc." (Doimo, 1993, 92).[12]

In sum, the impact or contribution of popular movements to expanding and deepening actually existing Brazilian democracy must be understood in the light of their embeddedness in and multilayered imbrication with these multiple other "counterpublics," which reach far beyond the community and thus counteract the movements' purportedly parochial and fragmentary tendencies. The proliferation of a broad array of alternative publics—variously entangled with and thus constitutive of the MP field—over the course of Brazil's ongoing democratization process has created multiple public arenas in which a variety of counterhegemonic or contestatory popular identities—based on gender, class, community, and so on—and political demands can be continually re/constructed.

From Resistance to Representation? The Intervention of Intra- and Intermovement Networks and Alternative Forms/Forums of Political Mediation

Beyond their decisive role in multiplying the number of alternative publics in which dissenting discourses on citizenship, participation, and democracy are invented and circulated, significant threads of Brazil's intra- and, especially, intermovement political/communicative webs have entered into the official or dominant public sphere. When in 1979, for example, the military regime imposed new strictures on the party system, the political opposition—long entangled with social movements and previously forcibly unified by military decree into a single party—imploded into at first five, and later many, political parties. Thus, multiple strands of MP and other movement webs and their discourses and demands found their way into several new political parties and, ultimately, into policy arenas.

Because social movement webs spanned into opposition parties during the transition period, subaltern counterpublics were able to carve out significant niches within dominant publics in postauthoritarian Brazil. When the opposition won control of several state administrations in the early 1980s, for example, some state and local governments—responding to long-standing movement demands to participate in policy formulation and thereby hoping to garner democratic legitimacy—created a variety of issue-specific citizen councils through which "representatives of civil society" would advise policymakers on matters of relevance to their particular social constituencies.[13] Because council members most often were appointed and not selected by those constituencies, however, their representativeness and legitimacy vis-à-vis social movements were significantly compromised. Still, some movement strands occupied these new institutional spaces in an effort to give greater public voice to the needs and interests of the socially and politically excluded.

By the 1990s, what we might call "council democracy" had become the order of the day throughout Brazil. At the local, state, and federal levels, hundreds of advisory or consultative citizen councils had been established in policy areas ranging from urban reform, to public health services, to child and adolescent rights, to African-Brazilian and women's rights. Though an analysis of the mixed performance, complex dynamics, and multiple contradictions of such councils is beyond the scope of the present essay, I underscore here the fact that council democracy has enabled a variety of movement webs to reach or spread into the official public sphere, and, in that sense, also represents a potential deepening and expansion of democratization.

The Workers' Party (Partido dos Trabalhadores or PT) (Gadotti and Pereira, 1989; Meneguello, 1989; Sader and Silverstein, 1991; Keck, 1992)—a radical democratic, leftist party fashioned out of the very intersections/crossings that were constitutive of the MP and other social movement fields—has been a particularly vocal advocate of council democracy. Elected in over three dozen municipalities in 1988, Workers' Party administrations set out to fashion new participatory and representative political institutions through the creation of popular councils (*conselhos populares*).

Elsewhere I have analyzed the multiple contradictions encountered by the PT's "experiments in radical democracy" (Alvarez, 1993). Here, I briefly highlight how the PT's political project was informed by the discourses and practices of the popular movement webs by which the party was traversed and with which the party itself was thoroughly imbricated. "Popular participation," together with the "inversion of local government priorities," became the twin pillars of the PT's municipal campaigns throughout urban Brazil in 1988. Both were seen as crucial to the party's goals of democratizing the relationship between poor and working-class citizens and the state and promoting greater economic and social justice. By investing in social services and infrastructure in the urban periphery, rather than privileging local business interests and the more affluent neighborhoods in the city, popular democratic PT administrations proposed to invert the historically elitist priorities of local government. The party's platform on popular participation, developed for that campaign, also clearly reflected the historic discourses deployed through popular movement webs:

> Participation is a political activity, of division and direct exercise of power. That participation should involve, therefore, the power to DECIDE on policy and CONTROL its execution. For this, the following five conditions are fundamental:
>
> 1. *political-administrative decentralization.* One cannot pretend that participation exists in instances without real decision-making power.
> 2. *the democratization of information.* The control of information constitutes a source of power. Without democratizing it, participation becomes a game with marked cards.
> 3. *planning.* The participation of people distanced from the day-to-day workings of the administration is impossible.
> 4. *creation of institutional channels for participation and control.* Participation is not a "gift" (*davida*) of the incumbents of power. It is a conquest of the population. It should, therefore, constitute a right of citizens, with clearly instituted democratic channels and rules.
> 5. *stimulus to the autonomous organization of the population* (popular councils, for example) and the recognition of diverse forms of political representation of the population. The creation of institutional channels of participation should not impede the population from organizing autonomously nor serve to coopt or to empty popular movements (*Documentos Políticos dos Pré-candidatos do PT*, cited in Paz et al., 1990, 17–18).

This conception of participation, especially the idea of the popular councils, was very much in keeping with the PT's distinctive popular democratic vision— one that both animated and was inspired by popular movement practices, such as those of the Popular Health Movement in São Paulo. These discursive tropes were not merely coopted nor appropriated from popular movements. Rather, they were constitutive of the popular movement field that the PT had an active hand in constructing and of which many members of the administration formed a part. Movement webs now stretched vertically into municipal institutional arenas, as many of the leaders and advisers to popular movements became public officials. The PT mayor of São Paulo, Luiza Erundina, for example, was herself a long-time political articulator of movements of the urban landless; her municipal health secretary was a *medico sanitarista* who had worked with the popular health movement since the mid-1970s. Members of Popular Movement Assistance NGOs filled the offices of the city hall and the municipal legislative chamber, either as appointed officials or as consultants to local government agencies or elected officials.

Beyond their growing overlap with council democracy, many activists involved in social movement webs have increasingly come to view critical engagement with formal processes of representative democracy as a complementary means for furthering the goals of empowerment and meaningful social/cultural citizenship. This was especially true after 1985, when civilian leaders from the ancien régime and conservative sectors of the political opposition assumed the reins of power in Brazil's first civilian federal administration in twenty-one years.

Notwithstanding their putatively "indiscriminate rejection of the institutional," for example, many intra- and intermovement webs became entangled in efforts to influence the drafting of the constitution that was to shape Brazil's postauthoritarian regime, thus working to break the hegemony of economic and political elites over the democratization process. Some active in loose-knit networks of movements and articulators, now formalized into coalitions such as the Constituent Assembly Popular Education Project, played a crucial role in mapping out national strategies, bringing movement leaders together to work toward the expansion of citizenship and representative democracy.[14]

To this end, the multiple intersections of intra- and intermovement webs were rewoven into more formalized coalitions or articulations of movement organizations, NGOs, labor unions, and party activists, such as the new "popular lobbies" established in Brasília in 1986 and 1987. Movement lobbies secured a "popular amendment" process, which provided that amendments to the draft constitution could be submitted for congressional consideration if signed by at least 30,000 registered voters and sponsored by at least three organizations of civil society.[15] The expansive mobilizational and organizational reach of numerous inter- and intramovement webs into important social and political institutions, such as the Catholic church, the academy, the media, parties and parliaments, was revealed in their ability to gather over 12 million signatures on 122 popular amendments—representing between 6 and 18 percent of the Brazilian electorate.[16]

Partially as a result of these efforts, the federal constitution allows for elements of direct democracy to be built into Brazil's political system at various levels. For example, Title One reads, "All power emanates from the people, who exercise it through their elected representatives or directly, pursuant to this constitution." The word "directly" was included at the insistence of popular lobbies and their progressive congressional allies and was fiercely opposed by the political right. The 1988 constitution provides for referenda, plebiscites, and "popular legislative initiatives" that require the endorsement of 1 percent of the electorate from at least five states.[17] It also recognizes the legitimacy and representativeness of civic associations and movement organizations. For example, it mandates that urban movement organizations be consulted in urban planning. It grants trade unions, professional associations, and other organizations of civil society the right to represent their members in any judicial or administrative instance.

Women's movement webs were similarly formalized in a concerted effort to influence the constitution drafting.[18] Through intensive lobbying by the National Council on Women's Rights—created in 1985 in response to movement pressures to promote progressive gender policy at the federal level—combined with women's movement-organized mass mobilizations, petition drives, and even sit-ins at congress to convince recalcitrant legislators, many items from the "women's agenda" made their way into the constitution. It provides for formal equality between the sexes and extends new social rights and benefits to women, including increased maternity leave (from 90 to 120 days), provides for paternity leave (though its duration is unspecified), expands social benefits and workers' rights to women workers, including domestic workers, and "extends provisions for childcare beyond the already existing obligation of employers so that it is now the general responsibility of the state to provide 'free care to children from zero to six years of age, in nurseries and preschools'" (Verucci, 1991, 559).

These movement lobbies are but one example of the configuration of an incipient social movement sector, composed of overlapping, heterogeneous, and polycentric movement fields, that are increasingly constituting a parallel overarching public sphere. And the constitution-drafting conjuncture represented a veritable watershed for Brazilian social movement discourses and practices. It prompted subaltern counterpublics to rethink their approach to the formally institutional, develop alternative practices of negotiation and dialogue with dominant publics, and translate reactive oppositional discourses and practices into proactive ones capable of being translated into policy in the official public sphere. Moreover, the manifold imbrications of various social movement fields began to be rewoven more purposefully into regularized forms/forums of inter- and intramovement dialogue and deliberation.

The MP field has created innumerable articulatory instances in the last several years. Some are locally or regionally based and sectorially focused, like the União de Movimentos de Moradia de Grande São Paulo (Union of Housing Movements of Greater São Paulo), created in 1987 in order to better coordinate land invasions and movement negotiations with local and state government authorities. Others are of national scope, bringing together both territorially based and sectoral movements, like the Central de Movimentos Populares (Popular Movement Central Coordination), founded in October 1993.

Popular Movement Assistance NGOs working in the housing and urban reform fields have also formalized national forums like the Forum Nacional da Reforma Urbana (National Urban Reform Forum). Its discourse centers on promoting citizenship rights, democratic governance, and the "social function of property in the city." Together with the União and other MP articulations, the forum worked to gather signatures throughout 1991 and 1992 to submit a "popular legislative initiative" to Congress that would create a Fundo Nacional de Moradia Popular (National Fund for Popular Housing) and now monitors federal government policy developments related to urban reform. Moreover, joint actions within the NGO field have been facilitated by the creation of the Associação Brasileira de Organizações Não-Governamentais (ABONG, or Brazilian Association of Non-Governmental Organizations) in August 1991, which by the mid-1990s had over 200 institutional members. As mentioned above, the feminist field—especially its NGO strand—has also witnessed the formation of more formalized or institutionalized issue-specific and regional networks.

Each of these movement articulations is informed by a dual logic: on the one hand, they work to deploy alternative conceptions of rights, citizenship, gender, and so on, in the social/cultural realm; and on the other, they seek to make incursions into official publics. And as each of these articulatory forms/forums overlaps with or is traversed by a number of other inter- and intramovement fields, they are beginning to cohere into an increasingly politically relevant, if internally politically and organizationally heterogeneous, social movement sector.

Since the late 1980s, articulatory movement forums have proliferated rapidly and are devising alternative forms of political mediation between civil society and the state. That is, because movement webs reach into and are entangled with official publics, the discourses and express needs and demands of subordinate groups now more often at least circulate and are debated within public policy arenas. In this sense, then, the alternative publics constructed by social movements both complement the party system and help compensate for its failure to adequately represent subaltern social groups and classes. "Ac-

tually existing" party and electoral legislation "favor weak parties, limit accountability, and encourage personalistic, clientelistic, and individualistic styles of
representation" (Mainwaring, 1991, 39). Given the historic weakness and lack
of programmatic and ideological coherence of the Brazilian party system, therefore, the growing cohesion of a social movement sector may in part counteract this mis/representation of subaltern counterpublics within the official public
sphere.[19] Rewoven and increasingly regularized, if not necessarily formalized,
inter- and intramovement networks might counterbalance this deep flaw in
Brazil's actually existing systems of political representation.

Power "Knots" and Democratic "Snags" in Social Movement Webs

To be sure, difficult questions regarding representation, accountability, and internal democracy *within* the social movement sector are far from re-
solved. And relations among the various strands and nodal points of intra- and
intersocial movement webs are far from smooth. Indeed, movement fields are
themselves mined by unequal power relations among individual participants,
organizations, and strands that have obtained differential access to material
and cultural resources and gained uneven avenues of influence in and interlo-
cution with official publics.

The institutionalization of strands of the feminist movement in the form of
NGOs, for example, has triggered considerable conflict and controversy within
the larger feminist field.[20] Many feminists I interviewed in the early-to-mid
1990s were quite wary of the potential "NGO-ization" of the feminist movement,
just as some were once troubled by its institutionalization and/or co-optation
by parties and the state. They were critical of what they viewed as elite-centered
and excessively state-centric strategies that underplayed the importance of continued feminist struggle in the realms of fomenting gender consciousness and
challenging patriarchal cultural norms.

Moreover, because resources provided by the international development
establishment enabled feminist NGOs to gather policy-relevant information and
maintain permanent staff charged with interfacing with government and media representatives, these more professionalized, policy-oriented strands of the
feminist field have become privileged interlocutors of public officials, the media, and bilateral and multilateral aid and development agencies. Even when
feminist NGOs explicitly deny that they represent the women's movement, they
are too often conveniently viewed as such by public officials and policymakers
who can thereby claim to have "consulted civil society" by virtue of involving
a handful of NGOs in a particular policy discussion. As one long-time activist
put it:

It has been common to refer to the NGOs as if they constituted the feminist movement proper. And it is also frequent for the members of NGOs to portray themselves as "representatives" of the feminist movement. All of the sudden, all of our reflections on the necessity of expressing plurality and difference has been forgotten. A new relationship of power has been established within the movement. We now form part of a scenario in which some possess the information, have access to sources of funding and their decisions, therefore, they are the ones who effectively decide . . . (Borda, 1993, cited in Schumaher and Vargas, 1993).

Problems of representativeness and other power "knots" in movement webs thus have been exacerbated by their increased interaction with dominant publics in postauthoritarian Brazil. As Maria Aparecida Schumaher and Elisabeth Vargas argue, such problems plagued feminism as well as the social movement sector in general in the 1990s:

In Brazil, NGOs emerge as new actors on the scene beginning in the 1980s. They were formed by professionals from the social area, in general ex-political militants, ex-exiles who, upon returning to their country, wanted to exert autonomous action, independent of the State. The experience of previous activism contributed to the establishment of a new relationship with popular movements. This new relationship, nevertheless, has often been confused with the representation of those movements. And women's NGOs don't escape this rule (Schumaher and Vargas, 1993, 363).[21]

The problem of representativeness is further complicated by the fact that NGO nodal points in movement webs typically are not membership organizations nor do they generally adopt routinized procedures or mechanisms that would make their actions more accountable to larger movement constituencies on behalf of whom they profess to act. Moreover, the organizational dynamics of more professionalized or institutionalized strands of movement webs, in the view of some activists, sometimes depart significantly from the alternative discourses and practices that typified more informal, militant groups. In the case of the feminist field, for example, Natalie Lebon found that "[f]eminists seem to have managed to integrate some organizational principles from feminist groups into their NGOs, yet their accountability to financing agencies is bound to impose some constraints. This accountability can push them to sacrifice principles of participatory democracy for greater efficiency and increased productivity" (1993, 23). Laura MacDonald similarly argues that "NGOs' activities are also often constrained by the requirements of international funders. Demands to display short-term efficiency and income-generating potential conflict with the long-term processes of collective learning necessary to unleash the democratic potential of local organizations" (1992, 11).

Similar democratic snags are evident in the MP field. Relations of power between middle-class advisers—who often have more direct access to material resources and official publics—and poor and working-class participants, for example, are seldom exempt from the paternalism (or, in the case of feminists, maternalism) and rigid notions of social place that characterize Brazilian society in general. Moreover, the participatory, nonhierarchical organizational forms and informal decision-making formulas professed by the MP do not prevent power from being exercised (sometimes quite) undemocratically within and between popular movement groups.[22] As MacDonald points out, "local organizations often reproduce existing social inequities. Local elites are often able to dominate leadership positions and use organizations to expand their privileges. Even organizations made up entirely of the poor are usually structured on the basis of gender" (1992, 11).

And given that the ethical-political field of popular movements is constructed partially as a negation of "older" clientelistic associational forms, MP discourse often fails to recognize the legitimacy of "Other" poor and working-class citizens' claims articulated outside their field (Coelho, 1992; Pereira da Silva, 1992; Doimo, 1993). As Doimo maintains: "A field . . . establishes frontiers of inclusion/exclusion, awakens militant expectations, offers a sense of the future, defines interlocutors, classifies other fields and regulates participation" (1993, 46). During my observations of the PT's popular councils in 1991 and 1992, a binary discourse of "us" (the MP) versus "them" (the SABs or non-MP organizations) pervaded discussions about the electoral procedures and other rules governing the councils, for instance. Now that their former party and NGO allies were in power, some in the MP seemed invested in reserving these new PT participatory spaces for those of like mind (Alvarez, 1993).

Of course, the exclusionary dynamics and the uneven power flows that typify movement webs pose challenging questions about how to democratize social relations *within* subaltern counterpublics—and certainly merit much fuller treatment than I can allot them here (Alvarez, forthcoming a). My principal goal in this essay has been, instead, to suggest that—however contradictory— the sustained public presence and proliferation of social movement webs have been positive developments for actually existing democracy in Brazil. In this sense, I concur with Fraser's assessment that:

> . . . subaltern counterpublics are [not] always necessarily virtuous; some of them, alas, are explicitly antidemocratic and antiegalitarian; and even those with democratic and egalitarian intentions are not always above practicing

their own modes of informal exclusion and marginalization. Still, insofar as these counterpublics emerge in response to exclusion within dominant publics, they help expand discursive space. In principle, assumptions that were previously exempt from contestation will now have to be publicly argued out. In general, the proliferation of subaltern counterpublics means a widening of discursive contestation, a good thing in stratified societies (Fraser, 1993, 15).

Further, though the mediating role of movement webs is rendered more problematic by issues of representativeness and accountability noted above, the growing articulation of "alternative" and "official" publics has nevertheless widened political/policy contestation within institutions of political society and the state.

Concluding Reflections

Brazil's precarious, elite-dominated democratization process has been seriously tainted by flagrant corruption, thwarted by chronic economic crisis, and tarnished by intensified inequality, violence, and human misery. But social movements are fashioning alternative democratic discourses and practices that continually destabilize the hegemonic discourses and exclusionary practices of actually existing Brazilian democracy.

I have tried to show that the multiple political, organizational, and discursive overlappings woven among a vast array of Brazilian grassroots and liberation movements—and between these and other organizations of civil society, political society, and the state—facilitated the articulation of dissenting conceptions of democratic citizenship and gave rise to innovative forms of direct action and political mediation. This hidden side of the Brazilian democratization process, I have suggested, contains vital lessons for those wishing to retheorize dissent, direct action, and democracy in the late twentieth century.[23]

Social movement webs constitute alternative or subaltern publics in which new cultural and political meanings are produced, dissent is made possible, and direct action can be imagined. As Jean L. Cohen and Andrew Arato (1992, 562) remind us, movement contributions to democracy "should be conceived not in terms of the achievement of certain substantive goals or the perpetuation of the movement, but rather in terms of the democratization of values, norms, and institutions that are rooted ultimately in political culture." This alternative measure of "movement success" is particularly relevant in a democratizing regime whose society remains ruled by rigid norms of social authoritarianism that often thwart the meaningful exercise of the formal rights of citizenship by the politically, economically, racially, sexually, or culturally marginalized.

In Fraser's sense, then, the articulatory practices of social movements can indeed be viewed as generating "parallel discursive arenas," where the subaltern can re/construct alternative interpretations of their identities, interests and needs (1993, 14). Brazilian social theorist, Vera Telles, similarly maintains that social movements are crucial to the "constitution of public spaces in which differences can be expressed and be represented in possible negotiations; spaces in which values circulate, arguments are articulated and opinions formed; and, in which, above all, the ethical dimension of social life can come to constitute a public morality through democratic *convivência* (acquaintance-ship) with the differences and conflicts they imply and demand . . . " (1994, 92). Many popular movement demands (such as those for urban services), for example, as well as many of the demands of feminists and other liberation movements, are unquestionably often targeted at institutions of the state. However, this should not blind us to the fact that movements provide the socially *and* politically excluded with critical, alternative public spaces in which they can re/construct culturally stigmatized, or even vilified, identities and claim a "right to have rights" not just to social services but to human dignity, cultural difference, and/or social equality. Because democratizing social relations—whether at the micro level of the household, the neighborhood, the community association or the macro level of relations between women and men, blacks and whites, rich and poor—is an express goal of Brazil's contemporary social movements, civil society must be understood as both their "terrain" and one of their privileged "targets" (Cohen and Arato, 1992, especially Ch. 10).

I have also tried to suggest that multiple strands of social movement webs increasingly stretch beyond the terrain of civil society and into that of political society and the state. Fraser's "dominant publics" must therefore also be understood as both the target *and* terrain of Brazilian social movements. In this sense, movement webs operate today in many more public spaces than is implied in what Alberto Melucci (1988) has called "submerged [movement] networks." And, I have argued, because movement webs reach into or are articulated with dominant publics and with each other, they have devised new modalities of political mediation that are irrevocably entangled with and complement, even when they do not (and perhaps should not) replace conventional institutional mechanisms of what positivist political science refers to as "interest aggregation."

Finally, the alternative conceptualization of social movements' contributions to democratizing Brazil proposed in this essay suggests that movements might be crucial for orchestrating what we might call an "ethical-political choreography" of civil society that could smooth the often rough edges of "institutionally engineered" democracy (Alvarez, forthcoming b). Democratization is more than just a technocratic/institution-building process; it is also an "art," a profoundly cultural process. Perhaps institutional engineering must be balanced by such a choreography—one that enables the fluid and creative articulation *in society* of needs, interests, and identities historically excluded from dominant democratic publics—if the foundations of Brazilian democracy are to be inclusive, solid and enduring.

Notes

I borrow the provocative phrase "actually existing democracy" from Nancy Fraser (1993).

As always, I am greatly indebted to the dozens of Brazilian movement activists who found time in their crowded schedules to grant interviews and share vital information and astute insights that were crucial for my analysis. I am also grateful to my colleagues at the State University of Campinas in the state of São Paulo—where I was a Fulbright–CIES visiting lecturer in 1992—the Federal University of Santa Catarina in Florianópolis, and the Centro Josué de Castro in Recife for their helpful feedback on earlier (partial) incarnations of this essay. Claudia Lima Costa has been a constant and patient interlocutor throughout the project, providing incisive, constructive criticism. I also thank Catia Aida Pereira da Silva and Carmem Priscila Bocchi for their research assistance in São Paulo during the fall of 1992. Finally, the analysis that follows benefited greatly from the critical suggestions of the participants of the Harry Frank Guggenheim–sponsored conference on "Dissent and Direct Action in the Late Twentieth Century," held in Otavalo, Ecuador, in June 1994.

1. For an analysis of the intraelite negotiations that narrowed the scope of Brazilian democratization, see especially Hagopian (1990), Alves (1988), and Smith (1987).
2. For comprehensive accounts of Brazilian military-authoritarianism and the transition to civilian rule, see Alves (1985), Skidmore (1988), and Stepan (1988).
3. For a critical assessment of the underlying political and methodological assumptions informing much of this early literature on Brazilian social movements, see Cardoso (1994).
4. O'Donnell and Schmitter (1986). Scott Mainwaring aptly summarizes this view:
   In virtually all recent transitions, a panoply of popular organizations struggled against authoritarian governments and on behalf of establishing democracy. Labor unions, peasant groups, neighborhood associations, and Church groups played prominent parts in the struggles that ended authoritarian rule. Without some initial cracks in the authoritarian coalitions, their impact was limited, but once such cracks appeared, they bolstered the efforts to oust autocratic governments (1992, 303).
5. I must begin with a note of self-criticism here. My own earlier work on women's movements (1990a) purposefully focused on their evolving relationship to the state and explicitly did not seek to explore their impact on cultural practices, social relations or civil society, per se. Similarly, the initial focus of my current, on-going project (1993) on social movements and radical democratic alternatives, similarly focused on the workings and manifest contradictions of "alternative," participatory institu-

tions demanded by social movements and created by the Workers' Party, making me, I suppose, a kind of "neo-neo-institutionalist," as my colleague Leigh Payne put it in her response to a version of the above-cited paper presented at the University of Wisconsin, Madison, in 1991. This essay, then, is an attempt to move beyond my own previous focus on the formally institutional.

6. This paper draws on fieldwork on Brazilian women's movements and transition politics conducted from November–December 1981, October 1982–October 1983, and July–August 1985. Much of the ensuing discussion draws particularly on field research conducted on popular movements' relationship to the State in São Paulo and Brasilia in June–July 1988 and in São Paulo and other Workers' Party–led municipal administrations from August–October 1991 and July–December 1992. I also lived and worked in Brazil, serving as program officer in Rights and Social Justice for the Rio de Janeiro Office of the Ford Foundation and conducted research "on the side," carrying on many long-standing conversations with movement activists and NGO professionals, from August 1993 through September 1996. The analysis presented here does not necessarily reflect the opinions of the Ford Foundation. Portions of the ensuing argument are drawn from my 1993 article entitled "'Deepening Democracy': Popular Movement Networks, Constitutional Reform, and Radical Urban Regimes in Contemporary Brazil." The present essay forms part of a larger book project on social movements, citizenship, and radical democratic alternatives in Brazil.

7. For the most exhaustive and compelling account of the institutional transformation of the Brazilian Catholic church, see Mainwaring (1986).

8. Urban popular movements, as movement analysts have stressed, are a "subset of social movements." As Scott Mainwaring explains, the term social movements encompasses

   a wide amalgam of movements, including the feminist movement, the labor movement, the peasant movement, the ecology movement, the human rights movement and others. . . . Urban popular movements attempt to improve urban living conditions, usually through demands on the state for public services including sewers, paved roads, better transportation facilities, better medical facilities, running water, and electricity (Mainwaring, 1987, 133).

9. On the influence of populist clientele networks on the political worldview of residents of São Paulo's urban periphery, see Caldeira's (1984) excellent study and Gay (1990). On the early history of the SABs, see Singer (1980) and Gohn (1991).

10. These activities often brought feminist activists into open conflict with the local church. On these tensions and on women's participation in CEBs and other church-related movements, see Alvarez (1990c).

11. I borrow this metaphor from Calderon, Piscitelli, and Reyna who discuss the "mosaic of Latin American diversity" manifest in the region's varied forms of contemporary collective action (1992, 22).

12. The religious symbolism that animated the CEBs also permeates the discourses of all "popular movements," as Doimo further notes: "Linguistic tropes such as 'pilgrimage,' the 'oppressed people,' and the 'liberation' are the great mark of the religious discourse of the 'popular movement,' many times followed by biblical images such as 'Kingdom of God,' 'Liberation of Egypt,' and 'Promised Land'" (1993, 110).

13. These ranged from councils on the status of women and councils of the black

community to neighborhood-based community councils. On the dynamics and contradictions of women's rights councils in particular, see Alvarez (1990b). See also Ardaillon (1989) and Schumaher and Elisabeth Vargas (1993).

14. This coalition brought together a number of Popular Movement Assistance NGOs, including ISER (Instituto de Estudos da Religiao), IBASE (Instituto Brasileiro de Analises Sociais e Econômicas), CEDAC (Centro de Ação Comunitária), SEP (Serviço de Educação Popular), CEDI (Centro Ecumênico de Documentação e Informação), CPO (Comissão Pastoral Operária), CPT (Comissão Pastoral da Terra), and FASE (Federação de Orgaos para a Assistência Social e Educacional). Together they launched the National Movement for Popular Participation in the Constituent Assembly. For a comprehensive account of their activities, see Whitaker et al. (1989).

15. Indeed, the constitution drafting process in Brazil was more open to genuine citizen input than were similar processes in other recent democratic transitions, including those of Spain, Portugal, and Greece.

16. The range stems from the fact that any registered voter could sign up to three amendments. As Whitaker et al. (1989) point out, if each citizen signed one amendment, then approximately 18 percent of the electorate can be said to have participated in the process. Alternatively, if each participating citizen signed three amendments, then that figure becomes 6 percent. They suggest that the most likely figure would be around 10 to 12 percent participation (Whitaker et al., 1989, 104). That this number of signatures was collected in so brief a time span is all the more remarkable when one considers that each signatory had to show proof of voter registration at the time she or he signed onto an amendment and each citizen could sign no more than three amendments.

17. Maria Victoria de Mesquita Benevides (1991) argues that these mechanisms create a framework for the exercise of "semi-direct democracy." See also Moises (1990).

18. Conservative legislators pejoratively referred to the women's movement lobbying efforts as the "*Lobby do Batom*" or Lipstick Lobby, a term that was reappropriated and resignified by the movement itself.

19. Scott Mainwaring (1991) succinctly describes the perverse consequences of Brazil's party and electoral systems for the economically and politically disenfranchised:

> Allowing representatives so much autonomy to attend to local clienteles bolsters elitist elements in the political system by dampening issues of broad-based class entitlement. Politicians run favors and obtain resources for individuals more than groups or classes. Where representation is so individualistic, party programs and class issues are undermined, to the detriment of the popular sectors. Privileged elites gain easy access to the offices and dining table of congressional representatives and state bureaucrats and thus can dispense with having strong corporate representation through parties. Popular interests, however, are not effectively represented through such informal channels (p. 40).

20. I analyze some of these conflicts—especially as manifest during national and regional movement activities in preparation for the U.N.'s Fourth World Conference on Women—in "Feminismos no Brasil e na America Latina nos Anos 90: Reflexoes sobre os Processos Regionais Preparatorios para a IV Conferencia Mundial sobre a Mulher," a paper delivered at the conference on "Fazendo Genero: Seminario sobre Estudos da Mulher," Universidade Federal de Santa Catarina, Florianopolis, Santa

Catarina, 30 November–2 December 1994. See also Lebon's (1993) incisive analysis of the NGO-ization of the feminist movement.

21. They go on to explain how the spread of NGOs in Brazil is intimately related to the erosion and inefficiency of the national state:

> The big multilateral agencies (United Nations, World Bank), in possession of voluminous funds for investment in the Third World, until the 70s, almost exclusively financed governments. The changing evaluation of the performance of official organs reoriented the flow of such resources. . . . The wastefulness, malversation of funds, the rotativity of government technical personnel, are at the origin of this shift. Thus, organizations of civil society came to represent an interesting alternative. Presenting a clearer action profile and presenting themselves as available for better defined partnership relations, the NGOs appear as an efficient mechanism for the implementation of public policies, be they progressive or not (pp. 362–363).

22. On what has been dubbed the "tyranny of structurelessness," which often typifies informal movement organizations, see Freeman (1984) and Phillips (1991).

23. My analysis, in a sense, looks at the flip side of the dimension of movements discussed by Evers (1985).

References

Alvarez, Sonia E. (1990a). *Engendering Democracy in Brazil: Women's Movements and Transition Politics*. Princeton: Princeton University Press.

Alvarez, Sonia E. (1990b). Contradictions of a Women's Space in a Male-Dominant State: The Political Role of the Commissions on the Status of Women in Postauthoritarian Brazil. In *Women, International Development, and Politics: The Bureaucratic Mire*, ed. Kathleen Staudt. Philadelphia: Temple University Press.

Alvarez, Sonia E. (1990c). Women's Participation in the Brazilian "People's Church": A Critical Appraisal. *Feminist Studies* 16(2):381–408..

Alvarez, Sonia E. (1993). "Deepening Democracy": Popular Movement Networks, Constitutional Reform, and Radical Urban Regimes in Contemporary Brazil. In *Mobilizing the Community: Local Politics in the Era of the Global City*, ed. Robert Fisher and Joseph Kling. Newbury Park, Calif.: Sage Publications.

Alvarez, Sonia E. (1994). The (Trans)formation of Feminism(s) and Gender Politics in Democratizing Brazil. In *The Women's Movement in Latin America: Participation and Democracy*, ed. Jane S. Jaquette. Revised and updated. Boulder: Westview Press.

Alvarez, Sonia E. (forthcoming a). Latin American Feminisms "Go Global": Trends and Challenges of the 1990s. In *Cultures of Politics/Politics of Cultures: Re/visioning Latin American Social Movements*, ed. Sonia E. Alvarez, Evelina Dagnino, and Arturo Escobar.

Alvarez, Sonia E. (forthcoming b). Para uma Coreografia Democrática: Movimentos Sociais, Cultura, e Cidadania. In *Archivo Edgard Leuenroth—20 Anos*, ed. Angela Araujo.

Alves, Maria Helena Moreira (1985). *State and Opposition in Military Brazil*. Austin: University of Texas Press.

Alves, Maria Helena Moreira (1988). Dilemmas of the Consolidation of Democracy from the Top: A Political Analysis. *Latin American Perspectives* 15(3):47–63.

Ardaillon, Danielle (1989). Estado e Mulher: Conselhos dos Direitos da Mulher e Delegacias de Defesa da Mulher. Unpublished manuscript.

Baierle, Sergio (1992). Um Novo Princípio Ético-Político: Prática Social e Sujeito nos Movimentos Populares Urbanos de Porto Alegre nos Anos 80. Masters' thesis, State University of Campinas.

Benevides, Maria Victoria de Mesquita (1991). *A Cidadania Ativa: Referendo, Plebiscito e Iniciativa Popular.* São Paulo: Ática.

Borda, Angela (1993). Movimento Feminista, Autonomia e Organizações Não Governamentais. *Fempress* 141.

Brant, Vinicius Caldeira (1980). Da Resistência aos Movimentos Sociais: A Emergência das Classes Populares em São Paulo. In *São Paulo: O Povo em Movimento*, ed. Paul J. Singer and Vinicius Caldeira Brant. Petrópolis: Vozes.

Caldeira, Teresa (1984). *A Política dos Outros: Os Moradores da Periferia e o Que Pensam do Poder e dos Poderosos.* São Paulo: Brasiliense.

Calderon, Fernando, Alejandro Piscitelli, and José Luis Reyna (1992). Social Movements: Actors, Theories, Expectations. In *The Making of Social Movements in Latin America: Identity, Strategy, and Democracy*, ed. Arturo Escobar and Sonia E. Alvarez. Boulder: Westview Press.

Cardoso, Ruth Corrêa Leite (1983). Movimentos Sociais Urbanos: Um Balanço Crítico. In *Sociedade e Política no Brasil Pós-64*, ed. Bernard Sorj and Maria Herminia Tavares de Almeida. São Paulo: Brasiliense.

Cardoso, Ruth Corrêa Leite (1988). Isso É Político? Dilemas da Participação entre o Moderno e o Pós-Moderno. *Novos Estudos do CEBRAP* (20):74–80.

Cardoso, Ruth Corrêa Leite (1994). A Trajetória dos Movimentos Sociais. In *Anos 90: Política e Sociedade no Brasil*, ed. Evelina Dagnino. São Paulo: Brasiliense.

Cardoso, Ruth Corrêa Leite and Julio Assis Simões (1990). Políticas Sociais: A Relação entre as Agências Públicas e seus Usuários. Mimeograph.

Coelho, Simone de Castro (1991). Os Movimentos Sociais e a Institucionalização da Participação Política—Alguns Conceitos Básicos. Mimeograph.

Coelho, Simone C. T. (1992). O Estado e os Movimentos Pró-Moradia: A Construção de uma Relação Democrática. Masters' thesis, University of São Paulo.

Cohen, Jean L. and Andrew Arato (1992). *Civil Society and Political Theory.* Cambridge, Mass.: MIT Press.

Dagnino, Evelina (1994). Os Movimentos Sociais e a Emergência de uma nova Noção da Cidadania. In *Anos 90: Política e Sociedade no Brasil*, ed. Evelina Dagnino. São Paulo: Brasiliense.

Diamond, Larry (1994). Rethinking Civil Society: Toward Democratic Consolidation. *Journal of Democracy* 5(3):4–17.

Diamond, Larry and Juan J. Linz (1989). Introduction: Politics, Society, and Democracy in Latin America. In *Democracy in Developing Countries: Latin America*, ed. Larry Diamond, Juan J. Linz, and Seymour Martin Lipset. Boulder: Lynne Rienner.

Doimo, Ana Maria (1993). Movimento Popular no Brasil Pós-70: Formação de um Campo Ético-Político. Ph.D. dissertation, University of São Paulo.

Evers, Tilman (1985). Identity: The Hidden Side of New Social Movements. In *New Social Movements in Latin America*, ed. David Slater. Amsterdam: CEDLA.

Fernandes, Rubem César (1994). *Privado Porém Público: O Terceiro Setor na América Latina*. Rio de Janeiro: Relume-Dumara.

Ferreira dos Santos, Carlos Nelson (1981). *Movimentos Urbanos no Rio de Janeiro*. Rio de Janeiro: Zahar.

Fraser, Nancy (1993). Rethinking the Public Sphere: A Contribution to the Critique of Actually Existing Democracy. In *The Phantom Public Sphere*, ed. Bruce Robbins. Minneapolis: University of Minnesota Press.

Freeman, Joseph (1984). *The Tyranny of Structurelessness*. First published, 1970. London: Dark Star/Rebel Press.

Gadotti, M. and O. Pereira (1989). *Para Que PT? Origem, Projeto e Consolidação do Partido dos Trabalhadores*. São Paulo: Cortez.

Gay, Robert (1990). Popular Incorporation and Prospects for Democracy: Some Implications of the Brazilian Case. *Theory and Society* 19:447–463.

Gohn, Maria da Glória Marcondes (1982). *Reivindicações Populares Urbanas: Um Estudo de Caso sobre as Associações de Moradores em São Paulo*. São Paulo: Cortez.

Gohn, Maria da Glória Marcondes (1985). *A Força da Periferia: A Luta das Mulheres por Creches em São Paulo*. Petrópolis: Vozes.

Gohn, Maria da Glória Marcondes (1991). *Movimentos Sociais e Luta pela Moradia*. São Paulo: Edições Loyola.

Hagopian, Frances (1990). "Democracy by Undemocratic Means"? Elites, Political Pacts, and Regime Transformation in Brazil. *Comparative Political Studies* 23(2):147–170.

Huntington, Samuel P. (1991). *The Third Wave: Democratization in the Late Twentieth Century*. Norman: University of Oklahoma Press.

Jacobi, Pedro (1989). *Movimentos Sociais e Políticas Públicas*. São Paulo: Cortez.

Keck, Margaret (1992). *The Workers' Party and Democratization in Brazil*. New Haven: Yale University Press.

Landim (Assumpção), Leilah (1993). A Invenção das ONGs: Do Serviço Invisível a Profissão sem Nome. Ph.D. dissertation, Federal University of Rio de Janeiro.

Lebon, Natalie (1993). The Brazilian Feminist Movement in the Post-Constitutional Era: Assessing the Impact of the Rise of Feminist Non-Governmental Organizations. *Florida Journal of Anthropology* 18:17–26.

Linz, Juan J. (1990). The Perils of Presidentialism. *Journal of Democracy* 1(1):51–70.

MacDonald, Laura (1992). Turning to the NGOs: Competing Conceptions of Civil Society in Latin America. Paper presented at the 1992 Meeting of the Latin American Studies Association, Los Angeles, California, 24–27 September 1992.

Mainwaring, Scott (1986). *The Catholic Church and Politics in Brazil, 1916–1985*. Stanford: Stanford University Press.

Mainwaring, Scott (1987). Urban Popular Movements, Identity and Democratization in Brazil. *Comparative Political Studies* 20(2):131–159.

Mainwaring, Scott (1988). Political Parties and Democratization in Brazil and the Southern Cone. *Comparative Politics* 21(1):91–120.

Mainwaring, Scott (1990). Presidentialism in Latin America. *Latin American Research Review* 25(1):157–179.

Mainwaring, Scott (1991). Politicians, Parties, and Electoral Systems: Brazil in Comparative Perspective. *Comparative Politics* 24(1):21–43.

Mainwaring, Scott (1992). Transitions to Democracy and Democratic Consolidation. In *Issues in Democratic Consolidation: The New South American Democracies in Com-*

parative Perspective, ed. Scott Mainwaring, Guillermo O'Donnell, and J. Samuel Valenzuela. Notre Dame, Ind.: University of Notre Dame.

Mainwaring, Scott, Guillermo O'Donnell, and J. Samuel Valenzuela, Eds. (1992). *Issues in Democratic Consolidation: The New South American Democracies in Comparative Perspective.* Notre Dame, Ind.: University of Notre Dame Press.

Martes, Ana Cristina Braga (1990). A Institucionalização dos Movimentos de Reivindicação Urbana—As Secretarias de Saúde e a Participação Popular (1979–1989). Masters' thesis, University of São Paulo.

Martins, Luciano (1989). Ação Política e Governabilidade na Transição Brasileira. In *Dilemas da Consolidação Democrática*, ed. José Alvaro Moises and J. A. Guilhon Alburquerque. São Paulo: Paz e Terra.

Melucci, Alberto (1988). Social Movements and the Democratization of Daily Life. In *Civil Society and the State: New European Perspectives*, ed. John Keane. London: Verso.

Meneguello, Rachel (1989). *PT: A Formação de um Partido, 1979–1982.* São Paulo: Paz e Terra.

Moises, José Alvaro (1982). Contradicões Urbanas, Estado e Movimentos Sociais. In *Cidade, Povo e Poder*, ed. José Alvaro Moises et al. São Paulo: Paz e Terra; CEDEC.

Moises, José Alvaro (1990). *Cidadania e Participação: Ensaio sobre o Plebiscito, o Referendo e a Iniciativa Popular na Nova Constituição.* São Paulo: CEDEC; Marco Zero.

Moraes Nehring, Maria Lygia Quartim de (1981). Família e Feminismo: Reflexões sobre Papéis Femininos na Imprensa de Mulheres. Ph.D. dissertation, University of São Paulo.

O'Donnell, Guillermo and Philippe C. Schmitter (1986). *Transitions from Authoritarian Rule: Tentative Conclusions about Uncertain Democracies.* Baltimore: The Johns Hopkins University Press.

Paz, Rosangela Dias, Marcia Aparecida Accorsi Pereira, and Flávio Jorge Rodrigues da Silva (1990). São Paulo: Privilegiar "a Reprodução da Vida." *Proposta*.

Pereira da Silva, Catia Aida (1992). Os Conselhos Tutelares da Criança e o Adolescente de São Paulo e os Segmentos Pró-Cidadania: Conflitos, Negociações e Impasses na Construção de Espaços Públicos. Masters' thesis, University of São Paulo.

Phillips, Ann (1991). *Engendering Democracy.* University Park: Pennsylvania State University Press.

Sader, Eder and Ken Silverstein (1991). *Without Fear of Being Happy: Lula, the Workers' Party, and Brazil.* London: Verso.

Saffioti, Heleieth Iara Bongiovani (1987). Feminismos e seus Frutos no Brasil. In *Movimentos Sociais na Transição Democrática*, ed. Emir Sader. São Paulo: Cortez.

Sarti, Cynthia (1989). The Panorama of Feminism in Brazil. *New Left Review* 173:75–90.

Schumaher, Maria Aparecida and Elisabeth Vargas (1993). Lugar no Governo: Alibi ou Conquista? *Revista Estudos Feministas* 1(2):349–364.

Singer, Paul (1980). Movimentos de Bairro. In *São Paulo: O Povo em Movimento*, ed. Paul Singer and Vinicius Valdeira Brant. Petrópolis: Vozes; São Paulo: CEBRAP.

Skidmore, Thomas E. (1988). *The Politics of Military Rule in Brazil, 1964–1985.* New York: Oxford University Press.

Smith, William (1987). The Political Transition in Brazil: From Authoritarian Liberalization to Elite Conciliation to Democratization. In *Comparing New Democracies:*

Transition and Consolidation in Mediterranean Europe and the Southern Cone, ed. Enrique Balorya. Boulder: Westview Press.

Soares, Vera (1994). Movimento Feminista: Paradigms e Desafios. *Revista Estudos Feministas* 2(2):11–24.

Stepan, Alfred (1988). *Rethinking Military Politics: Brazil and the Southern Cone*. Princeton, N.J.: Princeton University Press.

Telles, Maria Amelia de Almeida (1993). *Breve História do Feminismo no Brasil*. São Paulo: Brasiliense.

Telles, Vera da Silva (1994). Sociedade Civil e a Construção de Espaços Públicos. In *Anos 90: Política e Sociedade no Brasil*, ed. Evelina Dagnino. São Paulo: Brasiliense.

Valenzuela, J. Samuel (1992). Democratic Consolidation in Post-Transitional Settings: Notion, Process, and Facilitating Conditions. In *Issues in Democratic Consolidation: The New South American Democracies in Comparative Perspective*, ed. Scott Mainwaring, Guillermo O'Donnell, and J. Samuel Valenzuela. Notre Dame, Ind.: University of Notre Dame Press.

Verucci, Florence (1991). Women and the New Brazilian Constitution. *Feminist Studies* 17(3):551–568.

Whitaker, Francisco, João Gilberto Lucas Coelho, Carlos Michiles, Enmanuel Gonçalves Viera Felho, Maria da Gloria Moura de Vega, Regina de Paula Santos Prado (1989). *Cidadão Constituinte: A Saga des Emendas Populares*. São Paulo: Paz e Terra.

Faye Ginsburg

"From Little Things, Big Things Grow"

Indigenous Media and Cultural Activism

... [I]ndigenous peoples throughout the world are united by their common situation as disenfranchised people, whose existence depends on a moral claim but who challenge the First World to examine its institutions, structures, and values, which have left indigenous peoples powerless and dependent.

(Wright, 1988, 367)

Alternative television undercuts hegemonic control by introducing meanings of interpretations that lie outside the "preferred range." Formerly "unacceptable" interpretations, once public, begin to circulate and may actually become legitimate points of view. . . . Finally, because the production of alternative media frequently involves collective action and entails the expression of group interests, it may also lead to collaborative and organized democratic participation.

(Anderson and Goldson, 1991, 61)

Now, film and television, together with their cultural counterparts in painting, ritual performance, radio, music and theatre, occupy a key place in indigenous self-affirmation and political development. Aborigines and their representatives are not only negotiating the form of their representation but are increasingly shaping the structures and practices through which Aboriginal representation is secured . . . .

(O'Regan and Batty, 1993, 170)

Introduction

These quotes demarcate a discursive space—shaped by indigenous social movements and those creating alternative media forms—for one of the more unexpected phenomena of the late twentieth century: the development of film, video, and television production by indigenous people, who, over the last twenty years, have been using these media as new vehicles for internal and external communication, cultural and language maintenance, self-determination, and resistance to outside cultural domination. Since the 1970s, a small but influential cohort of indigenous cultural activists in many different locales around the world have recognized that new media technologies offer a form that not only "fits" comfortably with oral and performative traditions (Molnar, 1995, 171); they also recognized that "small media" provide a field of cultural production that can enhance struggles for indigenous rights. These range from preservation and revival of languages, ceremonies, and histories to interventions in representations of indigenous people as they are told and made by media institutions of the encompassing state societies and to the invention of cultural possibilities that suggest alternatives to a reified traditional past, a marginalized present, or an assimilated future. I map indigenous media onto this landscape of activism and media because it most closely resembles not only what I have seen, but it also reflects the perspectives of indigenous directors who see their media efforts on a continuum with movements for cultural and political autonomy by and for First Nations people. The perspectives of Aboriginal activists are very much tied to the struggle for land and religious rights that characterizes the concerns of First Nations or indigenous social movements in particular. While it is not within the scope of this essay, other marginalized peoples such as migrants or exiles, the poor, or sexual minorities base their advocacy on other rights-based discourses that build their claims on categories of human dignity and cultural rights.[1] All of these groups, over the last decade or so, have become interested in the social and political possibilities of alternative media practices as a means of intervention into the status quo on a number of fronts, initially articulated by film and video activists.

In this essay, I spell out some of the circumstances that have created the conditions for the development of indigenous media, and the relationship of these kind of media practices (what some scholars have called "small media"; see Sreberny-Mohammadi and Mohammadi, [1994, xx]) to certain contemporary social action and movements. I argue that these latest products of indigenous expressive culture are part of self-conscious efforts to sustain and transform culture in aboriginal communities, an activity that is linked to indigenous efforts for rights to self-representation, governance, and cultural autonomy after centuries of colonial assimilationist policies by surrounding states.

These efforts are not so much against the state, but express a desire to be recognized and granted entitlements and reparations within the terms of the dominant legal code.

Analytically, I use the term cultural activists in my discussion of indigenous media makers in a way that underscores their sense of both political and cultural agency in creating this work. The ethnographic material I use encompasses work and media makers from a number of indigenous groups; however, my main focus will be on that which I know best from primary research, the work of Aboriginal Australian media makers.

The development of indigenous media is also part of a global process of decentralization, democratization, and penetration of new media technologies, a process that has had multiple and sometimes contradictory effects on local communities (Raboy and Bruck, 1989). In the case of indigenous media makers, far from being "polluted" by contact with other cultural forms, as some have argued (Faris, 1992), they have taken on Western media technologies both as critics of the culturally destructive effects of mass media and as producers of their own work. Tony Bennett and Valda Blundell underscore this point:

> The "innovative traditionalism" of First peoples has, of course, always faced two ways. If . . . Western cultural resources have been drawn on to lend new forms of social mobility and adaptability to traditional indigenous forms, the use of traditional cultural resources to produce distinctive transformations of Western cultural forms and traditions has been equally important. The significance of such exchanges is clearly evident in the history of First People's relations to modern media (1995, 7).

Extending that argument, I suggest that indigenous media work is significant not simply as a transformation of Western technologies, but also as a new form of collective self-production that is being used self-consciously by indigenous producers to mediate historical and social ruptures within their own cultures and to assert the presence and concerns of First Nations peoples in the broader societies that encompass them.

Although some early and important work in film and TV production by Native North Americans occurred in the 1970s (Weatherford, 1990), indigenous media did not achieve the status of a small but dynamic "growth industry" until the mid-1990s. Contemporary producers include Aboriginal Australians; Maori; various Amazonian Indian groups, most notably the Kayapo (T. Turner, 1991); Inuit (Roth and Valaskakis, 1989); and a wide range of Native Americans from both the North and the South (Weatherford and Seubert, 1988). These efforts emerged in tandem with the development of multiculturalist identity politics—especially in Australia, Canada, and the United States—that, over the last decade, created new understandings of the relationship between cultural and political rights. Terence Turner makes a compelling argument for rethinking our understanding of culture in a way that clarifies how practices like indigenous media are linked to "the revolutionary principle that the protection and fostering of the human capacity for culture is a general human right and, as such, a legitimate goal of politically organized society" (1993, 428).

It is also important to recall how issues of cultural identity and their associated claims have distinct meanings for different kinds of social formations. Whereas diasporic or religious minorities may be engaged in struggles around language, religion, and immigration, land rights take on vital significance in the construction of indigenous identity. For example, Bennett and Blundell point out how Aboriginal claims to the land reflect a "territorial groundedness" that refuses "engulfment in a singular national imaginary . . . " (1995, 2).

To insist, in this case, on the relationship between activities for self-determination and cultural autonomy—whether these are very local efforts to sustain native languages or broader-scale movements for land rights—ensures that analytic attention to a phenomenon like indigenous media is not confined to an ethnocentric domain of study that would focus on their media productions as isolated texts. Gail Valaskakis has argued cogently that for First Peoples "resistance is cultural persistence . . . continually negotiated in the discourse and practice of everyday life" (1993, 238). This point is crucial to understanding why, for indigenous directors, the very creation of media work that both reflects and revisions their lives and histories is a kind of self-conscious and direct social action that establishes and reinforces the visible cultural presence of indigenous lives in a form that can circulate in and among many communities. International conferences, festivals, coproductions and consultations are an important dimension of social action on the part of First Nations peoples contributing to the emergence of a global network of cooperation that has been growing steadily since the 1970s.[2] The range of contexts—from the local to the transnational—is the "mediascape" (Appadurai, 1990, 7)[3] that shapes and is shaped by indigenous media makers, as interdependent arenas of social action. Thus, my use of the term indigenous (like First Nations or Fourth World), while always tied to a specific local perspective, is nonetheless explicitly intended to index their common political conditions as people disenfranchised by the colonial practices of European settler states. Despite the diverse cultural practices of indigenous people around the globe, their shared historical circumstances have become the basis of broader social and political movements for Aboriginal cultural autonomy and self-determination through which they have been constituting themselves in relation to local, national, and international politics.

Cultural Activism

My work is part of a small but growing area of interdisciplinary research, scholarship, and cultural criticism interested in understanding, empirically, the relationship between new media practices and social action. This position is articulated clearly in a recent groundbreaking book, *Small Media, Big Revolution: Communication, Culture, and the Iranian Revolution*. Authors Annabelle Sreberny-Mohammadi and Ali Mohammadi write:

> In the contemporary world, media are part of political problems and part of the solutions, essential elements of repressive political structures as well as vehicles for their overthrow. Media can be used by states to establish their definitions of the political, their versions of history; they are part of the ideological state apparatus, the forces of repression. At the same time, media can be the tools of popular mobilization, they can maintain alternative histories and promote oppositional culture—in short, they constitute the resources and forms of expression of popular movements. Especially within repressive regimes, when there appears to be no space for "political" activity, media foster the politicization of the "cultural" (1994, xix).

> ... Looking at the dynamics of media use can help us understand breakdowns in regime policy and ideology but also the mobilization of alternate identities and resources to fight against the state ... (1994, 3).

Following a similar strategy of analysis, but tailored to the circumstances of indigenous people living under regimes of "welfare colonialism" (Beckett, 1988), research on the use of new media forms by indigenous people demonstrates the importance of the forms to contemporary processes of social transformation as their production is linked, historically and intentionally, to struggles for Aboriginal autonomy and self-determination. As in my prior research on abortion activists (1989), I have found that focusing on people who engage themselves with new possibilities for their own collective self-production allows us to ask more general questions about the political possibilities inherent in self-conscious shifts in cultural practice. In a different context (Ginsburg and Rapp, 1995), I have discussed these processes as "transformative action," a term that directs attention to understanding human agency in a grounded way, without a priori categorizing cultural practices as either dominant/hegemonic or alternative/resistant. Rather, this concept helps us see the emergence of new social and cultural possibilities on a continuum, from the activities of daily life out of which consciousness and intentionality are constructed, to more dramatic forms of expressive culture (such as media or social protests). To understand processes such as transformation, of course, requires attention to larger power structures, constraints, and questions of historical change in the broader conventional sense, and as they are experienced, reconsidered, and embodied in daily life by cultural activists.

Many indigenous producers share this understanding. They see the capabilities of visual media to transcend boundaries of time, space, and even language can be used in part to transform historically produced social ruptures by renarrating, from their perspective, the relationships between indigenous histories and cultures and the encompassing societies in which they live. Their work reflects an insight articulated by Stuart Hall, who writes that "identities are the names we give to the different ways we are positioned by, and position ourselves within, the narratives of the past" (1992, 225). This perspective is articulated in the following statement by Alberto Muenala, a Quichua filmmaker form Otavalo, Ecuador, who also directed the first indigenously organized "Festival Latinamericano de Ciné de Pueblos Indígenas" in 1994.

> Cinema about indigenous peoples must chart a new route, one that shatters the established language of Indians as objects. The new cinema treats us as subjects, as protagonists and producers of our own histories. We suffer a colonization that has not allowed the development of a cinematographic language. Only through a rupture with colonizing messages, assuming our own identity, will we transform and develop new imagery (Muenala, 1994).[4]

As an analyst, my interest is to see how this kind of understanding plays out in the production, circulation, and reception of indigenously produced video, film, and television, and how these processes operate as assertions of the historical and contemporary cultural subjectivities of Aboriginal people. To underscore that point, I use the term cultural activism as an analytic frame for this phenomenon. The term indexes how indigenous producers self-consciously use these hybrid cultural forms as means of social action that are powerfully linked to the kinds of activities more traditionally identified as "political" in the social movement literature.

The language of cultural activism points, in turn, to a recognition of the necessity of recognizing "the field of cultural production" (Bourdieu, 1993) as a potential locus not only of social reproduction but of social transformation. My concern with demonstrating the links between "culture" and "social action" draws on Turner's argument regarding current shifts in the meaning and praxis of culture as a legitimate source of political rights, and his assertion that today " . . . [c]ulture, as such, becomes a source of values that can be converted into political assets, both internally as bases of group solidarity and mobilization, and externally as claims on the support of other social groups, governments and public opinion all over the globe" (1993, 424).

This understanding of culture corresponds to that of a generation of "cultural activists" most active in indigenous media work worldwide, people now mostly in their late thirties and early forties. I focus on cultural activists, rather than the media productions, as a starting point for a number of reasons. Articulating the cultural dimension of activism involves an inquiry into how actors situate their participation as a meaningful part of collective struggle. This actor-oriented approach is a distinct contribution ethnographic work can make to the literature on social movements, which tends to look at social institutions and collectivities with little fine-grained attention as to how individuals engage in particular kinds of cultural production as a form of social action.

Second, a focus on cultural activists allows one to see media as a dynamic aspect of social relations, a vehicle through which mediations take place (see also Riggins, 1992; Downmunt, 1993). This is an important alternative to the paradigms in media studies that, until recently, have tended to focus on the film/video text, media institutions, or the technology itself, rather than the social relations of production, circulation, and consumption of work, a perspective that has recently gained strength. Sreberny-Mohammadi and Mohammadi discuss work on "small media" in relation to recent discussions around Habermas's notion of "the public sphere." Small media, they argue, can help create a political "public sphere" by weaving a "web of political solidarity" and serving as "the carriers of oppositional discourse" (1994, xx).[5]

Third, this focus on cultural activists enables one to escape typological debates in recent discussions of social movements that are polarized between resource mobilization theory (Morris, 1992) and notions of symbolic capital associated with identity politics and new social movements (Melucci, 1985). In these debates, indigenous movements for cultural and political autonomy are rarely discussed, perhaps because they do not fall easily into these sociological types: by contrast, indigenous activists understand their efforts to gain control over the images of Aboriginal people as directly connected to struggles over rights *and* resources, ranging from land claims to satellite access. For example, the image of Australia as *terra nullius* was particularly powerful in justifying the colonial appropriation of lands from Aboriginal people from the seventeenth century until the present, a hegemonic legacy that was only challenged successfully in the 1993 Mabo decision (Rowse, 1992). In the end, because indigenous movements for cultural and political autonomy are rarely discussed in the literature on social movements, the academic discourse reproduces the Eurocentrism that constructs these people as marginal to the states in which they live.

Finally, a focus on cultural activists can help illuminate how particular social actors become involved in and understand the creation and circulation of media that are intended to stand for collective bodies. Although the actual number of people directly engaged in indigenous media is small, the impact of this work has been widespread in and among different communities, particularly in liberal welfare states such as Australia, Canada, and New Zealand, where there has been regular government support for everything from monolingual local media associations, to programming on national television, to subsidizing feature film work.

In indigenous media work, there is a density of involvement by a cohort of people born in the 1950s and 1960s, who see their work as part of their community's struggle for visibility on their own terms. Of those coming from more traditional backgrounds, most are well versed in ritual and sacred knowledge, fluent in native languages, and leaders in their communities or tied to leadership through kin ties. At the same time, many activists have had access to education in the dominant culture and are comfortable dealing with Western technologies, bureaucracies, and venues for showing media work, all of which have been key elements in successful indigenous media projects. Many of these people came to consciousness in the movements for indigenous rights that were developing in different sites during the 1960s and 1970s. As a result of those activities, and policy responses to them, many also had access to scholarships and training programs that gave them skills and knowledge, enabling them to enter into new areas of cultural work. Examples span the planet, from the Inuit Broadcasting Corporation in Canada's Arctic that provided the training ground for the award-winning Inuit video maker Zach Kunuk, to the establishment of the Aboriginal Programs Unit at the ABC, Australia's national broadcaster. This generation, then, is also one that is, perhaps uniquely, bicultural, and thus able to build bridges between domains because of their cultural abilities in different settings.[6] As Eric Michaels described Francis Jupurrurla Kelly, a key player in the creation of the Warlpiri Media Association established at Yuendumu in central Australia in the 1980s: "Jupurrurla is indisputably a sophisticated cultural broker who employs videotape and electronic technology to express and resolve political, theological and aesthetic contradictions that arise in uniquely contemporary circumstances" (1987, 26).

From their own life experiences, these cultural activists recognize that social change cannot simply be legislated, but requires a long struggle against racism that is pervasive in the dominant culture in multiple arenas. Activists of all ages have recognized the impact of negative stereotypes and the invisibility of Aboriginal people, cultures and languages in the mass media; many younger people began to resist directly through the creation of counter-images that circulate both in home communities and in the surrounding dominant culture. Hopi video maker Victor Masayesva, Jr., also the head of the Native American

Producers' Alliance, articulates this clearly in a recent essay on Native American media.

> The recent crop of commercial films and television programs on Indians purportedly from a Native American perspective is a half-lie. . . . How could such media goodwill produce such ill will from native communities? An answer starts with the recognition that it's not so far removed from the U.S. government offering to manage our lands and natural resources. . . .
>
> If film is about imagined time and space, it is borne from imagination of people each of whom have constructed those times and spaces differently. . . . Certainly I feel the power of sacred spaces of ancient kivas at the ruins of Chaco Canyon, Mesa Verde, Betattakin, and certainly our ancestral ruin Kawestima. Then why are we continually left out of the recreation of these spaces and times on film?
>
> But if we indigenous filmmakers were to showcase our true differences, we would infuse film with the same reverence we have for our oral and performing traditions. When reflecting on our ceremonies and rituals, we understand how crucial that relationship is. . . .
>
> Native American filmmakers have run out of the luxury of access to the creative old timers from whom language and song was the ultimate human creation, particularly when woven into ritual, ceremony, performance or worship. It is critical that we recognize and accept this situation and begin the changes that will stimulate profound and exciting films, originating from an indigenous aesthetic (1994, 21).

In looking at activists, it is important to recognize that the distribution of new media technologies can be socially fraught, as they offer high-status, relatively expensive, and desirable resources.[7] A preliminary overview in a variety of small-scale traditional communities—from central Australia to the northern Arctic to Amazonia—suggests that they are a complex product of preexisting social structures (e.g., relatively egalitarian vs. more hierarchical), and the ways in which media is introduced by outsiders who may serve as long or short term advisers/advocates.[8] Speaking generally, the sociological profile of indigenous media producers suggests a self-selected group of talented individuals who have had access to training and who also exercise leadership because of kinship and/or demonstrated ability. Yet they are rarely operating as individuals but as members of communities, raising important and provocative questions about the social organization of media use. On the local level in more remote communities, the politics of access to cameras and editing varies widely. They range from the apparent control of equipment and tapes by male leaders in Kayapo communities (T. Turner, 1991) to the community-based productions in Ernabella in South Australia, in which access is open to all age groups and across genders, although most decisions about producing work are carried out by a representative council of elders headed by a respected couple (N. Turner, 1990).

In urban settings where producers are likely to be accountable to large "white" television bureaucracies, questions of accountability are worked out quite differently than in remote areas where the primary audience is from the producer's own community. Additionally, collaborations with whites on productions potentially raises questions about what constitutes a truly indigenous work, and how authorship is organized in such cases. At the national level in Australia, a great effort has been made to open training programs to as many people as possible, although there has been disgruntlement that traditional remote settlements have received priority in media funding over urban populations. More broadly, there is dissatisfaction that funding is piecemeal and oriented toward training rather than development of a vital alternative media sector that recognizes its crucial role in the articulation of contemporary Aboriginal identity (Molnar, 1995). In these struggles over funding and licensing, one can see how the production of indigenous media is linked to the self-conscious aspirations for self-determination of contemporary Aboriginal producers—whether remote/traditional or urban/bicultural.

Self-Representation and Aboriginal Activism

In 1988, I took my first research trip to Australia to collect tapes and see what was happening "on the ground" and over the airwaves. Since then I have been following the work being produced by and with Aboriginal Australians who, over the last decade, have been using film and televisual media to create images of themselves that are seen in various contexts by Aboriginal and European Australians as well as overseas audiences.[9] Like indigenous people in other parts of the world, Aboriginal Australians recognize the power of visual media not only for their own communities, but also for changing the consciousness of the nations that encompass them. They insist that indigenous perspectives be increasingly heard and seen in an Australian polity that is finally beginning to take account of the rights of its Aboriginal citizens, not the least of which is the right to represent themselves. In this case, the correspondence between the political and the figural meanings of self-representation are totally appropriate. Indigenous media productions acknowledge the traumas of contact history and the contradictions of life in the present and, most importantly, take these stories as a means to envision a cultural future for indigenous people both locally and as part of larger social formations. Thus, these productions are both about and part of the construction of contemporary indigenous identities, another dimension of efforts to establish their voices and visions on their own local terms, as part of Australia's past and present, and in relation to a transnational network of indigenous people. As Helen Molnar has pointed out in her study of Aboriginal media:

> A significant feature of the indigenous media industry has been the forma- tion of indigenous media associations throughout Australia. The link between these associations and the community is very important, and is often misun- derstood by government departments. Many of the media associations have grown out of existing indigenous community organizations, because these organizations feel that the electronic media can be used to provide informa- tion on a range of social, cultural, economic and political issues in a form and language that is relevant to the needs of Aborigines (1995, 170).

The evident interest in media is apparent in the extraordinary development of this work since 1980, when only a few radio shows existed. Now, indigenous producers are in almost every sector of the media. A recent survey of Aborigi- nal involvement in media (not including the extraordinary growth in radio) counted 150 media associations, 80 small-scale television stations in remote communities (the Broadcasting for Remote Aboriginal Communities Scheme), 2 areal remote commercial television services, an Aboriginal Unit at the state- sponsored ABC and SBS television stations, and a representative body, The National Indigenous Media Association of Australia (NIMAA) representing the hundreds of Aboriginal broadcasters working in radio, video, and television (Molnar, 1995, 170).

The range of this work reflects the diverse experiences of contemporary Aboriginal people. Traditional people living in relatively unsettled areas of Aus- tralia and whose contact history may be as brief as a few decades, have been experimenting with video production strategies to suit very specific cultural concerns (Michaels, 1986). By contrast, urban-based producers may be ori- ented toward opportunities in national television to create documentaries and other kinds of programming on Aboriginal history and culture. Others, like Aboriginal filmmaker photographer Tracey Moffat, may be involved in mak- ing independent experimental and feature films, working comfortably within the structures of an international independent film world, albeit addressing problematic issues of Aboriginality. The scope of this film and televisual me- dia corresponds not only to differences in the experiences of urban, rural, and remote-living Aboriginal Australians, but also to diverse cultural, historical, and social backgrounds within these categories.[10]

The context for Australian Aboriginal involvement in visual media produc- tion cannot be understood apart from the legacy of social movements for Aboriginal rights. Strikes, freedom rides, and other forms of civil disobedience in the 1960s catalyzed constitutional changes that granted Aboriginal Australian voting rights in 1962 and Australian citizenship in 1967 and set the stage for the recognition of Aboriginal claims for land rights and cultural autonomy in the 1970s. However, the official beginning of the "Aboriginal civil rights movement" is popularly recognized as 26 January 1972, "Australia Day," which commemorates the "founding" of Australia. On that date in 1972, four young Aboriginal men erected a small tent on the lawns of the Parliament House in Canberra and declared themselves a sovereign nation. Their action succinctly dramatized the issue of Aboriginal land rights in the Australian imagination, which helped mobilize a period of confrontational activism of the Aboriginal Black Power movements in the 1970s. In response, the Labour government under Whitlam initiated a policy of Aboriginal self-determination and stopped all applications for nonindigenous mining and exploration on Commonwealth Aboriginal reserves.

As part of their demands, the activists insisted on Aboriginal control over media representation of their lives and communities, which quickly escalated into explicit interest in gaining access to production. As anthropologist and Aboriginal activist Marcia Langton recalled this period:

> ... During the 1970s and 1980s, the Aboriginal response to racist representation, especially in the large urban centres, was to demand control of representation. These demands for control and for funding of community-controlled media, have been expressed at every major film and media conference during the last twenty years. But demands and strategies for controlling representations do not by themselves work to produce a better representation of Aboriginal people.
>
> ... Rather than demanding an impossibility, it would be more useful to identify those points where it is possible to control the *means* of production and to make our own self-representations (1993, 9–10).

In 1979, Aboriginal country-and-western singer Essie Coffey, along with white filmmakers Martha Ansara and Alec Morgan, made the landmark documentary "My Survival as an Aboriginal." As the first film made with an Aboriginal director, this was a dramatic break with the ethnographic genre that focused on ceremonial and traditional knowledge with little or no reference to the conditions of welfare colonialism. By contrast, "My Survival" offered a first-person examination of the difficult conditions of "fringe dwelling" rural Aboriginal communities, considering not only their "dispossession and alienation from the inside out but also ... the strength of both the filmmaker and her culture

as they survive despite having such odds stacked against them doing so"
(Leigh, 1992, 1).

The question of Aboriginal media representation heated up quickly in the
1980s with plans for the launching of Australia's first communications satellite
over central Australia, which generated an acrimonious public debate about
the impact of "dumping" mainstream television signals into the lives of Aboriginal people living there. As one Aboriginal elder from the community of
Ernabella summarized the situation, unimpeded satellite transmission "will be
like having hundreds of whitefellas visit without permits every day" (Anmanari
Nyaningu, quoted in N. Turner, 1990, 44).

In part to preempt the impact of the satellite, two remote Aboriginal communities in that area developed their own video production and low-cost television stations (not yet granted licenses), the Warlpiri Media Association
(WMA) at Yuendumu and Ernabella Video and Television (EVTV) at the settlement of Ernabella. In the words of Frances Jupurrurla Kelly, a Warlpiri man
from Yuendumu who was one of the key players in setting up WMA:

> Warlpiri Media's history started from their own people . . . because they're
> worried about their culture, mainly kids, concerned about their future. Ideas
> didn't come from the Europeans, it came from ourselves in the community . . .
> because the satellite went up and that time if been too light for our culture
> we wanted to say something against the satellite or against television in our
> territories. . . . The community decided to chuck in for it. Everybody put
> money toward it themselves. They made ten grand—everybody chucked in—
> the buildings were from their own money. The store allocated three grand
> as a donation. We finally got buildings up and gear (quoted in Cohen, 1993,
> 1).

Around the same time, an existing regional Aboriginal radio and media association, the Central Australian Aboriginal Media Association (CAAMA) centered in Alice Springs, made a bid for the license for the satellite downlink, as
a symbolic assertion of the presence of Aboriginal people in central Australia.
After a long struggle (and much to their surprise), CAAMA won the license
and established Imparja, the first Aboriginally owned commercial television station in Australia. The year Imparja was established, 1988, was also crucial as
Australia's Bicentenary; it was marked by considerable protest by Aboriginal
activists and their supporters who renamed the event "Invasion Day," successfully drawing attention not only to an oppositional reading of the founding of
the nation, but also to the ongoing need in the present for redress of the brutal legacy of colonization. They demanded (and received) considerable government support for counter-events, with a particular focus on representation

as an issue (much like what happened in North America around the Columbus Quincentenary). For example, Aboriginal trainees at the national television station, the Australian Broadcast Corporation (ABC), protested the lack of attention to Aboriginal concerns in national television programming, an effort that resulted in the formation of the Aboriginal Programs Unit. The first work produced and from that unit (with a mix of Aboriginal and Euro-Australian staff) was a biting dramatic parody of 200 years of institutionalized racism. In Australia, "Babakieuria" was broadcast during 1988 as part of the counterdiscourse to the bicentenary celebrations.

Analytically, institutional responses to social protest such as the creation of the Aboriginal Programs Unit can be understood as part of the processes through which nation states like Australia constitute and reframe their "imagined communities" (Anderson, 1983) via the circulation of televisual and cinematic images of the people and places they govern. Through struggles around issues of representation one can see the processes whereby different versions of the "national" come to predominate. As other scholars have noted: "Anderson focuses on the 'birth' of nations, but within the nationally bounded political structure, different versions of the 'social imaginary' (Castoriadis, 1987) may constantly compete to define the collectivity" (Sreberny-Mohammadi and Mohammadi, 1994, 10).

Although the Australian zeitgeist since the 1970s has increasingly favored multicultural expression as an acceptable version of the Australian polity (Hamilton, 1990), it was only in the late 1980s, under increasing pressure from Aboriginal activists and media associations, that the government has given more support to Aboriginal media production, explicitly bringing them into the mediascape of the Australian "national imaginary." For example, in 1978, the government established a separate Special Broadcast Service (SBS) initially to serve non-English-speaking immigrant minorities. In 1988, the SBS expanded its policy to include the presentation of Aboriginal radio and television programs and to take as part of its mandate the correction of popular misconceptions about Aboriginal history and culture.[11]

All of these events were part of a slow process of change in Aboriginal policy over the 1980s, from "welfare colonialism" to self-determination, in response to the pressures placed on the government by Aboriginal activists.[12] As media scholar Tom O'Regan and activist Philip Batty explained,

> [p]olitical priorities, program developments, new conditions in television, broader developments in Aboriginal communities, and more sophisticated political and administrative structures are part of a sea change in which the recognition of Aboriginal cultural, political and social rights to participation

and autonomy is replacing older protectionist, paternalist and social disadvantage (therefore welfarist) agendas. . . . With the emerging ascendance of non-welfarist logics of cultural, economic and poltical rights by virtue of original inhabitance, Aboriginal spokespersons and representative structures have achieved a greater degree of formalisation. . . . In these circumstances Aboriginal voices can only be expected to become more strident and less accommodating of the existing Aboriginal social and cultural circumstances, including televisual arrangements (O'Regan and Batty, 1993, 185).

Additionally, positive representations of Aboriginal people are also part of the cultural capital on which contemporary Australia builds its economy in arenas such as tourism, political affairs, and the marketing of things Australian overseas. For example, the international circulation of a festival of film and television on indigenous Australians, as part of the Year of Indigenous Peoples in 1993, was sponsored by Australia's Department of Foreign Affairs and Trade.

These broader contexts—the political economy of media, the changing relations of Aboriginal people with the state, a history of social struggle, and an ever-expanding realm of media technologies and representations—shape the complex mediascape of Aboriginal media production and circulation. In terms of actual social relations, it means that Aboriginal producers are frequently in the uneasy position of working with and being funded by governing bodies responsible for the political circumstances that, in their media work, they are protesting.[13]

In the following section, I demonstrate how cultural activists understand this new and complex object—Aboriginal media—as an extension of their collective (vs. individual) self-production in a variety of domains, from the assertion of local cultural practices to more overtly political work. Regardless of generalizations that can be made, I also want to stress that Aboriginal producers from various locales and backgrounds—remote, urban, rural—come to their positions through quite different cultural and social processes. In communities where traditional Aboriginal cultural practices are still relatively intact, such evaluation is culturally very specific, corresponding to notions of appropriate social and formal organization of performance in ritual domains in which general principles of kin-based rights to tell certain kinds of stories and ceremonial knowledge continue to shape production practices (Langton, 1993, 65).

In ways that are both similar and different, urban Aboriginal media makers are also concerned with their media productions as a form of social action. Although their works are more typically understood as authored by individuals (Langton, 1993, 13), many urban Aboriginal producers nonetheless see themselves as responsible to a community of origin, (for example, kin and friends in the urban neighborhood of Redfern in Sydney); however, it is a sense of community less bound by specific cultural rules than that of people in remote settlements. This is especially true of those working for Australian state television who shoulder the specific burden of creating an "authentic" Aboriginal presence in the mass media and, more broadly, in Australia's national imaginary.[14] More generally, my point is that for many Aboriginal producers, the quality of their work is judged by its capacity to embody, sustain, and even revive or create certain social relations, although the cultural bases for coming to this position differ for remote and urban people.

On Location: Indigenous Media

My first example is drawn from a successful community-based Aboriginal media association developed at Ernabella, a relatively traditional remote settlement on Pitjantjatjarra lands in south Australia, just south of Uluru (Ayers Rock). Like many other remote Aboriginal communities, Ernabella has a highly mobile population that can vary from 500 to 1,500 over the course of a year. Founded by missionaries in the 1940s, it became self-governing by the 1970s and retains an infrastructure consisting of a community store, a town office, a police station, a primary school, a health clinic, a church, an art association, and local broadcast facilities.

In 1983, people at Ernabella, began producing video programs with the encouragement of white schoolteachers and advisers, in particular Neil Turner who settled in the community, learned the language, and facilitated the development of Ernabella Video Television (EVTV) from its inception to the present. Established in 1985, EVTV operates from a small video production, editing and playback facility and an inexpensive satellite dish that provides local broadcasts of work produced by EVTV as well as items selected from national television feeds. Determined to be as independent as possible from government subsidies, EVTV has supported itself successfully through a self-imposed tax on cold drinks in the community store, the sales of EVTV videos, and occasional public and private grants (Molnar, 1989; N. Turner, 1990; Batty, 1993).

Since 1983, EVTV has produced over eighty edited videos as well as thousands of hours of community television under the direction of a respected couple, Simon and Pantiji Tjiyangu and a local media committee made up of male and female elders. Their concerns range from monitoring the content of work shown—so that images are not circulated that violate cultural rules regulating what can be seen (e.g., tapes of women's sacred ceremonies are only accessible to appropriate senior women and are never edited)—and the timing of viewing so that television transmission, whether locally produced or the national satellite feed, does not interfere with other cultural activities. Far from turning Ernabella residents into "mere fringe dwellers on the periphery of national mass media networks" (N. Turner, 1990), EVTV has become a powerful force of cultural revival for all members of the community. As Turner has observed,

> Children at Ernabella have seen themselves on TV more than any other of the world's children. They still invade the studio most afternoons after school to dance in front of the camera and watch themselves transmogrified by special effects! The power of video for educational purposes became quickly apparent (particularly for formal English) as tongue-tied children soon developed confidence and special narrative styles for the camera (1990, 45).

Perhaps because the supervision of EVTV is largely in the hands of elders, the video work of Ernabella is distinguished by its emphasis on ceremonies, in particular the stories, dances, and designs associated with the *Kungkarangkalpa* (Seven Sisters Dreaming) (which explains the origins of the Pleiades constellation). In adapting such forms to video, EVTV producers include in their tapes the production process itself, which can involve the whole community, including children, dancers, story tellers, and video crew. For example, one sees in tapes such as *Seven Sisters Dreaming: Tjukurpa Kungkarangkalpa Tjara* (1985, EVTV) not just a performance as we understand it in the West. Dances and enactments of the story of the Seven Sisters are preceded by extensive preparation and participation by those members of the Pitjantjatjara community who are responsible for ritual knowledge and ceremony. This aspect of Pitjantjatjara ritual performance has been reconfigured to accommodate video production: the tape includes not only ritual preparation but also other participants offering their comments on the ritual as they sit at night by the campfire to view the day's rushes (Leigh, 1992, 3). Such reflexivity is not a Brechtian innovation; rather, it authorizes any reconfiguring of traditional practices for video as "true" and properly done.

Productions by EVTV are empowering forms of social action in a number of ways. First, they extend the power that ceremonies have to revive sacred aspects of the landscape, while at they same time they provide an activity that reinforces the social relations that are fundamental to this kind of cultural production. The work of EVTV also enhances the place of Pitjantjatjara among Aboriginal groups in the area among whom the tapes circulate. Every time a tape is seen, particularly that of a ceremony, it enhances their power and authority as ceremonial experts. In a parallel process in the dominant Australian regional culture, Pitjantjatjara have been recognized, increasingly, as noteworthy cultural "performers." Over the last decade, people from Ernabella have been invited to nearby cultural centers such as Adelaide to "perform," a process of cultural self-objectification that has been hastened by the community's ongoing video practices. Neil Turner assessed the impact of EVTV in the following way.

> Its production is seen as a cultural imperative involving the whole community, not as the prohibitively expensive preserve of a mystified elite offering luxury handouts. In fact, EVTV has turned the cultural hegemonist model on its head, using video to promulgate their own cultural product nationally and around the world. They perform their *inma* (ceremonies) in cities to enlighten those unfortunates who have lost their pre-literate oral heritage. The Seven Sisters has now been sent over the central satellite footprint to Adelaide, Canberra, Sydney, the Philippines, Hawaii, Austria, Berlin and London (Turner, 1990, 45).

Knowledge of these issues is important to understanding the value of EVTV tapes as a form of social action that crosses over cultural borders, reaching other Aboriginal and non-Aboriginal audiences. The process of creating tapes has strengthened the community's sense of itself as having a strong hold on its language, law, and cultural practices; in addition (and crucially, given the current situation), such processes and their continued practice are key to any land rights claims that they make.

Since the early 1980s, the demand for more Aboriginal participation and visibility in the Australian mediascape has been increasing, not only for local access to video in remote areas, but also for more Aboriginal representation on mainstream national television. This concern is not simply about equal access but a recognition that distortion and/or invisibility of Aboriginal realities for the wider Australian public can have a direct effect on political culture. Continuing exclusion of work by Aboriginal people from Australia's media institutions has sharpened Aboriginal awareness of the connections between political enfranchisement and the need to control their own images in the public sphere.

In terms of content and staffing, aboriginal people are still virtually absent from Australia's three commercial television networks (with the exception of Stan Grant, an Aboriginal journalist, who was recently appointed anchor on *Real Life,* a nightly current affairs program) (Langton, 1993, 21). However, two important efforts to increase an Aboriginal presence on public television were initiated in 1989: (1) the Aboriginal Programs Unit (APU) of the Australian Broadcasting Corporation (ABC), the state-owned national television station that reaches all of Australia; and (2) the Aboriginal Unit of the Special Broadcast Service (SBS), Australia's state-funded station set up to provide culturally and linguistically appropriate programming, both imported and locally produced, for Australia's many ethnic communities.

In April 1989, a number of Aboriginal media activists worked with the Special Broadcast Service to develop a thirteen-part TV series devoted to Aboriginal issues, called "First In Line," the first prime-time current affairs show in Australia to be hosted by two Aboriginal people.[15] The producers and crew were primarily Aboriginal and consulted with communities throughout Australia for items stressing the positive achievements of Aborigines (Molnar, 1989, 38–39). Eventually, "First In Line" was discontinued, and an Aboriginal Unit was established with Rachel Perkins at the head, a young Aboriginal woman who had trained at the Central Australian Aboriginal Media Association (CAAMA) in central Australia, and who is the daughter of Charles Perkins, a well-known Aboriginal activist/politician and former sports hero. She has been creating programming through the use of work from regional and local Aboriginal Media Associations. In 1992–1993, she commissioned "Blood Brothers," a series she coproduced with Euro-Australian filmmaker Ned Lander. The series of four one-hour documentaries broadcast in 1993 are on different aspects of Aboriginal history and culture told "through the personal lives of four prominent Aboriginal men" (Perkins, 1992). These include (1) Darby Jampijinpa Ross, a Warlpiri elder who has been instrumental in fighting to retain traditional culture and law; (2) Rupert Max Stuart, an Arrente man, now a respected elder, who was falsely accused of the rape and murder of a white Australian girl in 1959 and jailed for twenty-five years; (3) Kev Carmody, a nationally known musician and songwriter, considered by many to be the voice of protest for black Australia; and (4) Charles Perkins, who in 1965 as one of the first Aboriginal students at Sydney University organized freedom rides to challenge the racist conditions under which Aboriginal people lived in rural towns in New South Wales at that time.

The documentary about Charles Perkins, "Freedom Ride," written and produced by his daughter Rachel Perkins, retraces the history of this initial stage of the Aboriginal civil rights movement through the retrospective accounts by Perkins and his fellow protesters, both black and white, as they revisit the places where they had carried out civil disobedience over twenty-five years ago. This piece strategically refuses any imagery of Aboriginal people in "the victim position," except by an immediate juxtaposition to a positive social/political response. In reaching out to a mixed but still predominantly white national audience, "Freedom Ride" is also a reminder of the possibility of white activism on behalf of Aboriginal rights at a contemporary moment when political separatism can serve as an excuse for apathy. Using archival footage, recreations of historical scenes mixed with oral histories, and contemporary verite footage, the documentary is powerful testimony to how political consciousness was created in everyday experiences of discrimination and transformed through direct action, much of it inspired by knowledge of the American civil rights movement gained in part through the mass media. In a particularly poignant moment, Charles Perkins recollects a solidarity visit from an African American delegation and how unexpectedly moved the Australians were when the visitors sang "We Shall Overcome," which they had heard many times on radio and television. This example of the role that the mass media played historically in creating contact between social movements in different parts of the world is a reminder that the documentary itself is embedded in a context of social action in which its presence on national television is yet another level of assertion and insertion of a rarely visible Aboriginal presence and perspective on Australian history. Despite the success and importance of these efforts, the SBS has a relatively small audience and budget and as of 1994, it is unclear whether the Aboriginal unit will be sustained.

Much like the SBS Unit, the Aboriginal Programs Unit (APU) of the state-controlled and -funded Australian Broadcasting Corporation (ABC) was also established to give voice to Aboriginal concerns on national television: however, the ABC has a much greater reseource base and reaches a larger audience. In 1987, the ABC set up an Aboriginal Programs Unit (APU),[16] but it was not until 1989 that their first Aboriginally produced and presented program, "Blackout," a weekly magazine show on Aboriginal issues, began broadcasting on a Friday evening time slot. (In 1992, it was awarded the United Nations Human Rights Media Award.) Additionally, the Unit programs occasional series such as "The First Australians," an eight-part series of independent documentaries on Aboriginal topics broadcast on Thursday nights in 1992.[17]

Frances Peters, a Kamilaroi Aboriginal woman who grew up in New South Wales in the 1960s and went to the university in Sydney (where she also performs frequently as a vocalist), joined the unit in 1989 as a researcher for "Blackout." The following year, she produced and directed her own first half-hour documentary for "Blackout," "Oceans Apart," for which she also wrote and performed the music. The piece is based on the lives of three Aboriginal women who were raised in white families; as adults, they reconnect with their Aboriginal heritage either directly, by seeking contact with their families of origin, or through cultural activities in the arts, communications, and education. Peters chose as her subjects women who "don't look Aboriginal," who are sophisticated and middle class, and who are anything but victims. This was a deliberate strategy to subvert conventional stereotypes of Aboriginal people in the dominant media, which tend to focus on men, traditional bush-living people engaged in ceremony or painting, or urban dwellers represented as social problems. The women's unusual narratives offer extraordinary examples of the possibilities of recapturing a contemporary indigenous identity in the face of tremendous forces of assimilation. "Oceans Apart" is also powerful for the striking differences in the women's lives despite their common struggles: Peters takes care to draw attention to the diversity of Aboriginal experiences. Frances Peters explained her choice as an effort to avoid treating Aboriginal people as issues: "They are speaking on behalf of themselves, from a personal point of view and therefore the political comes from the individual, the issue comes out of what is happening and the person's experience, rather than putting the experience up, and having the people speak on behalf of the experience. So by dealing with it on a personal level, we find that it is stronger politically as well" (interview, 1992).

Additionally, while the history of Aboriginal children being taken away and placed with white families is one of the more tragic legacies of the government's assimilationist policy toward Aboriginal children of mixed descent, "Oceans Apart" avoids becoming a simple attack. By allowing the women's stories to guide the piece it makes viewers aware of the costs of institutional racism as we are drawn into their lives, enabling us to see both the consequences of policy and the ways that they have managed to overcome them by finding alternative routes back to Aboriginal kin and communities.

Conclusion

People like Frances Peters and Rachel Perkins are part of a generation of cultural activists who came of age when the struggle for Aboriginal civil rights was already a social fact. Their efforts resemble the more remote-living Aboriginal media makers discussed above, insofar as they are concerned with their work as part of a range of activities engaged in cultural revival, identity formation, and political assertion. Their positioning (along with that of other producers) intersects and is influenced by emerging Western theoretical discourses in the arts built on frameworks of multiculturalism discussed earlier, which emphasize "cultural diversity as a basis for challenging, revising and relativizing basic notions and principles common to dominant and minority cultures alike, so as to construct a more vital, open, and democratic common culture" (T. Turner, 1993, 413).

Aboriginal producers working in national television are engaged in more than the creation of media images of themselves that alter their place in the world of representations; they see it clearly as a form of social action, but one that has its base in face-to-face relations. Through their work in televisual media production, they have been able to assert the multiple realities of contemporary urban Aboriginal life, not just for their own communities but in the national public culture where Aboriginal activism and political claims are generally effaced from the official histories.

The social relations built out of indigenous media practices within Aboriginal communities and with the dominant society are helping to develop support and sensibilities for indigenous actions for self-determination—a point underscored by communications scholar Helen Molnar in a recent article on indigenous media development in Australia:

> . . . Aborigines and Islanders are using the electronic media to create new means of distribution, and to restore the communication links destroyed by European colonization. Indigenous broadcasting, while largely community based, can potentially be transmitted locally, regionally, and nationally, informing Aborigines and Islanders about each other, thus strengthening indigenous self-identity (1995, 73).

As a form of transformative work, indigenous media is expressive of changes in indigenous consciousness rooted in social movements for Aboriginal empowerment, cultural autonomy, and claims to land. Together, these form a continuum of activities for Aboriginal self-determination vis-à-vis the state that understands the crucial connection between rights and representation. Self-presentation in popular media is seen as a key part of this process. The production and circulation of indigenous media are creating new arenas of cooperation and consciousness, from the revival of local cultural practices, to the insertion of their histories into national imaginaries, to the creation of new transnational arenas that link indigenous media makers around the globe in a common effort to make their concerns visible to the world.

Strategic Reflexivity

Given this agenda, it is crucial to consider the role of one's own research in such projects of social transformation. What is the boundary between engaged scholarship and social action at moments when culture—as an objectified social fact—is increasingly a shared object of interest? In working with indigenous media makers, it has been crucial that I identify the relationship of my research to *their* project. As a scholar, teacher, and film curator, I am understood as someone who can help draw attention to indigenous media in and out of the academy; more importantly, I can help constitute and expand the discursive space for it, a task that a number of indigenous intellectuals have themselves called for (e.g., Langton, 1922).[18] Although there has been increasing interest in programming indigenous work at mainstream cultural institutions and film venues—The Museum of Modern Art and The American Museum of Natural History in New York, or Robert Redford's Sundance Film Festival—this work is still largely absent from the canon of cinema studies and is only just emerging as a topic in visual anthropology and media studies. For this and other such work that is new and sometimes marginalized, research-ers like me can play an important role in bringing this work into view, so to speak, by developing courses, writing, building video collections and develop-ing programs that will expose people to this media and the mediamakers and provide analytical frames for understanding them.[19]

I write about this not as self-justification but as part of a perennial discus-sion of the role of scholarship in processes of social transformation. It is valu-able to "discover" empirical examples of cultural critique (a long tradition in American anthropology, as Marcus and Fischer have argued [1986]), and to create texts that reflect a more dialogical epistemology, but I am more inter-ested in how we understand our work, strategically, as a mode of social action and intervention, in relation to and collaboration with the projects of those we study. Working with cultural activists such as the indigenous media makers discussed in this essay, for example, it is clear that academics do not have a monopoly on innovative models of cultural processes, more inclusive social structures, or hybrid cultural forms, though we may articulate them differently. In other words, I am arguing that our reflexivity be more than textual, and that it begin by considering how our research is part of a social world shared with our subjects. In our work, we can identify how new social imaginaries are emerging out of peoples' daily lives, map points of potential innovation and ac-tivism, and—through our discursive and institutional practices—build on these findings to enhance the possibilities for positive social change.

Notes

I thank Richard Fox, Orin Starn, and the participants in the conference they orga-nized on social movements; they gave me helpful comments on this paper. John Borneman, who reviewed the book for Rutgers, also gave me useful advice. The fieldwork on which this work is based could not have been done without the help of Fred Myers in 1988 and Francoise Dussart in 1992 in the logistics and languages of Aboriginal research in the field and out; I am deeply grateful to both of them. In addition, I thank the following people in Australia who shared their time and insights with me: Philip Batty, Annette Hamilton, Freda Glynn, Francis Jupurrurla Kelly, Ned Lander, Marcia Langton, Mary Laughren, Michael Leigh, Judith and David MacDougall, Michael Niblett, Rachel Perkins, Frances Peters, Nick Peterson, Tim Rowse, David Sandy, Neil Turner, and Peter Toyne. For research support, I am grate-ful to the Research Challenge Fund of New York University (1988) and the John Simon Guggenheim Foundation (1991–1992). Portions of this piece were drawn from two essays (Ginsburg 1993b and 1994).

The title, "In Little Things, Big Things Grow" is taken from the title of a song by Aboriginal musician, historian, and activist Kev Carmody, which in turn became the title of a video documentary made about him for the "Blood Brothers" series produced as part of Aboriginal programming for Australia's SBS television channel.

1. I thank John Borneman for pointing out the importance of clarifying this distinction.
2. In line with recent work in anthropology and cultural studies, I view indigenous media as part of a problematic social formation through which differing notions of Aboriginality are envisioned in indigenous communities, in the Australian "national imaginary" (Hamilton, 1990), and in international networks concerned with indigenous people.
3. This term was created by Arjun Appadurai as one of five scapes of interaction that account for the current global cultural economy, in this case created by new media technologies and the images created with them (1990).
4. Translated by Victor Zamudio Taylor in 1994.
5. The authors define small media as:

   . . . a popular rubric for various kinds of mediated alternatives to state-run broadcasting systems, but the definition of non-mass media has never been very precise. From Schramm's (1972) attempts to define "big" and "little" media, to definitions of "group media" (Media Development, 1981), "community media" (Byram, 1981; Wade, 1981), or "radical media" (Downing, 1984), what has been crucial is a notion of these media as participatory, public phenomena, controlled neither by big states nor big corporations. Thus the distinction between "big" and "small" cannot depend on particular kinds of technologies or even their putative audiences, but rather on the manner and use of all technologies (Sreberny-Mohammadi and Mohammadi, 1994, 20).

6. Bennett and Blundell argue that "in societies like Australia and New Zealand, the field of operations for the 'organic intellectuals' of First Peoples is comprised by the interstices between their communities and the structures of government" (1995, 8).
7. I thank Orin Starn and Richard Fox for directing my attention to this point in their comments on an earlier version of this paper.
8. This point is often overlooked (but see O'Regan and Batty, 1993) and might explain, for example, the noticeable differences in community participation in two different longstanding media associations in central Australian communities, WMA and EVTV.
9. I have been researching the relationship of the development of film and video by Aboriginal Australians to the construction of contemporary indigenous identities in a number of contexts. In the summer of 1988, the fall of 1989, and the spring of 1992, I carried out field and archival research in Australia (including extended interviews and acquisition of productions for further analysis) with a number of Aboriginal producers working in independent film, in local media associations based at remote communities, and in Aboriginal television units. I have also been following government policy regarding media production and funding via documents, tribunal proceedings, and interviews with bureaucrats and administrators. (See Appendix and Ginsburg [1991, 1993a, 1993b] for a more detailed description of field sites).
10. Unfortunately, this diversity has rarely been accounted for by those setting broadcast policy, despite an ideological climate favoring multicultural expression as an acceptable version of the Australian nation (Molnar, 1990; Rowse, 1992).
11. Since the 1996 elections, when a much more conservative government was elected, it is unclear what the future of government-funded television will be.

12. For example, by 1990, the Department of Aboriginal Affairs was replaced by the Aboriginal and Torres Straits Islanders Commission (ATSIC), a $5 billion bureaucracy that is supposed to be responding to Aboriginal community structures rather than government imperatives.

13. Such contradictions, are inherent to the ongoing social construction of "Aboriginality." In concrete terms: "'Aboriginality' arises from the subjective experience of both Aboriginal people and non-Aboriginal people who engage in any intercultural dialogue, whether in actual lived experience or through a mediated experience such as a white person watching a program about Aboriginal people on television or reading a book" (Langton, 1993, 31).

14. Although the opportunities of such positions are obvious, there is some concern on the part of Aboriginal filmmakers that they are expected to confine their work to conventional or romanticized representations of Aboriginality, what Haitian anthropologist Michel Rolph Trouillot calls "the savage slot" (1991).

15. Michael Johnson and Rhoda Roberts were the hosts for thirty-eight programs, which aired Tuesday nights at 7:30 p.m.

16. While the state-controlled and -funded Australian Broadcasting Corporation (ABC) had been training Aborigines since 1980, by 1987 only seven Aborigines were employed there. That same year, the prime minister established the Aboriginal Employment and Development Policy (AEDP), which requires all industries to have 2 percent Aboriginal employment by 1991 (Molnar, 1989, 36–38).

17. As of 1993, the APU had six Aboriginal staff who produce "Blackout," a weekly late night program on Aboriginal affairs, as well as occasional documentaries and dramatic works. As such, it has been a precedent-setting model for including indigenous people and their concerns in the imaginary of the nation state and beyond.

18. My research is part of an ongoing effort to address what Aboriginal anthropologist and cultural activist Marcia Langton has identified as " . . . the need to develop a body of knowledge and critical perspective to do with aesthetics and politics . . . on representation of Aboriginal people and concerns in art, film, television, or other media" (1993, 28).

19. At NYU, I have established a Center for Media, Culture, and History, where we have been organizing conferences, screenings, and fellowships to bring indigenous makers to New York to meet each other and create links with the world of independent and alternative film and video production, a world whose institutional bases are in New York.

References

Anderson, Benedict (1983). *Imagined Communities*. London: Verso.

Anderson, Kelly and Annie Goldson (1991). Alternating Currents: Alternative Television Inside and Outside of the Academy. *Social Text* 28:56–71.

Appadurai, Arjun (1990). Disjuncture and Difference in the Global Cultural Economy. *Public Culture* 2(2):1–24.

Batty, Philip (1993). Singing the Electric: Aboriginal Television in Australia. In *Channels of Resistance: Global Television and Local Empowerment*, ed. Tony Downmunt. London: British Film Institute.

Beckett, Jeremy (1988). Aborigines and the State in Australia. *Social Analysis, Special Issue Series* 24(December):5–22.

Bennett, Tony and Valda Blundell (1995). First Peoples. *Cultural Studies* 9(1):1–24.

Bourdieu, Pierre (1993). *The Field of Cultural Production: Essays on Art & Literature.* New York: Columbia University Press.

Castoriadis, Cornelius (1993). *The Imaginary Institution of Society.* Cambridge, UK: Polity Press.

Cohen, Hart (1993). Unpublished paper.

Downmunt, Rony, Ed. (1993). *Channels of Resistance: Global Television and Local Empowerment.* London: British Film Institute

Faris, James (1992). Anthropological Transparency, Film, Representation and Politics. In *Film as Ethnography*, ed. P. Crawford and D. Turton, pp. 171–182. Manchester: University of Manchester Press.

Ginsburg, Faye (1989). *Contested Lives: The Abortion Debate in an American Community.* Berkeley: University of California Press.

Ginsburg, Faye (1991). Indigenous Media: Faustian Contract or Global Village? *Cultural Anthropology* 6(1):92–112.

Ginsburg, Faye (1993a). Aboriginal Media and the Aboriginal Imaginary. *Public Culture* 5(3):557–578.

Ginsburg, Faye (1993b). Station Identification: The Aboriginal Programs Unit of the Australian Broadcasting Corporation. *Visual Anthropology Review* 9(2):92–96.

Ginsburg, Faye (1994). Embedded Aesthetics: Creating a Discursive Space for Indigenous Media. *Cultural Anthropology* 9(3):365–382.

Ginsburg, Faye and Rayna Rapp (1995). Introduction. In *Conceiving the New World Order: The Global Politics of Reproduction*, ed. Faye Ginsburg and Rayna Rapp, pp. 1–18. Berkeley: University of California Press.

Hall, Stuart (1992). Cultural Studies and Its Theoretical Legacies. In *Cultural Studies*, ed. L. Grossberg, C. Nelson, and P. Treichler, pp. 277–294. New York: Routledge.

Hamilton, Annette (1990). Fear and Desire: Aborigines, Asians, and the National Imaginary. *Australian Cultural History* 9:14–35.

Langton, Marcia (1993). *Well, I Saw It on the Television and I Heard It on the Radio.* Sydney: Australian Film Commission.

Leigh, Michael (1992). *Cultural Focus, Cultural Futures.* Canberra: Department of Foreign Affairs and Trade.

Marcus, George and Michael Fischer (1986). *Anthropology as Cultural Critique.* Chicago: University of Chicago Press.

Masayesva, Victor Jr., (1994). Through Native Eyes: The Emerging Native American Aesthetic. *The Independent* 17(10):17–22.

Melucci, Alberto (1985). The Symbolic Challenge of Contemporary Movements. *Social Research* 52:789–816.

Michaels, Eric (1986). *Aboriginal Invention of Television: Central Australia 1982–86.* Canberra: Australian Institute for Aboriginal Studies.

Michaels, Eric (1987). *For a Cultural Future: Francis Jupurrurla Makes TV at Yuendumu.* Melbourne: Art and Criticism Monograph Series.

Molnar, Helen (1989). Aboriginal Broadcasting in Australia: Challenges and Promises. Paper presented at the International Communication Association Conference, March.

Molnar, Helen (1990). The Broadcasting for Remote Areas Community Scheme: Small Vs. Big Media. *Media Information Australia* 58(November):47–154.

Molnar, Helen (1995). Indigenous Media Development in Australia: A Product of Struggle and Opposition. *Cultural Studies* 9(1):169–190.

Morris, Aldon D. (1992). Political Consciousness and Collective Action. In *Frontiers in Social Movement Theory*, ed. A. D. Morris and C. McLurg Mueller. New Haven: Yale University Press.

Muenala, Alberto (1994). Culture as an Instrument for Indigenous People's Identity. Translated by Victor Zamudio Taylor. Film Notes for Video Viewpoints, 23 May 1994. New York: Museum of Modern Art.

O'Regan, Tom and Philip Batty (1993). An Aboriginal Television Culture. In *Australian Television Culture*, ed. Tom O'Regan, pp. 169–196. Sydney: Allen & Unwin.

Perkins, Rachel (1992). Brochure for Blood Brothers Series.

Peters, Frances (1992). Interview.

Raboy, Marc and Peter Bruck, Eds. (1989). *Communication For and Against Democracy*. Montreal: Black Rose Books.

Riggins, Stephen Harold (1992). *Ethnic Minority Media: An International Perspective*. Newbury Park, Calif.: Sage Publications.

Roth, Lorna and Gail Valaskakis (1989). Aboriginal Broadcasting in Canada: A Case Study in Democratization. In *Communication For and Against Democracy*, ed. Mark Raboy and Peter Bruck. Montreal: Black Rose Books.

Rowse, Tim (1992). *Remote Possibilities: The Aboriginal Domain and the Administrative Imagination*. Darwin: Northern Aboriginal Research Unit, Australian National University.

Sreberny-Mohammadi, Annabelle, and Ali Mohammadi (1994). *Small Media, Big Revolution: Communication, Culture, and the Iranian Revolution*. Minneapolis: University of Minnesota Press.

Trouillot, Michel-Rolph (1991). Anthropology and the Savage Slot: The Poetics and Politics of Otherness. In *Recapturing Anthropology: Working in the Present*, ed. Richard G. Fox, pp. 17–44. Santa Fe: School of American Research Advanced Seminar Series.

Turner, Neil (1990). Pitchat and Beyond. *Artlink* 10(1–2):43–45.

Turner, Terence (1991). The Social Dynamics of Video Media in an Indigenous Society: The Cultural Meaning and the Personal Politics of Video-Making in Kayapo Communities. *Visual Anthropology Review* 7(2):68–76.

Turner, Terence (1993). Anthropology and Multiculturalism: What Is Anthropology that Multiculturalists Should Be Mindful of It? *Cultural Anthropology*, 8(4):411–429.

Valaskakis, Gail (1993). Parallel Voices: Indians and Others. *Canadian Journal of Communication* 18:283–298.

Weatherford, Elizabeth (1990). Native Visions: The Growth of Indigenous Media. *Aperture* 119:58–61.

Weatherford, Elizabeth and Emelia Seubert (1988). *Native Americans on Film and Video*. New York: National Museum of the American Indian.

Wright, Robin (1988). Anthropological Presuppositions of Indigenous Advocacy. *Annual Review of Anthropology* 17:365–426.

Yoshinobu Ota

Appropriating Media, Resisting Power

Representations of Hybrid Identities
in Okinawan Popular Culture

The very power of the insight depends on the powerful error (in my opinion) that they make.

Michael Taussig (1993, 248–249)

Introduction

The signing of the San Francisco Treaty in 1952 between the United
States and Japan meant that the entire Ryukyu islands south of Okinawa would
be placed under American military occupation.[1]

In 1954, Colonel Pardy, a character in *Teahouse of the August Moon*, ordered
a former associate professor of humanities, Captain Fisby, to guide the people
of Tobiki (an imaginary village), Okinawa, to construct the school and the
townhall so that he might teach them the idea of democracy and lead them to
practice it in village political affairs. Following the "democratic" procedure they
had learned from him, the villagers decided to first have a teahouse before
any other building; a teahouse in this social context functioned more like a
nightclub. After the captain failed to promote the area's folk craft by which he
hoped to improve the village economy, he was forced to permit selling bottles
of *awamori* ("brandy" made of rice/millet) to the U.S. military base nearby so
that the villagers could recover their economic loss. Becoming impatient of
the apparently slow pace of democratization in Tobiki, Colonel Pardy suspected
the captain's sanity and sent a psychiatrist, Dr. McLean, to examine him. But
the doctor devoted most of his time to his hobby, horticulture, and frequented

the teahouse. Angered, the colonel ordered the destruction not only of the teahouse but also of the awamori factory. At this point, the colonel heard from Washington that the Tobiki case had been recommended as a model for village development in Okinawa, and a group of politicians were planning to visit the village to see what it was like. Now the colonel had to order the villagers to rebuild these buildings just destroyed.

Thus runs the story of the movie *Teahouse of the August Moon* (directed by Daniel Mann, 1956) based on the novel by V. Sneider. It is fraught with many stereotypical images of Okinawans, as any Hollywood movies on non-European peoples tend to be. In fact, many Okinawans at that time protested the way in which the movie portrayed Okinawans as being, for example, a people with no interest in education and an inclination toward hedonism. In 1954, when the American military government proposed to stage a theatrical version of this novel as a way to bridge the gap between the locals and the Americans, it met strong opposition from many Okinawans.

Although I do not reject the criticisms put forth by the Okinawans at the time, I propose another interpretation of this movie. In my view, it is a comedy that demonstrates the popular tactics (de Certeau, 1984, 30) of local people who must make do within the constraining order to create a space of plurality in which they could render more manageable the social conditions forced on them. This is by no means a dominant reading of this movie as a cultural text; however, it does offer a way of conceptualizing a process of identity formation currently popular among young Okinawans.

In this paper, I discuss a process in which a version of local Okinawan identity has been constructed through the mediation of mass media, in particular, television broadcasting. As Faye Ginsburg (1991) astutely notes, media should be understood not only as a cultural product but also as a social process. In other words, in addition to understanding media as representation—a common meaning associated with the term media—it could also be regarded as a process of mediation itself, a "creative tool in the service of new signifying practice" (Ginsburg, 1991, 93). Media mediates the dichotomies between power and resistance, between acquiescence and refusal, between the dominant and the subordinate, and, in this particular case, between the mainland Japanese and the Okinawans (see Madden, 1992; Turner, 1991, 1992; Michaels, 1991). Moreover, a similar mediation exists within Okinawan society between old and young. As a result of this complex process of mediation, Okinawan identity is represented in the local mass media as hybrid, incorporating many elements of Japanese mass media, local Okinawan practices, and experiences of living around U.S. military bases. This hybridity is significant not only because it denies the existence of an original or given Okinawan cultural essence, but also because it decenters the powers of discourses that disseminate through the same mass media images foreign to the young people in Okinawa. For example, Okinawa has been a popular tourist destination for the Japanese mainlanders. Its semitropical climate has been exploited in the mass media to produce images of an exotic tropical paradise where locals swim in the aqua water, catch fish as they please, and speak fluent English (because of the presence of U.S. military bases). Living in a society mediated by these images, the Okinawans can become strangers in their own society (Ota, n.d.b; cf. Hall, 1990, 233).

One source of this process of identity formation arises from the activities of a theatrical group in Koza, Okinawa Prefecture, Japan. First, I explore the fact that a series of television shows this group has been producing are an indigenization of Japanese "television comedies" (*conte* in French, *konto* in Japanese pronunciation). Then, I propose that through consumption of these television shows, young Okinawans empower their existence and forge a positive identity in Okinawan society, where they are often marginalized by two different discourses. On the one hand, discourse among the adult members of the society often categorizes the youth as being alienated from "true, authentic" Okinawan tradition. On the other hand, the discourse in Japanese mass media about Okinawa attributes young Okinawans with identities so fantastic that one of a few means of resistance would be to parody them. These discourses, in other words, transform the young people into "Okinawan subjects," with stereotypical essentialized characteristics of those living in the marginal area of Japan. I contend that by appropriating the mass media, one of the main sources of producing homogeneity throughout Japan, this theatrical group accentuates images of heterogeneity and emergent diversity for young Okinawan viewers. They learn to formulate their own identities in opposition to hegemonic discourses that position them at the margins of Japanese society and interpellate them as Okinawan subjects.

Activities of this theatrical group may be interpreted as a form of cultural mobilization and resistance through mass media, articulating the voices of the marginalized—in this case, young Okinawans. In the past, social movements have oscillated between complete identification with the mainland Japanese (rejecting the Okinawan lifestyle and dialects), and total immersion in things Ryukyuan to the extent of becoming "nativist." In light of this often-taken-for-granted dichotomy, the current historical conjuncture is unique because it circulates hybrid representations and because these are consumed by the young, who produce a sense of self neither traditionally Japanese nor purely Okinawan. In the following section, I offer a brief history of how Ryukyuans have been represented—an important subject since social movements in Okinawa and Okinawan communities in Japan have arisen through the struggles against such representations and since this history illuminates the peculiarity of the current youth movement.

Social Movements in Okinawa and Okinawan Communities in Japan

Prior to the 1609 invasions by the Satsuma feudal clan, the Ryukyu kingdom had prospered independently for over one hundred years through its trade relationship with China. It was this profit from trade with China that Satsuma wanted to control. After the military intervention, Satsuma acquired the northern part of the Ryukyu kingdom, a series of small islands including Amami, Kikai, Tokunoshima, Erabujima, and Yoron, and forced the kingdom into subordination. One expression of this subordination was an annual tribute from the Ryukyu kingdom to Satsuma. Through this, Satsuma monitored the profit accrued in trade between China and the Ryukyu kingdom. The relationship between the kingdom and the Satsuma clan changed drastically from one of equal partnership to one of subservience and dominance. After 1639, when the Tokugawa shogunate closed Japan's door to the outside world, Satsuma held onto its profits by tapping into the trade relationship between China and the Ryukyu kingdom.

Although certainly sharing common ancestries, the Ryukyu kingdom had been, from the perspective of the Japanese, an independent country, which kept its contact with Japan minimal. The idea that the Ryukyus were not part of Japan was used to justify Satsuma's invasion and exploitation. Among the Ryukyuans, there was popular sentiment that China would come and rescue them from Satsuma domination. For its part, Satsuma devoted a considerable effort to emphasizing the alienness of the Ryukyu kingdom: official visitors to the Tokugawa shogunate (*keigashi*) were ordered to wear Chinese clothes and play Chinese music (Miyagi Eishô, 1982; Kamiya, 1990).

This external and internal identification with China changed when certain political decisions were made in 1879. First, in 1872, the Ryukyu kingdom was incorporated into Japan as Ryukyu (feudal) clan. Next, in 1879, the Ryukyu clan was renamed as Okinawa Prefecture and made part of Japan. Through the educational system established in Okinawa Prefecture, the Ryukyuans were transformed gradually into Okinawans, subjects of the Japanese Imperial body (Arakawa, 1981).

This political restructuring of Ryukyu islands brought into play hierarchical concepts of center and periphery, perfection and degeneration, modern and premodern, progress and stagnation, rationality and irrationality, through which the relationship between Japan and Okinawa was understood (Ota, n.d.a). As Japan moved along its road to modernization, the Okinawans were left out of this process, marginalized, and labeled "backward" and "lacking in hygiene and work ethic." For example, on visiting an "Anthropological Exhibit" of the Fifth Domestic Industrial Fair in Osaka in 1903, an Okinawan man was shocked to see, under a thatched roof, two Okinawan women dressed in local attire playing a *sanshin*, a local three-stringed instrument. The guide pointed at them with his whip, exclaiming "these things here!" Appalled at this humiliating display of his fellow country people as curiosity objects, the visitor quickly wrote a letter to the editor of *Ryukyu Shinpô*, protesting furiously that the Okinawans had been presented as if they were animals, along with the Ainu, Koreans, and others.[2]

Marginalized constantly by the gaze of the mainland Japanese, Okinawans themselves organized social movements in the 1920s and 1930s under the name of "betterment of lifestyle movement" (*seikatsu kaizen undô*). This movement was most active in Okinawan emigrant communities in such mainland Japanese cities as Osaka, where many Okinawans migrated to work at textile factories. Daily face-to-face interactions with the Japanese intensified feelings of alienation among Okinawans. The history of this movement is very complex, and a thorough discussion of it is beyond the scope of this paper (cf. Tomiyama, 1989). I simply note here that it changed from a movement organized by left-wing activists fighting against discrimination by the Japanese into one led more by the upwardly mobile; from a movement for Okinawans to become proud of their Okinawan roots and cultures to a movement for them to become more like the Japanese, forgetting dialects, not playing sanshin, not drinking awamori, and so on.[3] By the end of the 1930s, this movement became almost synonymous with the social process of "subjectification by the emperor" (*kôminka*).

From 1945 to 1972, American military forces occupied the Ryukyu islands. As a preparation for governing the Ryukyu islands the Office of the Chief of Naval Operation prepared a book entitled *Civil Affairs Handbook: Ryukyu Islands*.[4] Utilizing information (translated from Japanese into English by second-generation Japanese Americans) collected between 1934 to 1940, one of the major conclusions of the handbook was that the Okinawans were not Japanese and that they constitute a minority subject to discrimination, like other minorities in Japan. Following a suggestion in this book, the military government supported local cultural activities (such as "traditional" singing and dancing) because the promotion of Ryukyuan identity was interpreted as a deterrent for the more visible and consequential social movement in the 1950s and 1960s, the movement to "return to Japan" (*sokoku fukki undô*).[5] With political hegemony clearly in hand, the U.S. military government considered the local tradition solely in instrumental terms. That is, it was a means to encourage Okinawans to think of themselves as distinct from the Japanese and a way to help legitimize the U.S. presence in Okinawa by asserting a self-image of a patron that understands local tradition. Thus, U.S. military rule placed a negative sanction on Okinawan identification with Japan, while encouraging cultural autonomy; consequently, Americans have never been a part of the Okinawan "imagined communities" (cf. Anderson, 1983).

Since identification with Americans has been limited, Ryukyuan identities have always oscillated between two ideological interpellations: a complete identification with the Japanese (or, in a very limited historical case, with the Chinese), on the one hand, and a total identification in some objectified aspects of Ryukyuan tradition such as music, dancing, food, and clothing, on the other. These present a choice similar to the familiar one between a desire to enter modernity, now expressed in the slogan "catching up with the mainland Japan" (*hondonami*) and a desire to return to a "pure, authentic" past (nativism).

Another construction of Ryukyuan identity seems to have emerged in a visible form in the last ten years. Neither the language of modernity nor the idiom of nativism could capture this "third space" of hybridity (Bhabha, 1990, 211). In the theoretical language of Mary Louis Pratt (1992, 6), such a possibility is characteristic of a "contact zone" like Okinawa, where the subordinate and the dominant, the Okinawans and the Japanese, are both surrounded by the very visible U.S. military presence. The process of "transculturation," the effort of the subordinate or marginal group to invent a culture from materials transmitted to them by the dominant culture often occurs in a contact zone. In other words, popular culture emerges as a result of negotiating with the dominant culture: "popular cultures are the product of . . . the *people's own reflections* about their living conditions, and *conflict-ridden interaction* with hegemonic sectors" (García Canclini, 1993, 22).

The conceptual clarification above corresponds to an important Okinawan term, *chanpurû*, or mixing. This refers to hybrid representations circulating in the mass media for the young people. In the following section, I discuss the meaning of this term as it has emerged in a discourse on Okinawan culture.

Mixing (Chanpurû)

The term chanpurû in an Okinawan dialect referred originally to a style of popular cuisine that mixes everything available at hand. After World War II, Okinawans began using canned pork imported from the United States, mixed with local ingredients such as vegetables (bitter cucumber and gourd), *fu* (wheat-gluten bread), tofu, and *sômin* (vermicelli). The resulting dish has been *the* most popular one among Okinawans.

Although the term was in circulation far before the 1980s, it was not until the early 1980s that it gained frequent usage in mass media, overflowing from the original culinary domain in the direction of other cultural domains, particularly those of music and theater. It is increasingly used to signify the regional culture of Koza, a city developed around the Kadena Air Force Base.[6] In the domains of music and theater, Teruya Rinsuke is considered the first individual to mix Ryukyuan instruments with amplified Western instruments to accompany a comedy performance. He is a musician/comedian who created a stage musical show called *watabushô* (literally, "fat man show").

Teruya Rinsuke was born in Osaka in 1929; in 1936, he returned with his parents to Koza, Okinawa, near the Kadena Air Force Base. Completely taken in by the narrative performances of silent movie narrators, Teruya Rinsuke developed an interest in verbal performance at an early age. During World War II, he met an eccentric dentist cum parodist, Konaha Bûten, who impressed young Rinsuke very much with songs such as the following:

> I heard about this Hitler [*hittorâ*], a very famous Hitler
> When he swings [his bat], he never fail to get a run [*hitto*]
> England, America, France, Holland, and all he knocks them out
> Hitler [*hittoâ*] here, Hitler [hittorâ] there.

As Teruya Rinsuke recounts it today, this was not a song to praise Hitler's deeds because in an Okinawan dialect the sound hittoâ means "will to steal"; therefore, Hitler is a thief. This spirit of critique, Teruya Rinsuke says, is always present in Kohana Bûten's performances (Teruya, 1992, 95–96).

When Okinawa was severely damaged, and when many people of Kadena lost their lands, which had been converted to runways in the air force base, Kohana Bûten and Teruya Rinsuke began visiting people's houses to entertain them with music and performances. Because the American occupational force operated with an assumption that Okinawans enjoy theater and music much more than food (which was then scarce; see Miyagi Etsujirô 1992), the officers even encouraged Bûten and Rinsuke to visit different villages around the air force base. Accompanied by his sanshin, Rinsuke sang songs such as a "song of rejuvenation," which is still an important part of his repertoire:

> My eldest son is the chief cook at the base.
> My second son is working at the PX.
> Even my mother is working at night [illegally], exchanging money.
> Finally I've got some money, and feel much better.
> I feel rejuvenated.
>
> (*Umarikawaribushi*, A Song of Rejuvenation).[7]

Today, Rinsuke recalls a motto of Bûten: "It is easy to laugh at the weak, but it is much more fun to laugh at the strong." He touches on this point frequently in his performance.

Working at his grandfather's musical shop in Koza, Rinsuke was exposed to many kinds of popular music that American GIs listened to. Influenced by the music, Rinsuke modified his own sanshin into a four-stringed instrument and started performing a mixture of singing, narration, and performance, a combination that he later called "*watabushô*." Many residents of Koza still remember the popularity of his watabushô.[8]

"From the world [*yû*] of China to that of Japan, and then to the world of America, and finally, back to the world of Japan," is a common expression heard these days. Many Okinawans recall their history in terms of the politically dominant with whom they have been negotiating their lives, and because of whom a highly creolized culture of contact zone has emerged.[9] As an organizing metaphor for the lifestyle of Koza, some started to represent their culture in terms of chanpurû, a creolized cuisine of Okinawa. In a recent interview, Teruya Rinsuke states: "This is good, but that is bad. That is good, but this is bad. That is not what chanpurû is. Left as well as right, up as well as down, everything is good, that is what chanpurû means. That is called chanpura-ism" (from an interview broadcasted on NHK, 30 September 1993). His statement needs to be understood as one spoken by an Okinawan conscious of his social position in Japan. It is not to be taken as a sign of mere creolism without explicit recognition of power differentials, the kind of position that confounds various cultural activities of mix-and-match, obliterating in the process differences between the privileged, cosmopolitan and freely traveling and the less privileged, local and stationary.

This articulation of local culture in terms of a "relativizing" spirit of mixing is quickly becoming a main conceptual nexus tying together many local performing artists. Rinsuke's son, for example, is the leader of an internationally recognized music group, Rinken Band, instrumental in bringing a form of dancing called *kachâshi* to club scenes in London. Two male vocalists of the band used to be members of the theatrical group, Shochiku Kagekidan, on which I will elaborate in the following section.

The center of these creative musical and theatrical activities is Koza, a town of 50,000 people who have thrived on the economy of Kadena Air Force Base since 1945. Koza is distinct from Naha, the largest city in Okinawa Prefecture: Koza is a provincial town, while Naha is the political and economic center for the prefecture. The people of Koza, however, often regard themselves as purveyors of Okinawan culture, whereas they see the people of Naha as "Japanized" [*hondoka*]: "Naha is a smaller Tokyo," some Koza residents state flatly.

This valorization of Koza is not derived from a simple association of the countryside with "timeless tradition" and the city with the decay of such tradition. The relationship between these two cities is too complex to allow for such a simple dichotomy. For example, some people of Naha (and more precisely, Shuri) appropriate the city's historicity (as the seat of Ryukyu kingdom) as symbolic capital for the assertion of their purity, originality, and authenticity. But, to the people of Koza, Okinawa cannot be defined historically with reference to the legacy of Ryukyu kingdom alone because, although such a definition may effectively resist the hegemony of mainland Japan over Okinawa, it marginalizes Koza's inhabitants in relation to those of Naha (and more precisely, Shuri).

This qualification is important because in November 1991, the Shuri castle—the symbol of the Ryukyu kingdom's power and glory—was reconstructed and used as a main site for a television drama, *Ryûkyû no Kaze* [The Wind of Ryukyus]: *Dragon Spirit* (broadcast on NHK every Sunday for six months in 1993). Discourses on Okinawa in terms of this historical representation have been dominant in mass media throughout Japan. But many contemporary Okinawans either remain indifferent to this historical symbol or critical of it because it is, to many, a reminder of social hierarchy within the Ryukyu kingdom (Ota, 1993, 401). For this and other reasons, the television show had one of the lowest ratings in Okinawa Prefecture from among a series of shows of this kind produced by NHK since 1972. It is against this background that the activities of a theatrical group, Shôchiku Kagekidan, must be considered.

Shôchiku Kagekidan *(Creating Laughter in Radical Ways)*

Shôchiku Kagekidan (笑築過激団) written in Chinese script) has produced various shows on the local television network (RBC) as well as live stage performances since its formation in 1983.[10] Shôchiku's most popular television show is called *Owarai pôpô* (now renamed *Dêji owarai pôpô*), which has been broadcast on RBC since 1991. The main part of the show consists of short stand-up comedies (conte), a form that is alien to the long theatrical tradition of Okinawa. Prior to producing a series of Owarai pôpô, the group's main format was more in line with "traditional" stage performances of *Uchinâshibai* (Okinawan theater). The group consciously adopted the conte form from television shows produced in mainland Japan and broadcast in Okinawa. Even in June 1993, TV comedy shows produced in mainland Japan had the highest popularity rating in a survey conducted by one of the local newspapers (*Ryukyu Shinpô*).[11] Thus, Shôchiku, once a consumer of television comedy shows, became a producer of comedy shows for local consumption.

The founder of Shôchiku, Tamaki Mitsuru, was born in Koza in 1958. He remembers his primary school days when a student was punished if he or she spoke in a local dialect: a teacher gave the errant student a card (*hôgenfuda*) with the words, "A Dialect Spoken," written on it. This student, in turn, was supposed to catch another student for speaking in a local dialect. Students who accumulated more than three such cards had to participate in cleaning their classroom for that day. However, when Mitsuru went to a high school in Kumamoto, Kyushu (part of mainland Japan), he heard local students speaking in a Kumamoto dialect and realized that it was all right for some people to speak their own dialect. He often wondered why this was not the case in Okinawa.

Dropping out of college to become an actor, Mitsuru joined a performing art group in Tokyo; however, he was told that he would never have a role unless he could speak flawless standard Japanese. He returned to Okinawa to join an Okinawan theater group. Since the group performed traditional Okinawan plays with historical themes, performances were strictly in the Okinawan (Shuri) dialect. Not accustomed to speaking in any "pure" dialect, he had to learn Shuri almost as a foreign language. By then, the young Okinawan spoke in a mixture of standard Japanese and various local dialects, the linguistic form called *Uchinâ Yamatoguchi*. He also knew that no more than 20 percent of his peers could understand such a "proper" Okinawan dialect, and he wanted to perform on stage in the Uchinâ Yamatoguchi, which most young people his age could understand.

Despite such adaptation, Tamaki Mitsuru appreciates a continuity from Okinawan traditional theater. In his productions, performers are allowed to improvise as they please, a feature of traditional theater in Okinawa. His group performs with traditional Okinawan theater groups. The most recent production was *Tobiasato* (Flying Asato), a story of a legendary Okinawan man, Asato Shûshô, who tried to fly in defiance of the kingdom's prohibition on flying, which was thought to defile the power of the sky deity. The act immediately translated as a crime against the kingdom's power to control the supernatural realm.

From the perspective of Okinawan purists, Mitsuru's shows represent the decaying of Ryukyuan culture, a degradation of the timeless authentic Ryukyuan tradition that is embodied in dialects, traditional dances, and classical Ryukyuan songs. But from the perspective of upwardly mobile, education-conscious parents, his shows represent aspects of the Okinawan lifestyle they want their children to overcome; they do not want to expose their children to such "backward" aspects of their own society. These two criticisms against Mitsuru's group's performances reiterate two versions of social movements that existed earlier.

While television disseminates information produced in mainland Japan to Okinawa and contributes to replacing local, heterogeneous perspectives with a more homogeneous one, Shochiku's limited exploitation of the television network has enabled him to present a view of Okinawan culture that is different from the view that it is waning and decaying. In Tamaki Mitsuru's words:

> What I have been doing is mostly conte, and people usually view our performances as nothing serious, just for fun, even if sometimes I think we are making a serious commentary on something. It is my ultimate dream to deliver evening news in Uchinâ Yamatoguchi. What I wanted to do is to recover the potential of media in Okinawa from the dominance of Japanese [*Yamato*] television networks. It is "high jack the media" (*mediajakku*) that I wanted to do (Interview, 1993).

His theater performs locally in high schools throughout the Okinawa Prefecture and nationally, traveling to large cities in mainland Japan such as Osaka and Tokyo. He appears frequently on local television talk shows, discussing his view of Okinawan culture and his theatrical activities. Mitsuru started performing as a comedian at private occasions like weddings and "birth year" (*shônenyui*) parties. His breakthrough came when he was given a chance to perform in Janjan, a famous theater in Naha. In 1981, he formed a theatrical production, but some members left the group and each now pursues a solo career. Together with them, Mitsuru envisions disseminating his understanding of Okinawan culture through the entertainment industry.

Presented below are transliterated texts to show examples of Shôchiku's performances. The first short piece is called *Zoo*. (The Best of *Owarai pôpô*, vol. 2). The scene presents a conversation between an Okinawan zookeeper and a young helper from mainland Japan:

> "Hello, chief. I brought a lion," said the young man from mainland Japan.
> "OK. (Take it) 'over here, over here' [*kumakai, kumakai*]."
> "Well, now a 'bear' [*kuma*]," (kuma means bear in Japanese).
> "Chief, here is a bear."
> "OK, over there, over there [*ama, ama*]," says the chief, without looking up.
> "Well, well. Now he wants me to bring a horse," the young man misunderstands ama for *uma*, "horse."
> "Here is a horse."
> Surprised, the chief says, "What have you been doing? Where is a lion?"

This conte presupposes the power difference implicit in the conversations between a Japanese mainlander and a local person. As discussed before, a linguistic performance marks Okinawan people in their dealings with the mainland Japanese.[12] Since 1879, when the Ryukyu kingdom was annexed to Japan, the policy of the Japanese government has been to eradicate regional dialects: in Okinawa, through elementary and secondary education, students are taught to devalue their dialects in favor of standard Japanese, the language spoken in the center of economic and political power. As a consequence, many young Okinawans can no longer speak dialects, although they can still comprehend them. Moreover, their speech patterns are highly creolized in Uchinâ Yamatoguchi, a mixture between Okinawan dialects and the standard Japanese. Middle-aged Okinawans, who could command dialects more freely, speak disparagingly of this linguistic mixture, while others bemoan the fact that the youth are yet unable to speak proper Japanese. It is these two hegemonic discourses that position young Okinawans on the margins of their own society and that Shôchiku Kagekidan's short comedies struggle against. Their strategy is to create a person who could take advantage of the highly creolized culture of Okinawa, from whose position the two hegemonic discourses are subverted, if only for a moment, by the power of carnivalesque laughter (cf. Jenkins, 1994).

In *Zoo*, the butt of the joke is someone who could not understand the dialect. Inscribed in the daily lives of young people is the hegemony of the mainland Japan, while that hegemony is relativized by the Okinawan who is also able to comprehend standard Japanese. The young Okinawan, like Said's (1990, 366) "exile," cultivates a plurality of vision. In addition, young Okinawans are marginalized in their own society through a discourse of traditional Okinawan culture in which they are said to be influenced too much by the mass culture of mainland Japan. This kind of discourse on authenticity is also the target of Shôchiku's production. Let us consider a piece called *yâsan [yakuza]* (The Best of *Owarai pôpô*, vol. 2):

> A gang passes on the street a man from mainland Japan. Bumped into the shoulder,
> "My, my [*akijamiyô*]," says the gangster.
> "You . . . are 'you a gangster' [*otaku yâsan*]?" (This is an expression in standard Japanese).
> "I am full. I've just finished eating a lot of sashimi [*namasuba châkami watamicchon*]."

While in colloquial expression, yâsan means a yakuza (street gang) in standard Japanese, the same sound also means hungry in the dialect. In the dialect, a street gang is called *ashibâ*. If a viewer did not know vernacular speech, the point would be missed completely; such a viewer may be out of touch with colloquial Japanese expressions, perhaps someone who understands the dialect alone. The privileged one in this case, even more clearly than in the earlier example, is the one who occupies the creolized linguistic position.

Shôchiku Kagekidan sometimes deals with even more complicated subject positions, representing experiences of local people living around the Kadena Air Force Base, the largest U.S. military base in the Far East. These people must negotiate standard Japanese, the regional dialect, and English. Below is a conte, *Uchinâ Eigo Kôza* [Okinawa English Lesson], based on a current social condition of Koza:

Kamadû: "Hey, good morning, *Hancho*.[13] My name is . . . Mike *Choison* [Tyson?]"

    Jirâ: "Oh, my name is Sakkâ Hanson [a name of professional wrestler?]"

    Kamadû: "Yes, from today, both of us are classmates, right, but you are sitting on my chair" [spoken in an Okinawan dialect, but with an intonation simulating English].

    Jirâ: "Oh, a wrong seat? . . . Oh, sorry, sorry."

    Kamadû: "Oh, the bell is ringing. A teacher will come soon. . . . OK, now he is coming."

    "Stand up. Bow."

    Teacher: "All right. Hello (*Chûya mabirâ*), everyone. Let's open to page 32."

    Jirâ: "*Naberâ* [gourd]?"

    Teacher: "This is a pen [spoken in English]. Kamadû, how do you say it in an Okinawan dialect?"

    Kamadû: "Oh, [in an] *uchinâ* language, '*kurepenyaibî*'."

    Teacher: "Good. Next, Jirâ . . . What is this? Say it in a dialect."

    Jirâ: "*Kure nûyaibîgatai.*"

    Teacher: "No, since you are male, not *tai*, but *sai*. Like a rhinoceros [*sai*] in Africa."

    "OK, now Kamadû. Stand up, please [spoken in English]"

    Kamadû: "Yes, Kamadû."

    Teacher: "Yes, Kamadû?"

    Kamadû: "Oh, teacher, it's a joke. My name is Kamadû. Yes, I do [spoken in English], they rhyme well [*goro nicchon*]."

    Teacher: "OK, now I see. . . . 'Oh, my God,' how do you say it in a dialect?"

    Kamadû: "'Oh, my God,' in a dialect . . . *Akisamiyô*."

    Teacher: "Very good. You are very good. How about, 'Fuck you'?"

    Kamadû: "Oh, 'Fuck you' . . . *Yanawarabâ* [a bad child], *sarissayâ*"

    Teacher: "Very Good. Sit down. Next, Jirâ. Stand up, please."

    Jirâ: "Yes, Jirâ."

Teacher: "What? Why?"

Jirâ: "Yes, Kamadû, OK? Yes, Jirâ."

Teacher: "Oh, no."

Kamadû: "Hey, hey. In my case, my name is Kamadû. Yes, I do. They rhyme well. Your name is Jirâ. Yes, I do. Yes Jirâ. They don't rhyme at all."

Teacher: "Did you get it now? OK, Jirâ, 'Kill you.' How do you say it in a dialect?"

Jirâ: "OK, in a dialect . . . 'Yanawarabâ, takkumisaresayâ, koroshi-teshimisaniyâ' [the latter half of what he says is meaningless]."

Teacher: "No. Look [at] me. Eye is [sic] open. Teeth, mm. Shinasarissayâ."

Jirâ: "Shimisamashiniyâ." [trying to imitate the grimace of the teacher].

Teacher: "You are a stupid man [tottorô]!" [as he hits Jirâ on the head].

Jirâ: "Shinisarindô!"

Teacher: "Oh, that's the way to say it. A nice accent."

Jirâ: "Shimisamashiniyâ"

Teacher: "Again, like that. You are a really stupid man [tottorô]."

Jirâ: "Tottorô?"

Kamadû: "Tottorô, a nice man, same, same [tottorô means 'nice man']."

Jirâ: "Oh, thank you, teacher."

Teacher: "OK, next. Do you know Rinken Band? This is one of their songs. It goes, 'Nîsêtâ, Mâkaiga/Wattâ Tanmê Kêîtî/Hijâjû Usagigâ' [Young men, where are you going?/Because my grandfather is drunk/I am taking him a bowl of goat soup]."

Jirâ and Kamadû: "Yes, We know that song."

Teacher: "Hijâjû, Usagigâ, translate that into English."

Jirâ: "Oh, pantomime, OK? Yagi [goat] soup, rabbit. . . ."

Teacher: "Rabbit? Why, rabbit?"

Kamadû: "Oh, teacher, sir, probably, usagi, rabbit [in a standard Japanese, usagi means rabbit]."

Teacher: "Again, you are very stupid. A fool you are. Rabbit? Now, Kamadû, show him a model of being a good student."

Kamadû: "[singing] I take [a bowl of] yagi soup."

Teacher: "Oh, you are very good. Very good. There goes a bell. That's it for today."

Kamadû: "Stand up. Bow."

This conte favors the viewer who can migrate between three linguistically constituted subject positions: the first position is that of English, the second of standard Japanese, and the third of a mixture of Okinawan dialect and standard Japanese [Uchinâ Yamatoguchi]. But English spoken in this conte is very transparent in that it does not call for much knowledge of the language beyond that shared by young people. Moreover, most of the dialogues among the three are conducted in an inflected Uchinâ Yamatoguchi, the lingua franca of young Okinawans. By favoring the speaker of this linguistic form, it is Jirâ, who has an inadequate understanding of it, who is marginalized.[14] Since Jirâ is obviously not an American soldier, his incompetence is easily attributable to the dominant Other in Okinawan society. His persona becomes a metaphor for someone from mainland Japan rather than for the American soldier he was supposed to represent.

I would like to call attention to here ethnic stereotyping. Fujiki Hayato, the actor playing Jirâ, said: "My mother owned an electric appliance store right next to the gate of the Kadena base. Each weekend many soldiers lined up in front of the store to buy radio cassettes. One day I was with my mother at the store, when this 'black' man came up to the front of the line and started dancing as he held the radio cassette on his shoulder. This image I recalled when I played that part." Thus, Fujiki relied on his own memory rather than on ethnic stereotypes to create a concrete image embodied in Jirâ.[15]

In the first half of the conte, both Kamadû and Jirâ creatively translate elementary English expressions such as "This is a pen" and "What is this?" into Uchinâ Yamatoguchi. Every schoolchild in Japan steps into the world of English as they learn expressions such as these. At school, where standard Japanese is the medium of instruction, these expressions are never translated into Uchinâ Yamatoguchi. For example, "This is a pen" and "What is this?" are rendered directly into the kind of "language" (dialect), the young people are accustomed to hearing and using. "Oh, my God" and "Fuck you"—perhaps expletives they hear from GIs in Koza—are not translated literally, but they are made to correspond creatively to expressions already existing in the dialect: *Akisamiyô* is an interjection, whereas *Yanawarabâ* is a common phrase for scolding and intimidating a child.

Translating English expressions into the language that constitutes their everyday experiences (without intervention of the language that normally marginalizes them) opens up the possibility for relativizing, if just for a moment, the power relationship inscribed in linguistic interactions: their lingua franca, Uchiniâ Yamatoguchi, is no less appropriate than standard Japanese as a medium of translation. Viewers' laughter is a testimony that these translations are creative means to reconceptualize their distance from standard Japanese.

The success of the latter part of the conte depends on parodying this power relationship by which the young Okinawan people are constituted as speaking individuals. For example, Jirâ does not understand the meaning of the expression tottorô. Since it is in Uchinâ Yamatoguchi, someone who cannot comprehend it is excluded; in this context, that person cannot be the GI whose role Jirâ is supposed to play. Thus, it is more natural to see Jirâ as a metaphor for the Japanese mainlander since he cannot translate properly usagigâ and since he rendered it as rabbit. In fact, usagi in standard Japanese means rabbit. In contrast to Jirâ, Kamadû occupies the position homologous to that of the young Okinawans who can migrate between different linguistically constituted positions.

For the young Okinawans, speaking either in Uchinâ Yamatoguchi or in standard Japanese signifies acceptance of a world already constituted by social meanings that sometimes disempower them. While speaking in Uchinâ Yamatoguchi immediately marks them as distinct from the mainland Japanese (because of its "alterity"), speaking in standard Japanese also marginalizes them in their linguistic interactions with Japanese mainlanders because of their "imperfect" use of the language. In other words, they are different because they speak a dialect hardly comprehensible, and they are inferior because they speak imperfectly (cf. Tsing, 1993, 26). These experiences of exclusion are even more exacerbated by a nativist discourse on the need to preserve authentic Okinawan culture and by a modernist discourse on the need to Japanize.

Only recently, with the addition of two female members to his crew—Kohatsu Yayoi and Kishaba Izumi—has Tamaki Mitsuru begun producing conte on gender differences in Okinawa. His relatively recent undertaking of this social issue is rather surprising because a discourse on Okinawan culture often highlights femaleness as its distinctive characteristic: for example, the spiritual predominance of the "sister" (unari) is well known among folklorists and anthropologists and females possess the power to bless the household head. I have not yet seen any conte addressing gender ideology in Okinawa, as it crosses the field of social marginality discussed to date.

Discourse on Okinawan tradition is gendered, like colonial discourse in India and other places. A recent feminist critic, Horiba Kiyoko (1990, 57), interprets a social movement after World War II to abolish the practice of "bone-washing" (senkotsu)—the removal of flesh from bones of the deceased at the end of the seventh year after burial—as a movement to liberate women from men. In her analysis, men assigned to women a job that nobody likes to do, in the name of tradition; therefore, a discourse of modernity is in complex ways intertwined with a struggle between men and women. Tamaki's theatrical group has not yet addressed this issue.

The popularity of Owarai pôpô must be examined in light of the processes of marginalization that young Okinawans experience daily. To do so, I present interviews conducted with high school students in Urasoe, Okinawa Prefecture.

Popularity of Owarai Pôpô among the Youth in Okinawa

Owarai pôpô has been on the air every Friday night (0:45 a.m. to 1:20 a.m., RBC network) since 1991, and it has been one of the most popular programs among high school students in Okinawa.[16] The result of my questionnaire from students at Urasoe Commercial High School in Okinawa indicates that they like the show very much because: (1) the show uses many dialects that they understand (Uchinâ Yamatoguchi); (2) the show is based on familiar things and events that they feel close to; (3) the show is full of conte that can be appreciated only by young Okinawans and this makes them feel superior to someone who couldn't understand these jokes; and (4) the show reflects the "true" Okinawa [in the eyes of the students]. One student said:

> I did not watch *Ryûkyû no Kaze*, because I did not like it. It was about the past; I am not that interested in a history of Okinawa. Pôpô is fun. I watch with my brothers, if they are around, and sometimes with my friends. They use the language we speak at school, and I feel close to the show; I can relate to their show.

Another student continues:

> *Ryûkyû no Kaze* does not look real; it does not feel like it is taking place in Okinawa. . . . In Pôpô I find out more about Okinawa, something like "Okinawanness" (*Okinawarashisa*), even if sometimes the show is nothing but inside jokes. I do not think the people from mainland Japan understand these jokes. That's why I like this show.

High school students seem to consume the Owarai pôpô as part of a process of understanding their own lives in contemporary Okinawan society.[17] They watch it neither to gain information nor to enjoy dramatic development; they watch it because they want to laugh at the conditions in which they find themselves since, "laughter . . . constitutes a special perspective on experience" (Stam, 1989, 87). In other words, they learn to interpret their daily experiences of being caught in hegemonic relations through the comic perspective of the show, a perspective reserved specially for (sub-)culturally hybrid beings.

As I have noted, all the conte in Owarai pôpô are conducted in the highly creolized Uchinâ Yamatoguchi, the lingua franca of the young people of Okinawa. They also use it to communicate with others outside their circle; however, using it brings the speaker into a certain social relationship vis-à-vis the community of speakers of dialects much more grammatically rigid than Uchinâ Yamatoguchi and of speakers of standard Japanese. These two communities are hegemonic over young people, so their lives are saturated with power-laden relationships as soon as they begin speaking. Such relationships are not seamless, but are ruptured. Shôchiku's television shows offer a model of understanding these relationships by actively constructing a series of conte based on these ruptures in the hegemonic relations that subsume Okinawan daily lives; viewers appropriate such a model for interpreting their experiences in a subversive way. In other words, viewers feel privileged to laugh at social conditions that in their daily lives only disempower them. Laughing at representations of these conditions is a means to affirm their own hybrid identities not in terms of loss, decay, or corruption, but in terms of multiplicity appropriate for the current condition in Okinawan society.

Tamaki Mitsuru and his wife Tazuko receive many fan letters and apparently read them carefully, for sometimes they incorporate responses in their theatrical productions: in fact, Tamaki Mitsuru asked me if it was all right for me to develop a conte out of my own involvement with the group. He found it flattering as well as comic that someone would take a scholarly interest in his activities. Although I need to investigate further, I suspect that the interaction between viewers and his theatrical group is an important perspective on Shôchiku's television output.

Tamaki's effort to represent Okinawanness as products of negotiations and interpretations of encounters between Okinawans and the Japanese is important because he consciously resists various discourses of modernity and tradition. His aesthetic is popular not only in the sense that it is mass entertainment, but also in the more critical sense of opposing dominant discourses that disempower youth (cf. Bennett 1986). His popular representation is hybrid in terms of the language (Uchinâ Yamatoguchi) it uses as well as the medium (conte) in which it is performed.

This sort of hybridity is characteristic of postcolonial "contact zones" (as Prat calls them), where unified, rigid, and monolithic representations of Self and Other are displaced by more permeable visions and identities, those produced in processes of making due and bricolage. Certainly, I do not want to ignore the violent and damaging quality of social and cultural intrusion from mainland Japan. But I want to emphasize that in politically and economically marginal places such as Okinawa, it is common to find the appropriation of cultural elements and forces from the dominant—a process of "cultural reconversion" as García Canclini (1992) defines the terms for the Latin American case.

In the margins, the already lost and therefore unrecoverable, is the experience of the whole, as Ivy (1995) has recently observed of Japanese cultural representations. Thus, there can be no holistic Okinawan experience even in the margins where anthropologists and folklorists have tended to fantasize a traditional culture thriving in pure form. But out of this fragmentation, is the sense of Okinawanness is created anew, as evidenced in, for instance, a local production of Owarai pôpô and enthusiastic responses to it by young viewers.

I am drawn to Shôchi Ku's theatrical activities not only because they challenged the often-assumed concept of culture as a bounded, integrated entity, but also because I see in their activities the importance of the role of culture in political change. García Canclini (1995, 261) nicely summarizes this point, writing about Mexican culture:

> When we do not succeed in changing whoever governs, we satirize him or her in Carnival dances, journalistic humor, and graffiti. Against the impossibility of constructing a different order, we establish masked challenges in myths, literature, and comic strips. The struggle between classes or ethnic groups is, most of the time, a metaphorical struggle. Sometimes, starting from metaphor, new transformative practices slowly or unexpectedly invade the picture.

Conclusion

I have discussed the identities of young Okinawans more as a process or articulation rather than as a reflection of a fixed essence. In other words, such identities must be definable in relation not only to the dominant Other, non-Okinawans, which emerges in a discourse of modernity, but also to the dominant Other internal to Okinawan society, the pure Okinawan of nativistic discourse. In discussing the notion of chanpurû, or mixing, for example, I have stressed its power to destabilize both discourses—that of modernity and that of nativism—and cultivate a third space from which to articulate identities meaningful for the youth.

There is a potential in some of Tamaki Mitsuru's talks to view such a process as itself fixed, a hermeneutically sealed quality of the area of Koza—an indication that his discourse of Okinawan culture may become localized. But there are new patterns of political articulation emergent in Okinawa. In the summer of 1993, Okinawan musician Kina Shôkichi organized the *Nirai Kanai Matsuri* (Message for the Earth, original in English), a four-day festival: Nirai Kanai refers to the imaginary island of spiritual and material abundance in Ryukyuan mythology. In addition to a variety of musical events, the main part of this festival consisted of a series of panel discussions on the present conditions of indigenous peoples in the world. Kina and his organizers invited Denis Banks, a leader in AIM, and representatives from the Australian Aboriginal people, the Maori, the Ainu, and the Ami (from Taiwan), among others. On one of the panels at the festival, the Ainu, the Korean Japanese, and the Okinawans discussed their experiences of marginalization in Japanese society (cf. Sjöberg, 1993).

The combination of political interests among the three groups has never been articulated; I think this is rather surprising, even if one takes the element of "hype" (since 1993 was "the International Year of the World's Indigenous Peoples") into consideration. As the indigenous people of Hokkaido, a land that began to be colonized about the same time that the Ryukyu kingdom was annexed to Japan, the Ainu have been much more visible in Okinawan media than ever: some still continue resurrecting a claim that both the Ainu and the Okinawans are "lost brothers and sisters" because of the similarities in their physical appearance.[18] During the 1920s and 1930s, when the *seikatsu kaizen-undo* ["betterment of lifestyle movement"] was a major social movement for the Okinawans in Osaka, the movement carefully avoided any reference to and comparison with other minority groups in Japan. In fact, many Okinawans were then convinced that they were different from the Ainu, the "backward" people of Hokkaido: in many letters, Okinawan people criticized the Anthropological Exhibit at the Fifth Domestic Industrial Fair, where both the Ryukyuans and the Ainu were displayed, but showed little sympathy for the Ainu. Now, the pendulum has started swinging in the opposite direction.

This new articulation of political affiliation between the Ainu and Okinawans is also evident in a comparison, made by Ainu and Okinawan speakers, between two cultural ethos: *ureshipa moshiri* (a life in harmony with nature) among the Ainu, and *ichariba chôdê* (those we meet are all brothers) among Okinawans. These ethos are presented in contrast with those considered to be dominant in Japan at large: a neglect for natural conservation in favor of industrialism, an indulgence in materialism and an ignorance for those who are historically marginalized. In short, Ainu and Okinawan spokespersons articulated their mutual interests together, perhaps for the first time in history, against the dominant Other, the Japanese, using a discourse of environmentalism, spiritualism, and multiculturalism. Moreover, their presentations of Ainu and Okinawan selves are transnationally configured in global cultural networks of native peoples. A festival such as Nirai Kanai Matsuri is an example of newly emerging alliances among the native peoples of the world with the possibilities for further transnational cooperation (Ginsburg, 1994, 378).

Okinawans, like other Japanese mainlanders from Wakayama Prefecture, Hiroshima Prefecture, and Kumamoto Prefecture, have emigrated all over the world since the early part of this century: Hawaii, islands in Micronesia, and countries in South America including Brazil, Argentinia, Bolivia, and Peru. Now, these emigrants' children and grandchildren are coming back, either temporarily or permanently, to Okinawa (and other parts of Japan wherever jobs are available) to take advantage of Japan's booming economy.[19] Alberto Shiroma (from Peru) is one such person. He has been active in the musical scene in

Koza, and formed a Latin rock group, Diamantes. Their song, "Ganbateando," whose title itself is highly syncretic, is about the very difficult life of "guest workers" in Japan. The song became a hit in 1993, supported by many Okinawan youth.[20] I do not suggest that the support for this song has come solely from sympathy that they feel for guest workers. But, in contrast to mainland Japan where there are often feelings that guest workers will cause an erosion of authentic Japanese culture (already mixed and pluralized), Koza is a place where it is appropriate for such a song to win support.

As Shochiku's television shows and these more recent examples show, popular culture forms—theater and music, in particular—have been important sources for articulating Okinawan identity as mixing (chanpurû). As Gilroy (1993, 99) suggests, the strength of the concept of diaspora is its power to resist binary opposition between "folk cultural authenticity and pop cultural inauthenticity"; the concept of mixing dislocates these distinctions. As much as the question of what constitutes authentic black music/culture is a bitterly contested issue, the same question has also arisen in discourse on Okinawan music/culture. In this process of articulating cultural differences, an invocation of authentic Okinawan tradition bestows only a partial identification. From the perspective of the marginalized youth, their engagement with Okinawan society becomes "performative"; that is, representations of their cultural differences undermine the notion that cultural mobilization always needs to invoke the authentic Okinawan tradition. Bhabha's (1994, 2) following comment applies well to the Okinawan case: "The borderline engagements of cultural difference may as often be consensual as conflictual; they may confound our definitions of tradition and modernity; realign the customary boundaries between the private and the public, high and low; and challenge normative expectations of development and progress."

Thus, in a time of rapid social transformation, discourses of the narrative of originality and authentic subjectivity become theoretically and politically important for those who want to theorize a process and means of struggle and resistance on the margins of society.

Notes

I thank the founder of Shôchiku Kagekidan, Tamaki Mitsuru, his wife, and manager, Tamaki Tazuko, for their hospitality when I visited their home on 13 October 1993, to discuss a paper (in Japanese), "Hybrid Representations: Television and Popular Culture in Okinawa."

I am also grateful that they sent me many video tapes of their stage performances; their insights and comments are incorporated into this paper. My thanks also to Mr. Tôme Mitsumasa, who helped me with a questionnaire distributed among the students of Urasoe Commercial High School. I presented a shorter version of this essay, "Production and Reception of Hybrid Representations: Media and Formation of Local Identity in Ryukyuan Popular Culture," at the 92nd annual meeting of the American Anthropological Association, Washington, D.C., 17–21 November 1994. I have benefited from all the comments made about the paper during the conference; in particular, I thank Professors Richard Fox, Orin Starn, and Faye Ginsburg for their concrete suggestions for revision of this paper.

1. In this paper, I use the term "Ryukyu" and its adjective "Ryukyuan" in reference to a group of islands under the control of the Ryukyu kingdom until annexation by Japan in 1879. After that, islands south of Okinawa main (is)land in the Ryukyus were included in Okinawa Prefecture. Thus, I use the term "Okinawa" in reference to these islands after that date. The people of Okinawa main (is)land call their island *uchina*, which was rendered in Chinese characters (沖縄) as pronounced as Okinawa in Japanese.

2. Clearly, domestic industrial fairs in Japan, held eight times from 1877 to 1922, were versions of the world fair transplanted to the domestic context (Yoshimi, 1992, 126). The Louisiana Purchase Exposition in St. Louis, Missouri, 1904, brought indigenous people under the surveillance of an empire's gaze (Rydell, 1984). In addition, letters sent to the editors of the newspapers in Okinawa seldom showed sympathy for the Ainu, who were also objects of the imperial gaze at these so-called exhibitions. Until recently, various social movements in Okinawa characteristically have not consolidated their efforts to unite with those in other parts of Japan.

3. Complex historical as well as economic factors were involved in the changes of the characters of "betterment of lifestyle movement" for the Okinawans. One factor may be an enormous expansion of Okinawan communities in the Osaka area and the increase of friction between the Japanese residents, for what were urged to be changed were only those aspects that could become problematical in living among the Japanese (Tomiyama, 1989, 230).

4. G. P. Murdock is one of the three anthropologists from Yale University involved in authoring this work. Anthropology is deeply implicated in the governing of the Ryukyu islands: the American military government fully exploited the interpretation that Okinawans belong to a minority group. On the one hand, this encouraged ostensive signs of separation from Japan; on the other hand, it discouraged any signs of reunification with Japan. So, from the point of view of the American military government, raising the Japanese flag was considered a sign of resistance to its presence and rule in Okinawa. In 1987, burning the Japanese flag meant an act of defiance to the political marginalization experienced by the Okinawans (cf. Field, 1993).

5. The military government in Okinawa denied opening a Japanese literature department at University of Ryukyu. It also suggested rewriting all the textbooks used for primary and secondary education in "Ryukyuan dialects" (Miyagi Etsujirô, 1982, 240).

6. Kina Shôkichi, a musician born in Koza in 1948, is well known in the "world music market." In 1970, he named his back-up band Champluse (pronounced *chanpuruzu*). His song, *Hana* (flower) has been recorded in thirteen different languages, most recently in Malagasy (sung by Tarika Sammy, in "A World Out of Time," Shanachie 64041). His musical connections are not restricted to local associations, but extend

to such notables as Ry Cooder and François Breant, a producer of Salif Keita's highly acclaimed work, *Kô-yàn* (Island CCD 9836).

7. Nearly 200,000 people (94,000 Okinawan civilians, 94,000 Japanese soldiers, and 12,000 American soldiers) died in the battle of Okinawa, from April to June 1945. One of every four Okinawans died in this battle.

8. Rinsuke's legendary figure is well preserved in *Untamagirû* (a film directed by Takamine Go, 1989). This film was awarded a special prize at the 12th Film Festival of the Three Continents, held in Nantes, France, December 1989.

9. In Koza, I heard an elderly woman in a restaurant, saying "*Nêsan, aisuwârâchôdai*" [Miss, please give a glass of iced water]. Her pronunciation, clearly different from a Japanese vernacular expression, "*wôtâ*," indicates that this expression came directly into Okinawan dialects through contacts with the Americans at the military base.

10. The name of this group, Shochiku Kagekidan, is a parody of the more famous Shôchiku Kagekidan, written with entirely different Chinese characters; this latter group is a musical unit from mainland Japan (*yamato*).

11. According to a survey conducted by a local newspaper (*Ryukyu Shinpô*, 8 June 1993), the three most popular programs are shows of conte, whose ratings were as high as 45.5 percent.

12. Dialects spoken within Okinawa Prefecture are also quite diverse; these are as different from standard Japanese as French is from Italian (Lebra, 1966, 8).

13. The expression, "Hanchô," belongs to the biographical context of Tamaki Mitsuru's father. Right after World War II, his father was hailed by a GI, "hey, *hanchô*," meaning "boy"; however, his father thought it meant "a leader of a group," and thus interpreted as a compliment.

14. In fact, it is very difficult to decipher identities of both Jirâ and Kamadû. They appear to be acting the parts of American GIs learning an Okinawan dialect; Jirâ enacts a rather stereotypic image of an African American, listening to a radio/cassette player ("boombox") held on the shoulder. But Jirâ seems to have already acquired, almost as a habit, necessary responses in the dialect, as he reacts to the teacher's blow in a style that only a local person could possess. I spoke to Tamaki Mitsuru about this confusion of identities presented for the viewer. His response was: "When I was young, I knew this black soldier on the base, who could speak the dialect very well. I thought it interesting to depict how the Americans may learn the dialect. But, when Fujiki Hayato (Jirâ) and Gakiya Yoshimitsu (Kamadû) started practicing this conte, they also improvised a lot, and the end result is what you saw."

15. A discussion of ethnic stereotyping in Okinawa is beyond the scope of this paper. Nonetheless, it is necessary to closely examine and contextualize local experiences under the military government; in anthropological discussions an uncategorical, totalizing treatment of this issue in Japan is often proposed (e.g., Russell, 1991). Such discussions certainly alert the reader to more obvious stereotyping in Japanese mass media, but obscure various ways in which these stereotypes are articulated with social practices of empowerment in marginal areas of Japan such as Okinawa.

16. I distributed sixty questionnaires to students at the Urasoe Commercial High School. According to the results, 90 percent of the students are watching *Dêji Owarai pôpô*. Since the fall of 1992, Shôchiku has been visiting high schools in Okinawa Prefecture

and performing for students. I distributed the questionnaire at Urasoe Commercial High School a week before Shôchiku's first visit there.

17. In the near future, I plan to examine more thoroughly the consumption of the shows among the young (high school students).

18. As Kato Sango, one of the pioneers of Ryukyuan studies wrote in 1988, "the indigenous people of the Ryukyu islands are descendants of Ainu; this fact has been already proved not only by the evidence from archaeological excavation of *utaki* ["sacred places"] but also by similar place names existing in Hokkaido and the Ryukyus" (1975[1888], 29). There are many popular writings on this theme.

19. Descendents of Japanese emigrants are allowed to work legally; therefore, many workers came to Japan from Brazil and other countries that had a significant presence of Japanese emigrants to work mostly at blue-collar jobs that domestic laborers tend to avoid. The total number of workers from South America is estimated to be around 200,000 (Kuwahara, 1991, 89).

20. The following are the Spanish lyrics for "Ganbateando" (by Alberto Shiroma):

Era una noche oscura, ya nadie va caminado
Está con sus dos maletas, el DC-10 esperando
Con sueños e ilusiones, y una deuda pendiente
Ramón se va a trabajar al pais del sol naciente

Aqui lo que más le cuesta, es poder comunicarse
Entre tanta indiferencia, difícil es aguantarse
Aparte de la rutina, interminable y pesada
Hay gente que discrimina, y lo provoca por nada
Para matar la tristeza, que tiene en su corazón
Por la família que espera "Ganbatteando" va Ramón

(Chorus): "Ganbateando" sí, "Ganbateando" va, y seguimos "Ganbateando"

Así comienza la "Chamba," Ocho horas y con "zanyô "
Después de comer a dormir en el "Ryô,"
Y en sueño Ramón canta . . . Salsa!

(Chorus)

References

Anderson, Benedict (1983). *Imagined Communities*. London: Verso.

Arakawa, Akira (1981). *Ryukyu Shobun Igo* (After the Incorporation of Ryukyus into Japan, Vols. 1 and 2). Tokyo: Asahishinbunsha.

Bennett, Tony (1986). Popular Culture and the Return to Gramsce. In *Popular Culture and Social Relations*, ed. T. Bennett, C. Mercer, and J. Woolcott, pp. xi–xix. Philadelphia: Open University Press.

Bhabha, Homi (1990). The Third Space. In *Identity: Community, Culture, Difference*, ed. J. Rutherford, pp. 207–221. London: Lawrence and Wishart.

Bhabha, Homi (1994). *The Location of Culture*. London: Routledge.

de Certeau, Michel (1984). *The Practice of Everyday Life*, trans. S. Rendall. Berkeley: University of California Press.

Field, Norma (1993). *In the Realm of a Dying Emperor*. New York: Vintage Books.

García Canclini, Nestor (1992). Culture and Power: The State of Research. In *Culture and Power*, ed. Nestor García Canclini. Newbury Park, Calif.: Sage Publications.

García Canclini, Nestor (1993). *Transforming Modernity*, trans. Lidia Lozano. Austin: University of Texas Press.

García Canclini, Nestor (1995). *Hybrid Cultures*, trans. Chiappari and S. López. Minneapolis: University of Minnesota Press.

Gilroy, Paul (1993). *The Black Atlantic: Modernity and Double Consciousness*. Cambridge: Harvard University Press.

Ginsburg, Faye (1991). Indigenous Media: Faustian Contract or Global Village? *Cultural Anthropology* 6(1):92–112.

Ginsburg, Faye (1994). Embedded Aesthetics: Creating a Discursive Space for Indigenous Media. *Cultural Anthropology* 9(3):365–382.

Hall, Stuart (1990). Cultural Identity and Diaspora. In *Identity: Community, Culture, Difference*, ed. J. Rutherford, pp. 222–237. London: Lawrence and Wishart.

Horiba, Kiyoko (1990). *Inaguya Nanabachi* (Women Have Seven Sins). Tokyo: Domesu Shuppan.

Ivy, Marilyn (1995). *Discourses of the Vanishing: Modernity, Phantasm, Japan*. Chicago: University of Chicago Press.

Jenkins, Ron (1994). *Subversive Laughter: Liberating Power of Comedy*. New York: Free Press.

Kamiya, Nobuyuki (1990). *Bakuhansei Kokka no Ryukyu Shihai* (Ryukyu Islands under the Control of Tokugawa Regime). Tokyo: Azekura Shobo.

Kato, Sango (1975[1888]). *Ryukyu no Kenkyu* (Studies on the Ryukyu Islands). Tokyo: Miraisha.

Kuwahara, Yasuo (1991). *Kokkyô o Koeru Rôdôsha* (Labourers over the National Boundaries). Tokyo: Iwanami Shoten.

Lebra, William (1966). *Okinawan Religion: Belief, Ritual, and Social Structure*. Honolulu: University of Hawaii Press.

Madden, Kate (1992). Video and Cultural Identity: The Inuit Broadcasting Corporation Experience. In *Mass Media Effects Across Cultures*, ed. F. Korenny and S. Ting-Toomey, pp. 130–149. Newbury Park, Calif.: Sage Publications.

Michaels, Eric (1991). A Model of Teleported Texts (With Reference to Aboriginal Television). *Visual Anthropology* 4:301–322.

Miyagi, Eishô (1982). *Ryukyu Shisha no Edo Nobori* (Emissaries from Ryukyu Kingdom to Edo [Tokyo]). Tokyo: Daiichi Shobo.

Miyagi, Etsujirô (1982). *Senryôsha no Me: Amerikajin wa Okinawa o Doumitaka* (The Occupant's Gaze: How Did Americans View Okinawans?). Naha, Okinawa: Okinawashuppansha.

Miyagi, Etsujiro (1992). *Okinawa Senryo no 27 Nenkan* (27 Years of American Occupation). Tokyo: Iwanami Shoten.

Ota, Yoshinobu (1993). Bunka no Kyakutaika: Kankô wo tôshita Bunka to Aidentiti no Sôzô (Objectification of Culture: The Creation of Culture and Identity in the Tourist World). *Minzokugaku Kenkyu* 57(4):383–410.

Ota, Yoshinobu (n.d.a). Beyond Folklore Studies as Discourse: Politics and Representations of Ryukyu Culture in Japanese Folklore Studies and Tourism. In *Okinawa: Domination and Response at Japan's Periphery*, ed. K. Taira et al. Honolulu: University of Hawaii Press.

Ota, Yoshinobu (n.d.b). Power and Resistance in Tourist Discourse on the Ryukyu Islands: Appropriation of Tourist Representations for Identity Politics of Local Fishermen. In *New Directions of Tourism Studies*, ed. N. Graburn. Osaka: National Ethnological Museum.

Pratt, Mary Louis (1992). *Imperial Eyes: Travel Writing and Transculturation*. London: Routledge.

Russell, John (1991). Race and Reflexivity: The Black Other in Contemporary Japanese Mass Culture. *Cultural Anthropology* 6(1):3–25.

Rydell, Robert (1984). *All the World's a Fair: Visions of Empire at American International Expositions, 1876–1916*. Chicago: University of Chicago Press.

Said, Edward (1990). Reflections on Exile. In *Out There: Marginalization and Contemporary Cultures*, ed. R. Ferguson et al., pp. 357–366. Cambridge: MIT Press.

Sjöberg, Katarina (1993). *The Return of the Ainu: Cultural Mobilization and the Practice of Ethnicity in Japan*. Chur, Switzerland: Harwood.

Stam, Robert (1989). *Subversive Pleasure: Bakhtin, Cultural Criticism, and Film*. Baltimore: Johns Hopkins University Press.

Taussig, Michael (1993). *Mimesis and Alterity*. New York: Routledge.

Teruya, Rinsuke (1992). In *The Man of the Champurû (an interview with Morita Jun'ichi)*, ed. Tenkô Kikaku. Tokyo: Tokyo Shoseki.

Tomiyama, Ichiro (1989). *Kindai Nihonshakai to "Okinawajin"* (Modern Japanese Society and "Okinawans"). Tokyo: Nihonkeizaihyôronsha.

Tsing, Anna Lowenhaupt (1993). *In the Realm of the Diamond Queen*. Princeton: Princeton University Press.

Turner, Terence (1991). Representing, Resisting, Rethinking: Historical Transformations of Kayapo Culture and Anthropological Consciousness. In *Colonial Situations*, ed. G. Stocking, Jr., pp. 285–313. Madison: University of Wisconsin Press.

Turner, Terence (1992). Defiant Images: The Kayapo Appropriation of Video. *Anthropology Today* 8(6):5–16.

Yoshimi, Shunya (1992). *Hakurankai no Seijigaku: Manazashi no Kindai* (Politics of World Fairs: The Gaze of Modernity). Tokyo: Iwanami Shoten.

Ingrid Monson

Abbey Lincoln's
Straight Ahead

Jazz in the Era of the
Civil Rights Movement

Now that Abbey Lincoln has found herself as a Negro, I hope she can find
herself as a militant but less one-sided *American* Negro. It could help her
performance.

Jazz Critic Ira Gitler (Gitler et al., 1962a, 20)

Who knows more about the Negro than the Negro? Everybody else up until
this point has been exploiting the Negro. And the minute the Negro begins
to exploit himself, even if this was so, here comes somebody who says they
shouldn't exploit themselves. But who *should* exploit the Negro? Here's the
point: she has a perfect right to exploit the Negro.

Drummer Max Roach (Gitler et al., 1962a, 21–22)

In November 1961, jazz critic Ira Gitler (1961) published a dismiss-
ive review of Abbey Lincoln's album *Straight Ahead* (Lincoln, 1961) in the pages
of one of the leading jazz magazines, *Down Beat*. He accused the singer of "becoming a professional Negro," covering up poor musicianship with "banal" (i.e.,
political) lyrics, and mistaking propaganda for art (Gitler et al., 1962a). This
remarkable album—featuring compositions and arrangements by Mal Waldron,
Max Roach, Oscar Brown, Thelonious Monk, Randy Weston, and Julian
Priester—combines thick five-part horn voicings, poignant improvised solos,
and shifting textures, with Lincoln's expressive voice and lyrics. The musical
effect was modern, dramatic, and explicitly political through both song lyrics
and Nat Hentoff's liner notes—which stressed Lincoln's self-awareness as an
African American as central to her artistic voice. The album has become

something of a classic in the intervening years. The ensemble accompanying Lincoln, which included a number of the most respected musicians active at that time, is nearly identical to that which had participated six months earlier in Max Roach's and Lincoln's *Freedom Now Suite* (Roach, 1960)—Coleman Hawkins, Eric Dolphy, Mal Waldron, Booker Little, Julian Priester, Art Davis, and Walter Benton (Lincoln, 1961).

The *Freedom Now Suite*, whose cover art depicted African Americans at a lunch-counter, was recorded in August and September 1960 (about six months after the first Greensboro sit-ins) and was linked explicitly to political action through its performance as a benefit for the Congress of Racial Equality (Miscellaneous Benefits) and at the 1961 national convention of the NAACP in Philadelphia (Current, 1961). The *Freedom Now Suite*, however, did not receive the same scathing criticism as *Straight Ahead*. The impact and reception of *Straight Ahead* in 1962, as well as the public debate on "Racial Prejudice in Jazz" published in the pages of *Down Beat* in response to Gitler's review, must be viewed against a set of historical circumstances that included the success of African independence movements, the escalation of the civil rights movement, and the emergence of free jazz. Although white reaction initially was positive to changes in aesthetics and the new assertiveness of African American musicians, a tremendous polarization along racial lines in the professional jazz world had emerged by 1962.

I am interested in how a new African American musical and cultural sensibility came to be constructed in the jazz scene in the early 1960s, as well as in its paradoxes and relationship to broader political struggles and discourses. At stake in the discussion are several issues that anthropologists have been debating in recent years: the politics of identity, essentialism, the role of aesthetic practices in the constitution of cultural ideologies, and the role of musicians as agents of political advocacy. From a discourse-centered perspective, my aim is to show how the discourses of race, gender, music, modernism, and political action converge and inflect one another in the world of professional jazz at a particular moment during the civil rights movement. From a practice-centered perspective, I am concerned with how people chose to act upon these discourses and in what interactional settings various positions were taken. More specifically, I am interested in the way in which individual agents in the jazz world (musicians, critics, audience members, promoters, recording industry operatives) situated themselves, negotiated their statuses, and took action within these frequently conflicting social discourses.

The theme of what Paul Gilroy calls "ethnic absolutism"—an essentialized notion of identity—hovers as a backdrop to a central issue in this essay: a partial reconciliation of practice-centered and discourse-centered approaches to social analysis through an examination of the ways in which the charge of "essentialism" has been deployed in recent debates about race and ethnic identity. A tacit presumption in recent debates—that any demand for ethnic autonomy or self-determination is fundamentally essentialist in character—creates a problem in historical and social interpretation that a close reading of the 1962 debate over *Straight Ahead* and racial prejudice in jazz illustrates.

Yet the role of music and musicians in this era of political action was not only symbolic. There was a constant multi-layered dialectic among music as a symbolic means for asserting an African American identity, musicians as participants in explicitly political activities (such as benefit concerts for the principal civil rights organizations), and musicians as advocates for greater economic equity in the white-dominated music industry.

Straight Ahead: *The Public Debate*

The quotations that provide the epigraph to this essay are drawn from Gitler's review of *Straight Ahead* and the panel discussion organized by *Down Beat* magazine in reaction to it. Two consecutive issues of *Down Beat* were devoted to an edited transcript of the discussion, which included performers and critics Abbey Lincoln, Max Roach, Ira Gitler, Nat Hentoff, Lalo Schifrin, Don Ellis, Bill Coss, and Don DeMichael (Gitler, 1962a, 1962b).[1] The issues that dominated the discussion are very familiar: (1) social vs. biological explanations of cultural and musical difference, (2) whether reverse racism or "Crow Jim" existed in the jazz world, (3) who was entitled to evaluate or speak about jazz and the black experience, and (4) whether integration was an unproblematic social goal.

Roach and Lincoln criticized Gitler for having published a review that focused more on Lincoln's politics than the artistic merits of her performance. Gitler argued that he was justified in casting Lincoln as a "professional Negro" because in his view she was "using the fact that [she was] a Negro to exploit a career" (Gitler et al., 1962a, 21). That Gitler's charges were rooted in a discomfort with Lincoln's politics is apparent in his denunciation of the singer's involvement in a group called the Cultural Association for Women of African Heritage:

> She is involved in African nationalism without realizing that the African Negro doesn't give a fig for the American Negro, especially if they are not blackly authentic. I would advise her to read *A Reporter at Large* in the May 13, 1961, issue of the *New Yorker* or talk to a Negro jazzman of my acquaintance who felt a strong draft on meeting African Negroes in Paris. Pride in one's heritage is one thing, but we don't need the Elijah Muhammed type of thinking in jazz (Gitler et al., 1962a, 21).

The positions taken by Lincoln and Roach in the *Down Beat* panel were sharpened against the implicit and explicit charges made by critics Gitler and Don DeMichael that white musicians were discriminated against in the new political climate. Lincoln and Roach were called upon repeatedly to prove that they were not racist against whites, and, in response, they defended their right to speak from a privileged position by reason of their *social experience* as blacks. The central concern for many of the white participants was their belief that white musicians were not being hired by black musicians because of their race. "We might as well use the term Crow Jim," argued Don DeMichael. "To me, a lot of the Negro jazzmen have limited the people that they say swing—the people they will hire—to Negroes. They will say white guys don't swing, don't play jazz, and they have stolen our music." Lincoln added, "and they have," while DeMichael responded, "they haven't. I don't agree with you there" (Gitler et al., 1962a, 25). In the discussion that followed, Roach argued that the reason black players "nine times out of ten" stand a better chance of swinging is due to the greater exposure to the music that is the product of living in black social environments. Roach took great care to mention a black musician who immersed himself in classical music, had a doctorate in music, but couldn't swing because of insufficient exposure to jazz.

But DeMichael was not satisfied: "You're saying we are a product of our social environment; therefore jazz is learned. Why would a Negro boy learn jazz better than a white boy?" Roach answered, "My son—he listens to records all day. From before he was born—in his mother's belly—that's all he's been hearing." DeMichael responded, "So has my son," and Roach affirmed his commitment to a social explanation by saying, "All right. Then he stands a chance" (Gitler et al., 1962a, 25).

The ability of Gitler and DeMichael to construct the white jazz musician in a "one down" position relative to black musicians, as well as Max Roach's confidence that the better jazz musician would usually be the African American musician, emanates from the atypical position African American music holds relative to dominant European American cultural hegemony. As Burton Peretti has noted, while the cultural practices of white Americans have been treated as the mainstream of American history "white jazz history is an appendix to an African-American mainstream" (Peretti, 1992, 77). Music has been one of the few cultural practices in which non–African Americans have been willing to acknowledge the achievements, even superiority, of black artists—although not infrequently with an ideology that trivializes socially acquired musical knowledge as "natural," "untutored," and "innate."[2]

In jazz, the musical devices and aesthetics developed and widely practiced in African American communities have provided the standard against which the efforts of white participants in the music have been evaluated since at least the 1920s.[3] The history of jazz, which from its origins in African American urbanization (ca. 1890) through Lincoln and Roach's efforts in 1962 must be considered against the context of Jim Crow, reveals the repetitive character of the themes of discussion present in the *Down Beat* panel, especially those concerning appropriation and ethnic authenticity. The history of twentieth-century American popular music, indeed, is the history of an interracial encounter through music under asymmetrical economic, aesthetic, and political circumstances.

Race and Essentialism

A considerable, thought-provoking body of work has emerged critiquing the concept of race, essentialist ideologies of ethnic identity, and the privileging of vernacular experience in accounts of cultural difference.[4] Stuart Hall's critique of the "essentializing moment" turns on the tendency to reduce blackness to a racial, that is, biological category: "the moment the signifier 'black' is torn from its historical, cultural, and political embedding and lodged in a biologically constituted racial category, we valorize, by inversion, the very ground of racism we are trying to deconstruct" (Hall, 1992, 30). Kwame A. Appiah's attempt to find a "nonracialist foundation" for the "Pan-Africanist impetus" likewise centers on avoiding complicity in the racial logic of the dominator through simple inversion of racialist arguments (Appiah, 1992, 43). Appiah argues that race is a biologically meaningless term by presenting scientific work demonstrating that the chances of two human beings having the same gene at any random chromosomal locus is approximately 85 percent both *within* and *between* racial categories (Appiah, 1992, 36). The differences between the races, then, are primarily morphological rather than genetic: differences in skin, hair, and bone.

Paul Gilroy's critique of ethnic absolutism centers around what he believes is the exaggerated authenticity that the invocation of vernacular cultural forms confers upon critics, particularly black critics, who have been reluctant to "give up the qualified axiological authority that we fought so hard to attain" (Gilroy, 1994, 50). In arguing for a transnational diasporic perspective on the black Atlantic, Gilroy worries about the parochialism of vernacularism and argues that the critical community "should strive to act locally and think globally" (Gilroy, 1992, 193). He finds Americans particularly prone to "culturally protectionist" positions, even to the point of suggesting that some "Afro-American ethnicists . . . want to confine the Atlantic legacy within their own particular set of local, national, or nationalist concerns" (Gilroy, 1992, 197).

The problem, from the point of view of jazz history, is how easily the critique of essentialism and ethnic absolutism can be transformed into renovated charges of reverse racism, no matter how socially grounded are African American arguments for ethnically based identification. bell hooks has commented on the paradoxical aspects of postmodernism for African Americans. Arguing that while, on the one hand, the critique of essentialism is useful to promoting an understanding of the diversity of black experience, she notes that: "The postmodern critique of 'identity,' though relevant for renewed black liberation struggle, is often posed in ways that are problematic. Given a pervasive politic of white supremacy which seeks to prevent the formation of radical black subjectivity, we cannot cavalierly dismiss a concern with identity politics" (hooks, 1990, 26).

To Gilroy's broad questions about the discourses of ethnicity, I would add more pragmatic ones. (1) Under what circumstances have people taken ethnically absolutist positions? (2) Does it make sense to equate every rhetorical stance of ethnic assertiveness with a fundamental essentialism? (3) What roles do self-interest and the realignment of power play in the ideological stances taken? I argue here that the shape of African American claims to authenticity and exclusivity in the early 1960s must be read against a long-standing historical process of appropriation in American popular music, the immediate context of the civil rights movement, and the broader one of African independence movements. The very hybridity of the music, which has synthesized and transformed both African and European elements, as well as its leading role in the constitution of American popular musical culture, has ensured (as Gilroy has suggested elsewhere) that music has remained a site of "constant contestation" (Gilroy, 1991; Hall 1992, 29).

Modernism and the Cultural Logic of
Musical Appropriation

The issue of musical appropriation and ethnic authenticity have been dialogically intertwined throughout the history of jazz. The legal implementation of Jim Crow legislation in the 1890s created a de jure color line which homogenized diversity and internal divisions in African American communities. The legal basis for deciding who was and was not black was heredity, regardless of physical appearance. Although the discourse of race is repeatedly inflected by those of class, gender, and the economics of the recording business, the daily lives of musicians were shaped most profoundly by the side of the color line to which they were assigned. To read the early history of jazz is to learn the racial calculus of Jim Crow—which clubs accepted black patrons, which hired black musicians but did not allow black patronage, which clubs were "blacks and tans," and which musicians were light enough in complexion to be able to procure food for the rest of the band from a white restaurant. One learns, in addition, how mixed bands recorded long before they performed in public, and how resentful many whites were toward economically success-ful black musicians who dressed in fine clothes, drove large luxury automo-biles, or squired their musicians around in customized buses or railroad cars to avoid Jim Crow restrictions.[5]

While there was certainly a two-way cultural influence operating in music, the terms of the interaction were grossly unequal and defined by the asym-metrical political, social, and economic contexts of race. Earnest young white musicians, for example, could flock to South Side Chicago black and tans to learn from African Americans the sounds of the blues, the timbral possibili-ties of brass instruments, and a new rhythmic sensibility, but blacks were not allowed to be patrons in white performance spaces (Kenney, 1993, 103). The economics of musical performance, on the other hand, encouraged black mu-sicians to learn the repertories, dances styles, and large ensemble instrumen-tation of white dance hall orchestras, since many wanted to work in the more lucrative white dance halls. Being a musician in the 1920s was not a downwardly mobile occupation. Music was one of the few professions open to African Ameri-cans, and, as such, held out the possibility of upward mobility among urbaniz-ing migrants from the South. Kenney's account of Chicago's South Side documents the considerable irony that what was slumming to many white ra-cial border-crossers was an avenue to increased economic prosperity, cosmo-politanism, and independence for African Americans (Kenney, 1993, 3–60).

By the 1930s, the game of "cultural telephone," which characterizes the mainstreaming of African American musical sounds and aesthetics, was firmly in place. Band leaders such as Paul Whiteman and Benny Goodman actively sought the work of black arrangers such as Don Redman and Fletcher Henderson, but the vicissitudes of Jim Crow (which prohibited mixed bands) ensured that African American contributions to the new popular music were made invisible to the mass audience by the behind-the-scenes character of in-terracial interaction. Although white musicians such as Gene Krupa, Dave Tough, and Artie Shaw readily acknowledged their debt to African American music and musicians, mainstream American audiences witnessed the mass popularization of Fletcher Henderson's, Jimmy Mundy's, and Edgar Sampson's big band style through Benny Goodman's originally all-white band in all-white performance spaces.[6] The masses thus became familiar with such African American musical devices as riffs, walking bass, and shout choruses through the medium of white performance.

One of the principal contradictions of the swing era is the economic domi-nance of white bands despite the overwhelming aesthetic inspiration provided by African American music and musicians. Yet appropriation was seldom simple. On the one hand, the Benny Goodman orchestra came into popularity by playing many of the same arrangements that were written and recorded by Fletcher Henderson in the late 1920s and early 1930s (*Down South Camp Meeting* and *King Porter Stomp*). On the other hand, Goodman, with promoter John Hammond's strong persuasion, became the first swing-era musician to perform publicly with an integrated trio, when Teddy Wilson was included in a 1936 performance at Chicago's Congress Hotel. Goodman later included other African Americans in public—among them Lionel Hampton, Charlie Christian, and Cootie Williams—and refused to capitulate to demands from promoters that black members of the ensemble be removed for performances in Jim Crow venues. Goodman benefited materially by having the sound of the black musicians and arrangers in the band, but he also paid them well for their services. Nevertheless, the demographics and economics of the music market remain startling. The Paul Whiteman and Benny Goodman orchestras made far more money than their African American counterparts who were of greater aesthetic significance—Duke Ellington, Count Basie, Earl Hines, and Jimmie Lunceford—not through unmediated appropriation, but because the historical context of Jim Crow, U.S. demographics, racist ideology, and the economics of the recording industry gave them an incalculable structural advantage.[7] The market and "business as usual" within the recording industry quite simply worked in favor of the white musicians (Stowe, 1994, 94–140).

Recording industry businessmen counted on the financial naiveté of some African American artists. Count Basie in the late 1930s was fraudulently signed to a Decca contract that provided him no royalties and subunion scale for recording (Porter and Ullman, 1993, 153). Local 802 of the American Federation of Musicians was unwilling to abrogate the contract despite John Hammond's intervention on Basie's behalf and the fraudulent circumstances in which a signature had been obtained. Although many artists found themselves making more money than they ever had before, they did not realize how much they were losing to substandard royalty agreements. When differing contractual terms operating for white and black bands became known, there was deep resentment.

The repeated charge that white musicians have stolen black musical innovations turns on this repetitive cultural and economic cycle within American popular music. White musicians learned from black musicians, but greater commercial success came to white artists. The mass white public then comes to view the music, not as African American music popularized by white performers, but as "white music" (or everyone's music)—historical and cultural memory stopping at the color line. The same process of cultural erasure occurred in rock and roll: Elvis Presley and the Beatles popularized rhythm and blues musical figures and encountered an ambivalent reception among African Americans for exactly the same reasons that Benny Goodman did.

The development of bebop in the 1940s has been viewed as an assertion of blackness in music in reaction to the overcommercialization and white appropriation of swing (Lott, 1988). Spearheaded by Thelonious Monk, Charlie Parker, Dizzy Gillespie, Charlie Christian, Kenny Clarke, and Max Roach, bebop placed the improvisational aspect of jazz at a new level of centrality. The new rhythmic complexity of bebop, especially its drumming (which was developed from Jo Jones through Kenny Clarke and Max Roach), as well as increased tempos, greater harmonic complexity, and instrumental virtuosity, emphasized both the African American bedrock of the music (as developed via the Count Basie band) and a new self-conception of "artist" rather than "entertainer." Significantly, musicians didn't use the term bebop in the early 1940s—they called themselves "modern."

The sense of modern in the 1940s *included* a sense of ethnic assertiveness. If the modern rhetoric of "equality before the law" was mobilized by the growing political movement against Jim Crow, musicians mobilized the discourse of modernism to demand nondiscriminatory treatment as artists, as well as the end of Jim Crow practices within the music industry. African American jazz musicians led the way in employing the musical and aesthetic markers of modernism—innovation, formalism, technical virtuosity, progress—to articulate an improvisational aesthetic that demanded the respect and deference of white musicians and legitimated black creativity. Hence, the curious marriage of modernism and ethnic particularism that characterize the aesthetic and political debates within the jazz community in the 1940s through early 1960s.[8] At one moment, a musician might invoke the supposedly universalistic standards of modernism to argue for the artistic merits and legitimacy of jazz; at another, the same person might invoke an ethnic argument to counter appropriative and control moves on the part of white participants in the jazz scene. At one moment, the rhetoric of brotherhood and integration; at another, the "cultural protectionism" and separatist sentiment that Gilroy terms ethnic absolutism.

The history of this dialectic in relationship to the backdrop of the civil rights movement seems central to understanding both the particularity of U.S. cultural history and the tension between transnationalism and localism that is currently a topic of debate in African diasporic cultural theory. I can only offer a preliminary sketch here of the issues especially germane to the confluence of music, politics, and identity that emerged in the 1950s and early 1960s: (1) the transnationalism of the civil rights movement in the 1950s; (2) the relationship of the cold war to emergent African nations and the civil rights movement;

(3) the violent repression of moderate civil rights demands (adherence to *Brown v. Board of Education* and voting rights); and (4) African American pride in music as a cultural practice which "one ups" the white mainstream.[9]

Transnationalism and the Civil Rights Movement

Richard Fox (in this volume) talks about the way in which the U.S. civil rights movement appropriated and molded discourses of Gandhian non-violence to its own ends through processes he terms "hyper-difference" and "over-likeness." His point is that transnational cultural flows may generate cross-cultural interpretations that tend to exaggerate differences between the local and transnational (hyper-difference) or exaggerate similarity (over-likeness). If the look toward India was an important transnational flow shaping the civil rights movement in the 1940s (and it was characterized by these excesses of recognition and misrecognition), the look toward African independence movements in the 1950s and early 1960s provides another example.

In an interesting coincidence, the very same issue of the *Chicago Defender* that announced *Brown v. Board of Education* (22 May 1954) included an article about Haile Selassie and his upcoming visit to the United States (Daniels, 1954). On the same page a picture of Ghanaian (then Gold Coaster) Joe Appiah and his British wife Peggy Cripps appeared, with a caption that announced the birth of their son Kwame (yes, the Appiah cited earlier) ("2 African Princes," 1954). In subsequent weeks the optimistic glow in the wake of the *Brown* decision was intermingled with extensive coverage of Selassie's visit, including articles entitled "Selassie's Special Message for Negroes" (1954), "Selassie Eats with Ike, Gets Howard U. Degree (1954), and "Integration on Display for Selassie at Capital" (Hicks, 1954). In the last, James Hicks drew attention to the State Department interest's in mobilizing the *Brown* decision to counter Soviet criticism of U.S. racial policies. The continuation of Jim Crow policies was hurting the U.S. in the cold war.[10]

The convergence of civil rights and the continent of Africa in the pages of the *Defender* was hardly exceptional. Throughout the 1950s, black newspapers covered the independence movements and personalities of African nationalism on a regular basis. The independence of Ghana in March 1956 (Payne, 1957), Nkrumah's visit to the United States in 1958 ("Africa on the March," 1958; "Chicago Puts Out Red Carpet," 1958), the admission of sixteen African nations to the U.N. in 1960 ("Gain Admission to United Nations," 1960), and the treatment of African diplomats attending U.N. meetings in New York ("African Envoys Face Bias," 1960), are among the events covered in the pages of the *Defender*. The respectability of the new African leaders in the eyes of the world, the invitations to international independence celebrations received by prominent African American leaders (such as Adam Clayton Powell and Ralph Bunche), as well as a regular foreign news column (which as early as 1955 had a border announcing the geographic priorities of its coverage as "Africa, Asia, Caribbean, Latin America") established a transnational counterpoint to the decade's largely pessimistic domestic news about tolerance for school de-segregation and access to public accommodations. Incidents like the lynching of Emmett Till ("Nation Shocked," 1955), the ambushing of an NAACP office in Mississippi ("Ambush NAACP Office," 1955), the success of the Montgom-ery Boycott (Branch, 1988, 143–205), Governor Orval Faubus's armed resis-tance to the integration of Little Rock's Central High ("Faubus Vows No Retreat," 1957), Louis Armstrong's public denunciation of Eisenhower's inac-tion in Arkansas ("Satch Blast," 1957), increasing awareness that school de-segregation was not only a southern problem ("Chicago High Schools," 1957), and that the battle against Jim Crow was likely to be protracted ("Fisk Race Relations Institute," 1958; "Tuskegee Issues '59 Race Relations Report," 1960) galvanized African Americans across class lines. The parallel between African independence movements and the civil rights movement was increasingly drawn ("Tells Buffalo Meet UN," 1960) as the lunch counter sit-ins began in 1960. The dialectic of "recognition" between the struggle for African nation-hood and civil rights, I believe, had enormous consequences for the way in which black nationalist ideologies developed within the musical world in the early 1960s.

Music and Politics

The rhetoric of freedom resounded in the international and domestic political arenas, but was also a critical feature of the emerging aesthetic of free jazz. Freedom from the formal conventions of the jazz tradition—e.g., chord progressions, fixed-length song forms, and the obligation to play jazz "stan-dards"—came to be taken as an icon for political freedom, and African Ameri-can self-awareness by the mid-1960s. The marriage of modernism and ethnic assertiveness was taken to a new level with free jazz, and met with consider-able ambivalence from jazz audiences, musicians, and critics (both black and white), just as bebop did. Some fully embraced the new expressive aesthetic and its politics; others viewed the avant-garde dissonance of the music as de-rivative of classical aesthetics and alienating to the black masses. In addition, older bebop musicians viewed many of the younger free players as having failed to come up through the competitive ranks of the African American musical tradition the older musicians had pioneered.[11]

It has been customary in the jazz literature to conflate the advent of free jazz with the emergence of a radical political consciousness in the early 1960s.

_____ *Table 1* _____
Benefit Concerts in the Era of the Civil Rights Movement

Date	Location	Benefit for	Participants
5/28/54	Eastern Parkway Arena	Brooklyn NAACP	Ella Fitzgerald, Harry Belafonte
6/2/60	Wheeler Hall, University of California, Berkeley	Scholarship Fund for students expelled from southern schools for "anti-discrimination" activities	Oscar Peterson Trio, Cannonball Adderley Quintet
8/7/60	Village Gate	"Sit-In" CORE	Thelonious Monk, Jimmy Giuffre, Bill Henderson, Clark Terry
1/15/61	Village Gate	CORE	Max Roach and the *Freedom Now Suite*
1/27/61	Carnegie Hall	CORE and Reverend Martin Luther King, Jr.	Frank Sinatra, Dean Martin, Sammy Davis, Jr
5/19/61	Carnegie Hall	African Research Foundation	Miles Davis and Gil Evans
7/14/61	Philadelphia	NAACP Annual Convention	*Freedom Now Suite*, Max Roach, Abbey Lincoln, Michael Olatunji, Sarah Vaughan, Oscar Brown, Jr.
Fall 1961	San Francisco Opera House	NAACP	Miles Davis
6/62	Seattle	CORE	Dizzy Gillespie
2/1/63	Carnegie Hall	SNCC	Dave Brubeck, Charles Mingus, Harry Belafonte, Lorraine Hansberry, Tony Bennett, Shelly Winters
8/23/63	Apollo Theatre	March on Washington	A. Philip Randolph, Tony Bennett, Cozy Cole, the Golden Chords, Coleman Hawkins, Quincy Jones, Herbie Mann, Thelonious Monk, Charlie Shavers, Art Blakey and the Jazz Messengers, Billy Eckstine, Johnny Hartman, Ahmad Jamal, Terri Thornton, Carmen McRae, Dave "Alleycat" Thorne, Lambert, Hendriks & Bavan
8/24/63	Baltimore	"Steak-Out for the Cause"—CORE	Jimmy McGriff, Madhatters, Freda Payne

(continued)

Table 1. Benefit Concerts in the Era of the Civil Rights Movement *(continued)*

Date	Location	Benefit for	Participants
10/20/63	Five Spot	CORE	Billy Taylor, Don Heckman, Ted Curson, Bill Baron, Dick Berk, Ronnie Boykins, Kennie Burrell, Ray Draper, Ben Webster, Joe Newman, Horace Parlan,Frankie Dunlop, Edgar Bateman, Dick Kniss, Don Friedman, Ben Riley, Helen Merrill, Roy Haynes, Tony Williams, Frank Strozier
10/27/63	Five Spot	CORE	Bill Evans, Gary Peacock, Ira Gitler, Alan Grant, Paul Motian, Al Cohn, Zoot Sims,Sal Mosca, Dick Scott, Hal Dodson, Sheila Jordan, Jack Reilly, Dave Sibley, Prince Lasha, Paul Bley, J. R. Monterose, Eric Dolphy, Bobby Hutchinson, Joe Chambers, Ron Carter, Freddie Redd, Booker Ervin, Henry Grimes
11/25/63	Santa Monica Civic Auditorium	"Stars for Freedom"— CORE	Count Basie, Frank Sinatra, Sammy Davis, Jr., Dean Martin. Cancelled due to assassination of John F. Kennedy
2/10/64	Upsala College, East Orange, N.J.	CORE	Dave Brubeck
2/12/64	Philharmonic Hall	Voter Registration, SNCC, CORE, NAACP Legal Defense Fund	Miles Davis Quintet
9/20/64	The Scene, NYC	"Come Sunday, an Evening of Jazz for the Benefit of the Folks in Mississippi—CORE	Benny Powell, Frank Foster, Tobi Reynolds, Quentin Jackson, Dotty and Jerry Dodgian, Thad Jones Quintet with Pepper Adams
12/27/64	Village Gate	Freedomways	John Coltrane, Abbey Lincoln, Max Roach, Len Chandler
5/23/65	Private apartment in Greenwich Village	CORE	Randy Weston Sextet, James Farmer, speaking on his recent trip to Africa and the U.S. civil rights struggle

Sources: Drawn from Congress of Racial Equality Records, 1941–1967, State Historical Society of Wisconsin (Miscellaneous Benefits) and Topics Files at the Institute for Jazz Studies, Rutgers University, Newark, N.J. (New York Handbills).

Amiri Baraka (1963) so powerfully associated free jazz with African American political self-awareness, and so disdainfully dismissed much of hard bop as middle-brow music for the black middle class, that the association of avant-garde musical style with political radicalism became for many a generation later an unquestioned assumption. Even a cursory look at the mundane genre of the benefit concert, however, suggests that features of musical style do not predict political participation well. A partial list of benefit concerts for civil rights organizations and their participants is provided in Table 1.[12] The frequency of benefit events increased in the early 1960s, reaching a peak in late 1963 and early 1964. I do not wish to exaggerate the importance of participation in benefit concerts as a marker of political activism, but even this partial list of benefit concerts establishes that a complete aesthetic and political spectrum of the jazz community lent their names and services to the major civil rights organizations. From Tony Bennett to Prince Lasha, from Ben Webster to John Coltrane, Oscar Peterson to Charles Mingus, and Frank Sinatra to Gary Peacock there appears to have been something of a consensus that jazz performers, whatever their internal differences, had a duty to support civil rights.

In retrospect, it seems to be no accident that the controversy over free jazz erupted within the jazz community when it did. Ornette Coleman became the center of a heated debate after a much-publicized debut at New York's Five Spot in November 1959, but it is difficult to explain his dramatic rise without considering the volatility of the historical moment at which he emerged. Not long after Coleman's extended engagement at the Five Spot the Greensboro lunch counter sit-downs began. On 1 February 1960, four North Carolina Agricultural and Technical (A&T) students sat at a lunch-counter at the downtown Woolworth's in Greensboro, North Carolina and requested service (Chafe, 1981, 71). Within two weeks, similar sit-ins were taking place in Raleigh, Durham and Winston-Salem (Branch, 1988, 273). As Taylor Branch reported, the contagion of the student protests took the civil rights activists by surprise: there had been similar demonstrations in at least sixteen other cities in the three years prior to Greensboro but "few of them made the news, all faded quickly from public notice, and none had the slightest catalytic effect anywhere" (Branch, 1988, 272).

As 1960 continued, upheaval in both the political and musical worlds was in evidence. In April 1960, police fired into a crowd protesting apartheid in Sharpeville, South Africa. In June, Charles Mingus organized the Newport rebel jazz festival and in October recorded the "Original Faubus Fables" for Candid records—which included lyrics lambasting Arkansas Governor Faubus's attempts to prevent black students from enrolling in Central High School (Mingus, 1960a).[13] Max Roach and Abbey Lincoln recorded *Freedom Now Suite* in late August and early September (Roach, 1960), and Ornette Coleman recorded his historic *Free Jazz* (1960) album in December. In October, Martin Luther King, Jr. was arrested during a restaurant sit-in in Atlanta and sentenced to four months of hard labor on a state road gang (Branch, 1988, 358–361), while Fidel Castro took up a highly publicized residence at the Hotel Theresa in Harlem (Duckett, 1960). John F. Kennedy was elected president in November—after the black vote was swung by his small interventions on behalf of Martin Luther King, Jr. A further escalation in the civil rights movement occurred when the Freedom rides began in May 1961 (Branch, 1988, 412–491).

Even the most insulated, single-minded musician would have had difficulty evading news of the civil rights movement and African independence. Although musicians differed in the degree to which they participated in political events, it seems reasonable to suspect that nearly everyone had some awareness of these events and that they provided an interlocking counterpoint against which various events in the daily lives of musicians and the music industry were interpreted. There was an everyday pervasiveness to the civil rights movement and African independence in the late 1950s and early 1960s.

In comparison to Ornette Coleman's *Free Jazz* (1960), Max Roach's *Freedom Now Suite* (1960), Abbey Lincoln's *Straight Ahead* (1961) and Charles Mingus's *Original Faubus Fables* (1960a) were comparatively conservative in musical sound, but more explicit in political content. The liner notes to *Freedom Now Suite* begin with a quotation from A. Philip Randolph: "A revolution is unfurling—America's unfinished revolution. It is unfurling in lunch counters, buses, libraries and schools—wherever the dignity and potential of men are denied. Youth and idealism are unfurling. Masses of Negroes are marching onto the stage of history and demanding their freedom now!" (Roach, 1960).

The original cover art displayed a photograph of three young black men sitting at a lunch counter, while a white male waiter looked skeptically into the camera. The work announced itself as a partisan in the struggle for civil rights and African liberation. Just as Duke Ellington's *Black, Brown and Beige* portrayed a "tone parallel to the history of the American Negro" in sections entitled *Black*: "Work Song," "Come Sunday," "Light"; *Brown*: "West Indian Dance," "Emancipation Celebration," "The Blues"; and *Beige* (Priestley and Cohen, 1993), the sections to the *Freedom Now Suite* had explicitly political and historical titles related to black and African liberation: "Driva' Man," "Freedom Day," "Triptych: Prayer/Protest/Peace," "All Africa," and "Tears for Johannesburg." (The last composition referred specifically to the Sharpeville massacres that had taken place in the spring of 1960.)

Charles Mingus's "Original Faubus Fables" likewise made its political commentary explicit. Mingus had recorded an instrumental version entitled "Fables

of Faubus" (Mingus, 1959) a year earlier, but Columbia Records would not let
him include the lyrics, which included the following dialogue (Mingus, 1960a):

> Mingus (M): "Name me someone who's ridiculous, Dannie."
> Richmond (R): "Governor Faubus."
> M: "Why is he so sick and ridiculous?"
> R: "He won't permit us in his schools."
> M: "Then he's a fool." (Mingus, 1960a)

In comparison, Abbey Lincoln's texts on *Straight Ahead* are far more meta-
phorical. On the title track, Lincoln never mentions race or class but suggests
that for some the road is "smooth and easy," but for those who must use the
backroads, "straight ahead can lead nowhere." Lincoln continues her indirect
commentary on social change in "Retribution," where she says she doesn't want
a "silver spoon" or a "hand to hold, " she just wants to let the "retribution match
the contribution" (Lincoln 1961). Nevertheless, neither *Freedom Now Suite* nor
"Original Faubus Fables" generated a critical reaction of the magnitude of Ira
Gitler's denunciation of *Straight Ahead*, despite their more explicitly political
character. Lincoln, it seems, "took the heat for them all."

As a singer and a woman, Lincoln seems to have provided a more convenient target for musical and political criticism than Roach or Mingus. The compositions on *Freedom Now Suite* were all Max Roach's (three of them with the
collaboration of Oscar Brown, Jr.). Roach's position as one of the founding fa-
thers of bebop made him less vulnerable to the musical criticisms that Gitler
claims were the basis of his tirade against *Straight Ahead*, despite the fact that
the two albums had nearly identical personnel. The two principal differences
between the albums were first, that *Straight Ahead* was issued under Lincoln's
name, and second, that Lincoln was given compositional credit on four of the
seven pieces. Neither singers nor women have enjoyed the same prestige as
their instrumentalist male colleagues, and Lincoln was not widely known at
the time despite having previously recorded four albums under her own
name.[14] In the panel discussion, Gitler claimed that his two-star rating (out of
a possible five) was based solely on musicianship. In the review he stated that
"her bad intonation could be excused if it led toward the achievement of something positive"(Gitler et al., 1962a, 21).

Lincoln is far from the only jazz musician to have been accused of bad intonation—Billie Holiday, Betty Carter, Ornette Coleman and many others have
also received this criticism. Since pitch shading is an important expressive resource in blues and jazz, the notion that there is a pure standard of intonation
against which musicians should be judged is itself problematic, for the Western-
tempered scale is a compromise with the overtone series to begin with.[15] While

there are some passages in *Straight Ahead* where Lincoln could be described as deviating from the tempered scale, they are by far outweighed by the dramatic power of her singing against the haunting timbral colors of the band. It seems far more likely that Gitler unloaded his accumulated discomfort with activist musicians against a relatively vulnerable, female target.[16] Lincoln did not record another album under her own leadership until 1973 (Lincoln, 1973).

In the growing consolidation of diverse African American and non–African American constituencies around the struggle to end Jim Crow, it is not surprising that formerly accepted principles of interracial business as usual in the jazz world came under attack. The early 1960s witnessed several attempts on the part of musicians to organize themselves into groups that could circumvent the unfair financial deals they encountered in the recording and performing business. Mingus's dissatisfaction at the financial sum offered to him to perform at the Newport Jazz Festival in 1960 (Mingus, 1960b, liner notes) motivated him to organize the Newport rebel festival. An organization called the Jazz Artists Guild, which intended to book concerts and other events on terms more favorable to musicians, was created in the wake of the festival with Max Roach, Jo Jones, and Charles Mingus as its leading members. Although the organization did not last, there was a new assertiveness among musicians with respect to financial dealings, and a greater willingness to suggest that racism underlay a good deal of business as usual in the jazz industry. The reaction of white critics and musicians to this new atmosphere of politicization indicates that the ideology under which they had developed their relationship to black music—a generally color-blind ideology of interracial harmony—was shifting to a politicized ethnic ground that threatened to exclude them, or, at the very least, call into question their motivations and legitimacy.

One reaction to this political assertion by non–African Americans was to appeal to the universalistic aspect of jazz modernism. The higher principle of color-blind racial equality could serve to counter those segments of the political spectrum that appealed to racial autonomy as a principle of organization. That is, in any case, how I interpret the escalation in the charge of Crow Jim at the same time as African American musicians became more vocal about white racism in the music industry. In addition to Don DeMichael and Ira Gitler, Gene Lees and Dom Cerulli repeatedly raised the issue of discrimination against white musicians (Lees 1960a, 1960b; Cerulli 1964).

To return from whence we came, Don DeMichael's discomfort with Abbey Lincoln's ethnic stance turns on her apparent deprioritization of the rhetoric of interracial unity. DeMichael asked, "But when we talked in Chicago, you remember our talking about not the struggle for just one man but for all men"? And Lincoln replied: "I'm for that. Yet my struggle first is for my people" (Gitler et al., 1962a, 22). After an exchange in which Jim Hall's (a white musician's) merits as a guitarist for Sonny Rollins was debated between Gitler and Roach, Lincoln asked:

> Why is it that because I love my people and I want human dignity, must I be a racist? Why is that I say to you, Don. Dizzy Gillespie is a great musician. Does that mean that you are inferior? This is the whole thing. Because I say my people are worthwhile and should be free, does this mean I hate the white man?"
>
> Bill Coss: "No Abbey, it only means that if you say only my people can be [worthwhile],"
>
> Lincoln: "Only? That's true. But have I ever said this?" (Gitler et al., 1962b, 23)

While the panel discussion ended on a note of unity, it arrived there through the circuitous route of discussing what positions people might take in a hypothetical race war and a problematizing of the meaning of integration. The more the other interlocutors insisted on the rhetoric of unity, the more Lincoln insisted on a rhetoric of autonomy.

Discourse, Practice, and Vernacularism

The emphasis on ethnic difference (hyper-difference) in the rhetoric of the black separatism of the early 60s most certainly responded to the emphasis on likeness (over-likeness) in the rhetoric of universal brotherhood on the part of liberal whites; what is taken to be real within this context is certainly a matter of positionality. The polarized climax to Lincoln's and Roach's confrontation with Gitler is not simply a question of the triumph of ethnic particularism over color-blindness. Both ideological positions coexisted in Lincoln's and Roach's thinking. What seems to have been at stake is the practical deployment of these rhetorics in the realignment of power and moral authority within the jazz world. In this interactional setting Lincoln and Roach appealed to the higher cultural capital of African Americans in the discourse of jazz music. Gitler, DeMichael, and Coss countered with the charge of Crow Jim no matter how social the explanation for differences in musical capital. In thinking about the implications of *Straight Ahead* for contemporary debates about race and culture, we need to recognize the wedding of self-interest to the larger historical and ideological context of the controversy. The participants on either side of the debate over *Straight Ahead* defended their personal interests and social positions as well as matters of principle. This seems to me to be where the intersection of discourse and practice lie. Considering the interactional contexts in which various ideological positions are taken and the social action accomplished by them is thus crucial to the reconciliation of discourse and practice-centered modes of anthropological interpretation.

I conclude with two points about the issue of transnationalism, politics, and jazz. First, considering the relationship of the jazz industry to national and transnational historical issues has much to offer a rethinking of jazz history. Jazz often has been presented as a linear succession of musical styles operating independently of broader social events: from New Orleans jazz through swing, bebop, cool jazz, and hard bop on an inevitable trajectory towards the musical avant-gardism of the 1960s (Litweiler 1984, 1992; Schuller 1968, 1986, 65, 1989). In the prevailing modernism of the literature, the jazz avant-garde has even been viewed as the logical culmination of stylistic developments that compress into approximately fifty years a harmonic evolution paralleling European classical music—from diatonic harmony to atonality; from encumbrance by rules to freedom. Existing works that consider the relationship of jazz to historical events, on the other hand, often have transposed a linear model of history to the question of jazz and social awareness. Here the quest for social freedom has been mapped directly onto the search for freedom from musical form, and free jazz has been presumed to be the most politically inflected jazz style (Baraka, 1963; Kofsky, 1970). As benefit concerts and the debate over Abbey Lincoln's *Straight Ahead* suggest, there was a more complicated set of interrelationships between the social, political, and the musical in the late 1950s and early 1960s that become visible if we consider the contexts of the civil rights movements, aesthetic modernism, and African independence.

Secondly, although the transnational circulation of music effaces geographically bounded concepts of culture, it may actually intensify debates over ownership and control of particular musics. If a love of African American–inspired music is something that multiple cultural groups within the United States and abroad have in common, we need to remember that that space of cultural overlap is evaluated differently by members of different cultural groups according to their differences in everyday social experience. This truism of traditional cultural anthropology and ethnomusicology is harder to bring into focus in the context of the United States, where the rhetoric of the melting pot constructs attention to differences as divisive. To the extent that ethnic differences and differences in color continue to shape differences in social experience, I object to the recent postmodern trend toward labeling any invocation of shared ethnic experience as essentialist. Nor is it surprising when multiple cultural groups partially share a cultural practice such as playing and listening to jazz, that members of each participating group feel (partially) entitled to claim it as their own.

In the example of Lincoln's *Straight Ahead*, one constituency's pride, self-assertion, and political activism was another's reverse racism, and each felt their evaluation of a shared musical milieu to be obviously true. If cultural experience is something that naturalizes a particular group's accumulated experience as rational truth, differences in the evaluation of something that two or more groups share is unlikely to be experienced as simply a difference, but rather as unreasonableness or irrationality, over the same set of facts. There is an enduring paradox in the phenomenon of transnationalism and cultural hybridity in general: neither solidarity nor tension are exactly what they seem; for that which at one moment is capable of bringing diverse cultural groups together can at another be just as likely to tear them apart. This is neither cause for celebration nor despair—but a tension to keep in play when thinking about the way music functions in an increasingly transnational cultural world.

Notes

1. Abbey Lincoln and Max Roach are African American performers. Lalo Schifrin and Don Ellis are white jazz performers (Schifrin was born in Argentina and was a member of Dizzy Gillespie's band at the time; Ellis was born in Los Angeles). Ira Gitler, Nat Hentoff, Bill Coss, and Don DeMichael are white jazz critics.
2. For a discussion of the relationship of early jazz criticism to primitivism, see Gioia (1988).
3. Recent historical work on early jazz that informs my argument includes Peretti (1992) and Kenney (1993). Peretti provides a new look at the role of New Orleans and urbanization in early jazz history that subverts many taken-for-granted presumptions transmitted in jazz histories. Kenney provides a thoughtful account of white Chicago musicians who crossed racial boundaries in their pursuit of learning black musical styles—and their paradoxical attitudes about race and class.
4. I have in mind Anthony Appiah (1992, 28–46), Gayatri Spivak (1988, 195–221, 1992), and Stuart Hall (1992).
5. For a summary of the vicissitudes of the color line on early jazz, see Peretti (1992, 177–210).
6. The sound of jazz drew on African American musical tropes such as call and response, interlocking rhythmic organization, blues melodic inflection, and the vocal and spiritual tradition of the church, as well as on non–African American musical elements such as musical theater tunes, dance instrumentation, harmony, and European conceptions of the artist. Among the musical stylistic devices pioneered by African American bands are the four-beat walking bass, the rhythmic feel of swing, and consolidation of the rhythm section (Bennie Moten, Count Basie, Earl Hines), arrangments that set one instrumental section against another (Don Redman, Fletcher Henderson), and the sustained expansion of solo improvisation (Louis Armstrong and those he influenced). For a more exhaustive account of the musical devices used by these bands, see Schuller (1989).
7. For contrasting accounts of Goodman's career, see Schuller (1989) and Collier (1989). For an account of how the Congress Hotel performance came to pass, see Collier (1989, 171–176). For economic details of Paul Whiteman's career, see

Johnson (1979). For a description of the economics of the entertainment industry in the 1930s, see Stowe (1994).

8. For a longer discussion, see Monson (1995).

9. For a longer discussion, see Monson (1994).

10. See also *Chicago Defender* coverage of Fidel Castro's residence at the Hotel Theresa in Harlem in October 1960 (Duckett, 1960).

11. Trumpeters Roy Eldridge and Miles Davis, for example, were extremely critical of Ornette Coleman's music (Litweiler, 1992, 82).

12. Table 1 was compiled from fund-raising records of the Congress of Racial Equality (Miscellaneous Benefits) and handbills sent to Marshall Stearns (New York Jazz Clubs) announcing events in the late 1950s and the early 1960s. This list is by no means comprehensive and it overrepresents CORE fund-raising events to the extent of my reliance on CORE archival materials at the State Historical Society of Wisconsin.

13. The Newport rebel festival was held from 30 June–3 July 1960. A critical account can be found in Lees (1960c). A more sympathetic account can be found in Michael Cuscuna's and Nat Hentoff's liner notes to Mingus (1960b). Musicians who participated in the rebel festival included the bands of Mingus, Ornette Coleman, Randy Weston, Kenny Dorham as well as premier musicians of an older generation: Jo Jones, Roy Eldridge, and Coleman Hawkins. For a historical account of the escalation of the civil rights movement in 1960, as well as the labyrinthine political strategies that resulted in John F. Kennedy's election, see Branch (1988, 272–378), Meier and Rudwick (1975), and Carson (1981). Contemporary documents pertaining to the civil rights movement in this period can be found in Aptheker (1993), Carson et al. (1991), and Garrow (1989).

14. Lincoln's four previous albums were *Affair* (1956), *That's Him!* (1957), *It's Magic* (1958), and *Abbey Is Blue* (1959).

15. Fifths in the tempered scale are smaller than their naturally occurring size in the overtone series. Intonation systems, when studied cross-culturally, reveal themselves to be just as constructed as many other features of culture.

16. Lincoln confirmed this interpretation in an interview with me on 13 June 1995 (Lincoln, 1995).

References

"Africa on the March" (1958). *Chicago Defender* 54 (16 August):10.

"African Envoys Face Bias in U. S." (1960). *Chicago Defender* 56 (8 October):12.

"Ambush NAACP Office: Belzoni Grocer Describes Attack" (1955). *Chicago Defender* 51(3 December):1.

Appiah, Kwame Anthony (1992). *In My Father's House: Africa in the Philosophy of Culture.* New York: Oxford University Press.

Aptheker, Herbert, Ed. (1993). *A Documentary History of the Negro People in the United States.* Volume 6: *From the Korean War to the Emergence of Martin Luther King, Jr.* New York: Citadel Press.

Baraka, Imamu Amiri (LeRoi Jones) (1963). *Blues People: Negro Music in White America.* New York: William and Morrow.

Branch, Taylor (1988). *Parting the Waters: America in the King Years 1954–63*. New York: Simon and Schuster.

Carson, Clayborne (1981). *In Struggle: SNCC and the Black Awakening of the 1960s*. Cambridge, Mass.: Harvard University Press.

Carson, Clayborne, David J. Garrow, Gerald Gill, Vincent Harding, and Darlene Clark Hine, Eds. (1991). *The Eyes on the Prize Civil Rights Reader*. New York: Penguin Books.

Cerulli, Dom (1964). Crow Jim: No Gigs for Ofays. *Rogue* (January):53–55+.

Chafe, William H. (1981). *Civilities and Civil Rights*. New York: Oxford University Press.

"Chicago High Schools 70% Jim Crow—NAACP" (1957). *Chicago Defender* 53 (21 September):5.

"Chicago Puts Out Red Carpet for Ghana's Nkrumah" (1958). *Chicago Defender* 54 (16 August):1.

Coleman, Ornette (1960). *Free Jazz*. 21 December 1960. New York: Atlantic SD1364.

Collier, James Lincoln (1989). *Benny Goodman and the Swing Era*. New York: Oxford University Press.

Current, Gloster (1961). Fifty-Second Annual Convention Promises a Stepped-Up Crusade. *Crisis* 68(7):398–412.

Daniels, George (1954). "Meet America's Guest of Honor: Haile Selassie: The Big Boss of a Little Country." *Chicago Defender* 50 (22 May):3.

Duckett, Alfred (1960). "Why Castro Fled to Harlem: Youth Says Fidel Made Fool of 'White Folks'." *Chicago Defender* 56 (1 October):1.

"Faubus Vows No Retreat on TV" (1957). *Chicago Defender* 53 (14 September):1.

"Fisk Race Relations Institute: Predict Bitter Struggle Ahead in Fight for Full Integration" (1958). *Chicago Defender* 54 (26 July):3.

"Gain Admission to United Nations" (1960). *Chicago Defender* 56 (1 October):1.

Garrow, David J., Ed. (1989). *We Shall Overcome: the Civil Rights Movement in the United States in the 1950's and 1960's*. 3 vols. New York: Carlson Publishing.

Gilroy, Paul (1991, 1987). *There Ain't No Black in the Union Jack: The Cultural Politics of Race and Nation*. Chicago: University of Chicago Press.

Gilroy, Paul (1992). Cultural Studies and Ethnic Absolutism. In *Cultural Studies*, ed. Lawrence Grossberg, Cary Nelson, and Paul Triechler, pp. 187–198. New York: Routledge.

Gilroy, Paul (1994). "After the Love Has Gone": Bio-politics and Etho-Poetics in the Black Public Sphere." *Public Culture* 7(1):49–76.

Gioia, Ted (1988). *The Imperfect Art: Reflections on Jazz and Modern Culture*. New York: Oxford University Press.

Gitler, Ira (1961). Review: Abbey Lincoln Straight Ahead. *Down Beat* 28 (9 November):35–36.

Gitler, Ira, Max Roach, Abbey Lincoln, Don Ellis, Lalo Schrifrin, Nat Hentoff, Bill Coss, and Dan DeMichael (1962a). Racial Prejudice in Jazz, Part 1. *Down Beat* (15 March):20–26.

Gitler, Ira, Max Roach, Abbey Lincoln, Don Ellis, Lalo Schrifrin, Nat Hentoff, Bill Coss, and Dan DeMichael (1962b). Racial Prejudice in Jazz, Part 2. *Down Beat* (29 March):22–25.

Hall, Stuart (1992). What Is This "Black" in Black Popular Culture? In *Black Popular Culture: A Project by Michele Wallace*, ed. Gina Dent, pp. 21–33. Seattle: Bay Press.

Hicks, James L. (1954). "Integration on Display for Selassie at Capital." *Chicago Defender* 50 (5 June):3.

hooks, bell (1990). *Yearning: Race, Gender, and Cultural Politics.* Boston: South End Press.

Johnson, Carl (1979). *A Paul Whiteman Chronology, 1890–1967.* Rev. ed. Introduction by Irwin Shainman. Williamstown, Mass.: Whiteman Collection, Williams College.

Kenney, William H. (1993). *Chicago Jazz: A Cultural History, 1904–1930.* New York: Oxford University Press.

Kofsky, Frank (1970). *Black Nationalism and the Revolution in Music.* New York: Pathfinder Press.

Lees, Gene (1960a). Afterthoughts. *Down Beat* 27 (13 October):53.

Lees, Gene (1960b). The Great Wide World of Quincy Jones. *Down Beat* 27 (4 February):16–21.

Lees, Gene (1960c). Newport: The Real Trouble. *Down Beat* 27 (18 August):20–23+.

Lincoln, Abbey (1956). *Affair.* 5–6 November. Hollywood: Liberty LRP 3025.

Lincoln, Abbey (1957). *That's Him!* 28 October. New York: Riverside RLP12–251.

Lincoln, Abbey (1958). *It's Magic.* 23 August. New York: Riverside RLP12–277.

Lincoln, Abbey (1959). *Abbey Is Blue.* 25–26 March. New York: Riverside RLP12–308.

Lincoln, Abbey (1961). *Straight Ahead.* 22 February. New York: Candid CM8015; CCD 79015.

Lincoln, Abbey (1973). *People in Me.* 23 June. Tokyo: Inner City IC 6040.

Lincoln, Abbey (1995). Interview with author. 13 June. New York.

Litweiler, John (1984). *The Freedom Principle: Jazz after 1958.* New York: Da Capo Press.

Litweiler, John (1992). *Ornette Coleman: A Harmolodic Life.* New York: William Morrow and Company.

Lott, Eric (1988). Double V, Double-Time: Bebop's Politics of Style. *Callaloo* 11(3):597–605.

Meier, August and Elliott Rudwick (1975). *CORE: A Study in the Civil Rights Movement.* Urbana: University of Illinois Press.

Mingus, Charles (1959). Fables of Faubus. *Mingus Ah Um/Charles Mingus.* 5, 12, May. New York: Columbia CK40648.

Mingus, Charles (1960a). *Charles Mingus Presents Charles Mingus.* 20 October. New York: Candid BR–5012.

Mingus, Charles (1960b). *The Complete Candid Recordings of Charles Mingus.* 20 October and 11 November. New York: Mosaic 111 (3 CDs). Liner notes by Michael Cuscuna and Nat Hentoff.

Miscellaneous Benefits (1941–1967). Congress of Racial Equality Records, State Historical Society of Wisconsin, Madison Wisconsin. Series 5, Box 28, Folder 8.

Monson, Ingrid (1994). "Doubleness" and Jazz Improvisation: Irony, Parody, and Ethnomusicology. *Critical Inquiry* 20(2):283–313.

Monson, Ingrid (1995). The Problem with White Hipness: Race, Gender, and Cultural Conceptions in Jazz Historical Discourse. *Journal of the American Musicological Society* 48(3):396–422.

"Nation Shocked, Vow Action in Lynching of Chicago Youth" (1955). *Chicago Defender* 51 (10 September):1.

New York Jazz Clubs (various dates). Handbills. Institute for Jazz Studies. Topics files. Newark, N.J.: Rutgers University.

Payne, Ethel L. (1957). "World's Notables See Ghana Become Nation." *Chicago Defender* 52 (9 March):1.

Peretti, Burton (1992). *The Creation of Jazz: Music, Race, and Culture in Urban America.* Urbana and Chicago: University of Illinois Press.

Porter, Lewis and Michael Ullman (1993). *Jazz: From Its Origins to the Present.* Englewood Cliffs, N.J.: Prentice Hall.

Priestley, Brian and Alan Cohen (1993). Black, Brown & Beige. In *The Duke Ellington Reader*, ed. Mark Tucker, pp. 185–204. New York: Oxford University Press.

Roach, Max (1960). *Freedom Now Suite.* 31 August and 6 September. New York: Candid CCD 9002.

"Satch Blast Echoed by Top Performers: Nixes Tour, Raps Ike and Faubus" (1957). *Chicago Defender* 53 (28 September):1.

Schuller, Gunther (1968). *Early Jazz: Its Roots and Musical Development.* New York: Oxford University Press.

Schuller, Gunther (1986). *Musings: The Musical World of Gunther Schuller: A Collection of His Writings.* New York: Oxford University Press.

Schuller, Gunther (1989). *The Swing Era: the Development of Jazz 1930–1945.* New York: Oxford University Press.

"Selassie Eats with Ike, Gets Howard U. Degree" (1954). *Chicago Defender* 50 (5 June):1.

"Selassie's Special Message for Negroes" (1954). *Chicago Defender* 50 (12 June):1.

Spivak, Gayatri Chakravorty (1988). *In Other Words: Essays in Cultural Politics.* New York and London: Routledge.

Spivak, Gayatri Chakravorty (1992). Acting Bits/Identity Talk. *Critical Inquiry* 18(Summer):770–803.

Stowe, David W. (1994). *Swing Changes: Big Band Jazz in New Deal America.* Cambridge, Mass. and London: Harvard University Press.

"Tells Buffalo Meet UN 'Two Faced' in Africa" (1960). *Chicago Defender* 56 (8 October):10.

"Tuskegee Issues '59 Race Relations Report: 'Hesitancy' Seen in Facing Integration" (1960). *Chicago Defender* 55 (6 February):20.

"2 African Princes: One Loses Wife, Other Has Heir" (1954). *Chicago Defender* 50 (22 May):1.

Nathan Stoltzfus

Dissent under Socialism

*Opposition, Reform, and the West
German Media in the German
Democratic Republic of the 1980s*

Introduction

In August 1993, I sat again in the archives in which the East German
Communist Party had once kept its own private collections. I had last worked
there in 1988, as an exchange scholar living in East Germany. At that time, as
the Marxism-Leninism Institute, it held the notes on German history that party
leaders had deemed most important to a Marxist interpretation of history. The
archives registered a number of the recent phenomenal changes in German
history, but one symbolized them especially well: Egon Krenz. There he was,
the former head of state and party in the German Democratic Republic (GDR),
in a new guise as just one of about thirty researchers.

Some historians have argued that, since no shots were fired and no heads
had rolled, the fall of GDR communism could not represent a revolution: the
protest movement had not succeeded in sitting in the vacated seat of power,
because it had not used violence to finish off the old regime. But what would
have been the use of putting Egon Krenz before a firing squad, now that he
was dispatched to the archives? True, Krenz was perhaps interested in learning what he could or could not deny in court. Now that he (like every historian) was consigned to studying rather than exercising power, what could be
the harm in preserving his life? Krenz had never had a ground swell of support, in any case, to buoy him to power again. In a shiny-cheap leather jacket
and those special East German shoes that substitute Velcro flaps for laces,
Krenz was now an "Ossie" among the supremely self-superior Westerners,
many of whom were casting an extremely judgmental eye on files he had once

generated. Even the three-paragraph city histories printed on restaurant placemats around former East Germany now designate the state Krenz once presided over as, regretfully, a "Fehlentwicklung"—a false start.

There was no mass opposition movement in the GDR before mid-1989. It is true that many East Germans were quietly critical of the state and party. Many did not believe the regime's rosy propaganda pictures. Many might have known that the leading Socialist Unity Party (SED) was not always right, as it claimed. Yet although few East Germans were true believers in communism, the vast majority did adapt to the communist system. Many people had internalized fear of the regime, if not its rules and values. Thus, through these persons the system could expect to inherit new generations of fearful subjects.[1] Many East Germans who might have become dissidents voluntarily left for West Germany instead or were forced out by the East German regime when their dissent became problematic. These included persons most likely to be effective dissidents—intellectuals and well-trained workers. There was no strong intellectual opposition (comparable to Charter 77 in Czechoslovakia) nor a mass movement (comparable to Solidarity in Poland) in the GDR until the fall of 1989. That fall, the masses protested as the regime was losing orientation, then handed over power to Bonn, an indication that they were not used to resisting. The few persons who had been resisting the regime for years had kept their eye on a long-term reform of socialism, maintained behind the Berlin Wall; rather than attempting the wholesale overthrow of the system, they had (sometimes at great risk and sacrifice) sought to walk a narrow line between opposition that would end in jail or expulsion and opposition that, although not specifically illegal, might form a dissenting popular opinion.

This essay recounts the growth of dissent in Halle, a small city in East Germany's industrial heartland. Pockets of opposition like those at Halle were scattered around the GDR; they comprised the core and gave energy to the opposition movement, as it formed in 1989. The case of Halle raises a number of challenging questions about the contradictory contours of socialist rule in East Germany.[2] In what follows, I focus on three issues of broad concern for understanding the making of mobilization in the late twentieth century: the influence of transnationalism, the role of religion, and the impact of the media. The West German media presented the most effective means East German activists had for building dissent, but on the whole these media assisted reunification rather than the reform activists sought. As Halle's history will show, good inquiry demands careful scrutiny as to how dissent grows at the intersection of local thinking and regional and even global forces and how the expression of discontent may remake, as well as be remade by, preexisting structures of ideologies and institutions. Endeavors to define the terms of opposition between the local and the global, and the past and the present, led the dissidents of Halle into a belated discovery of the lack of realism in their original aim of reforming the communist system from within. At the same time, their struggles were not altogether in vain. When socialism collapsed in 1989, many activists turned the lessons of mobilization against the old regime to the new project of cultural pluralism and social democracy in the haunted land of a reunited Germany.

The Case of Halle

Although it is 128 kilometers southwest of Berlin and just 32 kilometers west of Leipzig, Halle had its own faction of dissent, with its own leaders and grievances. In this slow-paced country where the state monopolized initiative, where telephones and automobiles, like other technological developments that enabled communication and efficiency, were a luxury, Halle's dissidents were almost unaware of other currents of opposition within the GDR.[3] The state cast a pallor over all kinds of communication, information flow, and individualistic or artistic expression and it contributed to perpetual uncertainty about the limits of politics. Everyone knew the Stasi existed, but few, if any, knew exactly how pervasively it had penetrated society and their own lives. No one could be sure who exactly worked for that Orwellian monstrosity.

Many erred on the side of "being good"—by leaving untested the boundaries of what was or wasn't allowed. Many in Halle were workers at the infamously dirty chemical plants, Buna and Leuna, however, and far from being concerned with class struggle, they had very little self-doubt, according to one worker who later attended the university.[4] For them, the world was "in order." Most had their TVs and hobbies and looked to fill the small quota of personal expression they needed in dachas and nonpolitical family life.[5] Here or there, one or two had even managed to procure membership in the Communist Party, or perhaps a Trabant—the East German car and symbol (like the Mercedes in West Germany) of being solidly ensconced in the middle class. A foreigner arriving in Halle provided a head-turning spectacle. East Germans apparently felt they had the right to turn and gawk, open-mouthed, at anyone who looked foreign, for persons who stood out against the very restricted patterns allowed by the state were immediately obvious and of interest.

Within this environment, a small group of persons grew up with an extremely well-developed capacity for resisting the tide. In Halle, this happened among the generation in its twenties and thirties, during the late 1970s and early 1980s. Like many in their parents' generation, they were drawn to socialism's ideals, if less susceptible by this period to promises of a brighter future and less willing to merely accept the present "real existing socialism" as the best possible socialism. In retrospect, they speak fondly of the inner freedom and solidarity they had then. Now that they can live anywhere in Germany, they remain in Halle. As in the rest of East Germany, protest in Halle galvanized in opposition to militarization.

The lineage of dissent traces back to individual acts of opposition and civil disobedience following a 1962 state law that mandated male conscription into the army. In 1968, the participation of East Germany's National People's Army in overthrowing the Prague Frühling uprising led not just to isolated actions of dissent, but created a whole group of permanent dissenters among the younger generation. These dissidents were impressed by the substance and methods of the contemporary U.S. civil rights movement, readily adopting the black movement's nonviolent methods, in an example of how the strategies and ideologies of mobilization in one culture move to another—due in this case primarily to the electronic media of the later twentieth century.[6] One young Catholic from Halle, advised by his priest to follow his conscience and refuse to participate in the invasion of Czechoslovakia, was executed.[7] A decade later, a proposed law to make classes on military service obligatory for ninth- and tenth-grade schoolchildren became another locus of open dissent. The Catholic bishops of Berlin issued an official letter of protest and the Protestant church also made protests. But in contrast to the churches' achievements through protest on the issue of conscientious objections, their protests in 1978 made no difference, as these military service classes were made mandatory with a national law of 1 September 1978. Other church-centered protests followed against the further militarization of society, including one opposed to the official East German standard practice of providing kindergartens with toy weapons and other military paraphernalia and directives requiring military exercises for university students, with similarly little effect. At the highest levels, church protests were typically quiet, expressed through the nonpublic channels the state had established for complaints, and thus easily ignored.

Peace and disarmament were the issues that most effectively rallied church as well as popular opposition, especially in the early 1980s following Soviet and NATO decisions to station nuclear missiles on German soil, on opposite sides of the Iron Curtain.[8] Yet, in general, the churches, Protestant and Catholic alike, continuously operated in the interests of the state (i.e., by moderating opposition) as well as in opposition to it.[9] Initially, Halle and other GDR opposition was organized from under the somewhat sheltering roof of the church. But by the1980s, intellectuals began to organize on their own, outside the churches. In March 1982 the regime announced that in cases of national defense women, too, would be conscripted into the military. This regulation led to an important new development among the opposition nationally—one with a center in

Halle: women formed Women for Peace, a group organized outside of the church, which continued its opposition activities through 1989.

By the early 1980s, GDR human rights and environmental action groups developed with the assistance of ideologies and strategies from other countries. Beginning in the early 1980s, with strong support from the West German Green Party, persons concerned with the mounting environmental disaster throughout East Germany formed small groups to voice dissent. Even as the minuscule East German opposition developed, the state, with its desire for full acceptance as a player in international affairs, grew increasingly confident. During the early leadership of Erich Honecker, who replaced Walter Ulrich as head of state and party in 1971, East Germany revised its diplomatic identity.[10] In exchange for acceptance into international organizations and normalized diplomatic relations with the West, the regime made some concessions affecting the way it treated its citizens. The capstone of this development was East Germany's treaty agreements at the summit conference in Helsinki in 1975. East Germans took pride and new hope in their international acceptance. Questions that had been taboo previously were now openly discussed. Within several years of the Helsinki accords, East Germans began forming very small groups faulting the leadership for its human rights record and demanding more freedom.

The ascendance of Erich Honecker, who had personally supervised the construction of the Berlin Wall, at first seemed to signal reform, culturally and politically. It became clear, however, that Honecker was not interested in basic reform. As one leading Halle dissident, Lothar Rochau, said, "I and many others soon learned that we had mistaken a sunny winter day [Honecker's early reforms], for spring."[11] The Stasi, a massive, virtually independent police force, continued to expand its repressive presence. By the early 1980s, as it stood directly on the verge of an unforeseen growth of domestic opposition, the SED regime appeared to have eradicated most of the opposition leaders by pushing them across the border into West Germany, or by silencing them. When in the early 1980s the Stasi wanted to make a public example of the difficulties and sacrifices anyone in the "independent peace movement" faced, they threw Rochau and others of his fellow-organizers into jail.

Strategies and impulses for both the peace and environmental movements in East Germany came from West Germany and the United States. Lothar Rochau, born in 1952, was a local leader in both movements. He grew up in what the Stasi described as a "positive parental household . . . raised in a positive sense." His father was a member of the SED, who spent his weary afterwork hours in the service of the Communist Party. In October 1977, after a stint in the army and four years of training, Rochau took up a post in Halle as a deacon for church youth. For Rochau, Jesus of Nazareth appeared as a non-violent resister of status quo power structures, and this was the vibrant new deacon's message to the youth of Halle. Martin Luther King, Jr., the American minister and activist, was a contemporary model for Rochau. If he hadn't lived in the GDR, Rochau reflected in 1994, he would have studied history or philosophy. But in the GDR, theology provided the only alternative ideology, and the church the only alternative power structure.

When he arrived in Halle, the youth of the city did not exactly flock to his officially announced church meetings. Rochau decided that "if the youth won't come to me, I'll go to them." Night after night he sought them out in discotheques and bars, listened to them, and tried to help. The Stasi's interpretation of the new deacon's behavior was more paranoid: "Finally Rochau's real intention is clear: he is projecting his own restlessness onto others and inciting them to oppositional behavior." The open discussions he encouraged began to create inner freedom, Rochau remembered, and from this internalized feeling, actions resulted that were often not a strict opposition, but merely fun. Rochau organized hikes and excursions, but also readings and concerts of works from artists under suspicion by the state—Betina Wegener, Sarah Kirsch, and Rainer Kunze. Theologians feared by the state (such as Friedrich Schorlemmer) also showed up. Rochau's youth group grew to be one of the biggest in the GDR. Up to 700 young persons attended activities he organized. The Stasi grew increasingly threatening, forbidding Rochau to follow through with plans and interfering with his work in various ways.

The independent peace movement—called "independent" because it was organized outside of official SED Party auspices—was the focus of Rochau's work. The Soviet Union's decision to deploy SS 20 intermediate-range nuclear weapons, some within 32 kilometers of Halle, and NATO's response, to station Pershing and Cruise missiles in West Germany, goaded Rochau and the peace movement on. As the West German peace movement flourished in response to these new weapons, the West German electronic media carried the news across the border. Rochau organized petitions, gathered signatures, and organized demonstrations in Halle as if these were the most natural activities, rather than political opposition. In March 1981, the attorney general for Halle demanded of Rochau's bishop that the church fire Rochau. But the church only warned Rochau to stop stirring up unrest and, above all, to desist from any sort of "spectacular actions."

For the Stasi, educating and mobilizing public opinion was tantamount to "subversive actions against the state." Rochau, however, was driven by "questions of real socialism, of corruption, of the misuse of power, and of how to overcome that."[12] With four friends—one of whom, as he later discovered, was a Stasi informant—Rochau founded a group outside of the church to write a manifesto on the "situation within socialism as it actually exists in East Germany." According to the Stasi, Rochau was misusing his church position, looking for every conceivable occasion to hold his treasonous assemblies and activities within established church or state bounds, and testing the state's patience with his "search for legal room in which to carry out his work." The Stasi noted that "it is also remarkable that in Rochau's opinion, there is in the GDR no freedom of opinion and no human rights!"

By 1981, the Stasi was looking for every opportunity to put Rochau behind bars, but he had to be fired first. The Stasi used a variety of methods to encourage the Protestant church to do this, including efforts to lure him into sexual intercourse outside his marriage. Rochau's conflict with the state came to a head in 1983, the year Egon Krenz became a member of the Politburo and secretary of the party's Central Committee. When Rochau led a demonstration of about one hundred young people wearing white doves to symbolize peace in September 1982, the church gave him a choice between losing his job and taking another one. He refused to go, and the church fired him on 1 March 1983.

Rochau then helped organize his youth group to participate (uninvited) in the official annual FDJ celebration of East Germany's official peace movement on 19 May. Rochau's small group of 50 to 100 made an effort to mingle with the FDJ parade, an assembly of thousands of uniformed youth, but was immediately encircled by Stasi agents.[13] One of the Stasi's tasks was to prevent dissidents from actions that were noticed by the public. Yet, according to Rochau "we wouldn't have stood out at all, no one would have noticed us a bit, if the Stasi hadn't moved in to encircle us."

Although it was the Stasi's need for total control that led it to take actions that only revealed what it was supposed to hide, the Stasi could not see it that way. At this demonstration, Stasi agents prided themselves in having prevented it from taking a "mass effect" by the "engagement of operational forces!" Stasi records, filled with specialized jargon and code words, sometimes give the impression that the secret police lived partially in an imaginary but very predictable world. There is little evidence that the police could have conceived that its actions to stop dissidence could have actually spread news of it. Stasi paranoia and need for total control led it to overreactions where it more wisely could have ignored the "enemy."

Weeks later, Rochau and about one hundred forty others of his group met for a bicycle demonstration against environmental pollution. Earth Day in East Germany was 5 June. It was a commemoration derived from the West that gave GDR activists an opportunity to call their own leaders to account. The West

German Green Party had a strong interest in supporting GDR environmental activists, and the East German state's concern with international acceptance had led it to include Earth Day on the official calendar. Every year, this call to remembrance of the world's fragile ecology was marked on the calendar. And every year, predictably, there was never an official word or action concerning Earth Day. As was so often the case for the state leadership, saying was not always doing.

Marxist ideology and notions that socialism would bring heaven on earth had mobilized much talent and energy on behalf of the German socialist state in its infancy. But for the children of East Germany's founders, the dissidents born to the following generation, it was also the ideas of officially celebrated communism (pacifism and freedom) that lent them courage for entering into opposition and gave them opportunities for doing so. It is interesting to speculate about why the leadership marked Earth Day on the calendar, even though it did not want this to have the effect it was intended to have elsewhere around the world, or why it made such a spectacle of its annual commemoration of Rosa Luxembourg, even while banning the strikes and repressing the free discussions she passionately advocated. In any case, such official actions had the effect of publicizing the state's hypocrisy and gave dissidents confidence in their cause. In a search to find that narrow band of action between opposition that would end in jail or expulsion, and opposition that was not illegal and yet capable of mobilizing public opinion, East German dissidents found a foothold in officially celebrated ideas and personages.

East Germany's official recognition of Earth Day illustrates the global extension of the environmental movement, migrating with people and the media across borders. Especially in Halle, the dirtiest area in one of the world's most polluted countries, Lothar Rochau's group felt spurred to action by this official recognition. It was normal for the city's children to get sick three or four times a month, mostly because of the polluted air. As early as the late 1970s, the dissidents of Halle had met in discussion groups and workshops on the problem of pollution. For Earth Day 1983 they planned a bicycle demonstration. Under police summons, several members of Rochau's group were warned that such a demonstration was not permitted and thus would constitute a criminal act. The state loathed the attention this brought to a problem it refused to acknowledge, but Rochau's group nevertheless determined that some sort of action "had to be dared—on the condition, however, that each participant took full, personal responsibility."[14]

In the face of threats from the state, Rochau sought the support of the Protestant church. The church, however, showed "great reserve" and "recommended finding another, less spectacular way!" In a meeting, the group rejected this advice, knowing that publicity was its ally, just as silence was that of the state. Thrown back on their own wits, the group decided against wearing gas masks during the demonstration as "too provocative" but in favor of using a quote from former East German head of state and party, Walter Ulbricht. On one side of a poster they cited Ulbricht: "Chemicals Bring Beauty, Prosperity, and Bread." The other side asked: "At what Price?" On Sunday, 5 June, the brave group met in Halle's Church Square, the square opening onto the market in front of Halle's oldest church (Marktkirche), presided over by a statue of the most famous German born to Halle, George Frederick Handel. Organizers of the bicycle demonstration had expected thirty or forty persons, but more than three times that many turned out (only two of whom had applied to leave the GDR permanently). Then the organizers instructed everyone once again not to provoke the police, to follow all traffic rules (regulations limited bicyclists to riding in pairs, two abreast), and so forth.

Among a sail of banners and posters, the demonstrators made their way toward Halle's infamous Buna Chemical Works just outside the city, waving to the Halle residents who appeared on their balconies on this warm, sunny day and waved back. Without warning, police stopped the procession. About forty were arrested and taken to the police station. The others were made to identify themselves, warned that water cannons would be used against them if they continued, and released. In the short run, ". . . some became resigned," one demonstrator remembered. "In the long run, however, this action together with others changed things. Thereafter, there was always some action or other on the 5th of June."[15]

On 23 June 1983, the Stasi arrested Rochau. The prosecuting attorney fabricated a case of subversive agitation, illegal contacts with the West, and endangerment to the public order. The main piece of evidence against Rochau was a memorandum discovered during the house search following his arrest. It was a reflection on peace and East Germany's hypocritical claim to the world to be the "Peace State." As Rochau later admitted, he had unrealistically expected the loudly self-proclaimed Peace State to be more reluctant to throw its citizens in jail for pursuing peace. At the time of his imprisonment for a three-year sentence, two other dissidents from Halle had just been sentenced to nineteen months in prison. Katrin Eigenfeld, a thirty-seven-year-old librarian and fellow-organizer with Rochau, was arrested for organizing the "Friedensdekaden" demonstrations, in which up to 1,000 people walked across the city from one church to another.

It was Katrin Eigenfeld's arrest that her husband Frank recalls as the event that spurred him to seek out the Western media. Halle dissidents had wanted to reform their own country themselves, as an internal matter. They wanted reform, not the West of the Western media. It was only due to the media, in fact, that Frank Eigenfeld was introduced to the idea that publicity might help. In the fall of 1983 he learned through the Western media (rather than through other dissidents) that Sebastian Pflugbeil, an East Berlin dissident, had been released following a personal request to Honecker from Richard von Weisäcker, then the mayor of West Berlin, and the publicity attending this request.

Following the report on Pflugbeil, Frank Eigenfeld drove to East Berlin to tell his own story to the dissidents there. He discovered that very few, if anyone, in Berlin had even heard of his wife's arrest. From East Berlin, dissidents contacted Petra Kelly about Halle's dissidents. The recently founded Green Party, particularly parliament member Kelly, had begun to reach out and make connections with East German dissidents like no other West German political party ever had or would. Both West German Chancellor Helmut Schmidt and member of parliament Petra Kelly met with head of state Erich Honecker to request more tolerance for the independent peace movement. Rochau became one of the tens of thousands of East German prisoners whose freedom West Germany actually bought with hard currency at a rate of approximately DM 96,000 per prisoner.[16] Katrin Eigenfeld, following the intervention of Kelly and Schmidt, was released from jail, and at this point East German dissidents began consciously seeking contacts with the West German media as a means of protection from their state's arbitrary arrests and punishment.

The historian Dirk Philipsen has characterized as "hidden" resistance the subtle, virtually unnoticeable lack of support for the party and state that typified many East Germans, while pointing out that "it is only when people's thoughts, aspirations, and actions become effectively 'public' that they can produce tangible results."[17] Katrin Eigenfeld was considered a leading representative of "political underground activity," dangerous because of the form her opposition took: the Stasi characterized it as "öffentlichkeitswirksam"—shaping of public opinion.

Publicity and public confrontation were the enemies of the state, and those friends of the state who also disguised themselves as the friends of dissidents always urged the dissidents to avoid publicity and to work through official channels. Just as church officials urged Lothar Rochau to avoid "spectacular" actions, so, too, Wolfgang Schnur, the gracious East German attorney who represented virtually all East Germans when they got into trouble with the state, always urged them to avoid publicity. Coming across as someone with their interests at heart, Schnur won the trust of Halle's dissidents. The one theme Schnur urgently, repeatedly expressed to dissidents was that they must avoid publicity at all costs. Publicity would only hurt them, he warned, adding that he himself could only help as long as their actions raised no publicity.[18]

Church official Manfried Stolpe, who was then consistorial president, repeatedly, earnestly warned Rochau to "keep it down. . . . Go ahead and do what you need to do, just don't draw any attention to it."

But Rochau sensed as well as Stolpe that there was little oppositional value in any activity that wasn't public (and, as Stasi records later revealed, Stolpe was in fact working for the Stasi). It became clear to Eigenfeld and others that publicity was their key to influence. Eigenfeld knew that publicity had been Pflugbeil's ally, and that he had found out about Pflugbeil's case only through the media.[19]

In East Germany, citizens were instructed to express their complaints through official channels, the so-called letters of protest or *Eingaben*, just as the dissidents were urged to accomplish their goals only through the state's official representative, Wolfgang Schnur, the Stasi agent. East German socialism established channels it claimed were there to help the people, but which were actually there to help the power center maintain control. The state attempted to channel citizen complaints into a nonpublic and thus harmless form. East Germans were entitled to an official response within ninety days, but often received none. Frank Eigenfeld contrasted going public with dissent in the media with trying to achieve change as an isolated individual or small group. The GDR dissidents learned that public expression was important not only to their efforts to achieve reform at home, but could also comprise a protective shield against state repression.

Any publicity—not just the publicity of the media but even the localized publicity of what Germans call "mouth radio" or word of mouth—might somewhat protect individuals. People interrogated by the Stasi, for example, were instructed not to tell anyone of their interrogation. They learned, however, that one possible form of protection against further Stasi harassment was to expressly violate the Stasi's order of secrecy. One Halle woman had the serendipitous advantage of attending an office Christmas party directly after an interrogation. Normally, she would have followed orders and repressed the desire to talk, she said. But the party spirit, combining the presence of friends and flow of wine, conspired to loosen her tongue, so that she ended up telling of her interrogation to just about everyone she encountered.[20] When the wine wore off, she feared retribution, but neither that nor another interrogation took place. As former dissident Vacläv Havel has written, the expression of truth in public rather than the experience of fear in private, was an important, minimally personal, triumph of the individual over the state.[21]

Although she considered open discussions and protests a more effective (and risky) form of opposition, Eigenfeld continued to use Eingaben letters to confront the GDR leadership with examples of its own hypocrisy and to point out that her group's own goals matched those of the state (or at least the state's rhetoric). To the great irritation of the Stasi, leaders of the 19 May demonstration wrote official protests to high state officials. The Stasi called the presence of dissidents at the FDJ demonstration a "counter demonstration," but in their letters the opposition characterized their actions as those springing from a desire to participate in the national demonstration of will to peace.[22] Although their motivations sometimes included pleasure received from kicking power in the shins, dissidents were careful to go on record as friends of the state, citing official rhetoric.[23]

Seven months earlier, in October 1982, Katrin Eigenfeld had been a ring leader in another confrontation with the state leadership, the writing of another Eingabe complaint, this one sent directly to Honecker himself by the newly formed Women for Peace, of which Eigenfeld was a founding member. Against the state's decision that in cases of "national defense" women could be conscripted, the new women's group insisted that their own ideas must be the basis of their own decisions about whether to go to war. Massive accumulation of weapons would lead to a catastrophe, but this could perhaps be hindered by an "open discussion of all questions that arise."[24]

Perhaps because the state repressed open discussion, treating it as if it were one of the most dangerous of weapons, the East German opposition often exhibited a very high degree of trust in the process of open discussion itself. Since officials simply ignored letters from persons they did not want to deal with, it is not surprising that substantive letters of complaint from seasoned dissidents often concluded not with the matter that had caused the complaint, but with a request to be heard in person. In its Eingabe letter to Honecker, Women for Peace demanded a provision within the new military service law that would allow for conscientious objection, but concluded with a request for a discussion of such a provision. The Eingabe to Krenz about the peace demonstration on 19 May 1983, anticipating silence, ended with a question: what possible reasons were there for denying them a conversation with officials? The opportunity to meet face to face with the apparatus that was controlling their lives, became the substance of some Eingabe letters (and by 1989, on the run to preserve its power, GDR leaders kept promising to open up new levels of "dialogue"). Eingabe letters show that disciplined dissidents strove not to show fear of the state, even as they refused to allow the state to define who they were, or what claims they could make.

As they learned that they could make no progress through complaint letters, GDR dissidents began increasingly to express dissent openly, but also nonviolently. Like the West German political parties that negotiated with the East German leadership and ignored the opposition, Katrin Eigenfeld was counting on the long-term existence of communist East Germany, and much of her activism was geared toward long-term mobilization of popular opinion. Like other serious dissidents in the GDR, she rejected the use of violence. The GDR opposition, comprised of representatives of a wide variety of belief systems, was united in a belief in unarmed rather than violent forms of opposition. Eigenfeld's refusal of violence was not shaped by the Christian gospel, but by an effort to have influence. In September 1986, the Stasi secretly recorded Katrin's responses to a West German film about the terrorist Bader-Meinhoff (RAF) group. "In order to succeed," Eigenfeld said after seeing the film, "activities can only be carried out nonviolently." Later she added that "nonviolent actions would have borne more fruit. In that case I would have joined [the RAF] as well."

Like other intellectual dissidents, Eigenfeld often relied on the institution, if not the religion, of the Protestant church, an institution relatively independent of the state that provided rare space for open, public discussions.[25] The church also had access to the key resources needed for spreading opinion. The means for reproducing the printed page, such as they were in the GDR— mimeograph machines, dinosaurlike photocopiers—as well as paper itself, were all restricted to officially recognized organizations like political parties and the churches.

The opposition had to develop public means of encouraging expression of complaints, and this included not only the use of the media but the use of church sanctuaries. Just as word-of-mouth might somewhat protect East Germans from Stasi intimidation, so, too, open dissent within East Germany, even if it did not receive media publicity, was more effective than the dissent channeled into the official Eingaben complaint letters. During so-called lamentation prayer services held in church, for example, openly expressed complaints against the state were considered a form of prayer. Eigenfeld was one of the main proponents of Halle's so-called lamentation prayer meetings, which were organized primarily by her father, Christfried Gabriel, a Protestant pastor in Halle. One of the lamentation services that most aggravated the Stasi was organized by Halle's Women for Peace on the evening of 29 June 1984. It was held in the Marktkirche, the church at market square, Halle's largest, most centrally located Protestant church and later the site of citizens' movement demonstrations in 1989. Pastor Gabriel opened the service by inviting anyone present to "raise a complaint, which if honestly expressed from the heart, would not be misunderstood and used against them."[26]

There was a biblical precedent for lamentation by God's People, but the Stasi took these services to be political subversion. At least three Stasi agents attended and wrote separate reports on the 29 June meeting. In attendance were about one hundred fifty people, most of whom were young. About fifty raised their voice to make complaints. Following each testimony, the group joined in singing "Come let us make lamentation, it is now time, we must cry out, otherwise we will not be heard." Eigenfeld, the Stasi reported, inspired and encouraged those present to make a complaint.[27]

The police did not risk entering a church to break up a service the way they intervened against public street actions, but following the 29 June lamentation service, the Stasi drew up plans to repress any recurrence of these services. For the Stasi, the lamentation prayers were just another example of the church's general "misuse of a meeting for hostile-negative attacks on the socialist state and social order." Using its specific attack against the lamentation prayers as a point of leverage, the Stasi hoped to intimidate the church in general. It planned "offensive measures" to repress further lamentation services and the general use of the church building for subversive purposes, categorizing its efforts as "disciplining" and "causing insecurity." In addition, the Stasi attempted to mobilize evidence to imprison the opposition (for which cooperation with the state's prosecuting attorneys was necessary). Their offensive included confiscating tape recordings of the services, holding independent interrogations intended to frighten and intimidate, and interfering actively in the personal and public lives of dissidents to isolate and immobilize their efforts.

As they began to realize that open speech and publicity was a life-support system, the dissidents realized the need to fight for freedom of speech, and they began to develop initiatives for guaranteeing human rights.[28] This tended to increase contacts with West Germany. Contacts between East German and Western dissidents often occurred through groups with international concerns—Physicians for Social Responsibility, environmental groups, and human rights or peace movement organizations. One of the ways the state stifled dissent was to shove troublemakers over the border, and as more and more former GDR dissidents and malcontents made their homes in West Germany, they slowly helped establish contacts between dissidents who remained behind and were means of support for them in the West. A Stasi agent reported on 20 November 1987 that Katrin Eigenfeld has sought, through someone who has emigrated from GDR to West Germany, to be put onto a "central list," with the goal of becoming known to the Western media, in order to encumber the efforts of state organs to control her.

Media and Movement

The state and party expended a good deal of effort attempting to redirect or hinder certain social processes, and in turn start new ones. As Czech leader Vacläv Havel wrote, communism was an effort "to organize all of life according to a single model, and to subject it to central planning and control regardless of whether or not that was what life wanted."[29] In East Germany, fear of being noticeable in a political way bled into the more general fear of standing out in any way at all. Social conformity pressures, formed in part by the collective fear of arbitrary state power, could make even nonpolitical acts difficult. Confinement enforced the fear of social nonconformity and the sense that there were no alternatives. Citizens had little recourse to a variety of social settings and models. Oppression of public dissent resulted in "pluralistic ignorance," the condition in which various persons in disagreement about the regime actually perceived themselves as being alone in their dissent. In 1989, protests in the GDR showed how quickly dissent, once displayed, could spread.

Jürgen Habermas, a prolific philosopher on matters of the public sphere and problems of public communications, wrote that the effect of televising the GDR protests of 1989 was to draw in to the protests persons who otherwise would have remained uninterested.[30] The mass media had a decisive effect in making the protests contagious. Furthermore, by reproducing the street demonstrations on individual television sets around Germany and the world, the mass media actually magnified the "physical presence of the masses demonstrating in squares and streets." This transformation of the demonstrations into a "ubiquitous" event increased their "revolutionary force," an advantage not shared by the protesters of earlier German revolutionary periods in the nineteenth and early twentieth centuries.[31]

The West German electronic media—particularly television—bedeviled the GDR's struggle to control the world view of its citizens, helping to win, in the end, the political struggle Gramsci identified as a "cultural battle to transform popular vision."[32] Since the 1970s, about 90 percent of East Germans regularly consumed West German radio and television, as Honecker admitted to the SED Central Committee in 1973.[33] Although the GDR population largely accommodated the communist system throughout its existence, the Western media, through advertisements as well as programs, presented a view of capitalist democracy that most East Germans came to see as preferable. The state, which Gramsci has usually associated with control through force, was poorly equipped to stop the consensus forming in GDR civil society, based to a large extent on Western media, that West Germany was a better place to live, and thus lost hegemony.[34]

For the state and party, the Western media were a force that disheveled society and socialist norms. By the mid-1980s the Eigenfelds and national leaders of dissent such as Bärbel Bohley saw the West German media as a source of some protection against arbitrary police actions. West Germans, including members of the parliament and prominent journalists, planned to increase the visibility of certain East German dissidents through the West German media. A Stasi report of 18 October 1986 reported that Katrin Eigenfeld had discussed the effectiveness of publishing Eingabe complaint letters in the Western media. Another report of 9 March 1987 was a record of a meeting of West German TV's reporter Franz Alt with twenty GDR citizens in Bärbel Bohley's Berlin apartment. Those present discussed the possibility of support for the independent GDR peace movement through reports on West German television. In October 1987, Stasi agents reported the existence of a list of forty East Germans, including Katrin and Frank Eigenfeld, in the hands of Oskar Fischer, then a member of the West German parliament from the Green Party. These East Germans were to be named among official documents of international organizations such as the peace movement, for example. Their international profile would lend them a "protective shield" through a level of visibility in the West that might guard them from the worst abuses of arbitrary police-state punishment. In addition, the publicity was intended to pressure the state into allowing dissidents like Katrin Eigenfeld to attend international meetings of the peace movement, held in the West.

For the East German dictatorship, the West German media not only helped cause internal unrest, they also made it more difficult for the regime to punish its dissidents, since it wanted to avoid negative international publicity. When Katrin Eigenfeld considered publishing Eingabe complaints in the West German media, her intention was to reach East Germans. Ironically, the best way to do this was to send her complaint first to West Germany, so that it could be sent back into East Germany again through the electronic media and spread into living rooms around the GDR. Publication of her letters in the West could, at best, give Eigenfeld a prominence that would make her imprisonment problematic for the regime, while also encouraging dissent inside the GDR. Published letters describing a complaint that a wide section of the population empathized with her could create empathy for the author, so that her imprisonment because of it would become unpopular.

East German politburo members railed at the Western media, accusing them of not only exhibiting and thus spreading dissent but also of seditiously sowing social unrest. The media were an arm of Western states, former Youth Leader Egon Krenz complained, to defame the leadership and draw the youth away from socialism. In June 1987, as music from a rock concert at the Reichstag building in West Berlin wafted eastward across the wall, East Germans began gathering on their side of the wall in a crowd that grew until it spread for hundreds of meters along Unter den Linden Street. Each night, for several days in June 1987, the evening concert resumed, while the crowd in East Berlin grew bigger and more political, until it clashed with the People's

Police, as the regular street police were called. According to a Politburo report, all those in attendance had found out about the concert through the Western media (as if the Berlin Wall had actually stopped the music itself). In a further self-deception, this internal document also flatly denied the Western media reports that East Germans dissidents had called out "Gorbachev."[35]

Krenz claimed that there was no official attempt to portray East German reality rosier than it really was, and a counterpart of this official denial was a tendency to blame the Western media for just about everything politically unpleasant.[36] Of course, images in the Western media did open up great gaps between what people experienced and the official image of East Germany.[37] Furthermore the dissidents, wanting to embarrass the state with televised depiction of its arbitrary and hypocritical police activities, planned their actions in conjunction with West German television journalists, alerting them to be on hand to report the brutal police repression of the most minor and justified dissent.[38] By mid- and late-1989, as waves of East Germans pushed to leave their country, the Politburo blamed this, too, on the Western media. True, as the media advertised the increasing possibilities for escape, more and more East Germans found out about it, and more left. But several years later, after poring over the documents he had written and received as the most powerful man of state and party, Krenz readily admitted that the state, and not the media, had been to blame. The state and party had not responded well enough to popular opinion and morale, he said.[39]

The Western media gave image and voice to disaffected masses the regime hoped to successfully portray as a fringe. The *Ausreisewelle* of people who chose to leave the GDR permanently discredited the East German state, especially as it reached such massive proportions in 1989. Unlike these streams of people leaving, the crowds of East Germans who began protesting on the streets by September 1989 made the regime look weak and unable to put down mass opposition. Protests showed that an ordinary citizen might stand up to the regime, not just flee. But in portraying a regime armed to the teeth as incapable of using overwhelming force, the protests encouraged more emigration. A report from early October 1989, based on reports from and surveys of East Germans, concluded that the mass street demonstrations had emboldened people who otherwise might not have left to get up and leave. Until the street protests, and despite the waves of fleeing East Germans, the regime felt that it could generally maintain popular support. But the protests—open opposition that refused to run—made it impossible for the regime to overcome the negative popular attitudes toward socialism that kept coming to the surface.[40]

During the uprising of late 1989, West German television was a unifying and reinforcing force behind the opposition, whether that of emigration and exit, or protest and voice.[41] The media could only show the vast numbers of people emigrating, and thus perhaps increase those numbers. For those who chose to stay and exercise their protest as voice rather than exit, however, the Western media could do more, at least initially.

The electronic media augmented the opposition's efforts not just by protecting it somewhat, but also by spreading the news of dissent. The Stasi was less sensitive than the state to outside opinion, and, exercising power somewhat independently, was more prone than the state to ignore the pains of embarrassment caused by the media's spotlight on human rights and other abuses. But in October 1989, as the situation for the state grew critical, Honecker ordered the use of military force against the peaceful Leipzig demonstrators. Nevertheless, politics prevailed when on the critical night of 9 October Honecker's order was ignored. The media had helped display and spread dissent to a point where the prevailing leaders felt violence would be useless, and some police officers declared that they would refuse to use force.

Within the GDR, the Western media unified, spread, and focused the opposition of late 1989. The media fastened their attention on Leipzig and Berlin, and by September and October they were spreading the news of increasingly large protests, as dissent leapt up around the country. Many provincial places where the media would never visit began staging their own protests.[42] The effect of Western journalists was to take information out to West Germany and then send it back again to the millions all throughout East Germany, via television and radio. They acted like a giant microphone held on incidents of dissent, to disseminate the news of dissent, allowing others to feel solidarity in opposition. Television images of opposition disturbed the consciences of East Germans who justified their lack of opposition with thoughts that all opposition was impossible. General Major Hänel, the Stasi chief for Berlin, admitted in August 1989 that the dissent broadcast by the Western media was very likely creating a general sense of discontent, since the reasons dissidents gave for their discontent were widespread in the GDR.[43] One German journalist suggested a much larger role for the media when he suggested that East German border guards allowed East Germans through the Berlin Wall and into the West that fateful night of 9 November, only after and because of the enormous flood of TV lights, indicating that the eyes of the world were watching.[44]

As their most effective way of reaching the masses to shape popular opinion, the active use of the Western media was the East German dissidents' most influential assault on the state. It is their effort to shape popular opinion on a wide scale that distinguishes their opposition from the kind the political scientist James Scott has characterized as "weapons of the weak." These "everyday forms of resistance" are primarily those of stubborn refusal, used to perpetuate traditional lifestyles and needs. They are survival mechanisms registered in the "tenacity of self-preservation . . . in petty acts of noncompliance, in foot dragging, in dissimulation, in resistant mutuality in the disbelief in elite homilies, in the steady, grinding efforts to hold one's own against overwhelming odds."[45] The weapons of the weak are unlikely to more than marginally affect peasant conditions, but have "changed or narrowed the policy options available to the state," according to Scott.[46] GDR's activists first appealed to the media for preservation, then soon used them to magnify and amass dissent in their efforts not just to narrow state policy options, but to radically reform the state.

By attempting to shape opinion, East Germany's protest leaders were attempting to reform socialism and the government, rather than merely survive. In the decades before 1989, heightened expressions of "everyday resistance" in East Germany did actually limit the state's policy options, according to the East Berlin Protestant youth pastor, Wolfram Hülsemann. Insistent practice of church activities the state wanted to repress gradually led to the official acceptance of those actions, Hülsemann recalled. During the twenty years after the late 1960s he had detected a pattern: first the church took an action the state considered threatening, but over the years, as the church continued the action, the state gradually got used to that particular form of opposition and fell silent. Hülsemann began by preaching critical sermons in church that the regime considered threatening, and he was threatened. But he continued, and after a while the regime stopped complaining. By a decade later, he was making the same criticisms of the state outside of the church, at rallies, and the regime eventually got used to this, too. An important distinction between GDR activists and Scott's peasants is that they wanted to mobilize popular opinion rather than merely survive on their own traditional terms. Through the Western media these dissidents reached more persons than Hülsemann could in speeches, and threatened the state much more—but it was also in part through the media that the masses had learned to prefer the West to reformed socialism.

It was occasional access to the electronic media of the 1980s that distinguished the weapons of the GDR opposition from those of James Scott's peasant rebels, in form and possible effectiveness. The active use of the media in conjunction with mass, public dissent was the most assertive, threatening form that GDR dissidence took. And even though it was not as dramatic as fiery, violent revolution, it was a more intelligent choice. The police would have certainly shot into a street mob brandishing weapons, the "Chinese Solution" that hung over the air that fall would have descended in a brutal reassertion of the power of a regime armed to the teeth. An effective domestic challenge to the GDR regime was possible largely because of the radical changes in Soviet and

Soviet empire politics under Gorbachev. But if people like Katrin Eigenfeld and Lothar Rochau had not already decided before 1989 that nonviolence was the only way to express dissent, the huge conflict in 1989 would not have been nonviolent. And if the opposition had used arms, the police of a regime that was armed to the teeth would have used arms in turn—despite Gorbachev.[47]

In the late twentieth century, the media, especially TV, are in a position to somewhat enforce the human rights norms of the Western world by displaying egregious violations of these standards. The GDR dissidents' decision not to use violence was tactically sound because the Western media that were available in their struggle magnified the reasons governments throughout history have had for not using force against their own citizens, who are not armed. An armed attempt to overthrow the regime—in accord with standard definitions of resistance—would have been self-defeating and ineffective for mobilizing the popular opinion and growing the civic movement that GDR dissidents wanted. On the other hand, governments that shoot down scores of unarmed citizens appear like bullies and risk their aura of legitimacy, while governments putting down armed uprising often strengthen their image of legitimacy (which is why German leader Bismarck had tried so strenuously to incite his domestic enemy, the Social Democrats, to anarchy and armed street conflict). Honecker, like Bismarck, fell after advocating the use of police force against domestic dissidents.

But Honecker had not been reined in by a king, but by the forces of democratization, together with the force of the media. In the late twentieth century, as illustrated by the GDR's revolutionary autumn, the media (especially TV) have become a powerful new force—for change as well as for continuity. In our time, as popular opinion around the world becomes more important and is readily registered and accessible, it is more effective in some cases for citizens to act collectively without arms, for social change. The bully regime that forces its power down the throats of peaceful citizens has often lacked legitimacy in the eyes of the general public, but in the late twentieth century the eyes of the general public are much more numerous, and more present, with the increased presence of the media. The context of increasing democratization and slow spread of human rights allows for collective actions that are not violent, and yet may achieve the same revolutionary effects of the bloody, dramatic changes that have been called revolution.

But the media, however, are certainly not of themselves a revolutionary or reformist force. The sheer cost of operating electronic media indicates that it will, in general, operate as a force for the status quo. Germany's postwar divisions provided the context for East Germany's unique life and revolutionary moment, within postwar eastern Europe. Not only did neighboring West Germany bleed away the GDR's potential for resistance, as hundreds of reform-ists like Wolf Biermann were shoved from East to West Germany. For decades, the powerful West German media, broadcasting across the eastern border to its neighbors who spoke the same language and shared a common history, had portrayed a West Germany that East Germans, especially the young generation, considered superior to their own country. In 1989 the same media were in a position to promote the growth of dissent and the demise of the GDR, but they were in no position to promote the reform that the leading dissidents had wanted since the masses had already come to see unification as the quickest, surest way to the things in life they wanted.

Germany is considered a country of revolution, although there have been important occasions of mass, popular uprisings of which 1989 is only the most recent. There is a tradition of German protests, popular uprisings that have forced the dislocation of repressive regimes, revealing an obstreperous streak that contradicts the stereotypical image of Germans as a docile people. This streak of protest has been considerably widened by post–WW II social developments—the 1960s, the new social movements, the Green Party, and the GDR citizens' movement.

The dearth of a revolution in Germany does not indicate the dearth of mass, revolutionary actions by Germans. During the revolutionary periods of 1848 and 1918/19, as well as during 1989/90, however, conservative governments waited out revolutionary impulses before consolidating power on their own terms. In 1989, the media assisted this German model by assisting the dissent against a regime, while overall acting as an aid to the reunification that most of the opposition leaders tried to prevent.

Germany's postwar division was the unnatural result of WW II, and unification, a latent theme in the GDR, became an irrepressible force, based on the majority's conception of life in West Germany and the future this would afford them. Various conditions, including the Western media, had shaped this majority opinion of the West. Even as it had educated East German tastes with the products and choices of the West, the Western media, using Western categories and Western interpretations, also acted to assimilate East Germany into the West.

A Movement on the Way to Reform

The dissidents were actually reformers but they represented revolution to socialism as it really existed. The dissidents were in the process of building a movement, and formed the initial and risk-taking core of the citizens' movement in late 1989. But would they have become strong enough to reform communism from within, and, if so, how long would it have taken for them to do so? The opposition was not only small, it was also (as a movement) short lived. The GDR's rapid decline and fall did not allow the development of a real consciousness about resistance and a more sophisticated goal than instant unification, identification with the clearest model of a different, possible lifestyle.[48]

By November 1989, and the point by which it appeared safe to demonstrate on the streets of East Germany, dissident-reformers who wanted a "third way" like those discussed above, were no longer providing the ideas and foci of the protest movement. How are we to assess the extent and significance of the opposition in the GDR? It was their efforts, for example, members of Women for Peace later said, that had led to the state's decision to discontinue the implementation of the law to conscript women into the military, in cases of national defense.[49] In the reunified Germany, though, Women for Peace and others of the opposition as well have dissolved, and the chance and responsibility for each individual to make a career in the new Germany has in many cases undermined the focus on national politics that brought them together. Even if we admit that some GDR activists were heroic in their sacrifice and willingness to fight until the end, what difference, if any, did the opposition in East Germany make?

Obviously, the reformer-dissidents in the GDR did not find a third way, nor have they clearly influenced national postcommunist politics. They have nowhere near the influence of the reconstituted Communist Party (PDS).[50] Some still argue that they would have, however, had it not been for the immediate intervention of West Germany, following communism's collapse.[51] Other citizen movement leaders, however, have reflected that the East German voters instinctively knew that the citizen's movement was more capable of bringing the old regime to its knees, than in setting up a new form of politics to fill communism's void.[52] Joachim Gauck, who in the GDR was an opposition leader from Rostock, East Germany where he was a Protestant pastor, remembered that in 1989/1990 East Germans wanted to join West Germany and West Europe. They didn't want to be written off any longer, he said. They wanted the West German Mark. They wanted to participate in the Western political system. They wanted to be let out of their confinement, out of their depression, out of their identities as Europe's step-children.[53]

The citizens' movement was too small and developed too late to influence the GDR's 17 million to try a third way (and even the most idealistic of them, Bärbel Bohley, now says that the communist system was incapable of reform). However, the GDR opposition can claim some impact on Germany's society and politics today. In city and regional politics, the citizens' movement is represented in numbers well above that in the national government. In Halle, members of the former opposition continue political activism and comprise a significant faction in the city government. There are other signs that the movement's legacy in the short run is best detected at community levels and within individuals who continue to struggle to build a responsible citizenry. There are some signs that on local community levels it has increased the potential among individuals for the political participation.

Perhaps it is most difficult to measure the legacy of the citizens' movement. Drawing from the historian Rudolf Stadelmann's thesis that the revolution in Germany of 1848 wrought important psychological changes, it might be possible to argue that the citizens' movement also implanted the ideals of grassroots citizenship and democracy.[54] Wolfram Hülsemann, the youth pastor in Berlin, is concerned with teaching German youth political participation. He wants to change standard concepts of power and resistance to take into account civilian responsibility and the significance of individuals in the support of political systems, and he relies on social movements and examples of social power to do this. The 1989 opposition movement "gave citizens courage to speak their opinion openly and to make their own judgments," he said. As a teacher, the movement also helps him to accustom students to images of people power, because it is a form of political participation. The movement is thus important as a step to overcoming the passivity East Germans learned under communism. "When I talk to my young people, I speak of 'Revolution'" Hülsemann said. "I want them to have pictures from history that give them courage. I want to make them politically active, and make them courageous. I can do that by showing them how people tried to participate in East German politics."

The citizens' movement is now often characterized as not having had a vision about what was supposed to happen after communism collapsed. But will the constitutional propositions of the citizens' movement of 1989—now archive documents—also be implemented in time as were the constitutional proposals of another "failed" German revolution, the one of 1848? Part of the significance of the GDR opposition is their vision. The meaning of the citizens' movement is impossible to measure. But it represents a standard, an ideal—a broadening mass participation in politics generally, and an increased potential of citizens for seeing their own interests at stake in the oppression of others.

Notes

1. Michael Schmitz (1995, 24, 25, 82, 83) has emphasized the GDR's repression of individual initiative and sense of responsibility, and the concomitant production of authoritarian personalities. The Halle Therapist, Hans-Joachim Maaz (1990, 36), wrote that the GDR system repressed creativity and individuality from the cradle to the grave. Children grew up under authoritarian and repressive teachers, the schools

were the "training grounds" of the nation. The system deprived its subjects of love and bottled up their disappointments and wrath, breeding a nation of persons suffering under "emotional congestion." Unable to find their own way, children merely reenacted what their parents before them had experienced. Rather than protesting, parents actually preferred allying themselves with this "children-hostile" system to the embarrassment of bucking the system. (The joke among the dissidents in Halle, indicating Maaz discouraged dissident activism, was that during the 1980s there were two ways that they might lose friends—either through emigration to the West, or therapy with Maaz!)

2. I am writing a book about the roots, impact, and legacy of the protest movements of 1989 in the former German Democratic Republic, a close-up study of protest in the provinces, and the problems there of reunification. Protests in the provinces—not just those in Berlin and Leipzig—played an important role in determining national developments in the GDR, and the history of a single provincial city, with its splendid array of biographies, poignantly illustrates the central issues of conformity and resistance in a police state as well as the social costs of the new unification.
3. Philipsen (1993, 49) and my interview with Frank Eigenfeld, 18 August 1993.
4. Interviews with Lothar Rochau (Halle), August 1993 and May 1994.
5. The diplomat and writer Günter Gaus (1983) used the phrase "society of niches" to describe the withdrawal of East Germans into private life as a way of escaping the omnipresent attempts of the regime to control all aspects of life.
6. Interviews with Wolfram Hülsemann (Berlin), March and August 1993. See also Jarausch (1993, 49).
7. Interviews with Klaus Herold (Halle), March 1993. The official news said that this objector had been killed in action, but one of his comrades later told Herold of his execution.
8. Pond (1993, 35ff).
9. There is much literature on the roles the churches played in the GDR. See, for example, Beiser and Wolf (1992) and Pollack (1990).
10. On 21 June 1973, the basic treaty regulating and normalizing relationships between East and West Germany took effect. On 18 September 1973, the United Nations accepted the GDR's three-month old application for membership (West Germany also became a member that day). In May 1974, East and West Germany established permanent diplomatic representations with each other, and at the end of 1974, the United States opened its embassy in East Germany's capital, East Berlin.
11. Lothar Rochau, unpublished manuscript titled "Daten, Gedanken und Geschichten zu einer Biographie," from January 1984.
12. Stasi report on Rochau, January 1984.
13. The proclamation Rochau sought out for his group was carefully selected from the words of East Germany's first head of state, Wilhelm Pieck: "Whoever in Germany once again picks up a gun, should lose his arm."
14. An eyewitness account of this demonstration and preparations for it is in Peter Wensierski (1986, 131–133).
15. Ibid., p. 133.
16. Jarausch (1993, 17).
17. Philipsen (1993, 20, 33).
18. Ibid, p. 46.

19. My interviews with Frank Eigenfeld (Halle) August 1993 and May 1994 in which he stressed the value of media and publicity corroborate the earlier ones of Dirk Philipsen (1993, 46).
20. Interviews with Henry and E. Shramm (Halle), April and May 1994.
21. Havel (1990).
22. When I interviewed him on 28 April 1994 (Halle), Rochau, too, called this a "counter-demo." More clever tactically, however, was the way the opposition characterized their actions in their Eingabe to Krenz in July 1983: "We too wanted to participate, we too have legitimate concerns about peace—and we are disappointed and not just that but also alienated by this Stasi action."
23. In an official letter of 6 July 1983 to Egon Krenz (who was then the party's Central Committee member in charge of the FDJ), the dissidents said they were "friends, who felt obliged to participate, because of the common concern for peace and the continuous cycle of arming and counter-arming, which could lead to catastrophe." This description of the demonstration is taken from a report titled "Notizen zur Friedensdemonstration der FDJ am 19.5.1983 in Halle auf dem Hallemarkt," an unsigned document from a demonstration participant. One of the forms of self-defense for dissidents was to keep a diary of their experiences, especially of mistreatment by the police.
24. Women for Peace, Eingabe of 12 October 1982, from the personal archives of Katrin Eigenfeld, Halle.
25. With its 7 million members, the Protestant church was overwhelmingly more active in GDR opposition activities than was the Catholic church, with 1 million members.
26. Stasi report on Katrin Eigenfeld, 29 June 1984.
27. Ibid.
28. Interviews with Frank Eigenfeld (Halle), May 1994.
29. Havel, "The End of the Modern Era," *New York Times*, editorial page, 1 March 1992.
30. See, for example, Calhoun (1992).
31. Habermas (1990a, 48, 49).
32. Gramsci (1963, 2).
33. Honecker blamed the "ruling circles in Bonn" for the intrusion of Western media (see Holzweißig, 1989, 63). The area of Dresden behind the Erzgebirge was protected from West German electronic media and consequently known in the GDR as the "valley of the clueless."
34. For overviews of the various interpretations of Gramsci's concept of hegemony, see Ransome (1992) and Bleiker (1993, especially 27–31).
35. "Bericht über Ereignisse am 6., 7., und 8. Juni 1987 in Zusammenhang mit Rock Konzerten in Berlin (West) und Schlußfolgerungen." Stiftung Archiv der Parteien, IV 2/2.039/277 (Rockkonzerte 1987), 6–18. As an exchange scholar living in East Berlin at the time, I witnessed this street gathering and heard the often-repeated cries of "Gorby, Gorby."
36. "No one had the intention of representing reality as any nicer than it really is." (Egon Krenz, Halle, June 1989, Stiftung Archiv der Parteien, IV 2/2.039/112: Erbegnisse, Erfahrungen, und Problemen der Berzirksparteiorganisation Halle, p. 108).
37. Michael Schmitz has listed some of the most poignant contradictions between state propaganda and lived experience in the GDR, and calculated the consequences.

Schmitz, *Wendestreß*, p. 82. The dissident Ralf Hirsch said that West German media reports that contradicted East German media possibly lowered the level of frustration in the GDR by bringing the reality people experienced more nearly in line with what reality as it was described to them on TV. (Interview, Ralf Hirsch [Berlin] March 1993.)

38. Dissidents who staged the Rosa Luxembourg counterdemonstration in Berlin in January 1988, called ZDF television to alert them to their plans. (Interview with ZDF correspondent Michael Schmitz and Ralf Hirsch, March 1990.)

39. Interview with Egon Krenz (Berlin), 7 September 1993. Krenz (1993, 90) wrote after his fall from power that the Western media, given the limited sources of information available to GDR citizens, had been a crucial influence on East German popular opinion.

40. Stiftung Archiv der Parteien (Berlin), IV 2/2.039/317 October–December 1989, correspondence on the citizens' movement. Krenz's file also contains an informative letter titled "Information" (Berlin, 6.10.1989, from Verband der Freidenker der DDR, Zentralvorstand).

41. For Albert O. Hirschmann (1993, 173–202), the two forms of "exit" and "voice" worked hand in hand to undermine the state during the revolutionary autumn of 1989. Other historians suggest that the waves of East Germans who voted with their feet by simply leaving East Germany initiated the collapse of communism and, overall, probably put more pressure on the regime than did the protests. See, for example, Jürgen Habermas (1990b, 54–58), who contended that 1989 was not a "voice revolution" but an "exit revolution" (Jarausch [1993, 17–30]; Naimark [1992, 75]).

42. More work needs to be done on the motivation for and the effects of protests in the provinces on national developments (if dissent had existed only in Leipzig and Berlin, the state could have successfully repressed it).

43. Mitter and Wolle (1990, 117).

44. Dieter Buhl, "Window to the West: How Television from the Federal Republic Influenced Events in East Germany" (Cambridge: J. F. Kennedy School of Government, 1990), discussion paper.

45. Scott (1985, 350).

46. Ibid, pp. 30, 36.

47. The decision to protest nonviolently—collectively and individually—is analyzed in Opp and Voß (1993, 127–137). My interviews indicate that protesters chose nonviolent forms out of strategic as well as moral grounds. Neues Forum and other organizers of the citizens' movements strictly instructed opposition to proceed nonviolently (see Bahrmann and Links [1990, 170ff]).

48. See, for example, Schmitz (1995) and Bornemann (1990). Bornemann (ibid., p. 33), who identifies the GDR revolution as existing between the massive Berlin demonstration of 4 November and the collapse of the Berlin Wall on 9 November, called reunification a "corporate state takeover" and concluded that the East German sense of inferiority in the face of Western prosperity "sapped the revolution's strength."

49. Interviews with Katryn Eigenfeld and Heidi Bohley, August 1993. Some GDR activists continue to organize protests and political initiatives to reform their new government—the old Federal Republic. (Halle is a center of recent protests against the Kohl government, protests targeting the Defense Ministry in particular, and espe-

cially Germany's sale of more than thirty warships, produced in the GDR, to Indonesia, a state with a record of genocide and severe human rights violations.)
50. See the full analysis of the 1994 German elections in Conradt, Kleinfeld, Romoser, and Søe (1995).
51. Schorlemmer (1991). Schorlemmer (ibid., p. 35), for example, a prominent member of the opposition in the Halle region, concluded that the entry of West German political parties into East German elections, beginning in 1990, had "torn the revolution from our hands" (p. 35). He concluded that, had East Germans had only been able to choose from among indigenous East German parties in the early elections, the citizen's movement would have remained a stronger force. Jürgen Habermas (1992, 438) also suspected that "the population of the German Democratic Republic has been similarly shocked by the campaigns of the West German parties currently invading its territory."
52. Christoph Kleemann, cited in Probst (1993, 13). Probst (ibid., pp. 12–13) agrees, writing that, in popular East German opinion, the citizens' movement could offer no convincing alternative to the political and economic system of West Germany. East Germans were initially sympathetic to the citizens' movement, but the movement's ties to efforts to reform socialism and its ambivalence about unification alienated many. West Germany was the closest model for escaping the conditions of communism that East Germans knew.
53. As cited in Probst (ibid., p. 13).
54. Stadelmann (1970).

References

Bahrmann, Hans and Christoph Links (1990). *Wir sind das Volk: Die DDR zwischen 7. Oktober und 17. December*. Berlin: Aufbau Verlag.
Beiser, Gerhard and Stefan Wolf, Eds. (1992). *"Pfarrer, Christen, und Katholiken": Das Ministerium für Staatssicherheit und die Kirchen*. Neukirchen.
Bleiker, Ronald (1993). *Nonviolent Struggle and the Revolution in East Germany*. Cambridge: The Albert Einstein Institution.
Bornemann, John (1990). *After the Wall: East Meets West in the New Berlin*. New York: Free Press.
Calhoun, Craig, Ed. (1992). *Habermas and the Public Sphere*. Cambridge: MIT Press.
Conradt, David P., Gerald R. Kleinfeld, George K. Romoser, and Christian Søe, Eds. (1995). *Germany's New Politics*. Tempe, Ariz.: German Studies Review.
Gramsci, Antonio (1963). *Selections from the Prison Notebooks of Antonio Gramsci*, ed. Quintin Hoare and Geoffrey Nowell Smith. New York: International Publishers.
Guas, Günter (1983). *Wo Deutschland liegt. Eine Ortsbestimmung*. Hamburg: Hoffmann & Campe.
Habermas, Jürgen (1990a). *Struckturwandel der offentlickeit: Untersuchungen zu einer Kategorie der burgerlichen Gesellschaft*. Frankfurt: Suhrkamp.
Habermas, Jürgen (1990b). *Vergangenheit als Zukunft*. Zurich: Pendo Verlag.
Habermas, Jürgen (1992). Further Reflections on the Public Sphere. In *Habermas and the Public Sphere*, ed. Craig Calhoun. Cambridge: MIT Press.
Havel, Vacláv (1990). *The Power of the Powerless*. Armonk, N.Y.: M. E. Sharpe.

Hirschmann, Albert O. (1993). Exit, Voice, and the Fate of the German Democratic Republic. *World Politics* 45 (January):173–202.

Holzweißig, Gunter (1989). *Massenmedien in der DDR*. Berlin: Verlag Gebr. Holzapfel.

Jarausch, Konrad H. (1993). *The Rush to Germany Unity*. Oxford and New York: Oxford University Press.

Krenz, Egon (1993). *Wenn Mauern Fallen: Die Friedliche Revolution*. Vienna: Paul Neff.

Maaz, Hans-Joachim (1990). *Der Gefühlstau—Ein Psychogramm der DDR*. Berlin: Argon.

Mitter, Armin and Stefan Wolle (1990). *Ich liebe euch doch alle! Befehle und Lageberichte des MFS, Januar–Nobember 1989*. Berlin: BasisDruck.

Naimark, Norman M. (1992). "Ich will hier raus": Emigration and the Collapse of the German Democratic Republic. In *Eastern Europe in Revolution*, ed. Ivo Banac. Ithaca: Cornell University Press.

Opp, Karl-Dieter and Peter Voß (1993). *Die Volkseigene Revolution*. Stuttgart: Klett-Cotta.

Philipsen, Dirk (1993). *We Were the People: Voices from East Germany's Revolutionary Autumn of 1989*. Durham and London: Duke University Press.

Pollack, Detleve, Ed. (1990). *Die Legitmat der Freiheit:Politisch alternative Gruppen in de DDr unter dem Dach der Kriche*. Frankfurt: Peter Lang.

Pond, Elizabeth (1993). *Beyond the Wall: Germany's Road to Reunification*. New York: The Twentieth Century Fund, Inc.

Probst, Lothar (1993). *Ostdeutsche Burgerbewegungen und Perspektiven der Demokratie*. Cologne: Bund Verlag.

Ransome, Paul (1992). *Antonio Gramsci: A New Introduction*. New York and London: Harvester/Wheatsheaf.

Schorlemmer, Friedrich (1991) *Bis Alle Mauern fallen. Texte aus einem verschwunden Land*. Berlin: Verlag der Nation.

Scott, James C. (1985). *Weapons of the Weak: Everyday Forms of Peasant Resistance*. New Haven: Yale University Press.

Shmitz, Michael (1995). *Wendestreß: Die psychosozialen Kosten der deutschen Einheit*. Berlin: Rowohlt.

Stadelmann, Rudolf (1970). *Soziale und Politsche Geschichte der Revolution von 1848*. Munich: Bruckman.

Wensierski, Peter (1986). *Von Oben Nach Unten Wächst Gar Nichts: Umweltzerstörung und Protest in der DDR*. Frankfurt: Fischer Verlag.

Orin Starn

Villagers at Arms

War and Counterrevolution in Peru's Andes

The hamlet of Huaychao perches at the edge of an Andean moor just where it plunges into the green forest of the Amazon valley. When I arrived to visit with a Peruvian journalist in 1994, a group of villagers in tattered sneakers and ragged ponchos took us to the rockpile that marked the grave of seven guerrillas from the Communist Party of Peru—Shining Path.[1] In Quechua, they told of killing the young fighters in 1983 with stones and machetes to prevent the takeover of the village by the Maoist revolutionaries. Despite reprisals by the Shining Path, these fifty families had defended themselves with spears and slings in a stubborn refusal to abandon the inhospitable countryside, even if the danger of attack often forced them to sleep in the icy caves above the hamlet. The rubble of a dozen farmhouses and the stone church testified to the ferocious predawn attacks where more than thirty villagers had died. "We have suffered beyond suffering," said an old man of a war that had seemed without end.

Huaychao was the first stirring of a massive and unexpected uprising against the Shining Path. Most analysts have presented the capture of Abimael Guzmán in 1992 as the main reason for the unraveling of the insurgency that in the previous decade led the Peruvian government to place more than half the country under military rule. What was far less noticed in the hubbub over the arrest of the man regarded by his followers as "the greatest living Marxist-Leninist" was that the Shining Path's influence had already declined over much of the Andes. Their Maoist blueprint projected the encirclement of Peru's cities from the countryside to "put the noose around the neck of imperialism and the reactionaries . . . and garrot them by the throat," in Guzmán's words.[2] By 1992, however, more than 3,500 villages in the departments of Apurímac, Ayacucho, Huancavelica, and Junín had organized into what came to be known as *rondas campesinas* (literally, "peasants who make the rounds") to fight the Shining Path.[3] Despite the assassinations of hundreds of patrollers (or *ronderos*), the alliance of the peasants and the military pushed the Maoists out of former strongholds across the stony gorges and snowy peaks of the Peruvian interiors. The "scientific" logic of Guzmán's plan was upended in a reversal as startling as a *pachakuti*, the inversion of heaven and earth predicted in Andean mythology, as peasants rose in arms against a revolution waged in their name.

During the first years of the war, I subscribed to the conventional wisdom among progressive observers that the peasant committees were an imperial imposition of the Peruvian military. This view pivoted on an imagined contrast between the "independent" and "peaceful" patrols against stock rustlers in the mountains of northern Peru and their "manipulated" and "violent" counterparts against the Shining Path in the central and southern highlands. Rondas campesinas had a grassroots sound, thanks to the inroads against thievery and corruption of the northern movement.[4] The application of the label by generals and ministers to what were then known as "Civil Defense Committees" of the war zone seemed a blatant bid to blunt criticism from human rights groups and leftist politicians of these organizations as the violent puppets of the security forces. Only after a series of trips to Huaychao and dozens of other villages across the south-central Andes did I begin to question the negative view of the uprising against the Shining Path. Although it was never hard to see the troubling hand of the military, the vision and passion of so many villagers in the fight against the violent authoritarianism of the Shining Path shattered the view of these impoverished Peruvians as the brutish dupes of a repressive state. Many scholars in the 1960s and 1970s had overlooked the upheaval and flux that fueled the explosion of the Shining Path in the first place. A danger of oversight recurred in the 1980s and 1990s, in this case of missing the counterrevolution. With the slipperiness of a trickster at an Andean carnival, the rise of the rondas reaffirms the impossibility of explaining and containing the unruly and sometimes painful trajectories of Peruvian history within the immobile boundaries of preconceived categories and fixed expectations.

This chapter is a belated bid to understand the Andean counterrevolution against the Shining Path.[5] It revolves around a conviction that there is a need to move beyond the easy characterizations of the patrollers as either brutish Hobbesian thugs or noble Tolstoian defenders of pastoral traditions or national sovereignty. Close scrutiny will confirm the need to avoid a naive romanticism by delving into division and violence in the movement. Yet it throws into relief the surprising success of villagers in carving a measure of peace from chaos and violence and in restoring new pride among the inhabitants of the forgotten Peruvian interiors who had seemed to many observers to be little more than passive victims of the storm of history. I am now convinced that the counterrevolution forces a recognition of the heterogeneous and often crosscutting consequences of every initiative for social change and reaffirms the potential of mobilization from below to contribute to the struggle for justice and dignity in a perilous world.

Perhaps the most astonishing accomplishment of the patrols revolves around the remaking of Andean society. The initiative of thousands of villagers in the fight for livelihood and survival has inverted what many scholars and journalists had presumed to be the inevitable obliteration of mountain identity and peasant culture in the hurricane of the modernity. Ghost villages have returned to fragile life from Purus to Marccarraccay, security guaranteed in large measure by endless hours of peasants themselves on dangerous watch in the biting cold of the Andean night. There are attempts to redefine and recover what is means to be a peasant, an Andean, and a Peruvian against the grain of want and terror at the edge of the new millennium. "*Kachkaniraqmi*" (I still exist), as the great Quechua-speaking writer José María Arguedas insisted in one of his most famous poems.

To Revolt Against the Revolution

"From the Andes will flow like rivers the currents of renovation that will transform Peru," proclaimed Luis Valcárcel in 1928.[6] The young Peruvian anthropologist was one of the brightest stars in the constellation of activists and intellectuals who championed Andean rights in the first decades of the twentieth century. These thinkers attacked racism and contempt toward mountain villagers in the national culture. They asserted that the Andean majorities represented the guardians of an Incan tradition that could be the touchstone for cultural independence and national emancipation. The Mexican and Russian Revolutions quickened the advent of radical politics in Peru, and socialism intertwined with nativism in this fervent doctrine of betrayal and renewal that premised the imperative of a return to indigenous values to confront modernity's challenges. As Valcárcel concluded, an "Indian Lenin" would lead a "tempest in the Andes" to reinvigorate a national conscience that would recognize the Indian peasantry as an "inexhaustible fountain of vitality for Peruvian culture" and bring "emancipation for the American race."[7]

Valcárcel's vision provides an entry into the Andean counterrevolution against the Shining Path. The history of the rondas reaffirms the correctness of the insistence of the young Peruvian scholar to recognize the place of mountain villagers in remaking Peru. Nevertheless, it would be an illusion to return to his view of the Andean majorities as isolated and timeless, maintaining an Incan "solar pedigree" untouched "by the tides of history."[8] To understand the revolt against the Shining Path, one needs to be able to go beyond the misleading presumption of a rigid separation of country and city, indigenous and Western, and tradition and modernity. Such a view enables Andean lifeways to be seen as the changing products of invention and amalgamation in a crucible of flux and upheaval. Far from the primordial expression of an immutable tradition of Andean resistance or rebellion, the mobilization of the late 1980s and early 1990s crystallized a volatile chemistry of politics and economy that reflected the deep involvement of mountain villagers in a divided yet interconnected planet at the end of the century.

The example of Cangari–Viru Viru serves to introduce the history of the counterrevolution against the Shining Path. As I discovered on a visit in 1993, ninety families from the villages of Cangari and Viru Viru had banded together in 1991 to build this hyphenated hamlet on a dry ridge above the Cachi River in the department of Ayacucho. The inhabitants had built a mud wall and eighteen guard towers of adobe brick and red tile around the hilltop settlement. In the delicate light of the Andean dawn, an uneven stream of women and men headed down to the riverplain to tend to crops and animals. They returned in the evening, herding goats and cows up the winding footpath inside the walls. By eight p.m. the men on patrol for the night took their posts with one-shot homemade guns of iron pipe, shotguns, and Mauser rifles, peering out to the uninhabited badlands across the shallow river where a band of the guerrillas had retreated with the promise to return to "annihilate" the "miserable mercenaries" and "pathetic stooges" who had dared to revolt against their revolution.[9]

As late as 1991, the river plain was a stronghold of the Shining Path. The Maoists used safe houses in the dusty hamlets along and above the river to bomb pylons and to assassinate politicians and policemen in the town of Huanta, just five miles to the northeast of Cangari–Viru Viru. However, the situation had changed with startling rapidity in 1991 and 1992. Under a new commander of the local region who came to be known as *El Platanazo* (The Big Banana) for his unusual height and pale skin, the army began a campaign of persuasion and intimidation to fight the Shining Path. Meanwhile, the violence and uncertainty of prolonged war had eroded the faith of most villagers in what the first cadre to arrive in 1985 had promised would be the "quick and glorious victory of the revolution," all the more so as the deepening crisis of the national economy endangered even the livelihood and survival of Andean farmers. Thus, many villagers in Cangari and Viru Viru were willing to move into a joint settlement in 1990, even though they knew it was a declaration of war against the Shining Path. It took less than a month for most families to build adobe houses on the hill. Over the next year, the guerrillas launched three nighttime raids, slinging grenades into the village from a stony outcrop. Nevertheless, villagers suffered no casualties, dug in behind their earthen walls and an outer fence of brambles. Rather than spread fear, the attacks strengthened a feeling of common cause. Peasant society was reconstructed as villagers built a chapel, school, health post, and a dusty plaza named "Lucas" after a Cangari patroller killed in 1989. "We're living with much more tranquillity now than before," as one weather-beaten farmer explained under the hot sun of the desert hills in 1993.

It would be a mistake to think of Cangari–Viru Viru as a typical case in the broad canvas of the Andean counterrevolution. Even before the Incas, the mosaic of diverse ethnic polities already belied the concept of a single Andean culture or world-view. The rondas have proved no exception to the history of heterogeneity in the Peruvian Andes. The implementation of patrols coincided with resettlement in Cangari–Viru Viru and other villages on the Cachi River. In other areas, villagers built walls and mounted patrols in preexisting settlements, whether refugee camps or established hamlets or towns. The power of the movement also differed from the fledgling patrols in Ayacucho's Víctor Fajardo and Lucanas Provinces to the paraprofessional armies of the Apurímac Valley. However, Cangari–Viru Viru does reflect the rapid spread of the rondas. By 1993, almost every village had a defense committee across hundreds of rugged kilometers from Andahuaylas to Junín. Every night, thousands of peasants headed out into the uncertain darkness for their weekly or monthly turn on patrol. Sentry towers of wood or mud loom over hundreds of villages and towns, and patrollers staff hundreds of checkpoints along the pot-holed highways that criss-cross the interiors. "We have changed the war," as a patrol leader in Cangari–Viru Viru told me in 1993.

The Birth of a Counterrevolution

The most immediate explanation for the village revolt lies in the inflexibility of the Shining Path. Some of the first war analysts returned to the ingrained view of the Andes as an exotic place of primordial customs and millenarian dangers to postulate that the insurgency must be an Indian revolt to restore the Inca empire. These views overlooked the fact that the Shining Path was never an organic uprising of the Andean peasantry. On the contrary, it was founded by Guzmán and other white professors in the Andean university of Ayacucho as a vanguard party to lead what party propaganda insisted was the "Strategic Offensive of World Revolution."[10] A reserved yet self-confident man who favored the conservative suit of an Andean intellectual,

Guzmán came from a middle-class family in the desert town of Mollendo, arriving in Huamanga in 1962 to take a university post. Already convinced of what he called "the grandiose importance and transcendence" of Marxist thought, the new professor belonged to the Communist Party of Peru–Red Flag until 1970s, when, apparently dissatisfied with the unwillingness of Red Flag leadership to take up arms against the Peruvian government, he led a splinter movement to found the Shining Path.[11] At a boarding house on Pukacruz Street, later known to local pundits as *El Kremlin* (The Kremlin), Guzmán delivered long talks on dialectical materialism and scientific socialism, and earned the nickname of *Dr. Shampú* (Dr. Shampoo) for his ability to brainwash listeners. During those years, intermarriage sealed the bonds between the Morotes, Durands, and Casanovas, the nucleus of what came to be known as the "Sacred Families" for providing the inner circle around the baronial Guzmán. Revolutionary bravado and intellectual certainty prevailed in the new party leadership, and an eager, even fierce, anticipation of the war where Guzmán promised the "oppressors will be irretrievably smashed."[12]

The bulk of recruits were high school and university students from Ayacucho's shantytowns and countryside. In this respect, and despite claims of radical upheaval, the new party's internal organization replicated the colonial stratification of regional society, as a white professional elite commanded a mass of brown-skinned kids of humble origin.[13] Even if they remained in the low rungs of the party, however, young followers of the Shining Path were offered the seductive promise of an active role in an imminent revolution under the wise guidance of charismatic leader who seemed to speak in the omniscient, almost magical voice of scientific truth. The assertion that the time was right for armed struggle furthered the Shining Path's appeal to many students, whose impatience for action was, in many cases, heightened by personal experience of poverty and racism as the children of the dispossessed. "The reactionaries are sharpening their knives . . . we, too, must get our knives ready," wrote a party propagandist about preparations for the so-called ILA or *Inicio de la lucha armada* (Beginning of the Armed Struggle).[14]

Between 1980 and 1982, the Shining Path put to flight the poorly armed and badly trained police throughout the rugged countryside of Ayacucho and the neighboring departments of Huancavelica and Apurímac. Although the view of some American scholars of a peasant rebellion or agrarian revolt ignored the top-down character of the Maoist insurgency, there is no doubt that the followers of Guzmán won a measure of village sympathy in the war zone.[15] Many peasants were happy to see inefficient and corrupt authorities depart, and the punishment by the cadre of adulterers and thieves seemed to validate the promise of a new, more just order. The Maoist rebels' status as the new lords of the Andean countryside heightened readiness to cooperate in demands for food and lodging even among those who doubted the call for revolution. As yet unopposed in mountain villages, the Shining Path ruled in what one analyst has called a regime of "utopian authoritarianism."[16]

The Maoists' advance did not last. At the end of 1982, President Fernando Belaúnde declared the bulk of the south-central Andes an emergency zone, under military rule; he sent in Second Infantry Division to lead the fight to recapture the mountains. The racist ideology of contempt for Andean villagers converged with the ferocious anticommunism of the cold war to spawn a terrible counteroffensive of burned villages and mass killings. In 1985, Amnesty International attributed 1,005 cases of "disappearance" to the security forces, the majority poor peasants. The firestorm led many villagers to reconsider the wisdom of supporting the Shining Path, who in Cangari, Viru Viru, and many other villages had promised the collapse of "rotten old order before the glorious people's army." "They promised us everything, yet all we got was more misery and death," as one woman in Cangari–Viru Viru said. In an exodus of almost biblical scale, 600,000 fled to the shantytowns of Lima and Ayacucho to escape these years of terror and displacement that came to be known in the Andean countryside as *manchay tiempo* (the time of sadness).[17]

Shining Path rigidity hastened the erosion of support for the revolution. Even before the military's arrival, the cadre had revealed an incapacity to deal with the rowdy intricacies of village society. One miscalculation was a ban on travel to markets. Guzmán followed Mao in believing that peasant enthusiasm for revolution would lead them to cooperate in raising animals and crops only for themselves in order to starve the cities. The vision of autarkic villages ignored completely the centrality of markets in the Andes. The trek to town to sell potatoes or a team of oxen provided a source of income for buying kerosene, soap, school supplies, matches, and other essentials, even a touch of excitement in the form of an ice cream cone or Colombian *cumbia* cassette. Trade and commerce also figured in the thinking of many villagers as the best avenue to advancement and mobility, and indeed owning a market stall or cargo truck formed part of the yearning for progress and modernity that had spread across the Peruvian Andes in the twentieth century. The market ban was a catalyst of unrest in Huaychao and other villages in the Iquicha moors in 1982, and later in 1989 in Huancayo.[18]

Inflexibility also became a liability on the matter of justice and punishment. The execution of cattle rustlers or even corrupt officials won approval in many villages, refuting the romantic claim of some anthropologists about Andean peasants' belief in a simple ethic of "punish but do not kill." Nevertheless, the dependence on the Maoist typology of poor, middle, and rich peasants sometimes

led into showy trials where young commissars presided over the flogging and
sometimes even stoning or hanging of better-off farmers, even in the many
villages where the difference between the poor and the rich amounted to a
pair of cows or hectare of land in a hardscrabble countryside where no one
escapes the injuries of racism or poverty.[19] The murder of an uncle or *compadre*
enlarged a circle of resentment and anger along the lines of kin alliance that
map the uneven landscape of social relations in the Andean countryside.[20] As
a young farmer from a hamlet on the forlorn moors of Huamanga explained
to me in 1992, "They told us they fought for the poor, yet even the poor suffered from their justice."

Rigidity also proved a liability in confronting the counterrevolution. The
Savonarolan fervency of this brand of orthodox Marxism led into a social eti-
ology of purity and danger where anyone in a hamlet with a ronda became a
"mercenary," "traitor," "stool pigeon," and "blackhead" who had to be "pulver-
ized," "annihilated," and "destroyed." Reliable testimony exists of the hacking
to death of babies and children.[21] The mass killing of hundreds of villagers in
Lucanamarca, Sivia, and Santa Rosa only fortified a feeling of hatred for the
followers of Guzmán. "The order was to erase everything," remembers Peter,
a Shining Path deserter who from 1988 to 1990 helped raid, burn, and kill
in the bedraggled hamlets of the Apurímac Valley.[22] Many villagers began to use
the word *ñakaq* (night demons) to suggest the merciless brutality that placed
the revolutionaries even beyond the realm of the human.

Military Maneuvers

Government forces were beginning to show unexpected flexibility in
the meantime. Unlike nearby Argentina or Chile, the Peruvian military had a
tradition of populism, reflected in the agrarian reform and nationalization of
foreign companies under the presidency of General Juan Velasco Alvarado
(1968–1975). The army, in particular, had also served as a rare avenue of social mobility in Peru in the twentieth century, always with a sprinkling of dark-
skinned generals of humble origins. The ferocity of the counteroffensive of 1983
and 1984 displayed the most brutal and imperial face of the troops. Torture,
rape, and murder remained a part of the counterinsurgency in subsequent
years. Already by 1985, however, many officers recognized the need to com-
bine persuasion with intimidation, including "sociopolitical development" and
"civic action" to build support among the peasantry. Massacres declined, even
if Peru remained the country with the world's highest number of "disappeared"
from 1988 to 1991. More soldiers were recruited from local villages and provincial towns. Showy generals like Alberto Arciniega and Adriano Huamán
danced and drank at parties and posed for pictures as godfathers of babies.

Historian Jaime Urrutia was himself arrested and tortured by the military in 1983 in the Ayacuchan barracks of Los Cabitos. He concluded in 1994 that the army "has changed. . . [Officers] like the sadly celebrated Commander 'Butcher' . . . are no more than a bitter memory, and peasants no longer live in terror of disappearances and arbitrary arrests."[23] Although the memories of the counteroffensive's terror would survive in stories and songs, the military managed a partial shift from occupier to protector, outmaneuvering the Shining Path in the battle for the Andean countryside.

It should be noted that the Peruvian army's adaptability warns against an oversimplified view of the intrinsic evil of the Latin American militaries. To be sure, there can be no question of the moral urgency of deepening documentation of the horrible history of military torture and murder in Peru as well as in Argentina, Brazil, Chile, Colombia, Guatemala, and Paraguay, all the more so as epauletted generals and weak-kneed politicians enforce a forced forgetting of past crimes by amnestying accused soldiers and officers. At the same time, the effort to grapple with the role of militaries ought to recognize and examine internal debates and conflicts between and within branches of the armed forces, diversity of national traditions and histories of martial institutions across the subcontinent, and malleability in outlook and strategy with the shifting terms of regional politics and world events. Instead of stopping at the necessary charge of terror and brutality, there is a need to develop an anthropology of the powerful that would open up to careful scrutiny the institutions and ideologies of Latin American militaries, and, in this case, to expand understanding of the unexpected capacity of the Peruvian army to redraw relations with the Andean peasantry.

Promoting rondas became a cornerstone of the army's bid to redraw relations with Andean villagers.[24] The military's first and mostly unsuccessful efforts in 1983 and 1984 to organize the peasantry used bluster and violence, including the murder of those who refused to join. By the end of the decade, their strategy had become far more sophisticated and reflected the counterinsurgency's new mix of authoritarianism and populism. Quechua-speaking officers traveled to high-altitude hamlets in Ayacucho and Huancavelica, dressed in *chullos* and ponchos, to urge their "brother peasants" to take up arms against "the enemies of Peru."[25] To promote the image of profitable partnership, the military also promised, and sometimes provided, donations of tools, medicine, and food. In 1991, I attended a meeting of fifty patrol leaders at army headquarters in the Mantaro Valley, where a general mixed in promises of shovels and tractors with the exhortation to "continue in your rondas." The military later donated 200 Japanese trucks, as a reward, in the general's words, for their "collaboration" against the Shining Path. The threat of force did not disappear, and, in fact, some inhabitants of Quinua remember how a mustachioed lieutenant threatened in 1989 to take "drastic measures" against villagers who refused to participate in patrols. However, the inclusive rhetoric and material incentives encouraged the interest and sometimes even enthusiasm about patrols on display in Vinchos, Huaychao, and dozens of other villages. Hundreds of patrollers in ponchos and with spears and rifles flooded the squares of provincial capitals across the south-central Andes to march with troops in holiday parades in a tangible display of their unlikely alliance in the fight against the Shining Path.

Perhaps the most striking sign of the changed relation between the military and villagers came in 1991. The army began the massive distribution to Andean peasants of more than 10,000 Winchester Model 1300 shotguns. At ceremonies presided over by a general or even Peru's president, Alberto Fujimori, and with the Winchesters blessed by a priest as if for a Holy War, the arms were handed over to peasants in little plazas of hamlets and towns across the war zone. During the Conquest, the Spaniards rigorously banned Indians, even trusted auxiliaries, from possessing either horses or swords, the instruments of Iberian supremacy in the deadly arts of war. Giving out guns would have been just as unthinkable for the Peruvian officers in the first years of the fight against the Shining Path, when the military was no more trustful of Andean peasants' true allegiance than the original band of European conquerors.[26] Even after 1991, many peasants, including those in Cangari–Viru, complained that the allotment of four or five guns per village was inadequate. They also wanted automatic weapons, to match the Shining Path's firepower, with its Kalashnikovs and FALs stolen from the police, and radios to call the army. Yet the Winchesters were welcomed in hundreds of villages, the culmination of months and sometimes years of petitions to the authorities for means to defend themselves greater than machetes, spears, hand-grenades of "Gloria"-brand evaporated milk tins, gunpowder, and nails, and the one-shot *tirachas*. A national law in 1992 recognized the ronderos' right to arms. The measure codified the reversal of the colonial withholding the technology of war from Andean peasants, signaling the confidence of Fujimori and his generals in peasantry's commitment to the fight against the Shining Path.

The government used the rondas to assert success at rallying Peru's poorest inhabitants to the defense of democracy and nationhood. In 1993, the army trucked thousands of ronderos into Lima to march on 28 July, Peru's Independence Day. Newspaper photos and TV news footage overflowed with the "exotic" imagery of ponchoed peasants along with a sprinkling of Amazonian militiamen in jaguar-toothed necklaces and war paint. It was coverage that exhibited and even reinforced the old conviction of the perennial Otherness of

Indians and peasants. In this context, however, difference's charge electrified what Fujimori called "our crusade to eradicate the scourge of terrorism," as legions of villagers, Winchesters over their shoulders, marched through Lima's streets with columns of nurses, engineers, schoolchildren, and doctors and squadrons of policemen and soldiers. Despite what I will suggest in a moment was their marginalization from ronda leadership, women wearing the "traditional" garb of bowler hats and wool skirts also paraded with spears and guns, extending the guarantee of the government's ability to harness their peculiar powers, multivocality, and diversity, in this case, the "female" as well as the "Andean." The extremes of violence and reason, the Andean and the Western, the primitive and the modern converged in this spectacle of national unity, staged by the government as part of the cultural politics of state-building in the shadow of hard years of violence and suffering that had torn so deeply at the fiction of national unity and progress.

The parade was revealing both for what it marked and left unmarked. No acknowledgment was made of the war's human costs, and the triumphalism of the pageantry effaced the massive human rights violations committed by government forces under Fujimori and his two predecessors. Meanwhile, the Winchesters of the peasants looked like popguns next to the rocket-launchers and bazookas of the regular troops, in what amounted to a public reminder of the military's ultimate power. Sleek generals and ministers occupied the position of privilege on the reviewing stand, magisterially elevated above the marching columns of Andean villagers, reflecting the power of white over brown, rich over poor, and city over county. Indeed, the very existence of the rondas bespoke the second-class citizenship of peasants. Wealthy elites paid for Dobermans, armed *guachimanes*, or watchmen, electrified fences, and cement walls to protect themselves from crime and political violence. Poor villagers did not have money to buy security, and their only option became to organize themselves in yet another example of how racial and class inequalities govern even survival's logic in Peru. Even as it played on the politics of inclusion and diversity, the spectacle underlined the subordinate terms of the incorporation of Andean and peasant identity in the fabric of nationhood.

After the march in 1993, most of Cangari-Viru Viru's fifteen marchers stayed in Lima to visit with relatives in the shantytowns of Huaycán and Villa El Salvador. Eventually, everyone trickled back to the mountains, to the animals and the plots that offered a fragile livelihood. In Cangari-Viru Viru, life is hard: there are the rivalries of local politics, the worry about drought or floods, the lingering fear of Shining Path attack. And yet, in a precarious security guaranteed in large measure by their own initiative in the rondas, villagers also carve moments of reprieve, whether the quiet excitement of a new baby's birth or the raucous energy of the San Juan's Day fiesta. As loss and pleasure inter-twine in this forgotten corner of the mountains, the rondas form part of the latest chapter in an on-going history of trauma, transformation, and survival of Andean societies.

The Economics of Return

Peru's economic crisis also played a pivotal part in the mobilization against the Shining Path. Already in the throes of a prolonged recession since the end of the Velasco years, the country plunged into an economic tailspin that reached a nadir in the chaos of bankruptcy and hyperinflation at the end of the 1980s. Although austerity measures imposed by President Alberto Fujimori (1990–   ) ended hyperinflation, they worsened the already desper-ate condition of most families, belying the smug talk of government ministers and American bankers about a Peruvian economic miracle. Whether fleeing poverty or war, new arrivals from the south-central Andes ranked among the poorest of the poor in the grey squalor of Lima's straw-mat and cardboard huts, even more marginalized because these Quechua speakers had difficulties with Spanish. Regular employment grew scarcer with recession. Even those who found jobs as gardeners, servants, laborers or watchmen could not feed them-selves on monthly salaries that seldom topped fifty dollars. For many migrants, the old dream of Lima as a place of opportunity and possibility gave way to a new vision of an inhumane and heartless metropolis where, a villager in Huaychao told me, "no one cares if you live or die."

Urban sadness and starvation intensified desire to return to the Andean countryside. Cultural critic Mike Featherstone underlines that: "the doubts and anxieties [of global change and upheaval] are reasons why "localism," or the desire to return home becomes an important theme—regardless of whether the home is real or imagined, temporary, syncretized or simulated."[27] This was true of the Andes. Ever since the explosion of migration down to Lima in the 1950s and 1960s, the mountains have figured as an object of nostalgia and long-ing for new arrivals in the city. Streetsellers do a brisk trade in pirated cas-settes of songs by mountain balladeers that celebrate the Andes' provincial traditions and stunning landscapes. The travails for mountain villagers of mak-ing a living on the faraway coast generated an imagery of abandonment and orphanhood in some of the most famous anthems in Andean repertory, includ-ing "Adíos, Pueblo de Ayacucho" (Goodbye, Town of Ayacucho). By the 1990s, the cause of el retorno (the return) developed into an almost biblical vision of redemption and recovery for families who had witnessed the shattering of the dream of progress in the city. This was all the more so as a number of Peru-vian human rights organizations and international aid agencies began to defend the right of the Andeans displaced to return to mountain homes. Teofilo Rimachi, from Cangari–Viru Viru, had made only ten dollars for fourteen-hour days as a security guard at a Lima paper factory: "If I must suffer or die, I would rather it be here in my mountain home than in the misery of Lima."

Order had to be restored for return to happen. In the face of distrust of the police and the incapacity or unwillingness of the military to put a detachment in each hamlet across the Andes, patrols were the best—and often the only— guarantee of a measure of security. As in the case of the Ayacuchan settlements of Purus and Lucanamarca, whole villages began to return to rebuild in 1993 and 1994. Every man took a weekly turn on sentry duty in adobe guardboxes and on the rocky trails. The conversion of *retornante* (returnee) and rondero into synonyms in rural talk signaled the centrality of the patrols in resurrecting dozens of villages that were destroyed and abandoned in the 1980s. Returnees also strengthened the patrols in those settlements that had weathered the violent storm, sometimes putting to use their Spanish and familiarity with the city to broker between fellow villagers and town politicians and military officials. The return of the displaced consolidated the uprising against the Shining Path in the south-central Andes, as those who had stayed behind were now joined by those who were compelled by city hardships to see their futures in the remaking of Andean life.

It should be apparent that a variety of variables converged to fuel the revolt against revolution. The decision to mobilize demands an avoidance of monocausal explanations and simple formulas in favor of a close-grained yet flexible examination of the plural and often unexpected forces that lead to collective action. More broadly, it also underscores the need to insist on social analysis that avoids the extremes of an ungrounded culturalism or a deterministic economism to examine the inseparable intertwining of cultural meaning and political economy in human experience, in this case of the alchemy between the forces of disenchantment with the Shining Path, pressure from the state, crisis in the Peruvian economy, and longing for the Andes. In this sense, the rondas confirm the dictum of anthropologists John and Jean Comaroff about the need for social theory to grapple with the "the simultaneity of the meaningful and the material in all things," and warn against the false certainty of "neat oppositions, nice determinations, and nefarious teleologies" that "short-circuit(ing) the more complicated pathways of human practice."[28]

Huaychao was an anomaly in 1983. No other hamlet withstood the Shining Path's onslaught on the moors beneath the foreboding crag of Razhuillca, worshiped by many villagers as a spirit of pain and possibility. In the next decade, the panorama was transformed with the rebirth of tiny settlements across the sad beauty of the lunar landscape of windy grasslands and rocky peaks. War survivors had returned from the invisibility of the diaspora to throw tin roofs over the stony ruins of burned villages, and to build guardboxes and watch-towers to protect against attack. "We have only ourselves to defend ourselves," as Natividad Huamán said of the ongoing struggle to rebuild from the blood and ashes that still haunted the present.

The Politics of Counterrevolution

As late as 1994, many critics maintained a negative view of the rondas as an expression of the brutalization of the Andean majorities. They charged the military with organizing by force, forcing peasants to the front line of a vicious war. Some opponents of Fujimori and his generals also insisted on the danger of the resettlements and patrols devolving into paramilitary groups that "extort," "blackmail," "rob," and "pillage," pitting the poor against the poor to unravel the delicate fabric of Andean life.[29] "We cannot permit the persistence of these evil institutions that spread death," a senator from a socialist party told me from his Lima office in 1989.[30]

Such a one-sided view can no longer be sustained. To be sure, the Lima marches and authoritarian patriotism of official proclamations about the "hero-ism and loyalty of the patrols" concealed paradoxes and divisions within the patrols and resettlements and the heavy hand of the Peruvian military in the rondas. Yet prophesied apocalypse has not come to pass. Quite the opposite, the rondas have contributed to a radical reversal of the spiral of death in the Andes and the return of more than 50,000 refugees to hundreds of far-flung villages abandoned in the heat of the war. From Angola's eastern provinces or Colombia's Middle Magdalena, there are many places where militarizing the civilian population has widened the circle of suffering and death. The role of the rondas in reducing violence underscores the need to avoid the trap of grand generalization to recognize the multiple and sometimes unexpected pathways of peasant societies in the postcolonial world.

The Contradictions of Militarization

This is not to say that the rondas are by any means unsatisfactory or unproblematic. Whether the picture in the *Soldier of Fortune* magazine of "forc-ibly organized structures" or the denunciation by the Shining Path of "stooges of the armed forces," observers with little else in common have framed the patrols in old images of the manipulability and brutishness of poor villagers. Just as untenable is the naive revisionism that swings into the opposite extreme of the reverse and condescending stereotype of the disenfranchised peasants as a reassuring fountainhead of harmony and wisdom. Careful scrutiny always reveals division and paradox in even the most progressive struggles, whether bossism in Brazil's shantytown unions or the problematic predominance of male priests over female parishioners in Zimbabwe's Christian base communities. No initiative is ever wholly oppositional or wholly power serving, and even the most noble movements will always defy the desire to freeze them into a tidy Jacobin imaginary. Through a recognition of plural and sometime cacophonous crosscurrents, scholars will be far more likely to generate the kind of analysis that presses beyond the stubborn caricatures of the shiftless illiterate or heroic resistor, or of the downtrodden as either passive objects or free subjects of history.

Perhaps the most obvious problem in the rondas revolves around the military. As the Ayacuchan historian Ponciano del Pino asserts, the movement has come a long way from "an early history of forced service and stringent supervision by army commanders over peasant patrollers."[31] The army still maintains a direct influence, however, an accountability codified into Legislative Decree No. 741, which stresses that every committee "must be authorized by the Joint Command of the Armed Forces . . . and operate under the control of the respective Military Commands [in their region]."[32] The army's authority assumes a variety of forms that extend from mandatory barracks meetings to demands for overnight lodging for soldiers. Although less common than in the past, there are still incidents of army abuse and corruption, like the sale of bullets, supposed to be donated by the government, by officers to peasants. Whether from church and development groups or political parties, outsiders have always played a key role in mobilization in the impoverished countryside in the Third World, belying the too easy view of the autonomy and independence of peasant organizing in some scholarship in subaltern studies. At the same time, the presence of hundreds of bases and tens of thousands of troops across the war zone leaves the military with an unusual power over village organizing, even more so with unsettling memories of the recent willingness of the troops to meet opposition with violence and destruction. Far from a clean tale of independent uprising, military power over the rondas marks a partial reinscription of Peru's colonial hierarchy of town over country and state over peasantry.

The role of the military connects to the problem of gender. Perhaps stemming from a wish to maintain a romantic view of harmony and equality in Andean villages, many scholars have used the imagery of "complementarity" and "parallelism" to describe the relation between the sexes in highland South America. To be sure, women's centrality in rites of survival and renewal of planting and harvest warns against reducing gender in the Andes to a parable of patriarchy, even as the gender bending of boisterous carnival crossdressing and free love reveals and even revels in the unstable boundaries of masculinity and femininity. However, indicators of the bleak harshness of gendered inequality also abound in mountain hamlets: wife beating, reluctance to send girls to school, and exclusion of women from elected office. Several anthropologists have explored how women come to be defined as more Indian than men by virtue of the greater likelihood that they will not speak Spanish and assume more traditional dress and duties, like herding and weaving.[33] The mutual reenforcement of the subordinate categories of Indianness and femaleness reflects a convergence of hierarchy of gender and ethnicity that fixes village women in a doubly displaced position at the bottom of national society.

The rondas reflect the second-class status of women in Andean society. Since men were more likely than women to migrate to the city or to die in the war, highland villages took on a female face. Demography made the contribution of women into the backbone of the organizations. Sons and husbands could only patrol because mothers and wives took care of meals and childcare. Women also formed the last line of defense in most villages with clubs and kitchen-knife tipped spears. The female contribution to beating back the Shining Path was seldom acknowledged in village life or national society. To the contrary, the organizations abound in signs of subordination. Only men carry the guns that symbolize the new power of peasant patrollers. The elected positions of comando or Civil Defense Committee president remained the province of men in line with the long history of the almost total exclusion of women from village leadership. To be sure, the logic of subordination was never seamless. With men away on patrol with the army, a ragged band of twenty women in the hamlet of Pampalca beat off a raid by the Shining Path in 1983, averting the likely slaughter of the entire village. Several women spoke to me of the momentary metamorphosis from peasant housewives into warrior women in a way that seemed to challenge the usual hierarchy of gender meaning that connects femaleness to passivity and containment. "We have also struggled," as the widowed María Ccente explained from the dirt floor of her shack of adobe and bamboo. Even Ccente and others went on to paint the mobilization only as an emergency measure, however, and emphasized that men remained in command. "The people got macho," villagers of both sexes would tell me in an ideology of masculinization that summed up the privileging of the male and the repression and even erasure of the female in the counterrevolution.

A last and related problem revolves around hierarchy and leadership. Andean villages have always been far less harmonious and egalitarian than might be suggested by the organic-sounding label of "peasant community."[34] Rumors of misappropriation of funds or misuse of authority by local leaders, whether of irrigation committees or village councils, represent a familiar feature of the social landscape. "Small village, big hell," as a Spanish aphorism has it. The rondas are no exception. Many comandos and Civil Defense Committee presidents have faced accusations, in some cases justified, of everything from stealing money donated by the government to excusing relatives from patrol duty.[35] Some ronda leaders have close ties to the military, giving them undue leverage in local politics; in Junín's Comas, where a number of village presidents complain of a decline in their authority. In the extreme case of the Apurímac Valley, where the rapid growth of coca cultivation in the 1980s exacerbated a climate of uncertainty and volatility, the first leaders turned the rondas into personal fiefs. This was the case of schoolteacher-turned-denture-maker Pompeyo Rivera Torres, "Commander Huayhuaco," who operated as a jungle warlord before his 1989 arrest for drug trafficking.[36] All of these histories undercut the effort to reduce the rondas to a tidy tale of innocent peasants against evil guerrillas, or to imagine a uniform backing for the organizations.

An obvious lesson of even this abbreviated survey of the limits of the rondas centers on the heterogeneity of any kind of social mobilization. Thus, women play a different, and mostly subordinate, role than men, while leaders are better located than followers to gain from favors of politicians or army officers. The unified sound of the label of movement, no more than the familiar stand-bys of culture or society, should not be allowed to conceal the inevitable differences in interest and standpoint of the differently positioned participants in popular initiatives, always as much a messy arena of tension and struggle as an iron-clad juggernaut of collectivity and union. Instead of the unilateral focus on consensus of liberal and functionalist models, or, conversely, of fragmentation and partiality in some brands of poststructuralist theory, the rondas suggest the urgency of a sensitivity to the delicate and sometimes explosive dialectic of difference and commonality, polyphony and solidarity, and conflict and consensus in every bid for change around the world.

Heterogeneity and Risk of Relativism

A sensitivity to contradiction should not mean falling into a leveling relativism that ignores the inroads of activism from below in Latin America or anywhere else. Dozens of mobilizations from shanty-town soup kitchens in Honduras to battered women's shelters in Brazil have meant the margin of survival in daily life. As in the case of indigenous federations in Ecuador or mine-workers' unions in Bolivia, they can also challenge the very logic of cultural domination and political exclusion between the elite and the dispossessed, the white and the brown, the rulers and the ruled. Although they may not be the harbinger of revolution, the inroads of these initiatives make them more than just the glory of slaves, and offer a welcome sliver of hope in the struggle for justice and dignity in today's world.

Peace is the rondas' most obvious achievement. A dense constellation of factors lies behind declining violence. The capture of guerrilla leaders weakened Shining Path's capacity to kill and destroy, even as disappearances and massacres by the security forces declined with the military's populist turn. Meanwhile, the remnants of the insurgency still attacked patrollers and resettlements; in a September 1993 raid on the Ayacucho village of Matucana Alto, twelve Quechua-speaking farmers were murdered, including five children. However, there can be little doubt of the significant role played by the rondas in ending the war. Checkpoints and patrols pushed the rebels out of the Upper and Lower Tulumayo Valleys in Junín, where peasants, in the words of one leader, began to fight in 1990 with "clubs, machetes, rocks and slings."[37] With almost no help from the military, the rondas also expelled the Shining Path from another of the war's bloodiest battlegrounds, the Apurímac Valley. The organizations' massive expansion in 1990 and 1991 corresponded to a more than 30 percent decline in recorded casualties and deaths in the departments of Andahuaylas, Apurímac, Ayacucho, and Junín. "There are no more massacres, not even attacks, nothing," concludes Juan Pardo, the Commando in the village of Vinchos on the windy grasslands above the city of Ayacucho.[38]

Some patrollers have not shied from the use of violence. I cut a deal in 1991 with a taxi driver to take me to the district of Comas, six hours above the city of Huancayo. Halfway up the winding track, the muffler fell off the rusted Nissan, forcing us to backtrack. On the way down, we met a pick-up filled with ronderos. It stopped, blocking our path on a rocky curve. In the misty light of the mountain morning, I watched with a sinking feeling as twenty ronderos jumped off the bed, grabbed stones, crowbars, and shotguns, and moved, silently, to surround us. Fortunately, and at the last moment, one of the weatherbeaten farmers recognized the taxi driver as his cousin. Tension dissolved. "The terrorists ambush, and we have to be ready to defend ourselves," one of the gun-toting villagers explained, apologetically. Even so, my apprehension had not been altogether a product of negative stereotypes about peasant ferocity. Just a year before, Comas peasants had stoned thirteen suspected guerrillas, sliced off their heads, and taken them in a blood-soaked burlap sack to army headquarters.[39]

Any discussion of ronda violence risks a fall into the essentialist view of the intrinsic brutality of the Andean peasantry, on display in one Peruvian historian's incautious claim about "the frequency of unrestrained cruelty in peasant wars."[40] But it would also be irresponsible to ignore the ronda killings of "suspected subversives" from Cunya in 1983 to Paccha in 1992.[41] Understandable, if not justifiable, against the explosive background of fear, personal and village vendettas, and mass violence by the Shining Path and the military, these cases of summary execution undermine the inverse, and ultimately just as condescending, essentialism of the view of the rejection by Andean peasants of any use of deadly force.[42] Once again, the rondas defy the easy judgment or sweeping generalization, in this case as "life-giving" or "life-taking" or "violent" and "peaceful," and present the imperative of recognition of the mobile and multiple contours to the potential shape of any social movement.

I do not want to minimize ronda violence. The icy recording of the annihilation of captured guerrillas in a book of minutes from 1983 suggest how war's dehumanizing logic of violence and retribution could extend beyond the Shining Path and the military and into the patrols.[43] It must be emphasized that killings by patrollers have fallen substantially, however, and are now a relative rarity. The rondas are similar in this respect to their northern Andean namesakes. There, the lynching of suspected rustlers, although never as frequent as of suspected rebels in the center and south, also declined after a measure of order was reestablished and the threat to survival and livelihood diminished. In a surprising number of cases, former guerrilla supporters have even been reincorporated into village society, if they prove willing to abandon the doctrine of revolution at any cost. "We lived in misery, and it was understandable that some would make the mistake of joining the Shining Path," as Hugo Huillca, an organizer of the patrols in the Apurímac Valley, explained to me. The strong ideology of forgiveness was fortified by the influence of evangelical protestantism in this subtropical region just below the mountains of Ayacucho.[44] A number of comandos and Civil Defense Committee presidents in the Apurímac and Huanta once belonged to the Shining Path, a startling instance of the elasticity of the patrols in their evolution into a mass movement.

Today, even many critics admit the movement has contributed to a surprising resurrection of civil society, a broader benefit of the organizations. There are regular meetings of the entire village to discuss patrol business, whether fundraisers for guns or scheduling patrols. As in the northern patrols, all men in the village must patrol and attend assemblies. Skulkers may be fined or even whipped. Yet this participation no longer rests in most places so much on military intimidation as on the collective conviction among villagers that patrols are desirable. Army officials no longer name the comandos and Civil Defense Committee presidents in most villages. Open assemblies instead elect them like other village leaders, part of what historian Ponciano del Pino calls the *interiorización* (interiorization) of the patrols in Andean life.[45] A panoply of other civic organizations, like parent-teacher associations, women's clubs, and irrigation committees, have also been reactivated with the new security provided by the patrols, expanding the room for local participation in village organizations. Increasingly, too, the organizations have extended beyond a purely military mission. When cholera broke out in the Apurímac Valley's Palmapampa, for instance, patrol leaders traveled to Ayacucho to request rehydration salts from development organizations and the government. Many patrols even incorporate old modes of village cooperation, holding *faenas* (collective work parties), to build guard towers and walls, or, in the case of Chaca, a potable water project. A system of *chasquis* (messengers), after the Incan communication system, links villages in the upper reaches of Huanta so that word of guerrilla sightings and attacks is shared. In part, then, the organizations have proven to be "Andeanized," "peasantized," and "villagized," reconfigured to local logics of necessity and tradition. Rather than hastening the demise of mountain traditions or institutions, they have become a vehicle for the defense of village interests and life, and the definition of new ways of being Andean.

The broadest accomplishment has been to restore a sense of autonomy and pride in many war zone villages. Although the extreme poverty of the south-central Andes contributed to initial receptivity to the Shining Path, displacement and killing in the war's escalation spun the world into what peasants call *chaqwa*, Quechua for chaos and disorder. By contrast, many peasants speak of the patrols as a sign of their ability to be more than passive victims of uncontrollable forces. "We're no longer tame lambs to be led to the slaughterhouse," says the Quechua-speaking Civil Defense Committee president in Ayacucho's Vinchos.[46] In the Apurímac Valley, villagers even celebrate the anniversary of the founding of the local ronda with ballads, poems, and speeches. Now many villagers identify themselves as ronderos as well as by the older tags of kin ties, village, province, department, and nationality as Peruvians. Talk prevails in parts of the south-central Andes of superiority even to the military. "We're able to do what they never could," says one man in the village of Chaca in Huanta province, "that is, restore order, discipline, and dignity in these communities."

Perhaps the most moving measure of the patrols revolved around the redefinition of the rules of inclusion and citizenship in the Peruvian polity. Deference and privilege stood on display in the request of the ponchoed authorities that the white anthropologist raise the Peruvian flag on the gnarled flagpole in the icy fog of Huaychao. After I raised the banner, however, villagers took over the ceremony to end the school year. Although only a handful of villagers among the ragged collection of toothless men, skirted matrons, and children in sweatsuits and bowler hats spoke more than a few words of Spanish, everyone knew parts of the national anthem. They sang the ponderous song in a wandering yet unabashed chorus that carried across the forlorn plaza of the ravaged village. Then, a group of men asked me to take a photograph of them with the Peruvian flag, crouching around it like a soccer team before a big match. Imagery of the inhabitants of the Andes as part of the "other Peru" has pivoted on the fantasy of the mountains interiors as a timeless terrain of primordial exoticism beyond the modern nation, in this way making mountain villagers into foreigners and exiles in their own country. The concern in Huaychao with anthem and flag flew in the face of the logic of displacement and exclusion in the claim of one observer that Iquichan highlanders saw the nation as an "incomprehensible abstraction."[47] Peru was not two but one in this mapping of geography and nationhood that rejected the apartheid of separateness to lay claim to belonging in the imagined community of an Andean nation.

Huaychainos recoded the meaning of Peruvianness in the act of laying claim to it. Most of them had learned the language of nationalism in the army barracks, school textbooks, and Independence Day speeches in the main square of Huanta or over the radio from the presidential palace in Lima. The peasantry disappeared in these vehicles of orthodox patriotism that narrated the nation as an epic of treaty signings and brave battles by the bearded generals and top-hatted presidents of the creole elite. History books even whitened the Incas, as if to deny that brown people of Andean descent could have made a real contribution to national progress. In the reworking of nationalism in Huaychao, the Quechua pronunciations and scratchy harmonies of the national anthem transformed the flowery Castillian of the creole standard into the loud cacophony of an Andean ballad. Meanwhile, someone had painted a ponchoed patroller and the inscription of of "Civil Defense Committee of Huaychao" onto the Peruvian flag in a prickly iconography that relocated the Andean peasantry from the margin to the center of the nation. Only men posed around the banner, an unsubtle identification of male privilege and national destiny that thrust forward a stark reminder of the many lines of paradox and division within the movement. Still, a number of women in bowler hats and puffy skirts joined in conversation after the ceremony to raise the flag in connecting the patrols to a struggle for justice and dignity in a divided nation. "We've fought without recognition, we no longer want to be orphans in our own country," as one old man framed a peasant nationalism that lay claim to recognition and support from the political leaders who, in the 1980s, had abandoned the Andean citizenry to the bleak battle against the Shining Path.

I hope I have shown that the limits and achievements of the rondas cannot be neatly disentangled. "Systems of power are multiple," as anthropologist Lila Abu-Lughod underlines, "overlapping and intersecting fields."[48] A social movement may reenforce the operation of oppression at one level, yet cut against the grain of domination and misery at another. The rondas remain caught within the disturbing logic of militarism, sexism, bossism, even as they carve a promising stability out of the relentless fear and chaos of war. However, it should be just as clear that my own feelings tilt toward admiration, even astonishment, at the patrols' achievements. The mobilization of Andean villagers against the Shining Path proved to be an unexpected reminder of the capacity of even the forgotten and the dispossessed to reshape history against the grain of pain and injustice of an unforgiving world.

On my last night in Huaychao, the tortured melodies of Quechua hymns wafted through the bitter cold of the little settlement from the adobe-and-thatch shell of Pentecostal church. At least for now, however, apocalypse was forestalled. The next morning I was greeted by the lieutenant governor and municipal agent with a polite goodmorning and a request list to carry to the aid agencies in the United States, a list that included guns and livestock.[49] "We don't want to move anymore, and maybe life will be better from now on," said the older of the villagers. His grim optimism seemed to grow from the bitter knowledge that no future could be any more terrible than the suffering of an unforgotten past.

"Jeremiah" and "The Savage"

Some observers continue to paint the patrols in the old frame of the Peruvian Andes as place of primordial and millenarian customs. "Time stands still in the Andean countryside," writes one Lima journalist, as another compares the patrollers to "Atahualpa's Inca warriors."[50] Through the relentless attachment of the labels of "remote," "isolated," "faraway" to the inhabitants of highland South America, the grammar of exoticism locates the Andes at a distant margin from a presumed center of global society in Europe and North America. More productively, it may be possible to see the Andes and the patrols not as a strange emblem of the faraway and archaic so much as a revealing face of common predicament of upheaval and flux on a shrinking planet. "Mountains of my Peru. And Peru at the cusp of the globe. I can only embrace it," as poet César Vallejo wrote. His 1930 verse already emphasized the need to move beyond the fantasy of Andean primitivism to accept that the distinctive lifeways of mountain villagers can only be understood as part of the onrushing history of the present.[51]

One of the most striking dimensions of commonality in global modernity revolves around the interweaving of creation and destruction. Whether in the tight weave of a poncho or pride in Quechua, the fierce sense of independent identity in Andean Peru points the irreducible diversity of pathways through today's world. However, the war zone also reaffirms the double quality of modernity that juxtaposes infinite possibilities from computer technology to space travel and unfathomable horrors from Bosnia to Rwanda. The stone markers of mass graves and the burned shells of ruined villages signal the inerasable evidence of terrible destruction, even as the beauty of an Andean ballad or the energy of assembly of the rondas underscore the stubborn persistence of creation and renewal. "There is no document of civilization which is also not a document of barbarism" claimed Walter Benjamin about the inseparability of pain and vitality in a famous dictum about twentieth-century history.[52]

On a trip to Huanta in 1993, I visited a fish fry and soccer tournament in the cactus hills of the lower valley. People from Cangari–Viru Viru and many other resettlements and villages, including comandos like "Jeremiah" and "The Savage" raced and yelled, as they played next to the rubble of an experimental farm burned by the Shining Path five years before. One of the gun-slinging patrollers explained in Quechua-accented Spanish that the fish came from a new artificial pond, and that a nearby resettlement wanted to turn the soccer field into a tourist complex with a hotel, volleyball courts, and canoeing. It is hard to imagine a resort in mountains where guerrillas and soldiers had roamed for so long. But no one ever imagined that the patrols might forge peace from war in the first place, said the man with a sly laugh. Against the bustle of jokes and food and ballads of the Andean celebration, one can only hope for the sound of more of this laughter that insisted on the unfinishedness of history, and that the coming years will leave these men and women with something better.

Notes

Grateful thanks for comments to Carlos Iván Degregori, Paul Gelles, Gustavo Gorriti, Alma Guillermoprieto, Charles Hale, Robin Kirk, Donald Moore, Charles Piot, Linda Seligmann, Frances Starn, Randolph Starn, Ajantha Subramanian, Clare Talwalker, and to all the participants in conference on "Dissent and Direct Action in the Late Twentieth Century" in Otavalo, Ecuador. Responsibility for the final version is, of course, my own. A different and longer version of this essay appeared in *Cultural Anthropology* in the November 1995 issue.

1. Two of the best studies of the Shining Path are Degregori (1990) and Gorriti (1990). Both will soon appear in English from the University of North Carolina Press. For a fascinating look at the important role of women in the party, see Kirk (1993b). Palmer (1992) collects some of the best work on the Maoists in English. See Starn (1992a) for an overview of the abundant literature on the guerrillas.

2. Abimael Guzmán, "We are the Initiators" in Starn, Degregori, and Kirk (1995). This is a translation of the speech delivered by Guzmán on 19 April 1980 to call for the beginning of the armed struggle.

3. These figures come from an unpublished survey from 1993 of the Instituto de Defensa y Investigación Nacional (INIDEN) in Lima.

4. On the rondas campesinas in northern Peru, see Gitlitz and Rojas (1983) and Starn (1992b).

5. José Coronel (1992 with Carlos Loayza, 1994, n.d.) and Ponciano del Pino (1992, 1995) have done pioneering work on the rondas, and I am indebted to both of these Ayacuchan scholars for their insights in our many conversations. Other sources on the rondas include Starn (1993), Instituto de Defensa Legal (n.d.) and Degregori, Coronel, del Pino, and Starn (1996).

6. Valcárcel (1995, 219).

7. Ibid. (220–221).

8. Valcárcel (1950, 1, 1995, 220).

9. These quotes come from a party statement that a Huanta announcer was forced to read over the radio in 1990.

10. Guzmán in Starn, Degregori, and Kirk (1995, 312).

11. Central Committee of the Communist Party of Peru (1989).

12. Guzmán in Starn, Degregori, and Kirk (1995, 313).

13. Chávez de Paz (1989) offers statistics on the makeup of the Shining Path, based on judicial records.

14. Morote (1970, 1).

15. For an early view of the Shining Path as a peasant rebellion, see an otherwise insightful essay by McClintock (1984).

16. Degregori (n.d., 3).

17. Kirk (1991, 1993a) has done the best work on Peru's internal refugees.

18. See Coronel (n.d.) on Iquicha, and Manrique (1989) on Huancayo.

19. See del Pino (1992) for more on the issue of violent punishment by the Shining Path.

20. A compadre is a person who is in a relationship of mutual obligation and friendship, usually established between the parents of a child and the person they choose as its godparent.

21. See the reports on Peru from 1990 to 1993 of Amnesty International and Americas Watch.

22. Interview on 13 December 1994 in Huanta.

23. Urrutia (1993, 88).

24. The role of the military in seeking to organize peasants to fight guerrillas bears a similarity to the so-called civil patrols in Guatemala, although these organizations were much more rigidly controlled by the armed forces. See Americas Watch (1986) and a number of the essays in Carmack (1989) for more on the civil patrols.

25. A chullo is the wool cap often worn by peasants in high villages in the Andes.

26. The preceding president, Alan García, had handed over 200 rifles in 1988 to patrollers in the Apurímac, but Fujimori was the first to approve the large-scale arming of the peasantry.

27. Featherstone (1996, 47).

28. Comaroff and Comaroff (1993, xiii–xiv).

29. The quotes come from Burneo and Eyde (1986).

30. Interview with Andres Luna Vargas, 10 July 1989, Lima.

31. Del Pino (1991, 235).

32. Decreto Legislativo No. 741, 8 November 1991, reprinted in *El Peruano*, the Peruvian government's official newspaper, 12 November 1991, p. 101687.

33. See de la Cadena (1991).

34. Mossbrucker (1990) offers a useful analysis of the utopian strain of much of the scholarship on Andean communities.

35. These are the titles of the two main leadership positions in rondas. Comandos typically organize the day-to-day mechanics of patrolling, while the Civil Defense Committee presidents have broader roles in charge of calling village meetings and having relations with government authorities and the army.
36. See del Pino (1995) for more on the history of the rondas in the Apurímac Valley. Instituto de Defensa Legal (n.d.) offers more on "Commander Huayhuaco," including his involvement in massive human rights violations.
37. Quoted in Starn (1993, 47).
38. Interview with Juan Pardo, 12 December 1991, Lima.
39. This story made *The New York Times*—"Peasant Farmers Said to Kill Rebels," 14 March 1990, section 1, p. 13.
40. Manrique (1989, 167).
41. For an account of the events in Paccha, see Amnesty International (1992, 25).
42. Historian Nelson Manrique (1989, 167) makes the point about the brutality of peasant wars. Carlos Iván Degregori (1989a) takes issue with Manrique, and advances the case for the existence of a "punish but do not kill" ethic, in a response to Manrique. Although I disagree with the essentializing thrust of both sides in this debate, I want to emphasize my broad admiration for the work of both of these scholars, among the most perceptive observers of contemporary Peru.
43. This quote comes from the book of minutes from a village in Tambo Province in Ayacucho for a meeting on 26 November 1984.
44. Interview with Hugo Huillca on 12 December 1991, Lima.
45. Quoted in Starn (1993, 53).
46. Quoted in Starn (1993, 43).
47. Vargas Llosa (1983, 83).
48. Abu-Lughod (1990, 53).
49. Lieutenant governor and municipal agent are two of the main leadership positions in Andean villages, both villagers appointed by the government.
50. Quoted in Balaguer (1993, 15).
51. These lines come from Vallejo's *Poemas Humanos*, appearing in translation in Starn, Degregori, and Kirk (1995, 16).
52. Benjamin (1968, 258).

References

Abu-Lughod, Lila (1990). The Romance of Resistance: Tracing Transformations of Power 33 through Bedouin Women. *American Ethnologist* 17(1):41–55.
Amnesty International (1992). *Human Rights During the Government of Alberto Fujimori.* New York: Amnesty International.
Balaguer, Alejandro (1993). *Rostros de la Guerra\Faces of War.* Lima: Peru Reporting.
Benjamin, Walter (1968). *Illuminations: Essays and Reflections.* New York, Harcourt, Brace and World.
Burneo, José and Marianne Eyde (1986). *Rondas campesinas y Defensa Civil.* Lima: SER.
Carmack, Robert (1989). *Harvest of Violence.* Austin: University of Texas Press.
Central Committee of the Communist Party of Peru (1989). Interview of Chairman Gonzalo. Mimeo.
Chávez de Paz, Denis (1989). *Juventud y terrorismo. Carácteristcas sociales de los condenados por terrorismo y otros delitos.* Lima: Instituto de Estudios Peruanos.

Comaroff, Jean and John Comaroff, Eds. (1983). *Modernity and Its Malcontents*. Chicago: University of Chicago Press.

Coronel, José (1994). Comités de Defensa: Un proceso social abierto. *Ideele* 59(60):113–115

Coronel, José (n.d.). Violencia política y respuestas campesinas: Huanta 1980–1992. Unpublished manuscript.

Coronel, José and Carlos Loayza (1992). Violencia política: Formas de respuesta comunera en Ayacucho. In *Peru: El problema agrario en debate/SEPIA IV*, ed. Carlos Iván Degregori et al. Lima: SEPIA.

Degregori, Carlos Iván (1989a). Comentario a la década de la violencia. *Márgenes* 3(5–6):186–190.

Degregori, Carlos Iván (1989b). *Que difícil es ser Dios*. Lima: El Zorro de Abajo Ediciones.

Degregori, Carlos Iván (1990). *Ayacucho 1969–1979: El surgimiento de Sendero Luminoso*. Lima: Instituto de Estudios Peruanos.

Degregori, Carlos Iván (n.d.). Jóvenes y campesinos ante la violencia política. Unpublished manuscript.

Degregori, Carlos Iván, José Coronel, Ponciano del Pino, and Orin Starn (1996). *Las rondas campesinas y la derrota de Sendero Luminoso*. Lima: Instituto de Estudios Peruanos.

de la Cadena, Marisol (1991)."Las mujeres son más indias": Etnicidad y género en una comunidad del Cusco. *Revista Andina* 9(1):7–29.

del Pino, Ponciano (1991). Los campesinos en la guerra. O de como la gente comienza a ponerse macho. In *Peru: El problema agrario en debate/SEPIA IV*, ed. Carlos Iván Degregori et al. Lima: SEPIA.

del Pino, Ponciano (1995). Villagers at Arms. In *The Peru Reader*, ed. Orin Starn, Carlos Iván Degregori, and Robin Kirk. Durham: Duke University Press.

Featherstone, Mike (1996). Localism, Globalism, and Cultural Identity. In *Global/Local: Cultural Production and the Transnational Imaginary*, ed. Rob Wilson and Wimal Dissanayake. Durham: Duke University Press..

Gitlitz, John and Telmo Rojas (1983). Peasant Vigilante Committees in Northern Peru. *Journal of Latin American Studies* 15(1):163–197.

Gorriti, Gustavo (1990) *Sendero: Historia de la guerra milenaria en el Perú*. Lima: Apoyo.

Instituto de Defensa Legal (n.d.). *El papel de la organización social campesina en la estrategía campesina*. Lima: Instituto de Defensa Legal.

Kirk, Robin (1991). *The Decade of Chaqwa: Peru's Internal Refugees*. Washington, D.C.: U.S. Committee for Refugees.

Kirk, Robin (1993a) *To Build Anew: An Update on Peru's Internally Displaced People*. Washington, D.C.: U.S. Committee for Refugees.

Kirk, Robin (1993b). *Grabado en Piedra: Las mujeres de Sendero Luminoso*. Lima: Instituto de Estudios Peruanos.

Manrique, Nelson (1989). La década de la violencia. *Márgenes* 3(5–6):137–182.

McClintock, Cynthia (1984). Why Peasants Rebel: The Case of Peru's Sendero Luminoso. *World Politics* 27(1):48–84.

Morote, Osmán (1970) *Lucha de clases en la zona alta de Huanta (distrito de Santillana)*. Bachelor's thesis, Facultad de Antropología, Universidad Nacional San Cristóbal de Huamanga.

Mossbrucker, Harold (1990). *El concepto de la comunidad: Un enfoque crítico.* Lima: Instituto de Estudios Peruanos.

Noel Moral, Roberto (1989). *Ayacucho: Testimonio de un soldado.* Lima: Publinor.

Palmer, David Scott, Ed. (1992). *Shining Path of Peru.* London: Hurst.

Starn, Orin (1992a). New Literature on Peru's Sendero Luminoso. *Latin American Research Review* 27(2):212–226.

Starn, Orin (1992b). "I Dreamed of Foxes and Hawks": Reflections on Peasant Protest, New Social Movements and the *Rondas Campesinas* of Northern Peru. In *The Making of Social Movements in Latin America*, ed. Arturo Escobar and Sonia Alvarez. Boulder: Westview.

Starn, Orin (1993). *Hablan los ronderos: La búsqueda por la paz en los Andes.* Lima: Instituto de Estudios Peruanos.

Starn, Orin, Carlos Iván Degregori, and Robin Kirk, Eds. (1995). *The Peru Reader: History, Culture, Politics.* Durham: Duke University Press.

Urrutia, Jaime (1993). Ayacucho: Un escenario post-Gonzalo, ?ya?. *Ideele* 59–60:88–90.

Valcárcel, Luis (1950). Introduction. In *Indians of Peru, A Book of Photographs by Pierre Verger.* New York: Pantheon.

Valcárcel, Luis (1995). Tempest in the Andes. In *The Peru Reader: History, Culture, Politics*, ed. Orin Starn, Carlos Iván Degregori, and Robin Kirk, pp. 219–222. Durham: Duke University Press.

Vargas Llosa, Mario (1983). The Story of a Massacre. *Granta* (9):62–83.

Nancy Abelmann

Reorganizing and Recapturing Dissent in 1990s South Korea

The Case of Farmers

In spring 1995, the Seoul Broadcasting Company aired *Morae sigye* (Sandglass), which was seen by the vast majority of the Seoul viewing public. The twenty-six episode drama highlights the way the 1980s in South Korea remain a touchstone of popular and political discourse. Through the gangster underworld it explores the machinations of political and corporate power and corruption. Looking at the Kwangju Uprising, a civilian uprising in 1980 that resulted in 2,000 deaths, it examines the agency and consciousness of the Korean people, and looking at retraining camps for dissidents it spotlights state terror. In the series, the decade stands for extremes—excessive repression and dramatic dissent.

Against the 1990s, dubbed the "era of the new generation" and marked by the wane of dissent, the 1980s emerge as a social and political inferno. What was shocking for me was this drama's depiction of student activism—the life-blood of the decades-long saga of dissent. In *Morae sigye*, the student movement emerges not as the protagonist of a heroic epic, but rather as one artifact among many of a destructive maelstrom. This portrayal is in keeping with a widespread fatigue and even disgust with that culture of dissent. Many people distance themselves not only from the military authoritarianism of the recent past, but also from the righteousness and drama of dissent—from the totalizing projects of both the left and the right. When people recall the 1980s, they think of the infringements on personal life imposed by both the military state *and* the protesters. People remember *when* urban spaces were consumed by the violence of demonstrations and their suppression; *when* the government demanded sacrifice and restraint in the name of political stability, economic development, and nationalisms; and *when* the moral prerogatives of the left made those with progressive inclinations feel guilty that they couldn't do more. Thus, the culture of 1980s dissent is portrayed not for its progressive teleology but rather as a window on the pathological political and social character of its times. The 1990s, in contrast, are marked by a widespread growth of the middle class, the celebration of consumer capitalism epitomized by increasingly visible upper-class enclaves, and the extension of personal and political freedoms.

The 1980s has receded into history because of local and transnational social and political transformations that culminated in *munmin chŏngbu* (civilian rule) or democracy. This national transformation occurred in the relaxation of cold war politics precipitated by the Soviet break-up and German unification. The demise of the cold war challenged South Korea's long-standing rhetoric of control and authority; likewise, socialism's devalued currency unsettled the ideology of dissent. Both transformations, however, were incomplete. Into the 1990s, the Koreas remain one of the last flash points of the cold war. The machinations over North Korean nuclear power plants in 1994 resuscitated old language at home and abroad, especially in the United States. Furthermore, many South Koreans have not been convinced by the promise of civilian rule and the proclamation of a "New Korea." And many dissidents have resisted the easy embrace of consumer capitalism. Many of the old activisms continue; this is particularly the case for farmer activism, which I will consider in this essay.

Nonetheless, the aesthetics of the age are certainly new. The dominant activist aesthetic of the 1980s—the *minjung* (people) imaginary is by now a relic of *temps perdus*. Minjung, a noun and adjective that could in the 1980s be combined with almost anything—history, music, art, film, religion, economics, etc.—was obsolete by the 1990s with its "new generation," "civil society," and "civil movements." Minjung itself had been a sort of psycho-socio-historical complex/construct that fashioned agents of struggle for South Korea's postcolonial, divided nation, and military authoritarian politics. I have argued elsewhere (Abelmann, 1993, 1996) that it wrested legacies of anticolonial, antiimperial, and leftist struggle occluded by the dictates of the official memory of the cold war and of military authoritarianism. Counter-nationalists, the minjung protagonists were not simply the downtrodden, but profoundly national agents of epic struggle. By the 1990s, this celebrated minjung activism of the 1980s—of farmers, laborers, and urban poor—has seemingly fallen outside of the purview of public discourse. Minjung movements have become less and less easily contained in middle-class imaginaries, epics, or organizations of struggle. The activism of the 1990s, moreover, cannot be easily subsumed under a singular aesthetic or narrative of dissent. With civilian rule the objects of dissent are more dispersed and the narratives and organization of the dissent are more fragmented. It is in this context that the notion of *simin* (civil) movements now dominates the discourse of dissent. It is important to note that the discourse of civil movements is not entirely locally produced, nor were revolutionary or minjung ones before that. In keeping with Richard Fox and Orin Starn's introductory points on protest generally, such narratives and the dissent they structure take place at transnational or creolized crossroads.

If a minjung epic of struggle has waned, social struggle has by no means come to a halt in South Korea. The end of encompassing epics of dissent and the continuity of minjung activisms are revealed in a vignette in an editorial in a progressive weekly. Kim Chong-ch'ŏl (1994, 112) went to see an activist play called *The Dawn of Labor* (Nodong ŭi saebyŏk), at which a woman seated behind him told him: "Nowadays, it is really rare to find a college student who thinks to come to this sort of play. Today's guests are mostly people from labor unions. Throughout the 1980s, progressive theater troops performed at the labor unions, so the laborers didn't feel the need to come, but now they come." As the activism of farmers and laborers slips beyond the 1980s minjung imaginary and outside the 1980s movement structures, it becomes invisible because it doesn't conform to the watersheds as mapped by urban intellectuals.

This paper considers both discourses and practices of dissent in postminjung South Korea. In the global arena, South Korea is one among many instances of postauthoritarian, post–cold war societies—mirrored in this volume, for example, in Sonia Alvarez's discussions of the refashioning and reorganization of dissent in Brazil. Postminjung activism uses different registers and tactics and hence demands changed analytical prisms. As Fox and Starn suggest in the Introduction, we need to examine the terrain between everyday resistance and revolutionary war. Indeed, 1980s activism in South Korea focused on the end points of this continuum—believing both in "total overthrow" and in everyday resistance; that is, the dream of revolution was predicated on a belief in the existence of undiscovered or suppressed radicalism that took quotidian form (Abelmann, 1993, 1996).

My approach to social activism here follows a number of social movement theorists (Touraine, 1981; Melucci, 1985; Escobar and Alvarez, 1992) who take up the discursive production of social movements not as secondary concerns, but as constitutive of all activisms. These thinkers argue that we must pay attention to the struggle over meaning and culture in social protest. I believe that social activism is in constant dialogue with the past as memory, and the past as an ongoing social and political contest (Foucault, 1975; Nash, 1979; The Popular Memory Group, 1982). In the same way that contemporary farmer activism is a blind spot to much of 1990s discourses of dissent, dimensions of past activism have also been occluded in 1990s discourses and memory. As the excesses and extremes of the minjung era are tallied, 1980s' activism is wrested from its historical conditions of production and its own dialogue with the past. Ironically, the new social movement theory, which is so popular in the 1990s, imagines earlier activism—such as minjung activism—removed from its day-to-day life. Retrospectively, minjung is homogenized against what was in fact a vast array of competing practices and discourses. The occlusions of discourses of dissent have their own social life, which fashion current and future activisms. In the same way that the 1980s activism was articulated through particular historical aesthetics, 1990s activism fashions itself through the public discourses on and the memory of the 1980s.

Here I examine 1990s discursive shifts through the articulation of simin movements as compared with minjung movements, and the 1990s *sinsedae* (new generation) distinguished from the culture and orientation of the 1980s *undongkwŏn* (student activists). I then take up farmers' activism through 1990s' shifts in the rhetoric and practice of *nonghwal* (farming village activism), and through meetings in 1993 with ardent activists from the 1980s. I am particularly interested in farmers' dissent for several reasons. First, farmers and their perceived culture were central to the minjung imaginary. Farmers embodied a history of resistance, silenced by the cold war and authoritarian regimes; they also emerged as symbols of the costs of rapid industrial development—as the keepers of an anachronistic sector sacrificed to development. Additionally, farmers are important because their organizing continued and even escalated into the 1990s. This activism has been especially evident in the struggles against the Uruguay Round, which opens trade barriers such that it threatens rural survival in countries like South Korea with its petty farming. Even in the 1990s, Korean farmers remain principally small family farmers with average landholdings under a hectare. As members of a by now minority sector (well under 20 percent), their lives and subsistence are increasingly remote from the general public. Although the standards of rural living have improved remarkably over the last decades—the vast majority, for example, own televisions, telephones, and even washing machines—rural areas remain culturally quite remote. Still vital in the 1990s is the *nongch'on hwaltong undong* (nonghwal, farming village activism), college student trips to the countryside that spurned both student and farmer activism throughout the 1980s. Through exploring nonghwal, I will consider the relationship between social metaphors and aesthetic narratives of dissent and the life and course of activism itself. Nonghwal is particularly apt for analysis here because it has long been devoted to activating others and is self-conscious on the question of mobilization itself.

Drawing a Line: The "New Generation" and "Civil Movements"

Many South Koreans stress the difference between 1990s *hakpŏn* (those who entered college in the 1990s), and the 1980s hakpŏn.[1] South Korean anthropologist Cho Haejoang (1994, 143) reports 1990s hakpŏn's resistance and discomfort with 1980s students: as one student told her, he feels closer to his teachers who came of age in the 1970s than to his seniors from the 1980s. Cho (1994, 146) explains that 1980s students arrived at college campuses that were completely enveloped in the upheaval of the student movement. Even if not all students were *undongga* (committed activists), the vast majority shared the movement perspective and "carried the weight of the country's fate on their backs." Cho (1994, 147) continues that 1980s students saw the prohibition of campus newspapers, stood by as friends were taken off to be tortured, and experienced the sudden disappearance and even the suicides of classmates. Students came to feel that "the only way to live with a conscience is to be a *t'usa* (fighter). In the innermost recesses of their heart, the nonfighters lived with the sense that they were sinners" and were reviled by activist classmates (Cho 1994, 147). It is this extreme righteousness that the new generation rejects. Students today arrive at campuses that are no longer the playing fields of the police. Whirring in consumer capitalism and preparation for employment, the campuses "belong to the students again" (Cho 1994, 147). The posters of the Korean University Student Association Federation (the central student movement organization) that were once at the heart of campus life, have become "part of the campus scenery" (Cho 1994, 152). Cho describes this as the generation's "lighter feeling."

Although Cho Haejoang (1994, 146) sympathizes with the new generation's revulsion with the 1980s, she nonetheless acknowledges the remarkable historical role of the 1980s activists. "Especially if you think of their parents' [the Korean War generation] enormous allergy for social movements, this generation [is remarkable] for having promoted historical progress." She also laments the historical circumstances that produced the 1980s culture of dissent: the culture and educational system of military authoritarianism (1994, 147). They were taught to find the *right* answers and were ironically schooled in a military temperament that would later allow them to fearlessly and righteously combat these very institutions of oppression (Cho, 1994, 145, 147). With a clear enemy to *t'ado* (overthrow)—the military authoritarian regime—students put their lives on the line (Cho 1994, 149). One social commentator has even charged that with their military fatigues and mass rallies, the students glorified death and celebrated the military. Cho (1994, 149–150) laments that it was the 1980s' movements' single-minded obsessions, exclusions, and righteous self-sacrifice that have produced a 1990s "movement void": "[These movements] turned away from or even oppressed those contradictions that emerged from people's daily lives—so instead of readying people for the next era of social movements, they've silenced them." The new generation "has come to even hate the term 'social movement'" (Cho 1994, 151).

Paek Uk-in, a prolific social commentator, extends Cho's analysis of university student generations to the broader social and cultural generational divide across the late 1980s watershed. He argues that South Korea has moved from the "age of politics" that peaked in the 1980s to "the age of culture." In a pithy shorthand Paek (1993a, 28) notes, "this is no longer an age in which Im Sugyŏng could become a heroine." Im, a college student movement activist who defied the National Security Law and traveled to North Korea in 1989 to participate in an international youth congress, was immediately imprisoned upon her return. Paek's (1993a, 28) "age of politics" was epitomized in the culture and life-style of the *undongkwŏn* (student activists), which ran on prohibition, restraint, and discipline. Society in general was restrained by ideology (Paek, 1993a, 38) and governed by "[the] comparatively narrow frame of our *kungmin*'s (state people) consciousness and life-style" (1993a, 25–26) and "ideals of discipline, frugality, industry, and unconditional obedience" (1993a, 42).

Paek (1993a, 26) points out that in the age of culture, the youth has emerged as the "new generation," in contrast with their predecessors who were named for politics (e.g., the "4.19 generation"). The new generation instead distinguishes itself by its consumption and style—"leisure, sex, and beauty" (Paek, 1993a, 38). Liberated from the homogenizing effects of totalitarian politics and revolutionary responses, the new generation reflects the "accelerated nuclear fission into various groups differentiated by ways of life, thought, and consciousness" (Paek, 1993a, 25–26). Paek (1993a, 38) is less concerned than Cho about the lasting effects of military authoritarianism on this generation: "People are thinking now is the time to renounce ideologies that restrain you, and to follow your desires." Paek's 1987 watershed is thus a constellation of clear dyadic transformations in step with Cho's characterizations: politics to culture, production to consumption/life-style, laborers to middle class, restraint to indulgence, homogeneity to diversity.

Simin undong (civil movements) are distinguished from their predecessors in a similar way to the rendering of the new generation. As the students are fashioned in relation to undongkwŏn, citizen's movements are a complex response to, but not a full-fledged rejection of, minjung movements. In the first issue of the English-language journal of the Citizens' Coalition for Economic Justice (Kyŏngsillyŏn, Kyŏngje Chongŭi Silch'ŏn Simin Yŏnhap), the organization that is most widely considered to represent simin undong, there is a short interview that champions a new era of social activism. Cho Woo-Hyun, the organization's chairman of the Policy Research Committee, is described this way: "He views civil activities from a pure perspective *without* ideology and has an interest only in living with ordinary citizens through grassroots civic movements." The text elaborates:

> Professor Cho *didn't* make his start as a labor activist. He *wasn't* even concerned about the labor issue at first. Rather, he majored in Labor Economics *by chance,* and the American traditional methodology he studied in the U.S. led him to analyze the Korean labor situation. Considering his age when he came to take practical interest in laborers, the word of a forerunner may not be proper in describing him. Nevertheless, he will not fall behind any forerunners with respect towards love of laborers (Citizens' Coalition for Economic Justice, 1994, 19, emphasis added).

Although a seemingly unremarkable portrait, the implicit markers distinguish civil from minjung movements. Cho's perspective is "pure" and "without ideology." Never self-fashioned as an "activist" or "forerunner," he is instead an "ordinary citizen" driven in a "new direction" by the "Laborers' Great Struggle of 1987–88" (Citizens' Coalition for Economic Justice, 1994, 19). Minjung movements are by implication ideological, instrumental, tainted, and activist centered.

The implicit criticisms of Cho, Paek, and the Kyŏngsillyŏn vita above, call for a new sort of activism—what they call "new social movements." Paek (1993a, 25–26, 45–49) predicts that production-based movements will not be able to sustain themselves as the paradigm shifts from production to consumption and that movements will become fragmented to reflect the splintering interests of consumer and cultural identities. The notion of new social movements picks up on the Western new social movements (NSMs) literature and activism, which is focused less on the overthrow of big structures and more on struggles over what Jürgen Habermas calls the life-world, including gender identities, sexuality, ecological concerns, and meaning.

Most articulators of simin movements, however, do not entirely dismiss minjung activism. This is not surprising because so many of them were active during the minjung era. Paek (1993b, 237–238), for example, chastises simin movements for ignoring minjung interests: "Simin movement organizations need to humbly recognize the limitations of the movement-line that advocates operating within the system. Even if we sufficiently recognize the importance of simin movements' efforts to extend the space of *simin sahoe* (civil society) and to work within the system on policy formation, their long-term development will be thwarted because they exclude the interests of the minjung." Paek

(1993b, 237–238) concedes that minjung movements need to take up the spaces of new protest, of daily life: "Minjung movements need to embrace . . . those spaces employed by the simin movement organizations and the regional movements which have drawn the attention and support of the *taejung* (masses)." Paek imagines that simin and minjung movements can coexist, learning from and even incorporating each other's interests and tactics.

Chong T'aek-sŏk also calls for coordinated simin-minjung movement efforts. He explains that before 1987, minjung and simin movements were indistinguishable because of their shared enemy: the military authoritarian regime. Although it has disappeared, he still argues for unity because of the ongoing national division which transcends class (Chong, 1993, 199) and because if simin is to mean those people who have the right to legal freedoms and equality then "we can say that minjung are simin" (Chong, 1993, 204).

Some 1990s activists, however, have held fast to the principles of minjung terminologies and programs. In *Iron* (Theory), a journal that maintains the 1980s radical line, Kim Se-gyun (1993, 117) argues that simin is an "anti-minjung" bourgeois social category. He advocates the struggle for a minjung society outside of the system (p. 117). Kim criticizes the distinction that simin movement activists make between "production" and "daily life" (pp. 120–121). Daily life, he maintains, has been and continues to be central to minjung movements (pp. 120–121). As for the contemporary crisis of minjung movements, he makes a distinction between movements in which minjung participate and those with revolutionary platforms. He asserts that the former, minjung movements at the "taejung [masses] movement level," are not in danger, but that those at the "political movement level" are faltering (p. 131). The task now, he insists, is to resist all impulses to join forces with the simin or new social movements (1993, 136).

Together these activists respond to what they see as an alarming repositioning of minjung movements and of the minjung imaginary to the margins. Except for Kim Se-gyun, they all project a uniform culture of dissent across the 1987 divide when movements were united against the authoritarian state. This reckoning commemorates 1980s dissent in the same way that it was characterized by the 1980s authoritarian state—uniform in composition and focused on opposition to the state.

Farmer Activism into the 1990s

For farmers' movements, these divides are certainly untidy. Lives spill over the divide, across these sea-changes. I will now discuss farmer activism and nonghwal practices and discourses over this divide as a window on transformations "in the field." The relaxation of the cold war climate of violence and repression eliminated the once-powerful stigma and fear of rural organizing. By the late 1980s, activists could tell farmers that officials and police would extend more benefits to a well-organized oppositional village than to ruling-party-loyalist villages. As a barometer of social change, some activists in farmers' movements became village heads and ran for public office. Meanwhile, the formation of the National Farmers' Association (1987) and then the National League of Farmers' Associations (1990) sought to at once unify a number of national farmers movement associations and to support the autonomy of county-level associations. The National League of Farmers' Associations aimed to distance itself from activisms in which "farmers are merely objects to be lead" (CNCYCW, 1990, 1). The irony of such equations, however, is the impossible search for a pure peasant or subaltern politics. With the National League of Farmers' Associations spearheading activities, and the extension of membership and county-level organization, farmer activism achieved new visibility and social standing.

In addition to this continued simultaneous integration and localization of farmer activism, the mounting concern in the late 1980s and early 1990s over the Uruguay Round further coalesced farmer political consciousness and organizational awareness. Farmers feared the repercussions of imports from countries where the industrial agricultural economies of scale would easily dwarf their competitive ability. The comments of the National League of Farmers' Associations provincial activists at a public forum, "The Current Situation of Farmers' Movements and Organizational Challenges," are revealing. P'yo Man-su noted that while it might have been possible earlier that farmers didn't realize they weren't living well, such optimism is impossible in the face of the current import problem. He continued, however, that these understandings do not always translate into activism, as they can instead engender profound resignation and pessimism (Chŏnnong 2, 1990, 12). In a similar vein, Ch'oe Chin-guk remarked that although the problems facing farmers were perhaps more vague earlier on, the import issues pose a stark and very concrete reality and deeply implicate the United States (Chŏnnong 2, 1990, 13). Pak Pŏng-jun added that farmers increasingly sensed that they must solve their own problems and that they could be a powerful social force if they united (Chŏnnong 2, 1990, 13). He maintained that the farmers' fundamental ideas about activism were profoundly affected by the 1987 labor struggles, particularly the return visits of laborers for the August harvest festival in the wake of these struggles; laborers came home boasting "we fought ourselves and were given raises, and it is because of our struggle that the Labor Laws were reformed" (Chŏnnong 2, 1990, 12).

The confidence in dissent and mandate for democracy culminated in high-profile protests throughout the country against the impending Uruguay Round negotiations in 1993. In some regions, farmers refused to sell their rice to the government at the state set prices and blocked the Agricultural Cooperative Offices with sacks of rice (*Daily Report*, 1 Dec 1993, 29), and in others they staged funerals—clad in funerary clothes made from rice sacks—to symbolize the death of Korean farmers (*Daily Report*, 7 Dec 1993, 25). Demonstrations in Seoul in December 1993 had as many as 30,000 participants, the largest ever of farmers in the post–Korean War era.

The cause of protecting the integrity of Korean rice farming was mobilized as a veritable symbol of national identity and well-being.[2] In the December 1993 *Tong-A Daily*, for example, an editorial championed farmers as it chided the United States:

> Watching over the rice negotiations, our people are upset over the excessive pressure from the United States. . . . We believe that Americans are fully aware of the deep and long history of the love and affection that the ROK people have for rice. Our people's love for rice is the same whether one is a farmer or not. Therefore, Americans are well aware of the fact that for our people, rice is tantamount to life itself. . . . Military security is important for our people, but safeguarding our rice is just as important (*Daily Report*, 7 December 1993, 25).

Such rhetorical posturing aside, however, farmers' protests were depicted as the anachronistic struggles of people destined for demise. The stirrings of farmers at the South Korean periphery as they watched themselves being sold down the river in the name of "inevitable internationalism"—"the tide of the times," and "the course of history"—is a case of resistance against the global post–cold war ideologies of neoliberalism and free trade. Indeed, the state presented itself as the helpless periphery of these inevitable global tides; farmers, long construed in the public imagination as a repository of Korea's yesteryear— the good and the bad—appear now as ironically "conservative" combatants against the global trends of the times. It is in no way easy to figure the character of contemporary protest—in their various centers and peripheries, and vis-à-vis the divergent rhetorics of the times.[3]

Nonghwal Past and Present

Nonghwal has long been a highly self-conscious pursuit. Predicated on the interaction between social actors postulated as quite distant and distinct, it necessarily operates on particular models of mobilization, and on the apperception of activist Others. Also, self-conscious is the vision of a field of social activisms, what Sonia Alvarez calls the "webs of activists"—in this case the relation between the student movement and farmer protest. From era to era, nonghwal is revisioned and revised against nonghwal past.

The practice of nonghwal transformed considerably since its origins in the first part of this century. Student trips to the countryside in the 1960s and the early 1970s were service-oriented summer vacation visits reminiscent of similar activities in the 1920s and 1930s. From the vantage point of 1980s nonghwal, they were romantic, sentimental, and charity-oriented sojourns to the country's economic and cultural periphery (HKHY, 1985, 9). University "circles"—clubs devoted to hobbies, areas of study, religion, sports, and the arts—organized the visits to single villages; there was no overarching organization or a particular agenda. From the 1960s to the 1970s, nonghwal were devoted to direct service; they labored and promoted increased productivity in the villages. A Korean Christian Student League pamphlet (HKHY 1985, 10) criticized such efforts for maintaining and bolstering the existing state agricultural system and obscuring the structural contradictions of the agricultural sector.

Already by the early 1970s, there was a shift toward a more political "team nonghwal," mirroring the growing minjung orientation of the student movement. While the circle and religious group nonghwal continued, team nonghwal was organized universitywide and worked in conjunction with the student movement. The team, however, forged no relation to the escalating organization and activities of farmers' movements. Some asserted that nonghwal had an adverse affect on farmers' movements since it was often out of touch with village life and made disjointed, unreasonable plans that led to nothing but distrust and frustration. As the student movement became interested in mass movements in the 1980s, the KCSL nonghwal became linked to the student movement with its branches and underground structures in the academic departments. In efforts to bridge the gap between activist and nonactivist students, nonghwal was called upon to politicize nonactivist students. By this time, the countryside, although still largely associated with its economic deprivation, was also reified for its structural circumstances warranting revolution and its historical repository of activism.

The second half of the 1980s brought a drive to promote direct contact with farmers' movements. Introspection and dialogue became integral to nonghwal, as the schedule included daily discussion sessions with farmers aimed at raising their consciousness, and, in turn, daily self-reflection sessions to discuss the progress of this meeting of consciousnesses. Committed to considering farmers as subjects of history, just as they celebrated farmers' oppositional activity or culture, students also sought to explain farmer passivity and inaction.

In the minds of students, the new farmer-as-subject nonghwal had to transcend farmer-as-object nonghwal. Farmers should no longer be objectified as the recipients of student service in this view, or subordinated to the needs of the student movement. One college senior forthrightly told me that when he began college he saw no reason for nonghwal, but that in 1985, he came to realize its meaning for the student movement. Here the consciousness of the farmers is absent; the only consciousness that matters is the students' consciousness. Nonghwal was thus a useful "experience" for student movement activists—a chance to learn about the material conditions of Korean history. Particularly important, then, was the students' (often first) encounter with the grind of physical labor and material poverty. In contrast, the new nonghwal demanded an active dialectic between the student movement and farmers' movements, and between students and farmers. This nonghwal veered away from "serving," unidirectionally conscientizing farmers, or merely training student movement activists. As was stressed in nonghwal literature, a farmer-as-subject nonghwal must be long term, interactive, and experience centered. Long term referred to relationships between students and farmers, which were longer than one-shot summer vacation encounters. Interactive and experience centered pointed to a conscientization based on an understanding of, and an intimate interaction with, farmers' pasts and dreams. The primary goal of such a conscientization was to "awaken farmers to a realization of their own subjectivity": "Students, through a comprehension of the realities of farming villages, will personally experience the reality of their colonial territory-homeland and build an emotional link with farmers. . . . Farmers, through [their contact with] the students, will plant a consciousness to become the masters of society and get connections with students" (KTNHCW, 1987, 1, 4). Students had high hopes for this meeting of farmers and students: "it should solve the contradictions of history" (KTNHCW, 1987, 1, 4). This "new" equation, however, was problematic because students were still deeply committed to providing service, training student activists, and raising the consciousness of farmers; echoing in these words were long-standing paternalisms and social hierarchies.

In the 1990s, the meaning of nonghwal has shifted again. An anecdote from a visit to the North Chŏlla Province in 1993 may illustrate the shift in mood and sensibility. I attended a planning session with college students and farmers for the upcoming summer nonghwal. I went with several farmers from one of the villages where I had lived (during research in 1987) to the meeting that was held some distance away at a deserted school. I found that the charged atmosphere of the earlier covert nonghwal was gone. Students' romanticism of farmers had waned, as had farmers' idealization or fear of activist students. I was also struck by the more relaxed, and less politically charged exchanges between students and farmers. Both groups seemed less susceptible to the stock characterizations of epic narratives, such as the student North Korean sympathizer, the selfless student revolutionary, the peasant revolutionary, the communist peasant, and so on. Addressing the farmers and students, one nonghwal leader noted: "Nowadays many farmers quip that the students sent to their villages 'don't seem like undongkwŏn students—they don't seem sufficiently moral or upright.' These days when farmers want to criticize nonghwal students this is what they say." Farmers and students alike roared with laughter, recognizing the remarkable change in political tides. Several years ago, undongkwŏn was a code word for North Korean sympathizing revolutionary student activists, just the sort most farmers avoided. Now it was a standard for students to live up to. The laughter also reflected the topsy-turvy circumstances that had led farmers to become the primary activists and the arbiters of dissent. Farmers didn't mince words that they were doing the educating. One farmer-activist instructed the crowd: "The best way to create members for *nongminhoe* (farmers committees) is to be an exemplary farmer with extensive technical knowledge. For example, if you know a lot about green houses, after delivering lots of technical advice, with lots of nitty gritty detail, you can suddenly add 'by the way I'm a member'—that is how to instantly convert farmers." For the students' benefit, he added: "Don't think that it is only members (of nongminhoe) who have a *ttŭt* (a clear purpose). In fact that isn't the case at all. Rather it is often the nonmembers who have more ttŭt." Cho, one of the men I knew, yelled out: "Yeah, in our village people aren't active, but it doesn't mean they don't have ttŭt at all. You shouldn't think that farmers don't know anything—they know a lot."

In considering the distinctions that 1990s nonghwal students made vis-à-vis the 1980s nonghwal, it is important to remember that student activism is the dissent of age and generation cohorts. Furthermore, because student activism has been the vanguard of postliberation dissent in South Korea, the country's political struggles also take form in part as generational struggles. It is difficult to homogenize the experience of college students across gender, class, region, and religion, but there are some general features distinguishing the 1980s and 1990s generational struggles that are relevant here. Although the public profile and platforms of student movement programs and initiatives have been primarily articulated against the state, more private struggles have been taking place in families, between generations, away from the public eye. While students in the 1980s valorized the countryside for its legacy of dissent and its pressing social concerns, to many of their (mostly urban) parents the country represented a lifestyle and social reality that was not so distant. In the 1980s, the vast majority of the parents of college aged students were themselves first-generation urbanites who had toiled through South Korea's incredibly rapid period of development to leave the ways and lifestyles of the countryside far behind them. Widespread sensibilities and narratives posited rural villages as anachronistic reservoirs populated by those without the personal ability or zeal to succeed in the city (see Abelmann, forthcoming). This sense of the countryside was thus diametrically opposed to that of their activist sons and daughters who surveyed the anachronisms of the countryside not as the personal characteristics of individuals but as the social products of structural circumstances, and who saw in farmers a legacy of radical agency. Further, if students waxed romantic about village communalism, many of their parents remembered well the reality of the normative constraints of the surveillance of villages and of patrilineal groups residing in close proximity. Thus, where their children looked for indigenous socialism, they saw the excesses of patriarchy and the constraints on individual freedom.

For many families, the participation of their sons or daughters in activism was an affront to the family labor that had afforded this generation the luxury of post–secondary education and the promise of upward mobility. And in an era of enormous political repression, the real costs of student activism to family safety were great. These were some of the dynamics of the less public generational exchanges amid broader social struggles; this is not to say that all student activists struggled *against* their families, but such relations certainly were widespread.

In contrast, the generation of 1990s students—of course, it is impossible to distinguish clear or discrete generations—posits its youth against a different generational cohort of parents and in a radically transformed social context. By the 1990s, the middle classes have become more entrenched and class structure more fixed; the rural periphery, by now considerably smaller, has grown more distant temporally and materially and hence easier to invest symbolically beyond the real life trajectories of urban migrants. Also, enhanced standards of living and the confidence in democratic politics have engendered the search for things Korean and its associated rural nostalgia; in many ways the minjung imaginary had been popularized and politically sanitized. There is room now to explore Korean culture *and* to hold dearly to one's career paths and plans. There is also leeway to dabble in politics and social causes without relinquishing economic well-being and social mobility aspirations. Finally, with the wane of the grand narratives of development and dissent, there is social and discursive space for personal growth. At the same time, however, the society's economic competitiveness and its ever-increasing cosmopolitan connections and consciousness have made it so that the competitively minded cannot rest easy that proper educational credentials alone will necessarily ensure the good life. Thus, the career-minded new generation combines both the relaxations and pressures of its era. This generation combines its parents'

celebration of modernity with politically benign interests in "Koreanness"—
an outright embrace of consumer capitalism and the search for national identity. As Cho Haejoang suggests above, this generation of students is closer to
its parents and more distant from its 1980s student predecessors.

Not surprisingly, these new social circumstances and identities have thus
transformed the very spaces and identities open to social activism. Also transformed is the generational space of youth itself; if the 1980s students bore the
weight of the political ills of their era, and if their parents before them labored
in the service of development, the new generation emerges as an age, style,
and consumer enclave whose politics will be necessarily different. Nonetheless, as Cho points out above, the new generation is not self-styled—it bears
the legacies and socialization of earlier social and political regimes. In their
bartering over a new era, we find the tracks of earlier times; the emergence of
generations (or generational narratives) is inherently dialogic—stitched at the
interstices of public memory, intergenerational relations, and economic contingencies. In South Korea—where for so long youth led the struggles—these
changes have profound implications for the way in which the activisms of the
future will be narrated and executed.

Student publications from the nonghwal organizations at two high-profile
universities and a 1993 nonghwal guidebook published by the Korean University Student Association Federation reveal the changing discourses and aesthetics of nonghwal for the new generation. In keeping with the 1990s nonghwal
anecdotes above, the new nonghwal was built on refashioned images of both
students and farmers. Nonetheless, many features of earlier nonghwal appear
in these writings, challenging the facile ways in which the 1980s–1990s divide
is drawn.

Publications of the 1990s distinguish their nonghwal from the old and different ones of their 1980s *sŏnbae* (seniors). One 1987 hakpŏn student (figured
by the year of entering college), who had come back to finish college after his
military service, described "what comes to mind about the nonghwal of the
past," including "the sound of seniors' scoldings," "dozens of rules and regulations," and "surveillance" (ANH, 1993, 2). He wrote, "these are the things
that occur to me long before anything about the importance of farmer and student solidarity" (ANH, 1993, 2). Nonghwal need not be the stuff of such painful memories; instead, it should be a place for learning "enjoyable labor,"
"encouraging each other," and "fortifying our love for each other" (ANH, 1993,
2). Furthermore, he cautioned that if the nonghwal labor is too difficult, students won't learn the "joy of labor" (ANH, 1993, 2). As for the rules—dozens
of which jumped to his mind—"they should be applied on a premise of love
and encouragement rather than of exclusion and rebuke" (ANH, 1993, 2).

Finally, he declared, "let's be proud of our members and pass these warm summer [nonghwal] days even more warmly" (ANH, 1993, 2). A 1994 pamphlet noted that "when we hear about sŏnbae's nonghwal we think that 'times have changed, but that nonetheless we also do a great job at nonghwal'" (MKCH, 1994, 12).

The old nonghwal was also imagined according to what students assumed were very recent changes in villages. Many of these changes, including improvements in the material standard of living—not necessarily a sign of the relative prosperity or future prospects of the rural sector—and farmers' awakened consciousness, shocked the students. A 1994 nonghwal pamphlet offered "the details of one student's nonghwal account," in order to consider how to "get beyond" the "old nonghwal thesis" (MKCH, 1994, 7). One student reflected that with all of the recent economic problems with the agricultural sector he had expected to find farmers "living even harder," but was instead surprised to see how well they lived—"drinking OB beer, serving coffee, and educating their children in the city" (MKCH, 1994, 8). He conceded that although farmers were "somewhat excluded culturally," overall their lives weren't so different from their own (MKCH 1994, 8). The students were thus cautioned that when preparing for nonghwal it is a mistake to imagine "your grandmothers' and grandfathers' era" (MKCH, 1994, 9). They were told not to anticipate *toenjang* (a soup made from fermented soy beans that is considered humble fare) in the fields, but "*paekpan* (rice with many side dishes, considered urban fare) taken out from restaurants, and bread and beers at snack time in the fields" (MKCH, 1994, 9). They went on, however, to explain that these culinary transformations were not signs of wealth, but evidence that farm labor was in short supply in the countryside and that restaurant take-out food was actually cheaper (MKCH, 1994, 11). Furthermore, they stressed that villages are still marginal in their city-centered society (MKCH, 1994, 11).

In the same way that the students cautioned against images of downtrodden farmers that they assumed were at the heart of their seniors' nonghwal, they also warned against romanticizing farmers' "community." Solidarity with farmers, they described, is extremely difficult to achieve if students maintain unrealistic images of them: "We have to get beyond the idea that farmers are only about groups . . . or that it is only about dark and hopeless existence. . . . From this nonghwal forward, let's think about the reality of their cultural life." They gave the example that it is unreasonable to visit the villages expecting women to be singing traditional folk songs (*minyo*), when it is pop music that they really enjoy (MKCH, 1994, 44).

Some reflections, however, highlighted students' debt to the old nonghwal. A senior in 1994 wrote, "before farmers didn't welcome nonghwal, but thanks to the struggle of those before us, they do now" (MKCH, 1994, 3). Students also reflected that the unpalatable rules and restraints of past nonghwal were in step with their times. They were times of "violent politics" and "direct suppression" when "just to form a farmers' committee (*nongminhoe*) was to be treated like a *ppalgaengi* (red)": "Our seniors fought together with farmers just to be able to establish these committees. They had to appear very upright, and it was of necessity that they reflected on and were criticized for their mistakes" (MKCH, 1994, 12).

Students articulated concrete perspectives and programs in accordance with their understanding of changed circumstances. At the heart of the self-proclaimed "new nonghwal" was a refashioned vision of "student and farmer *yŏndae* (solidarity)." The solidarity was to be less total, less romantic, and more mutually instrumental. They acknowledged the fundamental divides between farmers and students, but explained that their brief interactions are mutually serviceable for strengthening both student and farmer activist groups (*haksaenghoe* and *nongminhoe*). This instrumental approach acknowledged that students' village presence can promote the farmers' committees, but entertained little romance of "conscientizing" farmers. In this sense, they imagined a transformed minjung. As for fortifying the student groups, the new nonghwal was less convinced that the experience of farm labor or the exposure to the lives of South Korea's dispossessed would enhance their organization or activities. Rather, they argued that nonghwal offers students the chance to get away together and to strengthen friendship and solidarity. Here, nonghwal is rendered more like a summer camp. "You should be able to feel the hand of the student committee [haksaenghoe] in the rich human relations" (HTCHY, 1993, 3).

In their discussions of student and farmer solidarity, students began with reappraisals of the minjung: "First let's throw out the question, 'is it only the fighting minjung who are the minjung'?" (MKCH, 1994, 9). The minjung conjures images of "striking laborers" and "dying farmers,"

> but in fact the concept of minjung refers to all of us who in the course of living encounter contradictions. . . . Isn't the fact that it is poor people who come to mind when we think of minjung a sign of our elitism? . . . Aren't all of our parents who struggle so hard to pay our school fees minjung? Or the people who clean and manage [the campus] for us, aren't they minjung? . . . Before we leave for nonghwal we have to think of ourselves as among the minjung (MKCH, 1994, 9).

Nevertheless, even if everyone was declared minjung, students wrote of farmer suffering and of the real differences between students and farmers. "Even if

we talk about solidarity, the positions are different. Farmers experience the contradictions directly. They are its subjects. Students experience them [the contra-
dictions] only indirectly and go to many efforts to solve them. . . . The reality
is that it is difficult for students to be the direct subjects of agricultural policy"
(MKCH, 1994, 11). Students still wrote about farmers' suffering and hardship.
The solidarity of the new generation was to be less political: "Extend the attention you have given, and your attachment to, your own [new generation]
lives . . . to your minjung siblings" (MKCH, 1994, 13). "[Nonghwal] isn't necessarily about anything political. You can talk to farmers about each and every aspect of life, and you can point out contradictions. . . . Go ahead and show
them your personal style. Build even greater trust with farmers. . . . Let's show
them [farmers] the kindness of the new generation" (MKCH, 1994, 13). Similarly, they warned against unnecessary "goal consciousness" that inhibited student-farmer relations: "Don't overdo it with the political talk" (MKCH 1994,
39). This instrumental solidarity was fashioned according to nonghwal's real
benefits for farmer and student organizing. Students wrote that nonghwal isn't
about service, but that it could be used to extend the students' realm beyond
the campus (MKCH, 1994, 10). Through nonghwal, student groups would also
become more *taejungjŏk* (popular based) (MKCH, 1994, 11). Although hopeful about nonghwal's potential for student organizing, students cautioned that
it couldn't be too purposive: "'Let's strengthen the student committee' can't become our slogan" (MKCH, 1994, 12).

Nongminhoe (farmers' committees), students imagined, are strengthened
when "we leave a good impression" (MKCH, 1994, 11). In this spirit, the students cautioned that in the villages they must be constantly mindful of what
might seem trifling details, that "even when taking a rest you must take note
of who is around you" (MKCH, 1994, 11). One pamphlet said that "nonghwal
should not be an activist space in which students are the proxy for farmers,
but . . . an activist space for autonomous farmers' committees" (HTCHY, 1993,
4). In a similar vein, a farmer's detailed account of nonghwal in 1991 reminded
students that because they do not understand the reality of farming villages,
they have a narrow sense of the impact of their visits: "It isn't that any single
person decided to join the farmers committee because of the students, but their
visit still strengthened the farmers committee" (Kim Sun-mi, 1991, 146).

In keeping with this softened student-farmer solidarity, there were new ideas
about a more egalitarian and democratic nonghwal organization. *Kyuyul* (rules),
a long discussion argued, should be about "attitudes or perspectives of life"
rather than constraint, interference, or control (MKCH, 1994, 33). Rules are
to be deliberated and decided on together "with love" (MKCH, 1994, 33): "Why
doesn't the [Nonghwal] Preparation Committee after the first day of nonghwal

meet with the trustworthy nonghwal members and together debate and decide on the rules. You can call the rules a 'lesson of love' and hang them where you are staying [i.e., nonghwal]" (MKCH, 1994, 34). *Sŏnbae* (upper-class men and women) were instructed not to intimidate their *hubae* (juniors): "When you are together with the farmers you [sŏnbae] must draw out the juniors to speak" (MKCH, 1994, 39). The new nonghwal was also supposed to be more fun. Students were reminded that it isn't just the farmers who need special activities. They recommended games for the students' healthy "group life" (MKCH, 1994, 41).

Unimaginable in 1980s nonghwal maxims were the many calls for student-student friendship—quite different from 1980s "comrades in struggle": "Ten days is a really long time for getting to know each other . . . eating together. . . . You can't always be put together or made-up for ten days" (MKCH, 1994, 41). One pamphlet appealed:

All of you near to me, my *tongji* (friends) . . . if you have a friend for whom you still have a bit of a prickly feeling somewhere in your heart, then work with them during nonghwal. Just as you will have a valuable experience [through nonghwal], how about taking an interest in what that friend is feeling, in what [nonghwal] has awakened in them. During these ten days together, let's strengthen our relationships (ANH, 1993, 1).

Calling for more fun, friendship, and less romanticism of farmers' hardship, the new nonghwal downplayed the importance of students' farm labor. If nonghwal was narrowly focused on students' farm labor, as they imagined it had been in the past, it would be a paltry affair: "Students would say 'Me too, I did labor,' and farmers would reflect 'There wasn't much work for students to do'" (MKCH, 1994, 11). Rhetorically, they asked, "If you go to nonghwal how would you feel about just laboring and getting evaluated?" and urged "Let's not make it 'Nonghwal! memories of tedious labor'" (MKCH, 1994, 41). Yet 1990s nonghwal notes still waxed enthusiastic about field work: "It is wonderful for farmers to know that their experience of pain [through labor] is not unrelated to your existence. . . . Getting to know people through labor is different than relating to a friend, but what an experience to be praised for your labor!" (HTCHY, 1993, 1).

From my return visit to the countryside to the various activities and ideologies outlined in 1990s nonghwal literature, it is clear that many aspects of 1980s nonghwal and minjung sensibilities have been disrupted. Farmer and student solidarity is to be forged not on the basis of unified engagements with the past and shared social visions, but instead on an understanding of mutual reinforcement. Nonghwal is not to be modeled after images of a communitarian rural village, but rather fashioned in accordance with the vicissitudes of 1990s' youth culture. Nonghwal is not to be the drab labor of personal sacrifice and restraint nor the training ground for broad based social dissent, but a colorful space where farmers might listen to pop songs and students can play games. Although students no longer consider farmers to be organic revolutionaries or duped masses, farmers are still symbols of hard labor and relative dispossession. Now, however, students sense that they do not have the rights to nor the responsibilities for farmers' struggles. These distinctions run parallel with those between minjung and simin movements. In the same way that the simin concept defines a fragmented space for middle-class dissent that is not articulated in a national imaginary such as minjung, the new nonghwal self-consciously delimits its own autonomy from farmers or epics about them. Nevertheless, it is not entirely divorced from the legacy of minjung representations. Similarly, the minjung-simin distinctions are never fully drawn. These various declarations of the new era are distinctions both drawn against and in part delineated by the older discourses and dialogues.

1980s Activists into the 1990s

Let me walk across the 1980s–1990s watershed through a brief revisit in 1993 to the modest network and remote landscape of a movement I examined from 1987 to 1988. The Koch'ang Tenant Farmers Movement (see Abelmann, 1996) was a late 1980s struggle in which some five hundred tenant farmers joined forces to fight against their corporate landlord. The struggle engaged student activists and professional organizers—so-called external activists—and city residents as the farmers traveled to Seoul to occupy their landlord's corporate headquarters. Koch'ang, located in the North Chŏlla Province, is on South Korea's southwest coast, one of the country's peripheries and a hotbed of political radicalism. Particularly active in the struggle was the long predominate farmer activism group—the Catholic Farmers' Union.

In my brief trip in 1993 I was struck by the messiness of this case, that the facts seemed to both endorse and defy easy periodization. Revisits are encounters with a constellation of barometers; one measures change across the biographies or the landscapes one knows best. These meetings, however, were in no way singularly emblematic of the times. That none of these farmers were active in movements focused on the impending GATT negotiations neither negates the widespread escalating struggles of this era nor reveals a particular local trend.

After decades of full-time activism, one of the central external activists from the Catholic Farmers' Union, Pae, had taken a high position in a new company committed to manufacturing food products from only home-grown (South Korean) grains. As he handed me his name card and fax number, he laughed at the seeming incongruity of his new status—the activist gone corporate. He had since split up with his wife—"I liberated her"—and he reflected that his years of activism, the spiral of his dissent, had diminished her confidence and autonomy. Remembering that his wife had been an ardent supporter of the activities in Koch'ang and an activist leader in her own right, I paused at this news and its obvious resonance with the second-wave U.S. feminism's response to the gender inequalities in the civil rights and new left movements. Since I had last seen him, Pae had arranged for his aging mother to return to South Korea from Chicago, where she and many of his relatives had been living for decades. Pae escorted me to a mountainous Buddhist retreat. He had built it with funds from a wealthy local physician whom he met recovering from a near fatal car crash. That day he introduced me to two visitors, both men who had passed much of the 1970s and 1980s in prison, who were there to rest and reflect. At this retreat nestled in beautiful hills some distance from the nearest city, Pae looks forward to quieter times in which 1980s activists can gather for reflection, meditation, and the achievement of personal as well as political goals. He was, as I had fondly remembered him, spirited and energetic, but these new guises—the corporate position and the religious retreat—bespoke new activisms, new sensibilities.

Cha had started his freshman year at a regional university, and his activism had begun with the tenant movement. He was now a newlywed farmer. During 1987 and 1988, he had been constantly frightened by the admonitions of the elders of his conservative kinship village and by the threats from local authorities. In 1993 we met at a cramped and busy lunch place in downtown Seoul where he unabashedly raised his voice about the ongoing political and economic injustices in South Korea, complaining that the so-called civilian government wasn't at all civil. I found the brazen tone of his words and his newfound confidence unbelievable. In the interim years he had become very active in the county farmers' committee. He had also worked on and off as a factory laborer in Seoul and had become involved in a national organization devoted to the "marriage problem" of rural men—that women are not willing to marry farmers. His new wife, a university-graduate Seoulite and former student activist, had agreed—against the demographic grain—to settle in his village where his family had modernized their farmhouse for her auspicious arrival. Although this marriage reminded me of those that some female student activists made in the 1980s, this case seemed different. There was no formal resolve about politicizing the village or strengthening the local farmers' committee. In a different vein, in keeping with the life-style orientation of simin movements and the individualistic flavor of the sinsedae (the new generation),

Cha talked at great length about the sort of marriage and family he wanted to have. Defying all cultural norms, in a patrilineal society, especially in a conservative kinship village, he and his wife are determined to have only one child, girl or boy.

Furthermore, he has already decided to send the child into the nearby hills alone to teach her or him self-reliance. He will never, he explained, indulge his child as he had been indulged as the youngest son and the one designated to stay back in the countryside to care for his parents.[4] He wants a free-spirited, independent child and that sort of marriage as well. This domestic vision, like his forthright political denunciations, would have been unthinkable several years earlier. Indeed, the entire constellation, his marriage to a former student activist, his confident political proclamations, and his vision for the next generation revealed social and personal transformations entirely at odds with the moment in which I had come to know Cha.

Song had been one of the most ardent activists. One of the poorest in his village, he bragged at length about his self-sacrificing activities in the movement and about his current experiments with organic farming. He explained that he continues to relinquish profits for social struggle, this time for environmental activism. He chuckled about the ironic fortune of the Chŏlla provinces: although the northwestern coast was impoverished because it missed out on state development programs, it was spared the environmental destruction of the rest of South Korea—"How lucky we are to have been excluded." Song repeated stories that he had told me many times before about his natural intelligence and his youthful cunning. With a different birth, he went on, he would be the equal of any elite today. He then launched into stories about his recent negotiations with professors and middle-class people in Seoul over his state-of-the-art organic farming. Remembering Song's irreverent manner and his ardent participation in demonstrations all over Seoul during the 1987 protests, it was interesting to see that he had settled into new dissent as he cultivated his garden.

Finally, I met Oh, an English major, who, after graduation settled in a rural village with her boyfriend for farming and farmer organizing. Her boyfriend, an activist from the early 1980s who had served a prison term for antigovernment activities, grew tired of the slow-paced rewards of rural activism. The couple decided to return to Seoul despite the derision of local activists who condemned them for deserting the cause and making it impossible to organize that village in future years. The cost of personal decisions like this one recall the 1990s' image of 1980s dissent—its rules, lack of charity, and hard edges. I was with Oh at a Seoul café in 1988, when she briefly left the table to join activists sitting nearby. It was painful even for me to overhear them denounce her selfish departure from the countryside. Back in Seoul, her boyfriend returned to organizing workers in small-sized firms, which had been overlooked in the 1987 labor struggles. She began teaching English and organizing at a neighborhood night school (*yahak*) for workers of all ages. By 1993, the couple had married, had purchased a small apartment in a working-class neighborhood in Seoul, and had had a daughter. Her husband, who had never finished college after his imprisonment, was taking classes to finish up his degree. He planned to graduate and obtain a teacher's certificate so that he could someday earn a regular salary and continue political activities on the side. Oh entrusted her daughter to her mother, visiting only on Thursdays and picking her up for the weekends, and continued to teach at the night school. The students included the wives of laborers, laborers and some middle-class housewives eager to learn English at no charge. By 1993, the 1980s divides between working and middle classes had blurred somewhat, and it had become harder for Oh to recognize the minjung in this crowd. Many people at that time had noticed that the *tabang* (cafés) in working-class neighborhoods were no longer so different from those in rich enclaves, and that laboring women had acquired the consumption tastes of the middle class.

Oh worries about where she is going with these activities. She frets that teaching English is becoming not the means to other political discussions and activism, but simply the end in itself. She mused that perhaps she is merely imparting bourgeois cultural capital. She is also concerned about her own forfeited postgraduate studies. She thinks about studying abroad, but her family responsibilities and financial situation seem to preclude this. She is debating over which credentials or employable skills might best carry her into the future. This couple's adjustment to the new era represents neither the culture of the new generation, nor of simin movements, but the old epics and activisms.

In these brief encounters with Pae, Cha, Song, and Oh there are glimpses of new spaces and aesthetics of dissent, but also of old imaginaries. In keeping with the waning of the minjung imaginary, Pae has turned his attention to the external activists themselves, a community in transition. For Oh, the raison d'être of night school has become much less clear. Farmers Song and Cha articulate their own activism on new fronts: organic farming, family structure, and childrearing practices. The dissent of the 1980s maps an era against which aspects of the present are reckoned, such as the personal costs of activism for Pae and the long-term effects of personal sacrifice for Oh. The brief vignettes explored here suggest the sorts of discursive articulations that will fashion generational positions of dissent. In her analysis of generational cohorts of women in China, Lisa Rofel (1994, 248) writes, "There is no one fixed space from which all Chinese women speak in a sovereign voice. . . . Chinese women stand in a variety of generational and class positions which have been discursively articulated in history." Likewise, these South Korean activists are neither self-styled free agents nor are they cultural dopes executing social codes; they are negotiating subject positions fashioned by South Korea's changed political-economic and ideological climate and by the contingencies of their own life trajectories.

Epochs and Epics

The idioms and direction of 1990s South Korean activism—in keeping with global idioms and circumstances characterizing NSMs—are much less totalizing than those of the 1980s. With the waning of grand narratives, however, it is easy to flatten the quotidian practices of dissent of earlier epochs—to conflate the composite of little actions and idioms with big discourses. Thinking about activism over generations and throughout lifetimes, it is imperative to be mindful of both continuities and ruptures—to interrogate the ongoing production of the past for its silences and occlusions. In the case of South Korea, it is not only lives that spill over the divides of changed local and transnational circumstances and idioms, but also persistent social problems. The lives of South Korean farmers, for example, are still very much authored by grand narratives (including internationalism, the free market, neoliberalism, and modernity) and the sites of power—the state, for example—are not enigmatic or dispersed. The consideration of dissent in the late twentieth century demands attention to the heterogeneous nature of the spaces and discourses of dissent—the coexistence of local legacies and idioms with transnational circumstances and the personal rendering of past activisms that live in the face of divergent public memories. Hopeful, then, for both the vitality of dissent and for the scholarship that both records and inscribes such dissent are the new ways of imagining the objects and practices of protest.

I have briefly explored the transformed discursive contexts of dissent from the 1980s to the 1990s in South Korea. The historicization of the 1980s—the marking of an epoch—inscribes the epics of today's dissent. These are not, however, complete or total; the epochs are variously rendered and porous, and the epics are heterogeneous, emergent, and dialogic. No doubt the decade will settle variously across diverse cohorts and be fashioned anew at the hands of multiple interests and in the play of memory and the imaginary. South Korea emerges as a case of profound social, political, and discursive transformation. It is against the backdrop of such changes that social analysis must take up dissent and direct action.

Notes

I am grateful to the conference organizers and participants for their careful comments on and helpful criticisms of this paper. The editors' queries and suggestions were challenging. I am indebted to several friends and colleagues for reading this paper: Judith Hopping, John Lie, Kathy Litherland, and Ann Saphir. Additionally, I thank Soo-Jung Lee for her considerable input. I am above all thankful for the research assistance of Soo-Jung Lee and Jesook Song and for my ongoing interchange with friends from the field.

Parts of this essay appear in Nancy Abelmann's *Echoes of the Past, Epic of Dissent: A South Korean Social Movement* (Berkeley: University of California Press, 1996).

1. Over the last few years, graduate students in the United States from South Korea have been interested in distinguishing the cultural and political differences of the various hakpôn. One recent Korean American immigrant who frequently returns to Seoul told me: "In [South] Korea each year is like a decade."
2. Although most South Koreans understood the inevitability of the opening of the rice market, they also registered overwhelming opposition to this eventuality (*Daily Report*, 7 December 1993, 26). To many, it augured the beginning of a virtual demise of agriculture, in which South Koreans are faced with the fact that production costs in South Korea are more than three times greater than in the United States (*Daily Report*, 7 December 1993, 28; 8 December 1993, 26). In addition to concerns for the farming sector, polls revealed other, more general, anxieties including: food security, the unsuitability of foreign rice for Korean consumption, the environment, and suspicions that foreign rice is contaminated (*Daily Report*, 8 December 1993, 26). The newspaper editorial of the National League of Farmers' Associations even suggested the significance of the rice market for unification: "One of the biggest reasons that the National League of Farmers' Associations is advocating 'unified agriculture' is that in a unified fatherland the security of our food supply is crucial and also because we believe that autonomous unification will only be possible when we are self-sufficient in our basic food supply" (Kim Tae-hwôn, 1993, 1). After the opening had been officially declared, the president and many government bureaucrats and elected officials made formal public apologies in which they assured the public, as in the words of President Kim Young-sam, that "we have exerted every possible means and method to save our rice, the flesh and blood of our nation" (*Daily Report*, 9 December 1993, 29).
3. I am grateful to Orin Starn for comments on the interesting position of farmers' politics in relation to the powerful ideologies of our times.
4. According to Korean patrilineal logic, the oldest son would be designated to tend the farm and care for the parents. With rapid rural exodus, however, these responsibilities often fall to the youngest son, left in the countryside after all his older brothers have left for the city.

References

Abelmann, Nancy (1993). *Minjung* Theory and Practice. In *Cultural Nationalism in East Asia: Representation and Identity*, ed. Harumi Befu, pp. 139–166. Berkeley: Institute of East Asian Studies.

Abelmann, Nancy (1996). *Echoes of the Past, Epics of Dissent: A South Korean Social Movement*. Berkeley: University of California Press.

Abelmann, Nancy (forthcoming). Women, Mobility, and Desire: Narrating Class and Gender in South Korea. In *Gender and Social Change in Late Twentieth Century Korea*, ed. Laurel Kendall.

Aegukchŏk nongch'on hwalttong ŭl wihae uri irŏk'e hapsida (For a Patriotic *Nonghwal* Let's Do It Like This) (1993). Pp. 1–6. Yonsei University. Cited as ANH.

ANH. See Aegukchŏk nongch'on hwalttong ŭl wihae irŏk'e hapsida.

Cho, Haejoang (1994). 90 nyondae sahoe undong e taehayo (Concerning Social Movements in the 1990s). In *kŭl ilki wa sam ilki*, Vol. 3 (Reading Sentences and Reading Life), pp. 141–177. Seoul: Tto Hana ŭi Munhwa.

Chon'guk Nongminhoe Ch'ong Yonmaeng Chunbi Wiwonhoe (National League of Farmers' Association Preparation Committee) (1990). The Founding of "Chonnong" and the Direction of Farmers' Movements (*"Chonnong" kyolsong kwa nongmin undong _i panghyang*). Seoul: National League of Farmers' Association Preparation Committee Policy Office. Cited as CNCYCW.

Chong T'aek-sok (1993). Han'guk simin sahoe wa minjuijuŭi ŭi chonmang (The Prospects for Korean Civil Society and Democracy). In *Han'guk minjujuŭi ŭi hyonjaejok kwaje: Chedo, kaehyok mit sahoe undong* (The Current Process of Korean Democracy: System, Reform, and Social Movements), Haksul Tanch'e Hyobŭihoe, ed., pp. 177–211. Seoul: Ch'angjak kwa Pip'yongsa.

Chonnong 2. See Chwadam: Nongmin undong ŭi hyonsangt'ae wa chojikchŏk kwaje.

Chwadam: Nongmin undong ŭi hyonsangt'ae wa chojikchŏk kwaje (Round Table: The Current Situation of Farmers' Movements and Organizational Challenges) (1990). *Chonnong* 2 (May):9–27. Cited as Chonnong 2.

Citizens' Coalition for Economic Justice (1994). Person in CCEJ. *Civil Society*, 1:19.

CNCYCW. See Chon'guk Nongminhoe Ch'ong Yonmaeng Chunbi Wiwonhoe.

Daily Report, East Asia (1993). 1–14 December:219–238.

Daily Report, East Asia (1994). 2 February:22.

Escobar, Arturo and Sonia E. Alvarez (1992). *The Making of Social Movements in Latin America: Identity, Strategy, and Democracy*. Boulder: Westview Press.

Foucault, Michel (1975). Film and Popular Memory. *Radical Philosophy* 11:24–29.

Han'guk Kidok Haksaenghoe Yŏnmaeng (Korean Christian Student League) (1985). Nongch'on hwaltong annaesŏ (A Guide to *Nonghwal*). Cited as HKHY.

Han'guk Taehak Ch'ong Haksaenghoe Yŏnhap, Nong-hak Yŏndae Saŏpkuk. 93 Yŏrŭm nonghwal t'oron cheansŏ (Discussion Proposals for 1993 Summer *Nonghwal*), pp. 1–17. Cited as HTCHY.

HKHY. Han'guk Kidok Haksaenghoe Yŏnmaeng.

HTCHY. See Han'guk Taehak Ch'ong Haksaenghoe Yŏnhap.

Kim, Chong-ch'ŏl (1994). Sinsedae wa yŏksa ŭi mulkil (The New Generation and the Waterways of History). *Han'gyŏre* 21(3 March):112.

Kim, Se-gyun (1993). Minjung undong ŭi hyŏnjejŏk wich'i wa chŏnmang (The Contemporary Position and Prospects for *Minjung* Movements). *Iron* (Theory) 7:102–139.

Kim, Sun-mi (1991). P'och'ŏn-gun nongminhoe ŭi yŏrŭm 'nongch'on hwaltong' (The Summer Nonghwal of the P'och'ŏn County Farmers' Committee). *Chŏnnong* 3:137–148.

Kim, Tae-hwôn (1993). Uri modu him ŭl moŭl ttae (The Time Has Come for All of Us to Gather Our Strength). *Chŏn'guk Nongmin Sinmun* (National Farmers' Newspaper), 1 September:1.

Koryŏ Taehakkyo Nongch'on Hwaltong Chunbi Wiwŏnhoe (1987). 87 nyŏn nongch'ŏn hwalttong charyojip (1987 Agricultural Action Resource Collection), pp. 1–164. Cited as KTNHCW.

KTNHCW. See Koryŏ Taehakkyo Nongch'on Hwaltong Chunbi Wiwŏnhoe.

Melucci, Alberto (1985). The Symbolic Challenge of Contemporary Movements. *Social Research* 52:789–816.

Minjok Kodae Ch'ong Haksaenghoe (1994). "1994 Nonghwal charyojip" (94 Nonghwal Resource Collection), pp. 1–83. Cited as MKCH.

MKCH. See Minjok Kodae Ch'ong Haksaenghoe.

Nash, June (1979). *We Eat the Mines and the Mines Eat Us: Dependency and Exploitation in Bolivian Tin Mines*. New York: University Press.

Paek, Uk-in (1993a). Taejung ŭi sam kwa han'guk sahoe pyŏnhwa ŭi yoch'e (Transformations in the Life of the Masses and of Korean Society) In *Han'guk sahoe undong ŭi hyŏksin ŭl wihayŏ* (For the Reform of Social Movements), ed. Nara Chŏngch'aek Yŏn'guhoe, pp. 17–49. Seoul: Paeksan sŏdang.

Paek, Uk-in (1993b). Siminjŏk kaehyŏk undong e taehan pip'anjŏk p'yongkka (A Critical Evaluation of Civil Reformist Movements). In *Han'guk minjujuŭi ŭi hyŏnjaejŏk kwaje—chedo, kaehyŏk mit sahoe undong* (The Current Process of Korean Democracy: System, Reform, and Social Movements), ed. Haksul Tanch'e Hyŏbŭihoe, pp. 212–239. Seoul: Ch'angjak kwa pip'yŏngsa.

Popular Memory Group (1982). Popular Memory: Theory, Politics, Method. In *Making Histories: Studies in History-writing and Politics*, ed. Richard Johnson, Gregor McLennan, Bill Schwarz, and David Sutton, pp. 205–252. London: Centre for Contemporary Cultural Studies.

Rofel, Lisa (1994). Liberation Nostalgia and a Yearning for Modernity. In *Engendering China, Women, Culture and the State*, ed. Christina A. Gilmartin, Gail Hershatter, Lisa Rofel, and Tyrene White. Cambridge: Harvard University Press.

Taehaksaeng Nongch'on Hwalttong (University Students' Agricultural Action) (1986). *80-nyŏndae minjung ŭi sam kwa t'ujaeng yŏksa* (The History of the Fights and Struggle of the People in the 1980s), pp. 406–427. Seoul: Pip'yŏngsa. Cited as TNH.

TNH. See Taehaksaeng Nongch'on Hwalttong.

Touraine, Alain (1981). *The Voice and the Eye: An Analysis of Social Movements*. Cambridge: Cambridge University Press.

About the Contributors

NANCY ABELMANN teaches in the Departments of Anthropology and East Asian Languages and Cultures at the University of Illinois at Urbana-Champaign. Her writings include *Blue Dreams: Korean Americans and the Los Angeles Riots* (with John Lie, Harvard, 1995) and *Echoes of the Past, Epics of Dissent: A South Korean Social Movement* (University of California Press, 1996). She is currently completing an ethnographic project on women and social mobility in South Korea and is about to embark on an ethnographic study of transnational, transgenerational educational mobility among Korean Americans in Chicago.

SONIA E. ALVAREZ is an associate professor of the Board of Politics at the University of California at Santa Cruz. She is the author of *Engendering Democracy in Brazil: Women's Movements in Transitional Democracies* (Princeton University Press, 1990) and the editor (with Arturo Escobar) of *The Making of Social Movements in Latin America: Strategy, Identity, Democracy* (Westview, 1992) and (with Evelina Dagnino and Arturo Escobar) of *Cultures of Politics/ Politics of Cultures: Revisioning Latin American Social Movements* (Westview, 1997). Alvarez's current research centers on the challenges to democratic theory and practice posed by the (re)configuration of national and transnational civil society. Her forthcoming book explores how social movements unsettle prevailing democratic discourses and practices in contemporary Latin America and engage in interpretative struggles over received meanings of citizenship, participation, representation, and democracy itself.

ARTURO ESCOBAR was born and grew up in Colombia. He is the author of *Encountering Development: The Making and Unmaking of the Third World* (Princeton University Press, 1995) and coeditor of two anthologies on Latin American social movements, *The Making of Social Movements in Latin America: Strategy, Identity, Democracy* (Westview, 1992) and *Cultures of Politics/Politics of Cultures: Revisioning Latin American Social Movements* (Westview, 1997). He has been working on the Pacific Coast of Colombia since the late 1980s, and is currently an associate professor of anthropology at the University of Massachusetts at Amherst.

A member of the Institute for Advanced Study in 1971 and a Guggenheim Fellow in 1987, RICHARD G. FOX is a professor of anthropology at Washington University in St. Louis and the editor of *Current Anthropology*. His publications include *Lions of the Punjab* (University of California Press, 1985), *Gandhian Utopia* (Beacon, 1989), and, as editor, *Recapturing Anthropology* (School of American Research, 1991).

FAYE GINSBURG has been studying social movements and cultural activists for the last fifteen years. She is the author of an ethnographic study of activists on both sides of the abortion debate, *Contested Lives: The Abortion Debate in an American Community* (University of California Press, 1989). She has been working with and writing about indigenous filmakers since 1990. Ginsburg is a professor of anthropology at New York University, where she directs the Center for Media, Culture, and History.

RAMACHANDRA GUHA has been a senior fellow at the Nehru Memorial Library in New Delhi, and the Institute for Advanced Study in Berlin. He is the author of a study of the Chipko movement in India, *The Unquiet Woods: Ecological Change and Peasant Resistance in the Himalaya* (University of California Press, 1990), and currently lives in Bangalore, where he is working on a biography of the missionary-anthropologist Verrier Elwin.

INGRID MONSON is an assistant professor of music and a Harbison Fellow at Washington University, St. Louis. She is an ethnomusicologist whose primary area of expertise is U.S. jazz and the author of *Saying Something: Jazz Improvisation and Interaction* (University of Chicago Press, 1996). She has also published articles in *Critical Inquiry*, the *World of Music*, and the *Journal of the American Musicological Society*.

YOSHINOBU OTA, who received his Ph.D. in anthropology from the University of Michigan, is an associate professor in the Graduate School of Social and Cultural Studies at the University of Kyushu, Japan. His research topics include folk religion in the Ryukushus, ethnic consciousness in Okinawa, and, most recently, the effects of tourism on Latin American communities.

ORIN STARN is an assistant professor of cultural anthropology at Duke University. He has written about the politics of violence and modernity in the Andes and is the author of *"Con los llanques todo barro": Reflexiones sobre las rondas campesinas, protesta campesina, y nuevos movimientos sociales* (Instituto de Estudios Peruanos, 1991) and *Las rondas campesinas y la derrota de Sendero Luminoso* (with Carlos Iván Degregori, José Coronel, and Ponciano del Pino, Instituto de Estudios Peruanos, 1996) and the editor of *The Peru Reader: History, Culture, Politics* (Duke University Press, 1995) and *Hablan los ronderos* (Instituto de Estudios Peruanos, 1993). He is beginning a new project on the return of war refugees to Andean villages in south-central Peru.

NATHAN STOLTZFUS is an assistant professor in the History Department at Florida State University and author of articles on National Socialism as well as *Resistance of the Heart: Intermarriage and the Rosenstrasse Protest in Nazi Germany* (Norton, 1996), winner of the Fraenkel Prize for best new manuscript in 1993.